MARYLAND'S GOVERNMENT

VERA FOSTER ROLLO

Cartoon illustration and cover design by Jean Karol

Maryland Historical Press
9205 Tuckerman Street
Lanham, Maryland 20706
1985

To Michael and Sally

TABLE OF CONTENTS

FOREWORD

This book has been written because the author believes that the government of a people should not be a mysterious process. Government should not be understandable only to a few trained minds! The governments of Maryland and the United States of America are ours and we play an important role in the process of government.

Even young citizens should understand most of the Constitution of Maryland since it contains the principles and laws by which we are governed. Actually reading the Constitution of Maryland and the Constitution of the United States is not as difficult as one might imagine. We have provided the actual documents so that the student may study them. True, explanations have been given, yet the documents themselves are most inspiring and informative.

Nothing more strongly underlines the value of the governments of Maryland and the United States than the times in which we live today. Newspaper headlines show that government is of no avail unless the governed consent to it, take part in it. That is the real strength—a partnership.

Though accepting responsibility for the writing of this book and the use of the facts I have been given, deep appreciation is due to Paul Krieger, attorney at law; Dr. Leo O'Neill, professor, College of Education, University of Maryland; Louis L. Goldstein, Comptroller of the Treasury for the State of Maryland; Dr. Verne E. Chatelain, emeritus professor of history, University of Maryland; Mrs. Alice Fringer; Mrs. Stephen Markey, teacher; William S. Ratchford, II, Maryland Association of Counties; Edwin J. Schamel, Chief Deputy State Treasurer; Douglas I. Malcom, attorney at law; and the late Judge R. Lee Van Horn.

Vera Foster Rollo
Lanham, 1985

ABOUT THE AUTHOR

For over thirty years Vera Foster Rollo has lived and written in Maryland. She has received from the University of Maryland a B.A. degree, a Master's degree in American History, and is currently candidate for a Ph.D. degree.

A civilian flight instructor since 1945, she continues to fly light aircraft in Maryland. For some years she worked as a reporter and freelance writer for aviation magazines. Later she was an editor for a national aviation magazine and then went on to do newspaper work, freelance articles, and finally, books on Maryland history and (at the college level) on aviation law.

She has a son and a daughter and two grandchildren. Among her leisure activities are travel, music, walking, flying and reading.

Other books by Vera Rollo are: *Your Maryland: A Complete History*, 1985; *A Geography of Maryland*, 1981; *Maryland Personalities; The Black Experience in Maryland*, 1981; *Henry Harford: Last Proprietor of Maryland*, 1977; and *Aviation Law: An Introduction*, 1985.

SECTION I
United States and Maryland Law: An Introduction

The Maryland State House, built 1772-1779, is the oldest in the nation still in legislative use. (Photo courtesy the Maryland Department of Economic Development.)

SECTION I   WORDS, WORDS, WORDS!!!

NOTE: There are often several meanings to a word. In this book we usually give the legal meaning.

NOTE: In Europe, for centuries Latin was the language used by most learned persons. Often laws were written in Latin. This is why many Latin words and phrases are still used in the vocabulary of the law.

annotated code, a set of laws with ''annotations,'' which are notes, comments, explanations.

beneficiary, one who benefits, or is expected to benefit from something (such as a will, a life insurance policy, or a property insurance policy).

citizen, an inhabitant of a city or town; a person who owes loyalty, allegiance, to a country and is entitled to protection from the government of that country.

code, an orderly set of laws; or a suggested set of laws and rules.

constitution, a: a general plan of government and a statement of goals.

contract, a legally binding agreement.

defendant, a person required to defend himself or herself from a legal action or suit.

dissenting opinion, a written opinion in which a justice (judge) disagrees (dissents) with the opinion of the majority of the panel of judges.

3

extradition, the surrender or delivery of an alleged criminal by one authority(such as a state or a country) to another one which has jurisdiction to try the charge.

federal, a federal government is a central government which helps rule several federated (joined together) smaller governments. Example: our United States government helps govern our federation of states.

felon, one who has committed a serious crime.

felony, a serious crime usually punishable by a long imprisonment.

fraud, deceit, trickery, cheating; **fraudulent,** deceitful.

inalienable right, a right that cannot be taken away, given up, or transferred.

indictment, an accusation; a formal charge by a grand jury.

jurisdiction, the power, right, or authority to interpret and apply the law.

legislator, a lawmaker; a member of any lawmaking group. Example: A member of the Congress of the United States or of the General Assembly of Maryland.

misdemeanor, a misdeed; a crime less serious than a felony.

negligence, neglectful; the failure to exercise the care that a prudent person usually exercises.

opinion, a judgment about a person or thing; a written statement by a judge or panel of judges giving the decision of the court and explaining it.

party, (several meanings), a group or person taking one side of a question or contract; a group organized for political action. (Example: the Democratic party or the Republican party.) Also, a social gathering.

petition, to ask; a serious request made in a formal way to an authority or government.

plaintiff, one who begins a lawsuit to enforce a claim.

precedent, previous acts, custom, or previous court decisions.

prosecutor, one who carries out a legal action against a person accused of breaking the law, to prove that person's guilt.

tort, a wrongful act (except one involving a breach of contract) for which the injured (wronged) party can recover damages (often money) in a civil action (law suit).

venue, the place where something happened; the place where trial is held.

CHAPTER 1

Why We Have a Government and Laws

You might say that our government and our law form a *social contract*. We elect people who promise to work for laws that we would like. In this way, we—through the people we elect—try to get the laws that we want. We *also* agree that if the laws are not just exactly what we would like to have, we won't argue but will agree to obey whatever laws the majority of the voters have chosen. This is very important.

For example, we have a law that tells us to drive on the right side of the road. This lets all of us drive along in a *fairly* calm and orderly way. If we had to decide which side of the road we wanted to take, every time we met another car, we would have a great deal of trouble! So, laws are just sensible rules.

Laws are written by legislators (lawmakers) in our Maryland General Assembly and in the Congress of the United States. Our representatives in the General Assembly and in the Congress of the United States try to please as many voters as possible.

If we do not like a law, then, we vote for people who promise to work to change that law. Or, we can ask (petition) the government for changes.

When we are in Maryland we are under Maryland laws. That is, we are in Maryland's "jurisdiction." We are in the area that is governed by Maryland law. Citizens of Maryland obey Maryland laws and regulations as well as quite a few federal (United States) laws.

We might say, "But I don't want to obey all these laws and rules. Who are these government people and police who say that I must obey?" The answer is—that you, as a citizen and a voter—are really the "boss." Members of the United States and Maryland legislatures are elected by us. The police and government workers are hired by our consent. They are our public servants. It is important to remember that this is your government and your law.

In a democracy, the majority rules. That means that the person running for office who gets the most votes, wins the election. Also, in our legislatures, a suggested law with enough votes wins, is passed, and becomes a new law.

Even our basic State law, the Constitution of Maryland can be changed. Every two years we voters may vote for, or against, Constitutional changes that the Maryland General Assembly may propose.

The Constitution of the United States can be changed. It is not a quick or easy thing to do, but it can be done. The members of the Congress of the United States can vote to amend our U. S. Constitution. The Congress and a certain number of state legislatures then have to agree to these changes.

Under our United States and our Maryland governments, we all have rights. We have the right to vote, live, work and to own things in peace. We have other rights, too. That is what government and law is all about. It is our government. The laws are ours, to help us, to serve us.

Where can we find out what the law is

Why are all these laws and rules not written down exactly in our Constitution of Maryland? Because it would be too long, too complex, too rigid (stiff, unbending). A constitution is a *general* framework for a government and its law.

The exact rules (regulations) are written down for us by the departments in our Maryland government. For example, the Department of Transportation is one of these departments. The Departments of Education and of Agriculture are others. As rules need to be changed, these departments can change them. Times change, so our rules must be able to change fairly easily. This gives us a flexible system. Yet, all these rules have to be based on the general ideas written into the Constitution of Maryland.

Maryland laws are written down in the many volumes of the *Annotated Code of Maryland*. A "code" means a set of laws. The Maryland Code is revised annually. The revisions come out each year in October.

The meaning of "Federal"

Before we go on, let's take a look at some terms. The word "federal" is important. We live in our state, as in other states, under many federal laws. That is, we obey laws of a central government, a federal government. Maryland is one of a federation of states, united under one national (federal) government.

The Constitution of the United States of America gives us a basic, general, legal foundation to federal laws.

The Congress of the United States and the President of the United States combine to write new federal laws. Then, if the law is passed, departments of the federal government write rules to carry out and enforce these laws.

The *Annotated Code of the United States* and the *Congressional Record* contain all these federal laws. Supreme Court rulings and the decisions of federal courts also help define federal law. These, too, are published.

Power not kept by the federal government belongs to the state governments. State law is very important. Each state has its *own set of laws*!

It is important to know the laws of the state. "Ignorance of the law is no excuse."

"Good Grief!" we may say. "How can we learn all those laws?" This book will help you. There are attorneys, lawyers, that can be hired to explain things. They can explain how we can begin a business or buy a home. Bank officers and real estate people, too, often know these rules. There are books to explain legal questions.

You do not have to wade through the many volumes of Maryland and United States codes, however, for generally most government departments have booklets for you. For example, the Maryland Motor Vehicle Administration, has free booklets about driving rules and automobile ownership.

There are offices in our state capital, Annapolis, which can help. The Office of Legislative Reference in Annapolis can send you copies of new laws and even proposed laws not yet passed by our Maryland General Assembly.

When you want to do something, find out what laws apply. It also helps to understand the general reasons for our laws.

Some basic reasons for laws

There are many laws but just a few basic ideas (principles) of law.

The basic idea behind our law is to let us all have the right to live in peace and safety together. A *crime* is an act by someone that takes our rights to be safe and peaceful away from us.

We have laws that say that we must let people keep things that they own. Taking something from an owner is not fair and is called stealing. A person who steals is known as a thief.

Good citizens take pride in being honest. We like to treat other people the way we would like them to treat us. A good citizen can be trusted. When given a job to do, we are reliable, trustworthy. We can be trusted with work to be done, with other people, with vehicles and tools, and with money. A good citizen is honorable, a good neighbor.

11

To be a good citizen what we are actually doing is being considerate of others. For example, we drive with care. We do not want to hurt ourselves or others. We want everyone to enjoy their driving. We want them to be safe as they drive for pleasure or for work reasons. We try not to harm or annoy others. We ask for the same consideration, right? We try to respect each other so that we can live together in peace, prosperity and friendship.

Both our federal and state laws are meant to give us freedom and safety. We cooperate in other ways, too. We give money in the form of taxes to pay for the people we hire to help us, to serve us. We employ police, teachers and many other government workers. Our taxes pay for roads, airports, bridges, hospitals, rescue services, schools and many other important things that we need.

Yes. There certainly are many laws and rules! But the basic ideas are really easy to understand.

CHAPTER 2

Legal Terms

Criminal Law

Misdemeanors in Maryland are crimes such as cruelty to animals, destruction of property, disorderly conduct or disturbance of the peace.

Felonies are crimes of arson, burglary, murder, robbery, rape, manslaughter, mayhem, stealing and others.

Infamous crimes in Maryland are treason, felonies and fraud.

Again, you can see that the basic ideas are simple. Our laws are meant to help us live fairly, happily and safely together.

There is a booklet, sold for about $1.00, which tells us a great deal about criminal law in our state. It is titled: **Digest of Criminal Laws**. You may order these from the Maryland Police Training Commission, 3085 Hernwood Road, Woodstock, MD 21163.

United States Criminal Law

Stealing and Plundering. All states in the United States have laws against theft and plundering. Persons removing aircraft radios and other equipment, for example, fall into this category of criminal. If the thief steals in an area outside the jurisdiction of a state, U.S. federal laws cover such felonious acts. An example of federal jurisdiction is an area under U.S. maritime (sea) law.

Murder. Likewise, murder is punishable under either state or federal law, depending on where such acts are committed and other considerations. Murder, or assault, committed in national airspace falls within the federal jurisdiction if occurring on an interstate carrier, such as an airliner.

Kidnapping. Kidnapping is defined as the taking of a person against his or her will, without authority, and with criminal intent to collect ransom for that person's safe return. It is a capital offense in most states. If a kidnapped person is carried across a state line, the crime then becomes a federal offense with a penalty of death.

Other Serious Crimes. Among other serious violations of state and federal laws are:

Robbery, the forceful and unlawful taking of property or money by threatening life or safety or harm.

Burglary, breaking and entering a building with the intent to steal.

Theft, a term indicating that something is stolen. The penalty varies with the value of the objects taken. Criminally receiving stolen goods is a felony if the goods are received by someone who knows the goods are stolen.

Arson, is the willful and malicious setting of a fire or burning.

It is a crime to attempt to commit a crime, even if the attempt fails. Carrying a concealed weapon is a crime.

Finally, to plead ignorance of the law is no defense. Citizens are expected to know the law and in any case to conduct themselves in a responsible manner.

A criminal record is hard to live down, too!

Questions:

1. What kind of crime might be carelessly breaking down a small fence?

2. Give two examples of a felony.

3. What right does stealing violate?

4. Suppose a driver breaks a law and causes an accident. Can the driver be excused from responsibility because he or she did not know about the law broken?

1979 Cessna Centurion

CHAPTER 3

Being "of Age" in Maryland

Young people are interested in knowing how soon they can drive a car, work, marry, join the military services or buy a home. Here are examples of the laws that tell us how old we have to be in Maryland to do various things.

An adult, in Maryland, is a person who is 18 years old or older. At this age, or older, one may vote, make legal contracts, marry, own property, join the military services. (You may own property at a younger age, but must have a guardian to help you.) The rules on drinking alcoholic beverages changed recently. As of July 1, 1985, the legal "drinking age" is 21 years of age.

Driving. You must be at least 16 years old to drive automobiles, motorcycles and trucks. Drivers between 16 and 18 years of age are issued a provisional driver's license. This lets one drive, but limits the driver to certain hours and conditions. If you are under 18 when you apply for a driver's license, you must have completed driver education training.

To drive buses or tractor-trailers, you must be 18 years old.

The rules you usually need to know, plus many safety tips, are available in a free booklet. You can get it from police stations or offices of the Motor Vehicle Administration. You may wish to write for one. Write to: Maryland Department of Transportation, Motor Vehicle Administration, 6601 Ritchie Highway, N.E., Glen Burnie, MD, 21062.

Flying. You may begin flight training at any age. To fly a plane alone (solo) you must have a flight instructor's signature and be at least 16 years old. At 17 you can qualify for a license that allows you to carry passengers. At 18 you may earn a commercial license. This allows you to fly for pay.

Young People. There are many Maryland laws to protect young people. Article 100, Section 4, of the *Annotated Code of Maryland*,

for example, gives rules for employing young people under 18 years of age.

Young people under the age of 18 must also obey laws about carrying weapons. All citizens must obey laws about weapons. For example, *no person*, except officers of the law, may carry a weapon of any kind on public school property.

Conclusion

Yes, we have looked at just a few of the laws and rules we live under in Maryland. We are fortunate in our freedoms. We also have many responsibilities. No system is perfect. No system can please every citizen. We have to keep working at our government and our legal system to make it as effective as we can.

After reading about law and government, the same simple ideas keep coming through—that we have the right to be free, to be safe and to enjoy our property. Laws are based on ideas of fairness and justice.

18

Suggested Publications

Public libraries have the *Annotated Code of Maryland* and many other interesting books on law.

Digest of Criminal Laws, Maryland Police Training Commission, 3085 Hernwood Road, Woodstock, MD, 21163.

Maryland Driver's Handbook, Maryland Department of Transportation, Motor Vehicle Administration, 6601 Ritchie Highway, N.E., Glen Burnie, MD, 21062.

The Maryland Manual, published regularly by the Maryland Hall of Records. Available from: The Hall of Records, Box 828, Annapolis, MD, 21404.

Questions:

1. Why do you think the Maryland laws were changed recently to raise the legal age at which one can buy and drink alcoholic beverages?

2. Name several things one can do at age 18, when one becomes "of age," an adult, in Maryland.

3. Is it legal for a person 12 years of age to drive a car on a public highway? Can that 12-year-old fly a plane, taking flight instruction, on a public airway?

4. In the 1700's, a girl 12 years old was legally at the "age of consent" and could marry. What is the "age of consent" for marriage today? (Generally speaking.)

5. Name three rights we have, thanks to our United States and Maryland laws.

CHAPTER 4

Generally Speaking: Words and Ideas Used in
U.S. Law

If you would like to know a little more about law, the following definitions and discussions offer a general introduction to commonly used terms and ideas found in U.S. law. (It is, of course, important to consult an attorney for detailed information in actual cases.)

Law in the United States is based on the Constitution. This document grants each citizen the right to live peaceably and unharmed, to enjoy a home, to own property and benefit from its use, to conduct businesses and to have many other rights. Citizens in turn are to respect the rights of others.

If existing laws fail, due to changing circumstances, to protect the rights of citizens, federal and state legislatures may revise or repeal laws or enact new legislation.

In effect, the law is a set of rules, regulations and court decisions designed to settle disputes. If the parties involved in a disagreement cannot reach agreement, they may take the dispute to the courts for a decision.

"**Case law**," refers to that law which evolves from court decisions made prior to the case in question. These prior decisions, or "precedents," are cited by attorneys in the courts to support the arguments of plaintiffs and defendants.

A "**plaintiff**," is the party bringing action (suit) against another party.

The "**defendant**," is the party being sued who must defend himself against the charge.

The term "**party**," is used rather than list all the possible combinations of persons or organizations that might be involved in cases.

"**Civil law**," is that which determines and defines the rights of the individual in protecting his property or person.

"**Criminal law**," is written to protect the community against the harmful and criminal acts of individuals. It also protects the accused person by granting a fair and prompt trial.

A **crime** is an offense against the state and/or the people of the state. The public prosecutor brings suit against persons indicted (accused of) crimes in order to punish them and to deter crime.

A **felony** is a crime punishable by death (capital punishment) or with a state prison sentence. These are very serious crimes. (Example: assault with a deadly weapon.)

A **misdemeanor** is a crime but not a felony, a less serious crime in nature. (Example: disorderly conduct.)

"**Common law**," is based on precedent, previous court decisions.

"**Statutory law**," is based on the acts of federal and state legislatures.

A "**remedy**," refers to some compensation or action taken to remedy the wrong done to a plaintiff, e.g., money paid, "**damages**."

Courts of **equity** deal with recompense involving more than money—an injunction, for example, to restrain some action, or to require the performance of some duty.

To make business transactions less complicated, most states have adopted the *Uniform Commercial Code*. This is a set of regulations relating to business transactions to offer uniform business law. Federal legislation, too, attempts to bring uniformity to business law with various acts, e.g., the *Federal Consumer Protection Act*, known as the "Truth in Lending Act."

Jurisdiction

Jurisdiction is the power, authority, capacity, or right to act. It indicates the authority of a court to hear and decide cases. It may refer to a kind of case, and/or to geographical limits within which a court is empowered to act.

Jurisdiction is also used to indicate a nation's power to govern in certain geographical areas or situations. The term does not mean ownership.

The states of the United States have jurisdiction over non-federal matters within their borders.

Finally, the term indicates the power to govern persons being or residing in a particular state, nation, or place.

Venue

In practice the term "venue" means the place or county in which an injury is declared to have been done, or a fact declared to have happened. It also means the county or geographical division in which an action (a suit, a court action) is brought for trial. Venue does not refer to jurisdiction at all.

Liability

The term "liability" is a broad legal one which includes all manner of responsibilities, obligations, debts, and assumptions of risks by a person or an organization. To be liable is to be obligated or bound by law, answerable, chargeable; compellable to make restitution.

Limited liability is that which is legally limited in some manner. Owners of stock in a corporation, for example, are liable only up to the total amount of their investment. Other property they may own or money they may have cannot be reached by suits brought against the corporation.

Strict liability is "liability without fault." The case is one in which neither care nor negligence, good nor bad faith, knowledge nor ignorance, will save the defendant. Often, manufacturers operate under strict liability.

Negligence

Negligence is the omission to do something which a reasonable person, guided by ordinary considerations, would do. It also implies actions which would not be taken by a reasonable and prudent person.

One is not negligent unless one fails to use reasonable care, under existing circumstances, to avoid probable danger or injury. The term is synonymous with "careless." One is negligent if one's actions resulted in damage or injury due to lack of care.

Bailment

In general, bailment is the delivery of goods or personal property to another for care or for some special object. The *bailor* is the person handing over the property; the *bailee* is the party receiving it. An example might be, the handing over of an aircraft or automobile for maintenance.

Libel

A libel can be, in tort law, an accusation in writing or print against the character of a person which affects his reputation, diminishes his respectability, and which discredits him. Disparagement of goods is a form of libel. In general, libel in this sense means a false accusation which dishonors a person or product.

Freedom of Information

Under the Freedom of Information Act of 1966, which was strengthened in 1974, one is entitled to information from government files. To request this information, write to the appropriate federal agency, giving enough information so that the material in question may be located with reasonable ease. Send the statement that this is a "Freedom of Information Act Request. Do not delay."

Requests must be answered within ten working days, upon receipt by the proper office.

Torts

In general, tort law is that which is designed to compensate a plaintiff for the failure of a party to carry out a duty owed the plaintiff. To recover damages, a plaintiff must show a breach of duty and that injury or damage has resulted.

A "tort" is a civil wrong, an act, or a failure in one's duty toward another, causing property damage or loss, or injury to an individual. It may also be a breach of the peace, a crime, hence a cause for prosecution under criminal law.

Civil law is divided into "equity" and "law". Wrongs resulting in damage or injury (torts) which can be corrected (remedied or relieved) by money payment (damages paid) come under the "law" portion of civil law. If money alone cannot remedy the wrong, then, in a more formal action, the courts may require action on the part of the person being sued (the defendant) to give relief to the person bringing suit (the plaintiff).

Contract law is usually separate from tort law because court action may be brought for breach of the terms of a contract. Additional tort action is possible only if personal injury or property damage resulted and came from participation in the contract. Negligence must be proven to recover damages.

To review: "tort" is defined as coming from the Latin term, "to twist", "to wrest aside". It is a private or civil wrong or injury, independent of contract. It is a violation of a duty imposed by general law upon all persons in their relations to each other.

Contracts

Contract law is complex and is affected by the state laws in which contracts are made. The following is a general discussion only. (No portion of this book is intended to replace the services of an attorney!)

Contracts to be enforceable must be clear to all parties concerned and entered into without fraudulent intent. Contracts won by means of unwarranted pressures or threats are also unenforceable. The terms of the contract, then, should be clearly stated. All parties to the contract should examine all conditions of the contract before signing or otherwise agreeing to the terms.

Contracts may be written, verbal, or implied. Written contracts are "express" contracts and are in force according to the terms when signed by all parties. Verbal contracts are those not written but understood by all parties with verbal terms offered and accepted.

Contracts imply action and payment for action, or the transfer of some property for payment or other benefit. Placing a plane or automobile in the hands of airport maintenance personnel implies an order for work and an agreement to pay for the services requested.

Since human memory is not infallible, it is good business practice to have a work order written out for maintenance and repair work and to have a sales contract for the purchase of an automobile or other item.

A contract has three essential parts: a *subject*, an *agreement*, and *consideration*. The subject is the object or goal of the contract. This must be a lawful one, since contracts to commit offenses or crimes are not enforceable. Also, whimsical and frivolous contracts are not enforceable. The agreement is based on the idea that a property or service is being offered on terms agreeable to another party. Consideration is, of course, the agreed upon compensation (money or traded-in property) to be paid. This does not have to be money but must be to the benefit of the offering party. Again, contracts to perform unlawful ends are not enforceable.

The parties involved in an enforceable contract must be of age and mentally competent. Convicted felons cannot give assent that will be supported by the courts. One enters into agreement with felons with this risk in mind. Corporations are regarded by the law as persons and can enter into contracts. Contracts begin with an offer communicated to a party. There must be a clear and explicit understanding of the offer on both sides. An offer with a serious intent and made in good faith is a binding one.

Recent court decisions have found an otherwise legal contract not binding because, viewed in the context of their commercial setting, the terms were so exploitative that they were an abuse of the bargaining process. (Example: *District of Columbia, Williams vs Walker-Thomas Furniture Company*.)

Implied contracts are those in which services or goods are offered by a business and accepted by a customer. It is implied that the goods are of reasonable quality as advertised and that great care will be exercised in performing services.

Insurance

Insurance is a contract entered into by the insurer and the insured. These contracts, commonly called policies, must contain the elements necessary for a valid contract. (See the contracts section of this chapter.) A policy usually provides, upon payment of a premium (a fee), that the insurer will reimburse the insured for any loss incurred

27

by that person *from certain stated causes*. These causes are also known as "risks."

In insurance, as in other transactions, we get only what we pay for. Each additional coverage has an additional premium to take care of the greater risk that the insurance company is to bear.

To be insured a policy must have a subject—for example, the life of a stated person, a building, or a vehicle. The risk against which the property or life is insured must be specified in the policy. The amount for which the insuror agrees to cover losses must be given. The time period covered must also be plainly set forth in the policy.

One must have the right to insure. That is, if one has no financial interest in an aircraft, a house, or other property, one cannot recover money for damage or loss of the thing insured. An owner, or a partner (part owner), accurately described in the policy is insurable. A person who has property left in his possession for storage or repair (a bailee) has an insurable interest because should a loss occur he may be held responsible.

In life insurance if the insured takes out the insurance that person can make anyone he likes the beneficiary. The beneficiary may even be a complete stranger. Should a person take out insurance on the life of another person, a question arises. The beneficiary in this case must have an insurable interest in the life of the insured at the time the policy is issued.

Legal Quiz:

1. Define the word "jurisdiction."

2. What is meant by "venue?"

3. If you are "liable," what does that mean?

4. Name ways one might be found "negligent" after an auto accident?

5. What is a "tort," in legal meaning?

6. Name three things contracts usually contain.

7. Name two types of persons who cannot legally sign a legal contract.

8. Is an insurance policy a contract?

Maryland Governor's Mansion. State House Circle, Annapolis, Maryland.

Photo courtesy Div. of Tourist Development, Maryland
Dept. of Economic and Community Development.

CHAPTER 5

The Individual

Each of us is a person, an individual. We have rights and responsibilities in our town or city, on our county, our state, our nation —our world.

The following paragraphs show how laws and customs see the person, the individual. As you read, try to understand the reasons for these rules.

The Individual: World Law

Nations have jurisdiction (power) over their citizens. The definition of a citizen varies according to nation.

Some nations, including Great Britain and the United States, allow naturalization. Naturalization is the voluntary act of becoming a citizen. This demonstrates the United States philosophy that citizenship is "alienable," that is, that it can be transferred. Some governments hold that only the place of birth is a person's homeland, that citizenship is something inalienable, not buyable, salable, nor transferable.

HEY, MICHAEL, THERE'S A GUY IN MY MATH CLASS WITH AN ENGLISH ACCENT WHO CLAIMS HE IS AN AMERICAN!

WELL, GRUNT, HE IS PROBABLY A NATURALIZED CITIZEN WHO WAS BORN IN ANOTHER COUNTRY BUT BECAME A U.S. CITIZEN.

A sovereign nation has the power to insist that one obey its laws while within its borders and can punish one if the law is broken. True, a person may escape into another nation. Then, only should that other nation agree to return him (extradite him) can he be seized and punished. Extradition is approved as a rule only for certain crimes that civilized nations recognize, plus acceptable proof of the crime.

Diplomats are generally immune from prosecution by other than their home state. Diplomatic agents also have some immunity.

One of the individuals considered an enemy of all maritime states is the "pirate." A pirate may be defined as one who seizes vessels, goods, and/or persons in transit on the seas.

A ship saving miles by using the Chesapeake and Delaware Canal, near Chesapeake City, Cecil County, Maryland.

Photograph courtesy the Maryland Div. of Tourist Development.

Are corporations treated as individuals under international law and custom? Yes. Corporations have the nationality of the state (nation) in which they are incorporated. Unincorporated associations have the nationality of the state in which their headquarters or controlling body is located.

Piracy. The ancient crime of piracy is with us today in the guise of hijacking of aircraft and also in the capture of small boats operating offshore. Piracy is sometimes termed a "marine felony," a robbery at sea. The crime may include burning of the vessel or aircraft, the murder and/or capture of the passengers and crew.

Piracy is a federal crime and is punishable by life imprisonment under federal law, 18 U.S. Code 1651.

Jurisdiction Over the Individual

Ships and aircraft have the nationality of their nation of registry. Aboard a ship on the high seas the laws of the nation of registry prevail. In port, unless called aboard by the ship's master or an aircraft commander, or unless the peace is being disturbed, officials of the port being visited by the foreign vessel or aircraft generally do not interfere with foreign laws and customs aboard that craft.

A nation controls its own registered aircraft and the passengers aboard them when the aircraft is being operated inside its national boundaries, while over its territorial waters, and while over the high seas.

Corporations hold the nationality of the nation in which they are incorporated. Groups not incorporated have the nationality of the nation in which their headquarters, controlling the operation of the group, is located.

A nation maintains jurisdiction over its citizens. We pause to note here that definitions of citizenship vary from country to country. Birth, residency, or the nationality of one's parents enters into the matter. Dual citizenship is also possible, with a person claiming citizenship in two nations.

The U.S. law claims as citizens all persons born in the U.S. or those who have been naturalized in the U.S. Also, a person born abroad to a parent who is a U.S. citizen (that parent must have resided in the U.S. at some time), is recognized as a citizen of the United States.

A nation has the right to require its citizens to obey its laws and to punish lawbreakers. This right extends to all persons within a nation's national boundaries. Embassy personnel and other diplomatic personnel are customarily exempted and are generally sent to their home nation rather than being punished in the foreign state.

Extradition

Foreign citizens who hold no diplomatic immunity can be fined or sentenced to prison or even executed for breaking the laws of the nation they are visiting. There are treaties between nations concerning this, yet many an American has served a sentence in a foreign prison.

Extradition is the voluntary surrender of a person by one state to another.

Questions:

1. What is an individual?

2. What is a citizen?

3. Do you have to be born of U.S. parents in the U.S. to be a citizen?

4. What is an "inalienable right?"

5. Define the word "jurisdiction."

CHAPTER 6

State and Federal Courts Systems

In this chapter a brief summary of the court systems of the United States will be given with a short description of their functions—what courts exist and what they do.

There is today very definitely such a thing as states' rights. Whatever powers not given to the federal government are reserved to the states, according to the Constitution of the United States.

As you know, there was at the beginning of our United States history quite a wrangle over this issue of states' rights. Finally, the leaders of the various state governments realized that some rights must go to the federal government or else thirteen quarreling, divided and weakened small countries would exist. In the interest of all, certain states' rights had to be given up.

States' Rights

Government is seen as least harmful when nearest the people. At a distance it is perceived as being monolithic and tyrannical. Many oppose the increasing centralization of our government but must admit the need for it in many cases—treaties, public waterways, ocean borders, domestic and international air transport, and in matters relating to public health, education, welfare and national defense.

Writers urge that the Federal government stick to those functions given it by the Constitution and leave the States to tend to their own affairs. When the United States began, the States claimed virtually all rights, under the Articles of Confederation. The Federal government was a figurehead designed to treat with other nations, serve as a clearing house of news and needs of the States, and when necessary, to coordinate efforts toward national defense.

The establishment of the Constitution in 1789 welded the nation together and allowed the Federal government (the President, Congress and Supreme Court) more power; e.g., power to raise money via import and export levies, etc. Even so, the States held on to a great amount of power.

To this day, there is a power struggle between the state governments and the federal government. Why pay taxes to Washington, D.C., which are to be used at home? Many hands may be used, and paid, to take and return the funds; goals seen at home are lost in the federal bureaucracy; and control of funds is lost to people contributing taxes.

Let us look at our state courts systems and our federal courts systems to see how some rights are kept at the state level, and others surrendered to a higher, federal, authority.

State Court Systems

Our English colonial court systems were fairly simple in nature. Most of the political power lay in the hands of the English governor and his council of advisors. These men, and they were all men, appointed judges from a tight circle of educated property owners.

Even today, differences in state governments persist which were generated in colonial times. If the state was originally settled under French or Spanish rule, then the state government is similar to that of the original country that established itself there. Also, the laws and court system may still contain practices and customs from the parent country. In Maryland, as in so many states, and in our national, federal, government, English law forms remain with us.

With an increase in the number of people in the colonies and the amount of business conducted, naturally, the courts responded by expanding to handle the increased litigation that arose.

After the American Revolution, political power now lay in the hands of the men in the state legislatures. Oddly, these were often the same men who had been powerful and active under English rule. Property rights and the rights to safeguard business debts were promptly written into early United States law. Only those rights which the landowners and educated elite could not monopolize, due to the pressures of the general population of free men, were slowly surrendered. Many members of the gentry feared mob rule and

distrusted the ability of citizens to rule themselves. This was a natural fear, for self government had not been attempted before on this scale and with these particular hopes for republicanism and democracy. Early American government was not democratic in reality but had democratic government as its eventual goal in many minds.

American courts did respond to popular demands. Unpopular judges were removed and unpopular decisions reviewed by state legislatures. Even so, a cry sometimes arose that the eventual decision in a case was "unconstitutional." The review of state actions by the Supreme Court to determine constitutionality is an American innovation. This tended to offer United States citizens a uniform and powerful legal system, and one less apt to be arbitrary and whimsical at the state level.

With the industrialization of the United States in the mid 1800's, the courts changed and became more specialized. For example, interstate cases arose from the development of a national railway system. Railways, to be useful on a national scale, had to have a fairly uniform code of laws in all states. Hence, federal regulation came into being, today evinced in the Interstate Commerce Commission (ICC), a federal commission to transcend state and municipal variations with a uniform interstate code. Even so, the states demand taxes and certain operations concessions from interstate carriers. So, certain federal agencies were set up, and federal rules imposed on interstate business.

State Courts

Today, our state courts offer a part, or a combination, of the following courts:

The State Supreme Court which acts as a court of appeals for cases tried in a lower court in the state. Some states allow cases to be heard in the State Supreme Court without being heard by an intermediate court. That is, a person may appeal immediately after a lower court hears his case, skipping the next higher court entirely.

Intermediate Appellate Courts which are used for cases referred to them from a lower court of limited jurisdiction. For certain cases in some states this is, in effect, the highest court of appeals within the state system. There are trial courts of general jurisdiction in which cases may begin, be initiated, and heard. If this court decision is satisfactory to the party bringing the suit and to the defendant, then that decision stands. (It may be that the decision is not really acceptable, yet neither party can spare the time or money to pursue the matter further.)

Trial Courts of limited jurisdiction are those hearing only traffic offenses, or only estate cases (for example, an Orphans' Court), and the juvenile courts.

Decisions made in the lower courts are important because *most cases* are heard at this level and *are not appealed.* Thousands of cases are heard at the lower level of the judicial system, while only scores or hundreds are heard at the highest court of appeals in a state. For this reason, then, these lower court decisions set *precedent* and become a part of the law. We cannot take for granted the idea, however, that only important cases are appealed. Generally speaking, every litigant does have access to at least one court of appeal.

All of our states have the above-discussed three general "layers" of courts.

A court of appeal *does not retry the case*. The judges *review* the court records of the trial and decide whether the lower court decision was legal and appropriate.

Maryland, in the 1970's, eliminated many courts of limited jurisdiction and did away with justices of the peace. New rules for the disciplining of the judiciary were formulated and voted into law by state referenda which amended the state constitution.

The American Bar Association (ABA) has worked out a model state court system. North Carolina has adopted the ABA system, for example, discarding its unwieldy, traditional court system.

One finds the lower courts presided over by a single judge. State courts of appeal, however, tend to have more than one justice "sitting" or "on the bench." These judges, generally, make up odd-numbered panels, such as three, five, or nine, in order to avoid ties. Majority decisions prevail, but dissenting opinions often make important points. Both dissenting and assenting decisions are quoted by attorneys and jurists (judges) at later dates in arguing similar cases.

It is important to understand that each of the states of the United States has a separate and often differing court system. True, all the states share the U.S. Supreme Court, a body of judges who interpret the Constitution. These judges (Justices of the Supreme Court) select out of the many cases referred to that court, ones that will make clear some aspect of the Constitution. That document was written in rather general terms and just how its provisions apply to modern legal matters requires constant interpretation, re-interpretation and even amendment. Without this flexibility our government would be unable to respond to the changing needs of the people governed.

The writers of the U.S. Constitution, however, made amending the document an involved and time-consuming process. This was done for the good reason that the Constitution may be changed only after due consideration and with time allowed for detailed debate and discussion of the proposed changes.

Yet, despite sharing our basic governmental document, the Constitution, and sharing a nationally standardized federal court system, the fact remains that *in the states there are separate court systems* peculiar to that state and often quite different from the court systems of other states. Similarly, a body of state law has grown up in each state, quite often not at all like the laws of other states. State laws are alike in that they are to conform to the general provisions of the federal Constitution. This, however, allows scope for considerable difference, as we shall see.

41

States jealously guard their powers. Citizens wish to retain as much control over their lives and laws as possible. Each local area wishes to be able to choose its own rules. Federal control means that someone in Washington, D.C. will be telling them how to spend tax monies, how much to pay in taxes, and what rules of law are to be followed. Naturally, in such a diverse nation as this one, each area has different preferences and needs; the local power granted by state governments is a workable way in which to retain local power.

States differ for several reasons. Historically, for example, as we have mentioned, Louisiana with its French background will differ markedly in state government background from Massachusetts with its English historical orientation. California will reflect in some of its laws its Spanish origins. Further, varying ethnic groups settled various

WHY CAN'T ALL THE STATES HAVE THE SAME LAWS?

BECAUSE THEY HAVE DIFFERENT NEEDS. MARYLAND, WITH IT'S WATER AND PORT NEEDS DIFFERENT LAWS THAN A STATE LIKE ARIZONA THAT IS LAND-LOCKED.

AND HISTORY!

portions of our nation and this difference is reflected in the court systems and the laws of the states. Some states are rural, some urban in nature. Some have powerful special interest groups involved in oil production, fishing, aircraft manufacturing, tobacco raising, grain production, and on and on in great number. We can see, therefore, how states guard their powers and how each may differ from the other.

One state need not necessarily follow precedents set via the same circumstances in another state. Hence, completely separate and differing sets of precedents may exist in the various states. Further, even the U.S. Supreme Court cannot overrule the decisions of the highest state court unless a Constitutional question is involved.

Surprisingly, many United States citizens do not realize that such variety of law and of court systems do exist in their country. Most of us are familiar with our own state laws and pay little attention to others.

The Federal Courts

The United States Supreme Court, of course, has nine judges, (called Justices) one of whom is named the Chief Justice. Here, too, majority decisions prevail yet dissenting opinions are not without importance. Basically, the Supreme Court adheres to certain principles of constitutional interpretation, that the powers of the federal government are those to be found in the Constitution, expressly stated or implied. Once a power has been established as belonging to the federal government by the Constitution that power can be broadly interpreted. All powers not granted the federal government by the Constitution are retained by the governments of the states.

The Supreme Court can pass on the constitutionality of state laws thus making the federal government superior to state governments and decisions. Further, the Supreme Court has the right to decide whether or not an Act of Congress is constitutional. The Supreme Court is the highest court of appeals in the United States, and its decisions become the law of the land.

United States Supreme Court. At the apex of our system is, of course, the United States Supreme Court.

The nine justices *select* certain cases to be heard. Hundreds of cases are appealed to this highest court of the land, yet few are heard. Those cases chosen are ones involving constitutional issues and interpretations needing review.

The Supreme Court can and does reverse itself as time, circumstances, and public perceptions cause changes in the national outlook. Nevertheless, the precepts of the Constitution give the Supreme Court a firm framework on which to build. Changes are hard fought, but this possibility of reversal, of even Supreme Court decisions, gives our court system the rather deliberate flexibility it needs.

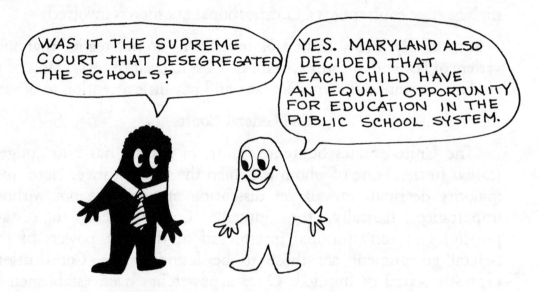

United States Courts of Appeals (Circuit Courts). Just below the United States Supreme Court are the regional United States courts which hear appeals referred to them from the state courts. By law, only certain cases may be heard. The cases may involve certain (substantial) sums of money, involve cases of persons residing in two or more states, or involve some federal factor. Again, may appeals are refused, not given a hearing.

Jurisdiction of U.S. District Courts. Under the National Aeronautics and Space Act as amended, the United States District Courts shall have original jurisdiction concurrent with the Court of Claims of civil actions or claims against the United States. These claims are those which are not to exceed $10,000.00, and are founded

44

on the Constitution, an Act of Congress, executive department order, a federal regulation, or any express or implied contract with the United States.

Subject to the provisions of Chapter 171 of the U.S. Code, District Courts have exclusive jurisdiction of civil actions or claims against the United States for money damages, injury, loss of property, or personal injury or death caused by the negligent or wrongful act or omission of employees of the United States Government. This applies under circumstances where the United States, if a private person, would be liable to the claimant in accordance with the law of the place where the act or omission occurred.

Pension suits and suits involving the Internal Revenue Service, however, do not come under the jurisdiction of the United States District Court.

The United States District Court has the power to remand cases to an appropriate administrative or executive body.

Authority to release funds for the settlement of claims and judgments is given under Title 31, United States Code 7242.

United States Special Courts. These are the special hearings held by various United States federal commissions such as the Interstate Commerce Commission (ICC), the Department of Transportation (DOT), and various boards. There are other special federal courts as well, which deal with particular aspects of federal regulation and are often ways of appealing decisions awarded in the state courts systems.

Federal Courts determine the intent of Congress in certain disputes. An example of this might be in interpreting the Act to Regulate Commerce. In the same way, state courts interpret laws formulated by state legislatures.

The Motor Vehicle Carrier Act of 1935 denies the Interstate Commerce Commission (ICC) control over in-state (intrastate) motor carriers operating legally under a state regulatory agency. Regulation at the state level is less pervasive in air commerce than in motor codes.

Supreme Court
of the United States

U.S. District Courts with federal and local jurisdiction	Administrative Quasi-Judicial Agencies	U.S. District Courts with federal jurisdiction only
(Virgin Islands Canal Zone Guam)	(Tax Court, Federal Trade Commission, National Labor Relations Board, etc.)	(91 districts in 50 states, the District of Columbia and Puerto Rico)
Court of Customs and Patent Appeals	Court of Claims	District Appeals from State Courts in 50 states
Customs Court		

The Congressional Role

The Congress of the United States sets broad policies and delegates regulatory interstate commerce powers to commissions and boards. Congress controls these boards via its power to deny or appropriate funds.

In the U.S. House of Representatives and in the U.S. Senate legislation and action is studied via committees. For example, the Interstate Commerce and Foreign Commerce committees study those subjects. These Committees deny or recommend legislation to Congress. Proposals for new laws are heard, evidence sifted, opinions voiced, and compromises worked out in Committees and then in Congress.

The Executive Role

The President of the United States has great powers. The chief executive has the overall power to recommend legislation to Congress and to administer the laws of the Congress. Certain veto powers are his.

He, or she, appoints members of commissions, although there is a limit as to how many members of a single party may be seated on any one board. Likewise, no one President may appoint to a commission a majority of the members.

The President may order investigations and studies. Recent studies have been made at Presidential request in the fields of air and surface safety, urban transportation, and in other areas.

The national budget is drawn up by the President and its recommended appropriations are presented to Congress. All commissions are in this federal budget, of course, and must submit requests annually to the Bureau of the Budget.

In international relations there are further powers of the presidency, in the President's power to negotiate by means of Executive Agreements with other heads of state.

Questions:

1. Why are the state legal systems in Maryland and Louisiana quite different in many ways?

2. Why were interstate federal commissions, such as the Interstate Commerce Commission, begun?

3. What is an appeal in the legal sense? An appellate court?

4. How can a "precedent" be used by an attorney in preparing a case?

5. Why do panels of judges in an appellate court total an uneven number? (For example: five judges, nine judges.)

6. Why is it so important that we agree to obey laws even though we personally might not think the law is just the way we want it?

Suggested Reading

See Rene Wormser, *The Story of the Law* (New York: Simon & Schuster, 1926), pp. 394-395, for the origin of United States state law policy.

Rene David and John E. C. Brierly, *Major Legal Systems in the World Today*, 2nd edition (New York: The Macmillan Publishing Co., Inc., 1978), pp. 328-33.

Stuart M. Speiser and Charles F. Krause, *Aviation Tort Law*, (San Francisco: Bancroft-Whitney Co., 1978), pp. 49-57. Also Vol. 2, pp. 435-37.

Gerhard von Glahn, *Law Among Nations*, 3rd edition (New York: Macmillan Publishing Co., Inc., 1976), pp. 422-24.

SECTION II
VOTING
AND OUR
MARYLAND GOVERNMENT

SECTION II   WORDS, WORDS, WORDS!!!

administration, performance of duties; management; a body of people who administer; also, the term of office of an administrative officer or body.

agenda, a plan for a meeting, a list of subjects to be discussed.

amendment, a change, an addition or a deletion (subtraction).

analysis, a study of something, an examination of something to discover its parts; **analyses,** the plural of analysis.

appeal, a request for a review of a court decision. An **appellate court** is one which hears appeals.

appointed, named to fill a position or office.

attests, declares to be true.

audit, a searching examination and verification of accounts; **auditor,** one who examines, verifies, declares to be true after examination.

bail, money left with a government agency which will be forfeited (not returned) should the arrested person "out on bail" not return for trial as promised.

briefs, in the legal sense, are legal arguments with notes on similar cases and decisions. These are written by attorneys to try to convince the court to decide a case in favor of the lawyer's clients.

budget, a detailed plan, a plan for spending money; one that is a **balanced budget** is one in which income and expenditures are the same, that is, they are in balance.

campaign, a connected series of actions designed to bring about a desired result; for example, a battle plan designed to gain a victory, or a plan to bring about some desired result.

candidate, one who offers himself or herself, or is proposed by others, for an office or an honor.

collateral, property (for example land deeds, stocks or bonds) handed over or promised as security. This may protect a lender or investors.

concurrent, acting together, jointly, with equal authority.

conventions, an assembly of persons who meet for some common purpose. (Example, to select a political candidate or candidates.)

countersign, a second signature that follows another signature, which attests (says, states) that a document is genuine.

court circuits, a series of places where courts meet regularly. The term comes from the days in which judges had to travel from place to place to hold court.

delegate, a person given the power to act for others.

docket, a list of court cases to be heard.

effect, the outcome; fact; the result of something that has been done or has happened.

election, the process of voting to choose a person to hold an office.

electors, persons qualified to vote in an election; an **electoral college,** is a body of electors; especially: one that elects the President and the Vice-President of the United States.

equity, dealing with matters of justice between conflicting parties.

fiscal, relating to financial matters (money matters).

General Assembly (of Maryland), the Maryland legislature, lawmakers; the Maryland General Assembly is a legislature made up of two "houses", the Maryland House of Delegates and the Maryland Senate.

general elections, those in which candidates of all parties and independent candidates compete for election to offices.

impact, effect of something or some action upon another. Examples: the effect of an oil spill on the ecology of Chesapeake Bay, or the effect of a law on the businesses in a state.

impeach, to charge a public official before a competent court with misconduct.

implications, results of an action or event; involvements; something implied.

inmate, someone held in an institution; a prisoner; a patient.

joint ballot, a voting together. Example: when the Maryland House of Delegates and the Maryland Senate vote together as one body.

jointly, together; the Governor and the Lieutenant Governor of Maryland run for office together. The President and Vice President of the United States are also "running mates," in campaigns and elections. The voter who casts a vote for one votes for both. The voter votes for a team.

jury, a body of persons sworn to test a matter submitted to them and to give their verdict (decision) based on the evidence presented. Example: in a jury trial, twelve people are selected to make up a jury.

lobbyists, persons whose job it is to try to influence public officials and legislators.

mandated, required by law.

nominee, a person chosen, suggested, for an office, a duty, a position.

officials, persons chosen to carry out the work of government. Leaders of formal government departments.

political platforms, the declared principles and policies of a political party.

primary elections, elections held to select by vote the candidates chosen to represent a political party.

qualifications, a list of items, experience, qualities needed to qualify for a position or to be a candidate for public office.

ratification, an agreement to a law, or an amendment to the Constitution, or to a plan of action, by the voters. It is the way voters may say "yes" or "no."

referendum, the practice of submitting to popular vote legislative measures; the **referenda,** is the plural of referendum.

registration (to vote), the formal act of registering to vote by entering in one's town or county, one's name, address and political party affiliation (if any).

replevin, a process of recovering personal property unlawfully detained or held.

senator, a member of a senate.

statute, a law; **statutory law,** laws relating to a statute or law.

transcripts, are complete written accounts of a court case; a complete written record of something.

veto, to refuse to approve.

vote, to express one's wish or choice by a vote; to cast a vote.

CHAPTER 1
Maryland, a General Description

MARYLAND GOVERNMENT

The government of Maryland is based on a written compact known as the Constitution of Maryland. The Constitution of Maryland, consisting of a bill of rights, the operational sections of the Constitution proper, and those amendments ratified to date, was adopted in 1867. It is the fourth constitution Maryland has had since the first was adopted in 1777 during the War for American Independence.

As Article 1 of the Declaration of Rights makes clear, the source of all power and authority for governing the state of Maryland is its citizens. The article states that "all Government of right originates from the People, is founded in compact only, and is instituted solely for the good of the whole; and they have, at all times, the inalienable right to alter, reform or abolish their Form of Government in such manner as they may deem expedient." Thus, although the responsibility for furthering the best interests of the citizens of Maryland is vested in specific officers and offices of state government, actual governing authority remains with the registered voters of Maryland. To be a registered voter, a person must be eighteen years of age or older, a citizen of the United States, and a resident of Maryland thirty days prior to the date of an election.

Recognizing that it would be too cumbersome for all persons to participate directly in the operation of government, the framers of Maryland's Constitution of 1867 followed the precedent established in earlier Maryland constitutions by providing for the delegation of power to elected representatives. To further guarantee the people's liberty, the Constitution of 1867 provided for the separation of powers of government into three distinct branches—the executive, the legislative, and the judicial—which exercise certain checks and balances on each other.

The *Executive Department*, consisting of various constitutional officers and agencies, is responsible for statewide implementation and enforcement of Maryland's laws and for providing executive direction and centralized administrative services. The chief executive officer is the governor, elected by the voters for a four-year term each even-numbered year that is not a presidential election year. The governor is responsible for ensuring that Maryland's laws are effectively executed, that certain appointments as provided by the Constitution or by law are made, that a budget is presented annually to the legislature, and as commander in chief of the military that the armed forces of the state are able to meet whatever emergency might arise. The governor may veto legislation passed by the legislature, and it is he who appoints judges to the state judiciary. The governor is assisted by the lieutenant governor, who runs for election on a joint ballot with the candidate for governor. Duties of the lieutenant governor are limited to those assigned him by the governor. The governor and lieutenant governor must each be at least thirty years old and a resident and voter of Maryland for the five years immediately preceding their election.

Other statewide executive officers are also provided for in the Constitution. The comptroller is charged with the general superintendence of the fiscal affairs of the state. The treasurer is responsible for accounting for all deposits and disbursements to or from the state treasury. The secretary of state attests to the governor's signature on all public documents and oversees all executive orders, commissions, and appointments. The attorney general serves as legal counsel to the governor, the legislature, and all state departments, boards, and most commissions. Each of these executive officers serves a four-year term. The people elect the comptroller and attorney general. The treasurer is selected by joint ballot of both houses of the General Assembly, and the secretary of state is appointed by the governor. An important agency of the executive department is the Board of Public Works, composed of the governor, the comptroller, and the treasurer, which is responsible for approving all sums expended through state loans, most capital improvements, and the sale, lease, or transfer of all real property owned by the state.

Until recently, Maryland, like most other states in the union, had experienced a steady proliferation of agencies, boards, and commissions within the executive department as the need for public services increased. Between 1969 and 1972 the General Assembly passed legislation creating twelve new cabinet-level departments, encompassing within them nearly 250 separate governmental entities. In order of their creation, the twelve departments are: Health and Mental Hygiene, Budget and Fiscal Planning, Natural Resources, State Planning, Personnel, General Services, Human Resources, Public Safety and Correctional Services, Licensing and Regulation, Economic and Community Development, Transportation, and Agriculture. The Department of Education was made a principal department in 1976, and in 1983 the Department of Employment and Training was created as the fourteenth department within the executive branch.

Material from the *Maryland Manual 1985-1986*, published by the State of Maryland, State Archives, Annapolis, MD.

Each state department, except for Education, is headed by a secretary, appointed by the governor with the consent of the Senate, who serves at the pleasure of the governor. Each secretary carries out the governor's policies regarding the particular department and is responsible for the department's operation. The Department of Education is headed by the State Board of Education, which appoints the state superintendent of schools to direct the department. Certain state agencies whose purpose or functions do not permit easy integration into one of the fourteen cabinet-level departments have remained independent, such as the State Department of Assessments and Taxation, the Public Service Commission, and the state universities and colleges. These permanent executive departments, agencies, and commissions are augmented by special study commissions and task forces at the discretion of the governor.

General Assembly is the legal designation of the Maryland legislature. The General Assembly is sometimes referred to as the "popular" branch of government, because its members are more directly representative of the electorate than are officials of either the executive or judiciary. Legislators are elected to both houses of the General Assembly from districts redrawn every ten years to ensure an equal representation based on the concept of "one person one vote." The geographical size of the districts varies according to population density, but in all cases are sufficiently small so that the electorate can be certain that their chosen representatives are familiar with the concerns and priorities of their specific area.

Like all states but Nebraska, Maryland has a bicameral legislature. The lower house is known as the House of Delegates and the upper house as the Senate. Representatives to both houses are elected in each gubernatorial election year for four-year terms. Candidates for the House of Delegates must be at least twenty-one years of age and those for the Senate at least twenty-five. The House of Delegates consists of 141 members, while the Senate has 47 members. Both houses convene annually on the second Wednesday in January for a 90-day session. Sessions may be extended by resolution of both houses, and special sessions may be called by the governor. The General Assembly is responsible for passing all laws necessary for the welfare of the state's citizens, for legislation dealing with the counties and special taxing districts, for determining how state funds are to be allocated, and for adopting amendments to the state Constitution. Bills may be introduced in either house, and when passed by both houses and signed by the governor they become law.

The General Assembly employs various committees—statutory, standing, and joint—to facilitate its work during and between sessions. The legislative branch also encompasses several state agencies. The Department of Legislative Reference assists in the preparation of legislation and maintains a library of material essential for legislators. The Commission to Revise the Annotated Code is involved in a multi-year reorganization and recodification of the laws of Maryland. The Department of Fiscal Services prepares financial impact statements and provides fiscal monitoring functions for the General Assembly.

One of the single most important tasks of the General Assembly, and one that requires close coordination and consultation with the Executive Department, is adoption of the annual state budget. The Constitution specifies that it is the responsibility of the governor to present the annual budget to the General Assembly within five days of the beginning of each legislative session. Unlike many other states, the budget of Maryland must not exceed anticipated revenues, thus preventing deficit spending and accounting in large part for the excellent bond rating enjoyed by the state. Reflecting the principle of separation of powers within state government, the governor must incorporate into the budget unchanged requests from the legislative and judicial departments, as well as the estimated expenses required for operating the public schools. Beyond these items and other obligations for certain state debts and the salaries of officials specified in the Constitution, the governor has considerable discretion in determining what programs and agencies to fund in the budget. The budget process is thus a major policy-shaping tool for the governor. Supplemental budgets may be submitted by the governor after adoption of the annual budget, but all requests for such funds must be matched by additional anticipated revenues. The importance and complexity of the state budget is indicated by the size of the annual request. In fiscal year 1985, total budgeted expenditures amounted to $6,952,765,551, or more than $1,598 for every man, woman, and child resident in the state.

The *Judiciary* is responsible for the resolution of all matters involving civil and criminal law in the State of Maryland. Judges base their decisions on statutory law, common law, or equity. As the population of Maryland has grown and society has become more complex, the judiciary has been reshaped to more effectively and efficiently deal with litigation and other matters requiring judicial determination. What has evolved is a four-tiered court system consisting of the District Courts,

Material from the *Maryland Manual 1985-1986*, published by the State of Maryland, State Archives, Annapolis, MD.

Circuit Courts, the Court of Special Appeals, and the Court of Appeals.

The District Court of Maryland, implemented in 1971 on a statewide basis in every county in the state and Baltimore City, is a court of limited jurisdiction that replaced the earlier local justices of the peace and county trial magistrates. The District Courts have jurisdiction in minor civil and criminal matters and in virtually all violations of the state Motor Vehicle Law. District Court judges are appointed by the governor for ten-year terms.

Appeals from decisions in the District Court, as well as more serious criminal and civil cases, are heard in the Circuit Courts. Circuit Court judges are nominated by special judicial selection commissions and appointed by the governor with the consent of the Senate. At the first statewide election occurring at least one year after their appointment, Circuit Court judges must successfully stand for election to continue in office for the term of fifteen years.

The Court of Special Appeals is the second highest court in Maryland. Like the state's highest court, the Court of Special Appeals is an appellate court. It was established by constitutional amendment in 1966 to ease the caseload of the Court of Appeals and to facilitate resolution of cases requiring appellate adjudication. Composed of thirteen judges, members of the Court of Special Appeals are appointed by the governor with the consent of the Senate for fifteen-year terms, subject to approval of the voters at the next election after their appointment. The Court of Special Appeals has exclusive initial appellate jurisdiction over any reviewable judgment, decree, order, or other action of a Circuit Court, except for appeals in criminal cases in which the death penalty is imposed.

The Court of Appeals has a long history in Maryland, dating from the first state constitution adopted in 1777. The Court of Appeals is the state's highest court, and the cases it reviews are limited to those of major importance where the decisions rendered bear largely on the proper constitutional interpretation of the law. The seven judges of the Court of Appeals, appointed by the governor with the consent of the Senate, serve fifteen year terms. Like judges of the Court of Special Appeals, judges of the Court of Appeals must win approval of the electorate at the first election occurring at least one year after their appointment.

Various units, boards, and commissions exist within the judiciary to facilitate operation of the department and to assist judges of the different courts. The Judicial Nominating Commissions present names to the governor when vacancies occur on any of the appellate or circuit courts. The Maryland State Law Library is the principal law reference library in the state. Also within the Judiciary Department are the State Board of Law Examiners, which conducts examinations for prospective members of the State Bar, and the Attorney Grievance Commission, charged with supervising and administering the discipline of attorneys.

These three branches of state government—the executive, legislative, and judicial—act in close harmony to preserve, protect, and extend the privileges and obligations provided to the citizens of Maryland by the state Constitution. All three branches represent the interests of the citizens of the State in their relations with other states and the federal government, and each works closely with and supplements the services of local, municipal, and county administrations. The checks and balances provided by the Constitution of Maryland ensure a certain beneficial degree of tension and proprietorship among the three branches of State government, and each carefully guards its prerogatives. The fundamental goal of State government as a whole, however, is to serve the best interests of the people. It is thus the citizens themselves who ultimately determine, through periodic elections, referenda, and amendments to the Constitution itself, the policies, functions, and extent of the government of the State of Maryland.

Material from the *Maryland Manual 1985-1986*, published by the State of Maryland, State Archives, Annapolis, MD.

MARYLAND AT A GLANCE

State Capital. Annapolis: The original capital was St. Mary's City. In 1694, the General Assembly designated Anne Arundel Town the capital. After Queen Mary's death in December 1694, Anne Arundel Town was renamed Annapolis for Queen Mary's sister and heiress apparent, Princess Anne. The government moved to Annapolis in February 1694/5, when the site was still known as Anne Arundel Town.

Population. 4,216,975 in 1980 census; ranked 18th among the states.

Government. The governor, elected by popular vote for a four-year term, is the chief executive of the State. Most State agencies are encompassed within one of the fourteen cabinet-level executive departments. Maryland's bicameral Legislature consists of a 47–member Senate and a 141–member House of Delegates. As of July 1984, the Senate has 41 Democrats and 6 Republicans and the House of Delegates includes 124 Democrats and 17 Republicans. The Legislature meets each year on the second Wednesday in January for 90 days to enact laws. The Maryland Judiciary consists of four court divisions: the Court of Appeals, the Court of Special Appeals, the Circuit Courts, and the District Courts. Local government exists in Maryland's 23 counties, 154 municipal corporations (including Baltimore City), and special taxing districts. Of the 50 states, Maryland is among those with the fewest number of local governments.

Area. In square miles: land, 9,837; inland water, 623; Chesapeake Bay, 1,726; total, 12,186. Ranks 42nd among the states.

Statehood. April 28, 1788, the seventh state.

Physiography. Divided into three provinces with progressively higher altitudes from east to west; Coastal Plain province extends from Atlantic Ocean to Fall Line; Piedmont or "Foothill" province from Fall Line to base of the Catoctin Mountains; Appalachian province from base of Catoctin Mountains to western boundary of State. Mean elevation, 350 feet; maximum elevation, 3,360 feet on Backbone Mountain.

Distances. Longest east-west, 198.6 miles—Fairfax Stone to Delaware Line; north-south, 125.5 miles—Pennsylvania line to Virginia line at Smith Point on south-shore mouth of the Potomac River; shortest north-south, 1.9 miles—Pennsylvania line

to south bank of Potomac River near Hancock; farthest points northwest corner to southeast corner at Atlantic Ocean, 254.7 miles.

Location. Highway distance from Central Maryland (in miles): Boston, 392; Chicago, 668; New York, 196; Philadelphia, 96; Pittsburgh, 218; Richmond, 143; Washington, D.C., 37.

Climate. Generally moderate, varies from mild to hot in summer and in winter from moderate in the east and south to very cold in the western mountains. Average annual rainfall, 42.90 inches; average seasonal snowfall, 25 inches ranging from 10 inches on the southern Eastern Shore to 110 inches in Garrett County. Average annual temperature 54.6 degrees Fahrenheit, with high temperatures in July, the warmest month, averaging in the low 80s and the low temperatures in January, the coldest month, averaging in the low 30s. Duration of the freeze-free period averages 185 days, ranging from 130 days in Garrett County to 230 days in the southern Chesapeake Bay area.

Chesapeake Bay. 195 miles long with 1,726 square miles in Maryland and 1,511 square miles in Virginia. Varies in width from 3 to 20 miles. Navigable for ocean-going ships and has two outlets to the Atlantic Ocean, one through the Chesapeake and Delaware Canal, one through the mouth of the Bay between the Virginia capes. The William Preston Lane, Jr. Memorial Bridge (Chesapeake Bay Bridge) spans 4.2 miles between Sandy Point, Anne Arundel County, and Kent Island, Queen Anne's County.

Chief Rivers. Potomac, Wye, Patuxent, Susquehanna, Choptank, Nanticoke, Elk, Magothy, Patapsco, Sassafras, South, Severn, Gunpowder, Tred Avon, Bush, Miles, Chester, Northeast, Wicomico, Pocomoke, and Great Bohemia.

Boating Waters. Twenty-three rivers and bays with more than 400 miles of water tributary to the Chesapeake Bay; Chincoteague Bay with 35 miles of water accessible to and from the Atlantic Ocean; an estimated (1984) 215 boat ramps and 31,000 boat slips.

Water Frontage. Sixteen of the 23 counties and Baltimore City border on tidal water. Length of tidal shoreline, including islands, 4,100 miles.

Material from the *Maryland Manual 1985-1986*, published by the State of Maryland, State Archives, Annapolis, MD.

Forest Area. More than 2,798,000 acres, or approximately 44 per cent of the land surface. Chief forest products are lumber, pulpwood, and piling. Nine State forests and one State forest nursery cover 127,369 acres.

State Parks and Recreation Areas. Thirty-five operational State parks covering 73,159 acres; 87 lakes and ponds open to public fishing; 9 State forests and portions of 15 State parks open to public hunting; 34 wildlife management areas, covering 80,385 acres, open to public hunting; 5 natural environment areas containing 13,753 acres.

Labor Force, Employment and Unemployment, 1983. Civilian labor force, 2,211,000; total employment, 2,058,000; unemployment, 153,000, or 6.9 percent. Non-agricultural workers (in thousands): Manufacturing—durable goods, 113.2; non-durable goods, 98.4. Non-Manufacturing—services and mining, 401.1; retail trade, 323.7; State and local government, 259.3; federal government, 130.6; construction, 95.4; finance, insurance, and real estate, 97.0; wholesale trade, 93.8; transportation, communication, and public utilities, 87.1. Total non-agricultural employment, 1,699.6.

Manufacturers, 1982. Number of reporting units, 2,319; total employees, 215,318; total wages, $4,412,028,463; total value added by manufactures in 1978 was $7,739.2 million. Most important manufactures: food and kindred products; primary metals; electric and electronic equipment; machinery, except electrical; chemical and allied products; and transportation equipment.

Selected Industries. Maryland's ten largest private employers: Automation Industries, Inc.; Baltimore Gas & Electric; Bethlehem Steel Co.; C & P Telephone Co.; IBM Corp.; Johns Hopkins University and Hospital; Marriott Corp.; Maryland Cup Corp.; Giant Food; Westinghouse Corp.

Agriculture, 1983. 18,000 farms covering 2,750,000 acres. Total farm receipts $1,055,000,000. Most valuable farm products: broiler chickens, $329,000,000; field crops, $340,000,000; dairy products, $220,000,000. Most valuable crops: corn, $134,000,000; soybeans, $71,000,000; tobacco, $28,000,000.

Mineral Production, 1983. Stone, 16,935,000 short tons, value $73,068,000; sand and gravel, 10,000,000 short tons, value $36,000,000; bituminous coal, 3,144,000 tons, approximate value $86,774,400; clays (excludes ball clay), 447,000 short tons, value $1,515,000; lime, 7,000 short tons; value of mineral production that cannot be itemized, $90,891,000; approximate total value of all mineral production, $288,653,400.

Seafood Production, 1983. Fish, 11,384,000 pounds, dockside value $3,848,000; crabs, 48,755,000 pounds, dockside value $16,055,000; oyster meat, 6,950,000 pounds, dockside value $10,198,185; clams, including soft-shell, hard-shell, and surf, 19,311,000 pounds, dockside value $10,437,000; American lobster, 76,000 pounds, dockside value $252,000. Maryland leads the nation in blue crab production.

Port of Baltimore. One of the leading ports in the United States, handling nearly 58,000,000 tons of cargo in 1981. Baltimore is the second-ranked container cargo port on the East Coast of the United States, with more than 4.4 million tons moved during 1981. Foreign commerce totalled 21,623,736 short tons in 1983. Baltimore is also one of the largest ports of entry for the importation of automobiles in the world, with 236,164 units arriving during the year. Other chief imports are ore, chemicals, petroleum products, gypsum rock, lumber, rolled and finished steel products, fertilizers and materials, unrefined copper, inedible molasses, sugar, and general cargo. Chief exports are grains, machinery, coal and coke, iron and steel scrap, iron and steel semifinished products, earth moving equipment, fertilizers, and general cargo. The World Trade Center in Baltimore, headquarters for the Port, serves as the center of international commerce for the region.

State Airports. The State owns and operates two airports, Baltimore-Washington International (BWI) and Glenn L. Martin State Airport. BWI has grown significantly, both in air service and passenger traffic. BWI reported 5,197,004 commercial passengers in FY 1983, an increase of 14.2 percent over the previous fiscal year. Twenty-five passenger airlines now serve the facility with over 570 flights a day. BWI also handles approximately 59 percent of the air freight in the Baltimore-Washington region, a total of 182,295,390 pounds in FY 1982. With several airlines now offering both passenger and cargo flights to a variety of international destinations, BWI is becoming a gateway airport for the United States, as well as serving the air transportation needs of the region. Glenn L. Martin State Airport is the largest general aviation facility on the East Coast. Handling primarily private and corporate aircraft, Martin is also the main base for Maryland's two air national guard squadrons and the Maryland State Police Aviation Division (MEDEVAC).

Material from the *Maryland Manual 1985-1986*, published by the State of Maryland, State Archives, Annapolis, MD.

State Railroads. The State currently runs three commuter and six freight lines. The commuter lines include two Baltimore-Washington lines and one Brunswick-Washington line. Freight lines include four on Maryland's Eastern Shore, one in Frederick County, and one in Carroll County. The five Class I railroads presently operating in Maryland cover almost 1,000 route miles.

Incorporated Cities Over 10,000 Population, 1980. Baltimore, 786,775; Rockville, 43,811; Hagerstown, 34,132; Bowie, 33,695; Annapolis, 31,740; Frederick, 27,557; Gaithersburg, 26,424; College Park, 23,614; Salisbury, 16,429; Takoma Park, 16,231; Greenbelt, 16,000; Hyattsville, 12,709; New Carrollton, 12,632; Laurel, 12,103; Cambridge, 11,703; and Aberdeen, 11,553.

Unincorporated Areas Over 20,000 Population, 1980. Bethesda, 83,022; Silver Spring, 72,893; Dundalk, 71,293; Columbia, 52,518; Wheaton-Glenmont, 48,698; Aspen Hill, 47,445; Potomac, 40,402; Essex, 39,614; Glen Burnie, 37,263; Oxon Hill, 36,262; Parkville, 35,139; Catonsville, 33,206; Suitland-Silver Hill, 32,164; Towson, 31,085; Security, 29,553; Lochearn, 26,904; Middle River, 26,756; Randallstown, 25,927; South Gate, 24,185; Pikesville, 22,525; Ellicott City, 21,784; Carney, 21,488; Severna Park, 21,253; Milford Mill, 20,334; and Arbutus, 20,163.

Education. Public Schools (1983–84) in Maryland include 749 elementary, 189 middle/combined, and 294 high schools, with an enrollment of 683,491 students; average cost per pupil (1983–84), $3,077. Public high school graduates, 52,446; percent intending to continue their education, 45.4. Nonpublic schools in Maryland (1983–84) include 323 kindergarten or pre-kindergarten, 305 elementary, 148 middle/combined, and 73 high schools, with an enrollment of 137,036. A tripartite system of public higher education in Maryland includes 17 community colleges, 8 four-year colleges and universities, and the University of Maryland. Among independent postsecondary institutions are 3 two-year colleges, 20 four-year colleges and universities, and approximately 206 proprietary schools. Federal funds support the U.S. Naval Academy in Annapolis.

Libraries, 1983. Twenty-four public library systems include 178 public libraries and 33 bookmobiles, with total collections of 10,664,267 items. School library media centers are located in 1,189 elementary, middle, and secondary schools, with total collections of nearly 14 million items.

The Maryland State Library Network provides resources to local libraries throughout the State. The Network is composed of the State Library Resource Center (Enoch Pratt Free Library, Central Building), three Regional Library Resource Centers (Eastern Shore, Southern Maryland, Western Maryland), four Metropolitan Referral Centers (Anne Arundel, Baltimore, Montgomery, and Prince George's counties), and academic libraries, including Catonsville and Essex Community Colleges, The Johns Hopkins University Libraries, Towson State University, and Libraries of the University of Maryland.

Medical Care, 1984. Personnel licensed to practice in the State: 11,588 physicians; 35,906 registered nurses; 9,403 practical nurses; 3,154 dentists; 1,409 dental hygienists. Licensed facilities: 84 hospitals, 201 nursing homes (comprehensive care), 20 alcoholic intermediate care facilities, 51 domiciliary care homes, 8 residential treatment centers for emotionally disturbed youth, and 11 mental retardation centers.

Principal Holidays.

New Year's Day, January 1

Dr. Martin Luther King, Jr.'s, Birthday, January 15

Lincoln's Birthday, February 12

Washington's Birthday, Third Monday in February

Maryland Day, March 25

Good Friday

Memorial Day, May 30

Independence Day, July 4

Labor Day, First Monday in September

Defenders' Day, September 12

Columbus Day, October 12

Election Day

Veterans' Day, November 11

Thanksgiving Day, Fourth Thursday in November

Christmas Day, December 25

Material from the *Maryland Manual 1985-1986*, published by the State of Maryland, State Archives, Annapolis, MD.

MARYLAND CAPSULE CHRONOLOGY TO 1968

c.10,000 B.C.	Indians known to have lived in Maryland by this date.
c.1000 B.C.	Indian introduction of pottery.
c.800 B.C.	Indian introduction of domesticated plants.
c.1000 A.D.	Permanent Indian villages established.
1498	John Cabot sailed along Eastern Shore off present-day Worcester County.
1524	Giovanni da Verrazano passed mouth of Chesapeake Bay.
1572	Pedro Menendez de Aviles, Spanish governor of Florida, explored Chesapeake Bay.
1608	Capt. John Smith explored Chesapeake Bay.
1629	George Calvert, 1st Lord Baltimore, left Avalon in Newfoundland, visited Virginia.
1631	Kent Island settled by Virginians under William Claiborne.
1632, June 20	Maryland Charter granted to Cecilius Calvert, 2nd Lord Baltimore, by Charles I.
1633, Nov. 22	The *Ark* and the *Dove* set sail from Cowes, England, for Maryland.
1634, March 25	Landing of settlers at St. Clement's Island.
1634/5, Feb. 26	First General Assembly met at St. Mary's.
1645	Ingle's Rebellion.
1647/8, Jan. 21	Margaret Brent denied right to vote in General Assembly.
1649, April 20	Religious toleration law enacted.
1650, April 6	General Assembly divided into an Upper and Lower House.
1652, March 29	Parliamentary commissioners hold jurisdiction over colony, curtailing proprietary authority.
1655, March 25	Puritans from Virginia defeated Gov. William Stone's forces at Battle of the Severn.
1657, Nov. 30	Lord Baltimore's claim to Maryland reaffirmed.
1664	Slavery sanctioned by law; slaves to serve for life.
1683, May 15	Headright system of land grants ended.
1685, Aug. 31	Printing press of William Nuthead used at St. Mary's City by this date.
1689, July–1690, May	Maryland Revolution of 1689.
1690, May–1692, April	Interim government of Protestant Associators.
1692, April–1715	Crown rule; Maryland governed as a royal colony rather than as a proprietary province.
1692	Church of England made the established church. Royal assent to establishment act given in 1702.
1694/5, Feb.	Capital moved from St. Mary's City to Annapolis.
1696	King William's School founded at Annapolis.
1715	Restoration of proprietary rights to Charles Calvert, 5th Lord Baltimore.
1718	Catholic disenfranchisement.
1727, Sept.	*Maryland Gazette* began publication at Annapolis.
1729	Baltimore Town established.
1732	Establishment of boundary line with three lower counties of Pennsylvania, which later became Delaware.
1744, June 30	Indian chiefs of the Six Nations relinquished by treaty all claims to land in colony.
1747	Tobacco inspection law enabled Maryland to control the quality of exports.
1755	Gen. Edward Braddock's expedition through Maryland to the west.
1763–1767	Charles Mason and Jeremiah Dixon surveyed boundary line with Pennsylvania.
1765, Nov. 23	Stamp Act resistance at Frederick.
1772, March 28	Cornerstone laid for State House in Annapolis.
1774, June 22	First Provincial Convention met at Annapolis.
1774, Oct. 19	Burning of the *Peggy Stewart* in Annapolis harbor.
1775, March 22	"Bush Declaration" signed, Harford County.
1775, July 26	Association of Freemen formed.

Material from the *Maryland Manual 1985-1986*, published by the State of Maryland, State Archives, Annapolis, MD.

1776, June 26	Departure of Robert Eden, Maryland's last colonial governor.
1776, July 3	Maryland Convention declared independence from Great Britain.
1776, July 4	Declaration of Independence adopted in Philadelphia. Engrossed copy signed by Marylanders William Paca, Charles Carroll of Carrollton, Thomas Stone, and Samuel Chase.
1776, Nov. 3	Declaration of Rights adopted by Ninth Convention. Church of England disestablished.
1776, Nov. 8	First State Constitution adopted by Ninth Convention.
1776, Dec. 20–1777, March	Continental Congress met at Baltimore.
1777, Feb. 5	First General Assembly elected under State Constitution of 1776 met at Annapolis.
1781, March 1	Maryland ratified Articles of Confederation.
1781, Nov. 5	John Hanson elected President of the United States in Congress Assembled.
1782	Washington College established at Chestertown.
1783, Nov. 26–1784, June 3	Continental Congress met at Annapolis.
1783, Dec. 23	Washington resigned commission as commander in chief of the Continental Army at State House in Annapolis.
1784	St. John's College established at Annapolis.
1784, Jan. 14	Treaty of Paris ending Revolutionary War ratified by Congress at Annapolis.
1785, Aug.	China trade begun with arrival of Canton cargo at Baltimore.
1785, Dec. 5	General Assembly endorsed Compact of 1785, an agreement with Virginia on navigation and fishing in the Potomac and Chesapeake Bay.
1786, Sept. 11–14	Annapolis Convention held to discuss revisions to Articles of Confederation. Maryland sent no representatives.
1788, April 26	Maryland ratified Federal Constitution.
1791, Dec. 19	Maryland ceded land for District of Columbia.
1796	Baltimore City incorporated.
1802	Property qualification for voting removed in local elections.
1803	*Viva voce* voting at elections changed to voting by ballot.
1807, Dec. 18	University of Maryland chartered as the College of Medicine of Maryland.
1810	Property qualification ended in voting for electors for president, vice-president, and congressmen.
1810	Free blacks disenfranchised.
1814, Aug. 24	Battle of Bladensburg.
1814, Sept. 12	British repulsed at Battle of North Point.
1814, Sept. 13	Bombardment of Fort McHenry, which inspired Francis Scott Key to write "Star-Spangled Banner."
1818	National Road completed from Cumberland to Wheeling.
1819, March 6	In *M'Culloch v. Maryland*, U.S. Chief Justice John Marshall interpreted Constitution to signify implied powers of federal government.
1824–1829	Chesapeake and Delaware Canal constructed.
1826	Jewish enfranchisement.
1827, Feb. 28	Baltimore and Ohio Railroad chartered.
1828–1848	Chesapeake and Ohio Canal constructed (to Cumberland by 1848).
1838, Oct. 3	Governor and State senators first elected by voters rather than by legislature.
1844, May 24	Samuel F. B. Morse demonstrated telegraph line from Washington, D.C., to Baltimore.
1845, Oct. 10	U. S. Naval Academy founded.
1850, Nov.4–1851, May 13 .	Constitutional Convention of 1850–1851.
1851, June 14	Second State Constitution adopted.
1854–1859	Rise of Know Nothing Party. Baltimore riots caused city to be known as "Mobtown."
1859, Oct. 6	Maryland Agricultural College opened at College Park.
1859, Oct. 16	John Brown's raid launched from site in Maryland on federal arsenal at Harper's Ferry.

Material from the *Maryland Manual 1985-1986*, published by the State of Maryland, State Archives, Annapolis, MD.

1861, April 19	Sixth Massachusetts Regiment of Union troops attacked by Baltimore mob.
1861, April 26	General Assembly met in special session at Frederick while federal troops occupied Annapolis.
1861, May 13	Gen. Benjamin F. Butler's Union forces occupied Baltimore.
1862, Sept. 17	Battle of Antietam.
1863, June	Confederates invaded Maryland en route to Gettysburg.
1864, April 27–Sept. 6	Constitutional Convention of 1864.
1864, July 6	Hagerstown held for ransom by Confederates.
1864, July 9	Frederick held for ransom by Confederates.
1864, July 9	Battle of Monocacy.
1864, Oct. 12–13, 29	Gov. Bradford declared Third State Constitution adopted after soldiers' vote was added to election totals. A test oath was required of all voters.
1864, Nov. 1	Maryland slaves emancipated by State Constitution of 1864.
1867, May 8–Aug. 17	Constitutional Convention of 1867.
1867, Sept. 18	Fourth State Constitution adopted.
1876, Oct. 3	The Johns Hopkins University opened in Baltimore.
1877, Jan. 16	Maryland-Virginia boundary demarcated by Jenkins-Black Award.
1877, July 20–22	Baltimore and Ohio Railroad strike riot at Baltimore.
1886, Jan. 5	Enoch Pratt Free Library opened in Baltimore.
1888–1889	Oyster Wars; fighting between Maryland and Virginia watermen on Chesapeake Bay.
1890	Australian secret ballot in elections adopted.
1894	First child labor law passed.
1902	Workmen's compensation law enacted, first such law in U.S.
1902	Compulsory school attendance law passed.
1904, Feb. 7	Baltimore fire.
1909, April 6	Matthew Henson, of Charles County, reached North Pole with Robert Peary.
1915, Nov. 2	Referendum and County Home Rule amendments adopted.
1916, Nov. 7	Executive budget process established by Constitutional amendment mandating balanced State budgets.
1920	Merit system established for State employees.
1931, March 3	"Star-Spangled Banner" adopted as national anthem.
1937	State income tax instituted.
1937, June 1	City of Greenbelt chartered, a New Deal model community.
1941, Dec. 7	*U.S.S. Maryland* among naval ships attacked at Pearl Harbor.
1947, July 1	State sales tax instituted.
1948	Montgomery County became first county to adopt charter form of government.
1950, June 24	Friendship International Airport (later BWI) began operation.
1952, July 31	Chesapeake Bay Bridge opened.
1955, Sept.	Desegregation of public schools begun.
1956	Voting machines used for elections throughout State.
1956, Dec.	Baltimore urban renewal begun.
1957, Nov. 29	Baltimore Harbor Tunnel opened.
1964, April 7	Public accommodations law enacted.
1967, June 21	Opening of Columbia, a planned city incorporating one-tenth of the land area of Howard County.
1967, Sept. 12–1968, Jan. 10	Constitutional Convention of 1967–1968.
1968, May 14	Proposed State Constitution rejected by voters.

Material from the *Maryland Manual 1985-1986*, published by the State of Maryland, State Archives, Annapolis, MD.

MARYLAND'S OFFICIAL STATE SYMBOLS

GREAT SEAL OF MARYLAND

The Great Seal of Maryland is used by the Governor and the Secretary of State to authenticate Acts of the Legislature and for other official purposes. The first Great Seal was sent from England shortly after settlement of the Colony. It remained in use, although slightly altered, until the Revolution. The State of Maryland then adopted a new seal similar in form and spirit to those of other states. One hundred years later, Maryland readopted its old seal (Joint Resolution no. 5, Acts of 1876). Only the reverse of this seal has ever been cut. The obverse, however, is still considered part of the seal and is used, among other things, for decorating public buildings.

REVERSE

The reverse consists of an escutcheon, or shield, bearing the Calvert and Crossland arms quartered. Above is an earl's coronet and a full-faced helmet. The escutcheon is supported on one side by a farmer and on the other by a fisherman. It symbolizes Lord Baltimore's two estates: Maryland, and Avalon in Newfoundland. The Calvert motto on the scroll is "Fatti maschii parole femine," usually translated "manly deeds, womanly words." The Latin legend on the border (the last verse of Psalms 5 from the Vulgate) is translated "with favor wilt thou compass us as with a shield." The date, 1632, refers to the year the Maryland charter was granted to Cecilius Calvert, second Lord Baltimore.

The obverse of the Seal shows Lord Baltimore as a knight in full armor mounted on a charger. The inscription translated is "Cecilius, Absolute Lord of Maryland and Avalon, Baron of Baltimore" (Chapter 79, Acts of 1969; Code 1957, Art. 41, sec. 74A).

OBVERSE

Material from the *Maryland Manual 1985-1986*, published by the State of Maryland, State Archives, Annapolis, MD.

64

STATE FLAG. Maryland's flag bears the arms of the Calvert and Crossland families. Calvert was the family name of the Lords Baltimore who founded Maryland, and their colors of gold and black appear in the first and fourth quarters of the flag. Crossland was the family of the mother of George Calvert, first Lord Baltimore. The red and white Crossland colors, with a Greek cross terminating in the foils, appear in the second and third quarters. This flag was first flown in its present form on October 25, 1888, at Gettysburg Battlefield for ceremonies dedicating monuments to Maryland regiments of the Army of the Potomac. It was officially adopted by Chapter 48, Acts of 1904. Chapter 862, Acts of 1945, requires that if any ornament is affixed to the top of a flagstaff carrying the Maryland flag, the ornament must be a gold cross bottony (Code 1957, Art. 41, secs. 72–74).

STATE FISH. By Chapter 513, Acts of 1965, the striped bass or rockfish (*Roccus saxatilis*) was designated as the official fish of the State of Maryland (Code 1957, Art. 41, sec. 71A).

STATE SONG. The nine-stanza poem, "Maryland, My Maryland," was written by James Ryder Randall in 1861. A native of Maryland, Randall was teaching in Louisiana in the early days of the Civil War, and he was outraged at the news of Union troops being marched through Baltimore. The poem articulated Randall's pro-confederate sympathies. Set to the traditional tune of "Lauriger Horatius" ("O, Tannenbaum"), the song achieved wide popularity in Maryland and throughout the South. "Maryland, My Maryland" was adopted as the State song in 1939 (Chapter 451, Acts of 1939; Code 1957, Art. 41, sec. 79).

Material from the *Maryland Manual 1985-1986*, published by the State of Maryland, State Archives, Annapolis, MD.

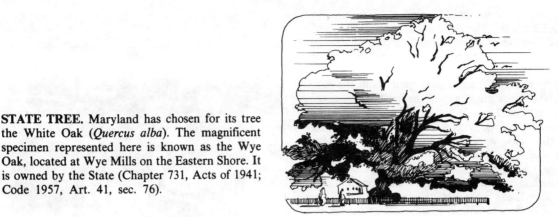

STATE TREE. Maryland has chosen for its tree the White Oak (*Quercus alba*). The magnificent specimen represented here is known as the Wye Oak, located at Wye Mills on the Eastern Shore. It is owned by the State (Chapter 731, Acts of 1941; Code 1957, Art. 41, sec. 76).

STATE DOG. By Chapter 156, Acts of 1964, the Chesapeake Bay Retriever was declared the official dog of Maryland (Code 1957, Art. 41, sec. 77B).

STATE FLOWER. The Black-Eyed Susan (*Rudbeckia hirta*) is the official Maryland flower (Chapter 458, Acts of 1918). A yellow daisy, or coneflower, it blooms in late summer (Code 1957, Art. 41, sec. 75).

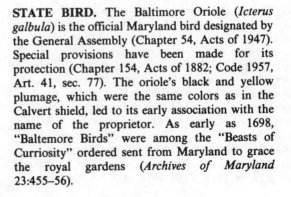

STATE BIRD. The Baltimore Oriole (*Icterus galbula*) is the official Maryland bird designated by the General Assembly (Chapter 54, Acts of 1947). Special provisions have been made for its protection (Chapter 154, Acts of 1882; Code 1957, Art. 41, sec. 77). The oriole's black and yellow plumage, which were the same colors as in the Calvert shield, led to its early association with the name of the proprietor. As early as 1698, "Baltemore Birds" were among the "Beasts of Curriosity" ordered sent from Maryland to grace the royal gardens (*Archives of Maryland* 23:455–56).

Material from the *Maryland Manual 1985-1986*, published by the State of Maryland, State Archives, Annapolis, MD.

MARYLAND SPORT. By Chapter 134, Acts of 1962, the age-old equestrian sport of jousting is the official sport of the State of Maryland (Code 1957, Art. 41, sec. 79A).

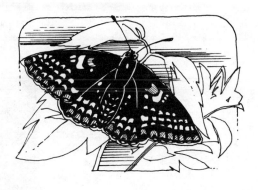

STATE INSECT. The Baltimore Checkerspot Butterfly (*Euphydryas phaeton*) was declared to be the official arthropodic emblem of the State by Chapter 253, Acts of 1973 (Code 1957, Art. 41, sec. 77C).

STATE FOSSIL SHELL. The shell of the Ecphora quadricostata (Say), an extinct snail, was designated the State fossil shell by Chapter 313, Acts of 1984 (Code State Government Article, sec. 13–311). The Ecphora inhabited the Bay and other East Coast tidal waters 5 to 12 million years ago. It is believed an Ecphora shell found in St. Mary's County, c. 1685, was the first North American fossil to be illustrated in European scientific works.

MARYLAND'S NICKNAMES. Maryland is known as both the Old Line State and the Free State.

According to some historians, Gen. George Washington bestowed the appellation "Old Line State" because Maryland's regular line troops served admirably in many Revolutionary War engagements.

The nickname "Free State" was created by Hamilton Owens, editor of the Baltimore *Sun.* In 1923, Georgia Congressman William D. Upshaw, a firm supporter of Prohibition, denounced Maryland as a traitor to the Union for refusing to pass a State enforcement act. Mr. Owens thereupon wrote a mock-serious editorial entitled "The Maryland Free State," arguing that Maryland should secede from the Union. The irony in the editorial was subtle, and Mr. Owens decided not to print it. However, he popularized the nickname in later editorials.

Material from the *Maryland Manual 1985-1986*, published by the State of Maryland, State Archives, Annapolis, MD.

Maryland State Comptroller Louis L. Goldstein reports on state revenues to the Governor and taxpayers.

Senator Charles McC. Mathias, Jr. (R-Md.) praises Secretary of Transportation Elizabeth Dole and Urban Mass Transit Administrator Ralph Stanley for releasing $24 million for the extension of the Washington Metropolitan area rapid transit system.

CHAPTER 2

National Elections and Qualifications for Voting in Maryland
Voting, Candidates and Elections: Legislators and State Officials

We have talked in a general way about voting and elections. Now let us take a closer look at the way we vote in Maryland. Let us see just how we select our legislators and state officials. Remember please, that all political and appointed officials can be either male or female.

You will often see in the following pages "he or she," "his or hers," used. It is rather awkward to keep saying this, yet we want to be accurate.

The General Assembly of Maryland

General: The legislature is called the General Assembly of Maryland. It has two "houses," (the House of Delegates and the Maryland Senate). (Article III of the Constitution of Maryland gives the rules for electing members of the General Assembly of Maryland.) As Article III, Section 1 of the Constitution of Maryland says: "The Legislature shall consist of two distinct branches; a Senate, and a House of Delegates and shall be styled the General Assembly of Maryland."

69

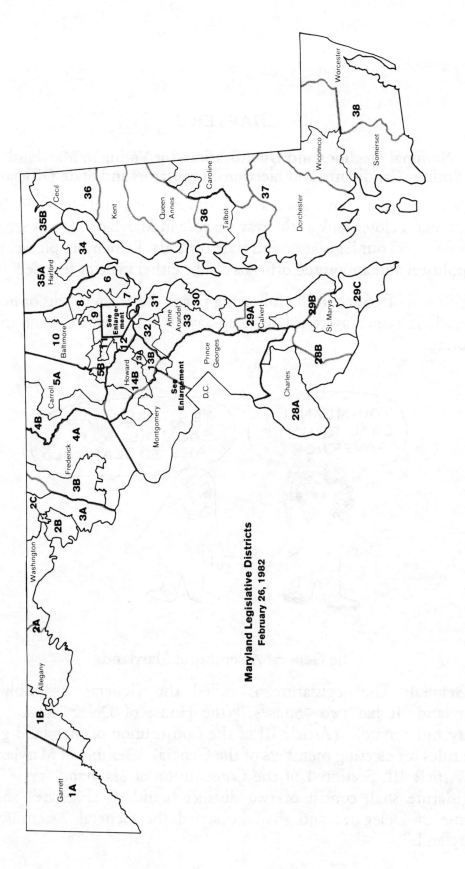

Maryland Legislative Districts
February 26, 1982

Material from the Maryland Manual 1985-1986, published by the State of Maryland, State Archives, Annapolis, MD.

70

A Constitutional amendment, ratified by the people on November 7, 1972, divided the State of Maryland into 47 districts for the election of the 188 members of the Senate and the House of Delegates.

Each *legislative district* elects one senator and three delegates. This makes a total number of 47 senators and 141 delegates.

Each district may be divided into three delegate subdistricts or may be one multi-member delegate subdistrict. *Each district must consist of adjoining territory, be compact in form, and of equal population.* (See Article III, section 1 - 4 in the Constitution of Maryland 1867, the present one, for details.)

In districts that contain more than two counties or parts of more than two counties, and where the delegates are elected at large by the voters of the entire district, no county or part of a county is allowed to have more than one resident delegate.

As directed by Article III, section 5, of the Constitution of Maryland, the Governor presented his Legislative Reapportionment Plan of 1982 to the General Assembly on January 13, 1982, and it became law on February 26, 1982.

Local election boards can give citizens information about the boundaries of local election wards, districts and precincts. Also, information may be obtained from local election offices as to how to register, where to vote.

Where one votes is determined by where one lives at a permanent address. This is where one is a "registered voter."

As Article II, Section 7 says: "The election for Senators and Delegates shall take place on the Tuesday next, after the first Monday in the month of November, 1958, and every fourth year thereafter."

You may wish to wrinkle your forehead (or whip out your calculator) to find out recent and coming election years. Do you get 1982, 1986, 1990? Good!

A candidate for public office is usually connected with one of the major political parties—the Democratic or Republican parties. In order to become the official candidate, or nominee, of his or her party, the candidate must defeat all other candidates in that party in what is known as a primary election. To become a party's official nominee for an office is important, because with it the candidate will receive many votes from members of the political party to which he or she belongs. These are votes that the candidate might otherwise not receive.

In Maryland, primary elections are held every four years on the Tuesday after the first Monday in November of an election year. During a primary election a voter is restricted as to how he or she may vote. In a primary election only those people who are registered to vote as a member of one of the political parties can vote. In a *primary election* they are picking a person from their political party whom they

YOU MEAN IF I AM A DEMOCRAT, I CAN ONLY VOTE FOR DEMOCRATS AND IF I AM A REPUBLICAN, I CAN ONLY VOTE FOR REPUBLICANS?

YES, THAT'S TRUE IN THE PRIMARY ELECTION.

would like to see run for office. Candidates selected in this way then run against the candidates selected by other political parties for the office in a general election. Voters who register as "independents" (not connected with any particular political party), are not eligible to vote for candidates in a primary election. Right?

Each legislative district contains voters who may elect one Senator and three Delegates. The candidates from the districts in each political party who received the most votes in the *primary election*, will then run in the *general election* against each other for office. A person who is an independent candidate can also run in the general election.

In Maryland, general elections for members of the General Assembly and other State officials take place every four years, on the even numbered years between Presidential elections. In the general election, if a person is registered to vote (unlike in the primary elections), he or she may vote for any of the candidates, *regardless of political party*. (That is, of a registered Democrat wishes to vote for a candidate who is a Republican, he or she may do so, and the other way around, of course.)

The candidates receiving the most votes will be the delegates and senators elected from their particular districts.

The General Assembly meets on the second Wednesday of January every year, for a period of ninety days. The General Assembly may extend this session up to another thirty days if three-fifths of the membership of each House agrees.

The Governor may call the General Assembly into session by Proclamation for emergency reasons, or due to extraordinary need. If called into additional sessions, unless for emergency reasons, then a majority of the members of both houses of the General Assembly must agree to meet.

Read the provisions of Article III to study the details of how the legislature of Maryland, the General Assembly, is elected, serves and is regulated. See how the system of "check and balances" operates with only certain powers given the legislature and others referred to the voters in various ways.

The Maryland House of Delegates

Elections for delegates to the Maryland House of Delegates are held every four years. For example, elections are scheduled for the years 1986, 1990, 1994, 1998 and the year 2002.

As we have noted before, there are 141 members of the House of Delegates. The voters of each of Maryland's 47 legislative districts elects three members of the House of Delegates. Every ten years, after the national census, the districts are checked to see that they still are all equal in population. This is to make certain that each voter has an equal and fair voice in selecting delegates and senators. At present there is one delegate in the House of Delegates for about every 30,000 people in the State (1980 census figures).

Once elected in a November election, the delegates go to our State capitol, Annapolis, and take office on the second Wednesday in January following that election.

In general, to be eligible to serve as a Delegate in the General Assembly of Maryland, a person must be on the date of the election: (1) a citizen of the State of Maryland, (2) a resident of the State for at least one year, (3) a resident of the district from which he or she is to be elected, for at least six months, and (4) the candidate must be at least twenty-one years of age.

Article III of our Maryland Constitution gives details of other qualifications that deal with conflict of interest, other posts held, and criminal records. Also, provisions are made for removing delegates through disqualification, resignation, death and other reasons.

The Maryland Senate

Members of the State Senate are elected in the same way as are the delegates to the House of Delegates. They must go through a primary election first (unless independent) and then a general election, before becoming a State senator. The term of office is four years in length.

There are 47 Senators, and they are elected from the 47 State senatorial districts in Maryland. (The areas having the most population are given the most members in the Senate. Baltimore City, for example, has several of these State senatorial districts.) There is one State senator for about every 89,000 people in Maryland (based on the 1980 census).

Officers of the State

At the same time that the delegates and State senators who will make up the Maryland General Assembly are being elected, the officers of the State are also elected for a four-year term. At this time, the voters choose the Governor and Lieutenant Governor (who run jointly), the Comptroller of the Treasury and the Attorney-General. Candidates for these offices, too, must run in a primary election (unless they are running independent of any political party). The winner is decided in a general election. The next gubernatorial election will be held in the year 1986. (Elections are scheduled every four years.)

The Secretary of State is appointed by the Governor. The Treasurer is selected by joint ballot (vote) of both houses of the General Assembly.

National Elections

Every four years the voters of our nation choose a President and VicePresident of the United States. The year 1988 will be a Presidential election year.

Political parties hold national conventions which are attended by people chosen from each state to represent their party. These national conventions determine which person from each party will be offered to voters across the country as its Presidential candidate. Then, each Presidential candidate chooses a person to run with him in the election for the post of Vice-President of the United States. The President and the Vice-President run jointly. A vote for the President is also a vote for the selected Vice-President. They run as a team, a pair. These conventions take the place of national primary elections.

People called "electors" are elected by popular vote in the states. When the votes for the Presidential election are counted for a particular district, usually the elector from that district must cast his vote for the candidate with the most votes.

Many states have the practice of *unit voting* by electors—that is—whichever Presidential candidate in that state wins a majority of the popular votes receives the votes of all the electors from that state.

These electors make up the Electoral College. The candidate who receives the most electoral votes is the next President. Electors meet at the same time in all of the states in mid-December following the Presidential election. The electoral college system is an old one and is not a very popular one. Many people feel that the electoral college system is undemocratic because the man with the most popular votes sometimes loses the election to the man having the most electoral votes! For example, in the elections of 1876 and 1888, this is exactly what happened. But this is the system by which we select our President, and with him or her, our Vice-President.

In Maryland and all other states, general elections are held on even numbered years to elect persons to go to Washington, D.C. as members of the Congress of the United States of America. These persons are chosen first by the political party to which they belong by means of primary elections in the states. Then, they run against candidates from other parties and against independent candidates for the position they seek. The person getting the most popular votes wins the election.

Some candidates want to represent their state as members of the United States Senate; others want to become members of the United States House of Representatives. As you know, *these two "houses" make up the national legislature, which is called the Congress of the United States.*

Oddly, only members of the lower House, the House of Representatives, are called Congressmen. Representatives serve four-year terms. Members of the upper House of the United States Congress, the Senate, are called Senators.

U.S. Senators are elected for six-year terms of office. Their terms overlap so that an experienced senator is always in office. That is, both senators from a state are not elected in the same election. Congressmen (members of the U.S. House of Representatives) are elected every two years for two-year terms. All of these elections to the Congress of the United States occur on even-numbered years. Every two years we select one senator and our U.S. Congress members (members of the House of Representatives).

Qualifications for Voting in Maryland
(Article I, Section I)

To vote in Maryland a person must: be a citizen of the United States; be at least 18 years of age; have lived (been a resident) in the State as of the time for the closing of registration before the election; be registered to vote with the Board of Election Supervisors in the county, or legislative district of Baltimore City, in which he or she resides.

A person does not have to be present in the State to vote. If that person is qualified to vote and has been registered, he or she may vote by mail. This is known as voting by "absentee vote."

A recent voting law allows new residents of Maryland to vote in Presidential elections if they have a permanent Maryland address and register before the registration books are closed. This is 30 days before the election.

A person wishing to vote in Maryland *must not*:
- be a lunatic, nor a person who is non compos mentis. (That is, voter must be considered sane.)
- have been convicted of an infamous crime or larceny, unless pardoned by the Governor.
- have been convicted of buying or selling votes.

CHAPTER 3
Introduction

ORGANIZATION OF OUR STATE GOVERNMENTS

You will recall that 13 colonies had governments based upon colonial charters, rather than constitutions. By 1775, however, these established governments were gradually falling apart because of the troubles with Great Britain. The Second Continental Congress then urged each colony to adopt such form of government as would guarantee the highest degree of happiness and safety for its people. In January of 1776 New Hampshire became the first of the 13 colonies to form an independent government under a constitution. Thereafter, South Carolina took similar action, as did most of the other colonies or states. The colonial charters of Connecticut and Rhode Island served as their constitutions for a number of years after they became states. Massachusetts approved a state constitution in 1780 which, although somewhat revised, continues to be the basis for that state's government.

While there were differences in each of the new state constitutions, certain things were similar. Each one recognized that the government could exercise only those powers granted to it by the people, and that the people had rights which the government must respect. The constitutions also divided the government into three branches—the executive, the legislative, and the judicial—with each branch having some controls over the others. It can be seen, therefore, that people in the United States actually live under Federal and state governments which are very similar in form.

The United States Constitution gives to the states those powers which are not granted to the Federal government and, at the same time, not denied to the states by the Constitution. Throughout our history this division of power has caused conflicts between Federal and state governments over the authority of each. For example, Congress passed the Tariff Act of 1828 which placed high taxes on imported goods. This pleased the northern states because it protected the sale of their manufactured products. The southern states, however, disliked the tax because it affected the exchange of their cotton, tobacco, and other products for goods manufactured in foreign countries. This tax brought about one of the first conflicts involving the authority of the Federal and state governments.

The southern states argued that the Federal government had been created by the states and, therefore, each state had the right to determine whether a law passed by the Congress was authorized by the Constitution. They further claimed that, if a particular state decided the Constitution did not give Congress the power to pass a certain law, the state did not have to obey it. This idea became the basis for what is known as the doctrine of "states' rights."

A famous debate on states' rights took place in the Senate in 1830. Senator Robert Hayne of South Carolina argued that his state had the right to decide that the Constitution did not give Congress the authority to pass the Tariff Act. Speaking for the northern states, Daniel Webster, a Senator from Massachusetts, answered by saying that the Federal government was created by the people and not by the states, and that the United States would soon break apart if each state insisted on obeying only those laws which it chose to accept. He ended his speech by saying, ". . . Liberty and Union, now and forever, one and inseparable!"

Webster was defending Article VI of the Constitution which declares that the Constitution shall be the supreme law of the land and shall determine what powers are given to the Federal and the state governments. He stressed the fact that under the Constitution the powers to govern are shared by the national and state governments. He argued that when the Federal government acts in accordance with the powers granted to it by the Constitution no state can nullify that action.

In this chapter you will read about the organization of the state governments.

Material from U.S. Government Printing Office publication, M-163, *Our Government*, revised 1973.

DISCUSS:

Why is it important for each state to have a written constitution?

MEETING NEW WORDS:

auditor: A person whose duty it is to examine financial records

convenience: Comfort; advantage; benefit

doctrine: A belief in certain things; a set of principles accepted as true

exchange: The trading of one thing for another; to give one thing in trade for another

inseparable: Cannot be divided; must remain together

nullify: To wipe out or destroy; to make meaningless

utility: A service or product which is useful

Fill in each blank with the correct word from the list above.

1. The southern states wanted to _____ the Tariff Act of 1828.

2. Webster said that liberty and the Union are _____.

3. The state _____ found a mistake in the financial records.

4. The northern states argued against the _____ of states' rights as interpreted by the southern states.

5. The cost of gas and electricity furnished by the public_____ companies is fixed by the state.

AS YOU READ

1. **Find out what powers are given to the states by the Constitution of the United States.**
2. **Find out how the executive, legislative, and judicial branches of state governments serve the people.**

ORGANIZATION OF OUR STATE GOVERNMENTS

The first 13 states had constitutions when the Constitution of the United States was written. The state constitutions gave to their people certain rights and a representative form of government which were very important to them.

Many people believed that the new Federal government might take away some of these rights or might change the form of the state governments. With this in mind, the writers of the Constitution made provision for the states to keep many of their rights, and further guaranteed to each state a republican, or representative, form of government. However, because the Federal Constitution also provides that it shall be the supreme law of the land, every state is bound by it and all state constitutions and laws must agree with it.

Content of State Constitutions

The constitution of each state provides the general plan for that state's government. It may also set forth the basis for other governments within the state, such as those of counties and towns. Other state constitutions may also establish governments for their larger cities.

A state constitution usually describes the purposes for which the state government is being created and lists the rights of the people living in that state. All of the constitutions declare that the final authority to govern belongs to the people of the state. They also tell how the government of the state and its communities shall be organized. Each state constitution generally lists the authority of each branch of the state government, establishes rules for the local governments, and provides a method for amending the constitution. It may also list different kinds of property that shall not be taxed by the state government.

Government Organizations Are Similar

The Federal and state, as well as the city, governments in the United States each have three branches of government. The following chart shows how the organization of government in the nation, the states, and the cities is similar.

Material from U.S. Government Printing Office publication, M-163, Our Government, revised 1973.

	FEDERAL	STATE	CITY
Legislative Branch	Congress—Senate and House of Representatives	State legislature—two houses in all states except Nebraska	City council or commission
Executive Branch	President, Vice President and President's Cabinet	Governor and governor's assistants	Mayor or city manager or city commission, and assistants
Judicial Branch	Supreme Court Federal courts	State courts	City courts

The Lawmaking Branch of State Governments

In all of the states except Nebraska, which has one lawmaking body, the legislative branch of the state governments has two houses. This is similar to the Federal government. The upper house is called the senate. The lower house may be called the house of representatives or the assembly. These legislatures may vary in size. In most states there are more members in the house of representatives than in the senate. Both senators and representatives must be chosen on the basis of population. The term of office of state legislators is whatever the state law declares it to be, usually two years.

State legislatures make laws in the same general way as the Congress of the United States. All members in each house cannot study every bill. Therefore, each house has a committee system similar to that of Congress. Each bill is referred to the committee organized to handle the subject matter to which the bill relates.

Any member in either house can introduce a bill.

The bill is then referred to the appropriate committee of that house for study.

If the committee approves the bill, it will be returned for consideration by the house from which it came.

After members speak for or against the bill, a vote is taken.

If the bill receives a majority of votes, it will be passed by that house.

If a bill has been passed in one house, it will be sent to the other house where it will go through the same procedure as it did in the first house.

If the bill is passed in both houses, it will be sent to the governor of the state.

If the governor signs the bill, it will become a law; if he vetoes it, the bill can become a law only if it is again voted upon by both houses and passed by the necessary number of votes.

The Executive Branch of State Governments

The chief executive in every state is the *governor*. His qualifications and term of office are determined by the state constitution. The governor has executive officers to help him carry out his responsibilities. These officers may be appointed by the governor or may be elected by the people.

The governor, together with his executive officers, enforces the laws of the state and sees to it that the work of the various departments is done properly. He may also suggest to the legislature what laws should be passed or changed. In some

Material from U.S. Government Printing Office publication, M-163, Our Government, revised 1973.

states the governor may appoint judges to state courts, while in other states judges may be elected by the people.

A majority of the states have:

A *secretary of state* who keeps the official records of the state.

An *attorney general* who is the chief law officer in the state. He advises the governor in legal matters, and helps to convict and to punish people who break the state laws. He represents the state in the courts.

A *state treasurer* who takes care of the state's money that comes from taxes, licenses, and fees. He also pays the debts of the state.

A *state auditor* who examines all the financial records of the state and the books of public officers.

The states generally have special officers whose duty it is to enforce labor laws. Other special officers enforce laws relating to the operation of public utility companies which furnish the people of a community with gas, water, and electricity. Each state also has special groups, called *boards* or *commissions*, that administer other state laws.

The Judicial Branch of State Governments

Every state government has a judicial branch consisting of a large number of lower state courts which have authority to try the two classes of cases—criminal and civil. Almost all civil and criminal cases involving state laws are first tried in these lower courts.

All states have higher courts which study the decisions appealed from the lower courts. These courts of appeals decide whether or not the correct decisions were made in the lower courts. The appeals court may agree with the decision of the lower court and dismiss the appeal. On the other hand, if it is found that a case was not correctly decided, the case can be sent back to the lower court for further hearing, or the court of appeals can change the decision of the lower court.

Attorney Addressing a Jury.

States can create courts to hear special matters. For example, there may be a children's court to try cases of children accused of having broken the law, and a court of domestic relations to hear cases involving disagreements between husband and wife.

Every state has a state court which is similar in function to the United States Supreme Court. Such a court has power to review decisions of the lower state courts, and its decisions interpreting the constitution and laws of the state are final.

The State Helps to Guard the Health of Its People

One of the most important services of a state is the protection of the health of its people. Most states have laws requiring that doctors, nurses, and persons who sell drugs must have licenses. These people must pass state examinations before licenses will be issued to them. The state examines many foods and drugs to be certain that they are pure. It establishes and maintains state hospitals for its people, and provides health examinations for school children.

Material from U.S. Government Printing Office publication, M-163, Our Government, revised 1973.

The State Educates Its People

State governments do many things to help educate their people. Each state sets certain standards of education for its schools. It passes laws that require children to attend school—public elementary schools and high schools are free. The state usually provides money to a school according to its needs. Many states establish and maintain colleges and universities where some, or all, of the expenses are paid from taxes. Most states provide adult education classes.

The State Protects the Lives and Property of Its People

The authority of a state to protect the lives and property of its people is called its "police power." This police power provides for the safety, comfort, and convenience of the people. Every state has a state police force. It also has a militia that can be called upon to work with local and state officers to protect the people and their property.

The state protects its people by regulating certain kinds of industry. Special officers inspect restaurants, factories, mines, and other places where people work. This is done to make certain that these places are clean and safe. By such inspection the hours during which women and chil-

Courtesy, University of Maryland

A State College.

dren work are also kept within legal limits. Public utility companies are regulated and the people are benefited by the establishment of fair rates for utilities, and are assured that health and safety standards are maintained.

The State Cares for Its Own Problems

When a country is new and it has many natural resources, such as rich soil, forests, oil, gas, and coal, people may become careless. They may forget to think about the millions of people who will live in the country years later. Should the people become careless, the soil may become poor, the forests may be cut down, and the oil, gas, and coal may be used up. The country would then be poor.

For many years the Federal government and the states have been teaching the citizens to care for natural resources. They try to teach the people how to keep soil from washing away, to plant crops so that one crop puts back into the soil what another crop used up in growing, to plant new trees as older trees are cut, and to preserve oil and natural gas supplies. By saving natural resources, our country will remain rich for posterity.

Photo by R. E. Bates

A State Hospital.

Material from U.S. Government Printing Office publication, M-163, Our Government, revised 1973.

83

A State Highway System.

Most roads are under the control of local governments but, since they are used by all the people of the state, part of the cost of building and repairing many local roads is paid by the state. The state and Federal governments work together in planning, building, and paying for cross-country highways.

Every day, in many ways, the state is part of the life of the people. They must help the state and themselves by obeying the laws, paying their taxes, working for better laws, and supporting law officers in carrying out their duties.

Each state is as good as the people who live in it. The state can be no better than its people.

CAN YOU DO THIS?

Complete each of the sentences below with the correct word(s) from this group:

commission	posterity	stressed
license	products	domestic relations

1. A person must pass a state examination before he can get a _____ to sell drugs.
2. The _____ court tried to bring the husband and wife together.
3. A special group called a _____ administers some state laws.
4. The governor _____ the need for new legislation.
5. Conservation assures to _____ the benefit of our natural resources.

Material from U.S. Government Printing Office publication, M-163, Our Government, revised 1973.

Answer these questions:

1. How did the writers of the Constitution make provision for the states to keep many of their rights?
2. Name the two houses of the legislative branch of state governments.
3. Which state has only one legislative house?
4. How can a bill become a law if the governor vetoes it?
5. Who is the executive authority of the state?
6. Which officers help the governor and how are they chosen?
7. What are some of the special courts which the state can create?
8. Over what cases do the state courts have authority?
9. What provisions do state constitutions contain?
10. What are some very important services which the state provides?

Talk about:

1. How are the three branches of the Federal and the state governments similar?
2. How does a state take care of its own problems?
3. Why can we say that a state is no better than the people who live in it?

Material from U.S. Government Printing Office publication, M-163, Our Government, revised 1973.

ORGANIZATION CHART OF
MARYLAND STATE GOVERNMENT

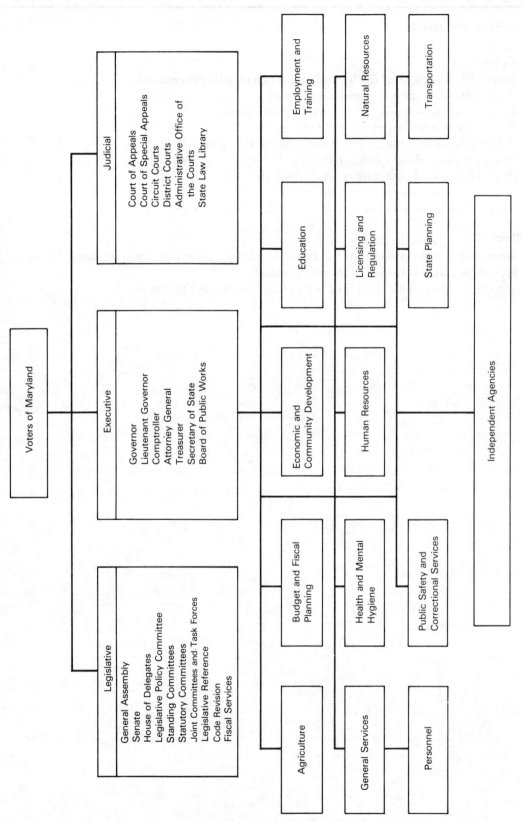

Material from the *Maryland Manual 1985-1986*, published by the State of Maryland, State Archives, Annapolis, MD.

Our State Government

Under the Constitution of the United States, all of the states, including Maryland, are promised the right to have a republican form of government. This is a government in which the citizens elect representatives who are responsible, answerable, to the people. These representatives govern according to law. Powers that the United States Constitution does not give to the federal government, or does not prohibit the states from using, are given to the states.

Because of those powers reserved to the states, Maryland and the other states can regulate, or govern, matters that affect citizens living in each state. For example, our Maryland government registers our births, records our marriages, regulates businesses, requires attendance at school and protects our lives and property. The State Government sets up many of our voting requirements. At the end of a citizen's life, Maryland's government records the death and provides laws to protect the heirs, the persons who are lawfully to have the deceased citizen's property.

The State of Maryland, then, has the power to regulate many things that we do. Those regulations under which we live are contained in the Constitution of Maryland, which is the *highest law* of the State, or in the laws of Maryland. The many laws of our State are published in books called the *Annotated Code of Maryland*. This code is revised each year to keep it up-to-date. Revisions are published every October.

In general: our laws are passed by the State legislature and all laws must agree with the Constitution of Maryland. Laws are passed and enforced to protect our freedom and to prevent us from interfering with the freedom of others.

Laws also provide for, and control, our State government. Like the federal government, the government of Maryland is made up of three separate branches: the executive, the legislative and the judicial.

Our State Government:
The Executive Branch

The Executive Branch is headed by six important officers. Four—the Governor, the Lieutenant Governor, the Comptroller of the Treasury and the Attorney General—are elected by the people. The Secretary of State is appointed by the Governor. The State Treasurer is elected by both Houses of the Legislature sitting together.

In addition to those officers, there are boards, commissions, departments and agencies that have been created by laws passed by the General Assembly which are responsible (answerable) to the Governor. They report regularly so that the Governor can know whether or not they are performing properly the tasks assigned to them. The Governor, in turn, reports to the General Assembly on the "State of the State."

Executive Branch

VOTERS OF MARYLAND

COMPTROLLER

TREASURER
Elected by Legislature

GOVERNOR

ATTORNEY GENERAL

Board of Public Works

LIEUT. GOVERNOR

SECRETARY OF STATE
Appointed by Governor

- Agriculture
- Budget and Fiscal Planning
- Economic and Community Development
- Education
- Employment and Training
- General Services

- Health and Mental Hygiene
- Human Resources
- Licensing and Regulation
- Natural Resources
- Personnel
- Public Safety and Correctional Services
- State Planning
- Transportation

INDEPENDENT AGENCIES

Executive Commissions, Committees, Task Forces, and Advisory Boards

Material from the *Maryland Manual 1985-1986*, published by the State of Maryland, State Archives, Annapolis, MD.

The Governor

Most of us think of the Governor as "the person who runs the State." We may not really know very much about his or her work. As the Governor of a booming state which has over four million people in it, we know that the Governor of Maryland is very busy. But what, we may wonder, *exactly* does our Governor do?

The Governor is the chief executive officer of the State and has great power. Some of this power is the result of having the right to select the people he or she wants to fill several important jobs in the State. True, the Maryland Senate must agree to these appointments, but still the power is there. It is needed to enable the Governor to govern our State effectively. Maryland may not be big in land area—it ranks 42nd in the nation—but it is big in terms of population, ranking 18th among the states of the nation. Our people (over four million of us) need a large number of government services.

Think for a moment of the money used in this work of government. About seven billion dollars a year is spent by the State of Maryland. The Governor, along with the Maryland General Assembly, has considerable power in deciding how all of this money shall be raised from taxes, investments and fees. Also, the Governor has a part in determining how it shall be spent. Each year he or she shows the Legislature a budget—a plan for spending money. This budget is discussed and then, when the members of the Legislature and the Governor agree, the budget is ready to be used.

The Governor's salary is $75,000 a year. Out of this, the Governor pays taxes and many personal expenses. Of course, some money is allowed the Governor to pay for certain travel expenses, for State social affairs and to pay for workers and equipment needed to do government work!

The Governor lives in a large mansion called Government House. It stands facing State Circle in Annapolis.

Across the street from Government House, in the center of State Circle, stands our graceful State House. Begun in 1772, it is the oldest State House in continuous use in the United States. There the

Governor has a suite of offices and a great reception room. From one wall of this stately room, Queen Henrietta Marie, for whom Maryland was named, sends a frosty painted glance across the room to the other walls where portraits of recent Maryland governors return her gaze.

One of the interesting, if not often used, duties of the Governor is that of being Commander-in-Chief of the military forces of the State. In times of emergency, the Governor has the power to send State Police or National Guard personnel into an area to help local forces safeguard the public. These emergencies include hurricanes, floods, serious fires and riots.

Another power given the Governor is that of pardoning a person who is a prisoner of the State. The Governor can transfer a person to another state for trial, when that person is accused of committing a crime in that state. In turn, the Governor can ask another state to transfer back to Maryland for trial a person accused of breaking a law in Maryland. (This transfer is called "extradition.")

A most difficult decision must be made by the Governor when asked to decide whether or not to stop, or delay, the execution of a person who has been sentenced to death by a court.

The Governor may submit to the legislature (the General Assembly) for approval, proposals for laws which he or she believes should be passed. The legislature makes the decisions on these. Another way in which the Governor influences lawmaking is, after both houses of the legislature have approved a proposed law, called a "bill," he or she may sign the bill which then becomes the law of the land. Or, the Governor may choose not to sign it, which is known as "vetoing" a bill. Then the Legislature must have a vote of at least three-fifths of each House to make the bill a law over the Governor's veto.

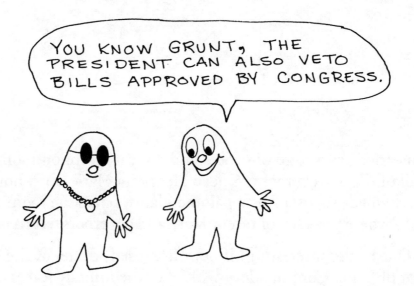

The Governor may inform the General Assembly at any time of the condition of the State.

When the Legislature is in session, the Governor is usually to be found in his or her offices in the State House, ready to talk with delegates or senators who would like advice.

The Governor serves a four-year term in office. During those four years he or she can be called upon to work long hours! While in office, our Governor works very hard doing many things. One of the Governor's duties is to serve on the important Board of Public Works. The other members of the Board are the Comptroller of the Treasury and the State Treasurer. These officials sit together to discuss the needs of the State. They make decisions on programs for the State involving many millions of dollars.

Since the Governor is thought of as the leader of his or her political party in the State, he or she makes speeches and attends many social affairs to try to help the party win elections. The Governor may be a member of the Democratic Party, the Republican Party, or some other party. The party he or she belongs to expects help in deciding party programs, so the Governor must attend meetings to help work out party plans.

Often the Governor must sit late at night at a desk, writing notes for a speech perhaps, answering letters, working out ideas for legislation that he or she thinks the General Assembly should discuss, looking over budget plans, and thinking of ways to meet the problems of Maryland.

Since the Governor is the head of the State of Maryland, he or she is often asked to welcome important visitors to the State, foreign visitors, groups of businessmen and club groups. These occasions can sometimes be a little startling. One day Governor Spiro Agnew walked out to accept the gift of a turkey from a group of turkey-growers. He found himself face-to-face, not with a frozen bird, but with a very large, very much alive turkey, sitting on his polished conference table in the stately reception room.

The Governor tries to meet as many people as possible. The

Lieutenant Governor helps with the chief executive's busy schedule. The work of the Governor is very interesting, for no two days are alike.

To be Governor of Maryland a person must be at least 30 years old and a registered voter and citizen of the State for five years before the election. In our State, the Governor may serve only two four-year terms consecutively (that is, in a row).

Each political party holds an election called a "primary election." In this election they pick the person they want to run for the office of Governor. Once their candidate is chosen, the members of each political party campaign for their chosen person. They work to convince the voters of Maryland that their's is the best candidate for the job.

Elections by which a Governor is chosen are held every four years. For example: 1986, 1990, 1994, 1998, 2002. Naturally, the person getting the most votes wins the election.

On the third Wednesday of the January that follows his or her election, the person chosen by the voters is officially made Governor of Maryland. The person leaving the office of Governor smiles, shakes the new Governor's hand and turns away to other work. The departing Governor probably feels both regret and relief at handing over that often hard, but always fascinating, position to another person.

Though the power of the Governor of Maryland is great, it is not permanent, nor is it complete. He holds office for a limited amount of time. If the Governor does not do the work faithfully, he or she may even be impeached and removed from office. This, of course, does not happen very often to governors in the United States, and then only for a very good reason. The power of the Governor is balanced by the power of the State Legislature and is regulated by the Constitution of Maryland and by Maryland law.

Still, the Governor holds people's lives in his or her hands, makes decisions that affect the millions of people in the State, and helps to collect and spend billions of dollars a year! This is important work and results in exciting years for the person holding the position of Governor of Maryland. Each Governor in turn serves the State and the people in the State. Each wins a place in the history of Maryland.

The Lieutenant Governor

The office of Lieutenant Governor was created by a Constitutional Amendment ratified by the people on November 3, 1970. The Lieutenant Governor is the second-ranking officer of the State.

Once a political party selects a candidate for Governor, that person selects a running mate to run jointly with him, or her, as candidate for Lieutenant Governor.

This officer of the State is elected for a term of four years by popular vote. The Lieutenant Governor runs for office "jointly" (together, as a team) with the Governor and, of course, at the same time in the same election.

The Lieutenant Governor's term of office begins, as does the Governor's, on the third Wednesday in January following his or her election.

To be eligible for the office, the Lieutenant Governor must be 30 years of age and must have been a resident and registered voter the five years before the election in the State of Maryland.

The work of the Lieutenant Governor? It is whatever the Governor decides. The Governor assigns duties to the Lieutenant Governor. (See the Constitution of 1867, Article II, sections 4,5,6 for more information.) The salary for Lieutenant Governor is $62,500 a year.

Should the Governor die, the Lieutenant Governor becomes the Governor. Also, the Lieutenant Governor serves as Acting Governor when notified by the Governor that the Governor will be temporarily unable to perform the duties of his or her office. (For more details, see the Constitution of 1867, Article II, sections 4,5,6.)

The Comptroller of the Treasury

The Comptroller of the Treasury is elected at the same time as the Governor, the Lieutenant Governor and the Attorney General. He takes office on the third Monday in January after the election and serves a four-year term. There is no limit set on the number of terms the Comptroller may serve. The salary is $62,500.

Why, since Maryland has a State Treasurer, is another important financial officer necessary? The reason is that the Comptroller has a different job. He is not the keeper of the funds; he is the man given the task of collecting the greater part of the vast amounts of money that go into the State Treasury. Also, he is, as the dictionary puts it, the "controller" of State money. That is, after the Governor prepares the annual budget and it is approved by the General Assembly, the Comptroller is the man who is responsible for its administration.

One of the important duties of the Comptroller is serving as one of the members of the Board of Public Works. The work of this powerful Board is described later in this section.

The Comptroller is also a member of the Advisory Council which meets with the Governor to talk over plans for keeping Maryland's finances in good condition.

The staff of the Comptroller of the Treasury has the responsibility of a great deal of careful accounting and record keeping.

Collecting taxes is a huge job. To do this work the Comptroller must plan the work of the tax offices well. Taxes come from many places. There is a personal income tax, of course. There is a corporate income tax, too; that is a tax paid by companies doing business in Maryland. Money also comes in from real estate taxes, retail sales taxes, motor vehicle fuel taxes, use taxes, gasoline taxes, admissions and amusement taxes. Taxes are also placed on tobacco and on all sorts of alcoholic beverages, such as beer, wine and liquor. It is the

Comptroller who controls and regulates the manufacture, sale, transport, storage and distribution of alcoholic beverages in the State. The Comptroller issues licenses to manufacturers, wholesalers, airlines, railroads, steamboats, transportation and storage companies.

Much tax money is paid back into county, town and city treasuries by the Comptroller.

Another very important task of the Comptroller of the Treasury is the protection of the credit of the State of Maryland. States, like people, sometimes need expensive items that cannot be paid for right away. To get money for these things the State may borrow money, but it must be paid back within fifteen years. The Comptroller must countersign the documents associated with State debts.

In Maryland, by law, each year the budget must balance. This means that if there is not enough money to pay for an agency's entire budget, plans must suddenly be changed so that the money will last. True, the Board of Public Works does have an emergency fund to help State agencies should this happen, but in general, the State budget must balance each year.

Each year the Comptroller makes a report to the General Assembly and to the Governor, giving a complete explanation of the spending and income of Maryland during the year just past. Indeed, he or she is called upon to make all sorts of studies, reports and decisions, so that Maryland's money may be managed properly. All checks drawn by the Treasurer must be countersigned by the Comptroller of the Treasury.

MY BUDGET NEVER BALANCES. I ALWAYS HAVE A PROBLEM WITH SPENDING MORE THAN MY INCOME!

The work of the Comptroller and his or her staff ranges from keeping records of public accounts, collecting reports on taxes paid into county and city tax offices, to making monthly inspections of the books of the Treasurer. It is the work of the Comptroller's staff, also, to prepare and supply all licenses issued by the Clerks of the Court. These include marriage licenses, business licenses and many others.

State-aided institutions send in reports to the Comptroller which tell how they have used the money given to them by the State. Such institutions are colleges, hospitals, libraries, historical trusts and other public service groups.

The Comptroller of the Treasury, upon request, furnishes information to the General Assembly, the Legislative Branch of the Maryland government. A General Assembly department does fiscal research, does certain auditing or checking work, and reviews the yearly budget so that the Department can explain the budget clearly to the General Assembly. The Comptroller receives the Legislative Auditor's reports and contacts various departments to follow the Auditor's recommendations. The Comptroller furnishes an estimate of expenditures in coming years to the General Assembly.

The Comptroller is "ex officio", that is, by reason of his office as Comptroller, a member of the Board of State Canvassers (election officials). This Board is given statements of the results of elections by city and county "canvassers," or counters of votes. The Board of State Canvassers then determines officially which person has the most votes and who has been elected to office.

Also, the Comptroller serves as a member of the Boards of Trustees for the three State retirement systems. These are retirement funds set up for employees of Maryland, for teachers and for policemen.

The Comptroller is an ex officio member, too, of the Hall of Records Commission which keeps important historical records and property for Maryland.

Yes, the duties of the Comptroller range far and wide and reach, in their effect, into every corner of the State.

The Comptroller, an elected official, is also a leader in his or her political party. He or she makes many speeches and appearances to help his or her party and must attend many meetings to help plan campaigns and party platforms.

As a State leader, the Comptroller is called upon to appear at scores of important meetings of the State, social affairs and official occasions.

To do his or her work he or she needs not only ability but must get and train a skilled staff. Comptroller Louis L. Goldstein often uses an oval table, which he calls his "round table." He gives much credit to his staff of efficient co-workers for carrying out the responsibilities of the office of Comptroller of the Treasury.

The Secretary of State

Under British colonial rule, the Governor of Maryland had a group of men to advise him. It was called the Governor's Council. After the American Revolution, the Governor of Maryland continued to have a Governor's Council. The office of Secretary of State was created by a Constitutional Amendment in 1837 to replace the Governor's Council.

The Secretary of State is appointed by the Governor. However, the State Senate must consent to the Governor's choice before the new Secretary of State can begin work.

The Secretary of State acts as the general secretary of the Executive

Branch of the Maryland government. He or she attests the signature of the Governor (which means that he or she declares the signature to be true and genuine) on public documents, commissions, warrants, proclamations and other public papers.

The office of the Secretary of State is a rich source of information for future students of history for it keeps a record of many State activities. The office keeps records on all people appointed by the Governor and on groups, called commissions, set up by the Governor to study certain State problems.

It is the responsibility of the Secretary of State to publish the election laws of Maryland and then distribute them so that they will be available to the people of the State. Persons wishing to run for state-wide office or for office in the United States Congress, must file their names with the Secretary of State. Also, all petitions for referendum, which are requests signed by a certain percentage of voters to ask that a law be voted upon in a special election to decide whether or not it shall become a law of Maryland, must be recorded with the Secretary of State. Later, when questions are asked of voters in these referendum elections, the results are given to the Secretary of State and he makes them known to the public. Candidates for public office must file with his office statements showing the contributions they have received and the expenses they have had during their campaigns for office.

When proposed amendments to the Constitution of Maryland are voted on by the voters, the Secretary of State announces the outcome. He also publishes (makes public in writing) the official results of elections held in the State. Legislative agents working to get certain problems and proposed laws brought to the attention of the General Assembly, must have their names registered with the Secretary of State. These agents are called "lobbyists." Their job is to promote the passage of certain laws in which they are interested by influencing legislators. Aside from having their names registered with the Secretary of State, the subjects of laws those lobbyists want passed must also be registered.

In the files of the Secretary of State are copies of the rules and regulations adopted by State officers or departments. These, the Secretary must publish, so that the public will know the latest regulations.

The Secretary keeps records on, and makes up the papers for, requisition and extradition. He also handles the paper work for pardons and commutations granted by the Governor. "Commutations" are reductions in prison sentences or reductions in fines charged a person by a court.

Now all this record keeping and making up of official documents might seem quite enough for one office, but the Secretary of State and his staff keep a great many other miscellaneous records and perform other duties. For example, the Secretary serves as the attorney for drivers, aviators and aircraft owners who are not residents of Maryland and who are involved in accidents in Maryland. The Secretary must keep the Great Seal of Maryland safe and ready for use when needed. His office keeps records of charitable groups. There, too, are recorded trademarks, trade names and service marks used in Maryland. The Secretary keeps records on trading stamp companies in Maryland.

The Secretary administers the State's notary statutes and issues notary public commissions. Applications, notary public manuals and related information may be obtained from the office of the Secretary of State.

The Secretary of State supervises the work of the Division of State Documents.

The Division of State Documents was created within the Office of the Secretary of State in 1974. The administrator is appointed by the Governor and is responsible for the administration of the State Documents Law (Code State Government Article, secs. 7–201 through 7–222, 11–101 through 11–129).

The primary duties of the Division are to print and distribute two official State publications: (1) the *Code of Maryland Regulations* (COMAR), the permanent compilation of the Governor's executive orders, all State agency regulations, and all opinions issued by the State Ethics Commission, and (2) the *Maryland Register,* a bi-weekly publication that serves as a temporary supplement to COMAR.

The *Register* prints all proposed, adopted, and emergency regulations of the State's administrative agencies, notices of public hearings and meetings, synopses of opinions of the Attorney General, proposed and adopted rules of court, hearing calendars of the Courts of Appeal, synopses of all legislation proposed, enacted, and vetoed each legislative session of the General Assembly, synopses of significant decisions by the Employment Security Administration's Board of Appeals, all

Executive Orders, all gubernatorial appointments, notices of bids requested and awards announced on all State contracts valued above $25,000, and any other document the General Assembly requires or the Committee on Administrative, Executive and Legislative Review (AELR) permits to be published. An index to the *Register* is published quarterly, with the last quarterly index being cumulative for the year. All adopted regulations, and Executive Orders that are generally permanent in nature, are periodically taken from the pages of the *Register* and integrated into COMAR by means of published supplements.

Administrative regulations are not effective (except emergency regulations) until notice of their adoption is published in the *Maryland Register.* The text of any document appearing in the *Maryland Register* and COMAR is the only official, valid, and enforceable text of that document. Any document appearing in the *Maryland Register* and COMAR is accorded judicial notice in all court proceedings.

Subscription information and free informational brochures pertaining to both the *Maryland Register* and COMAR may be obtained by writing or calling the Division's offices.

Material from the *Maryland Manual 1985-1986*, published by the State of Maryland, State Archives, Annapolis, MD.

Residential condominiums offered for sale in the State of Maryland must be registered with this office.

Commissions for special police and railroad police are issued by the Secretary of State for the Governor. These applications are processed by the State Police before being acted upon by the Secretary of State.

Every two years the Secretary, with the State Archives, takes part in the distribution of the Maryland Manual. The Manual has over 800 pages of information on Maryland and its government.

I SAW A COPY OF THE MARYLAND MANUAL IN THE LIBRARY. IT LISTS ALL THE PEOPLE ON COMMISSIONS AND STATE BOARDS. IT ALSO HAS PICTURES OF ALL OF THE STATE LEGISLATORS AND TOP OFFICIALS.

Though the work of the Secretary of State may sound very complicated, it is just this variety that makes it both so demanding and so interesting.

The Attorney General

The Attorney General is elected at the same time as the Governor. The Attorney General customarily takes office on December 20th that follows his election. He serves a four-year term. If elected, there is no limit as to how many terms he can serve.

The Attorney General must be a citizen of the State and a qualified voter. He or she must have resided and practiced law in Maryland for at least ten years prior to election. The Attorney General receives a salary of $62,500.

He or she is the chief legal officer of the State and represents Maryland in all legal proceedings. Before any State officer or agency uses administrative rules and regulations, the Attorney General must check them.

The Attorney General is also responsible for enforcement of certain laws which are designed to protect the public. These include consumer protection laws, antitrust laws and the Maryland Securities Act.

The Attorney General heads the Office of the Attorney General, formerly called the State Law Department and serves as legal advisor and representative for most of the boards, commissions, departments and officers of the Executive Branch of the Maryland government.

The Treasurer

Shortly after each gubernatorial election, the General Assembly elects a State Treasurer by "joint vote." This means that both houses of the General Assembly vote together on the matter. The Treasurer will serve a four-year term. He or she can serve any number of terms if elected by the General Assembly.

While visiting Annapolis, one may go into the Treasury Building, just off Church Circle. Glancing into the office of the State Treasurer, one sees a gracious, stately room. Appropriately enough, on the floor is a rug of glowing golden color! Chandeliers hang from the ceiling and shine in the light from tall windows. One might imagine the Treasurer of the State of Maryland sitting at the desk there, counting piles of money. Sometimes our Treasurer might wish that this were the true picture, but it is not. Instead, the Treasurer has duties that keep him or her more often in Baltimore City than in the more peaceful Annapolis. This stately room is meant more for formal occasions than for the everyday work of the Treasurer.

Let us look carefully at the work of the Treasurer and see if we can learn why this job is thought to be one of the most responsible and important ones in the State.

First of all, we know that Maryland's government collects and spends billions of dollars each year. Also, vast amounts are used in building our State in many ways. Money must sometimes be borrowed for the State; other amounts must be kept on hand for use; still other amounts must be invested. Yes, it is a complicated money picture, this State financial story.

The State Treasurer is a member of the powerful Board of Public Works. He or she serves on the Board with the Governor and the Comptroller of the Treasury. If you will look at our section on the Board of Public Works, you will see that it has great influence on the way that Maryland's government is run and on the way Maryland money is spent. So, this is one very important duty of the State Treasurer.

The office of the State Treasurer is responsible for:

(a) Receiving, paying out (disbursing), and accounting (keeping records) of State funds. This involves, for example, the work of keeping track of many bank accounts in many banks. Sometimes money is set aside for certain uses and must be kept in bank accounts until it is needed. Each month the Treasurer must publish reports on all these accounts in a large Baltimore newspaper.

To pay all the bills of the State, the Treasurer's office makes out thousands of checks a month! These range in size from small payments to pharmacists for Medicare medicine to huge welfare checks of millions of dollars sent to the counties and to Baltimore City. As you know, balancing a personal bank account is not always easy. You can imagine then the work involved in balancing amounts involving thousands of checks each month. Paying out money, or disbursement, is a big part of the work of the Treasurer's staff.

In a way then, the Treasurer does count Maryland's gold. He or she counts it as it comes in and as it goes out.

(b) The Treasurer keeps official records of investments and collateral. (Collateral is property, stocks and bonds perhaps, which may be sold if money is not repaid or given back as promised.) These records help the Department of Fiscal Services with part of its work. This department reports to the General Assembly. The Treasurer's office, then, keeps complete records on collateral and all money coming into the Treasury, being paid out and invested.

(c) The office of the Treasurer keeps accounts on the public debt of the State. It pays the interest on these debts and pays off the debt itself, as promised. The Treasurer is the official Registrar of State of Maryland bonds.

(d) In the Treasurer's office are kept records of deeds and information on all property owned by the State of Maryland.

(e) Money is sometimes set aside for some special purpose; for example, surplus money must be held by the State Accident Fund. This money must not just lie around in banks when it can be invested

and earning interest for its fund. So, the State Treasurer and his staff must invest this money. The Treasurer is also the "Custodian," that is, the keeper or caretaker, of all investments of the State.

(f) The Treasurer requires banks to furnish collateral to protect deposits of State funds in the banks. For every dollar kept in the banks, they must give the Treasurer stocks and bonds worth $1.10 to hold. He is official custodian of this collateral.

(g) Since Clerks of Court and Registers of Wills deposit money in banks for the State, the Treasurer asks these banks to give him collateral to protect these deposits.

(h) Insurance companies and out-of-state building associations doing business in Maryland must leave securities worth a certain amount with the State Treasurer. This is done to protect the people who deposit, insure or invest with these companies.

(i) The State Treasurer arranges for the sale of State of Maryland bonds. The State Roads Commission advertises and holds sales of State Roads Commission bonds. The money from the sale of these bonds is paid into the Treasurer's office, and he or she sees that the money is safely deposited for Maryland.

In addition to the duties just listed, the State Treasurer and his or her staff have many other things to do for Maryland. Though these are given in the following paragraphs very briefly, you can see that each is important and each requires a great deal of careful work.

These miscellaneous duties of the Treasurer's office include: handling of minutes and other paper work, including studies, as a member of the Board of Public Works; serving as a member of the Boards of Trustees of the three retirement systems of Maryland; serving as a member of the Board of Revenue Estimates; serving as a member of the State Board of Canvassers (boards of election officials); and serving as a member of the Maryland Industrial Development Financing Authority. The Treasurer also serves on other committees and acts as custodian for various funds in Maryland.

When asked by the General Assembly, the Treasurer and his or her staff study proposed laws or amendments to the Constitution of Maryland. The General Assembly is then advised on the financial effects of this legislation and in this way is helped to write good laws.

The Treasurer has the responsibility of placing insurance on State property. The Treasurer's office administers this insurance program and keeps track of the many policies, claims and records.

The Treasurer is called upon by the Governor and the Comptroller of the Treasury for special studies and reports. These help them plan both income and spending programs for the State.

Our State Treasurer is chosen for his or her knowledge of money matters. Who has the greatest knowledge of today's money affairs? It seems that the people heading large banking concerns would be most likely to have this experience and knowledge. So it is that, usually, our Treasurer is also the head of a large Maryland banking company.

Since Baltimore is a great financial center for Maryland, the Treasurer will spend much of his or her time there. In Baltimore he or she meets people and talks over ways of best serving Maryland in money matters. He or she visits the government agencies in Baltimore and attends to many business affairs there.

When the Treasurer is in Annapolis, there is little time to sit peacefully at the desk, golden rug underfoot, gazing out of the tall windows. Many tasks are given our Treasurer; and for all the responsibilities that officer must carry, he or she may perhaps be repaid by the knowledge that few people hold positions of such trust in Maryland.

The Board of Public Works

This very important Board of Public Works is made up of the Governor, the Comptroller of the Treasury and the State Treasurer. The term "public works" means buildings, lands and other property owned and used by the public; in this case, property owned by the State of Maryland

The Board of Public Works must approve all money spent on land, buildings or other public facilities, except for money set aside for State roads, bridges and highways. This sounds quite simple, but the power to give contracts for spending State money makes the Board a very powerful one. The Board also decides where State offices are to be located and approves renting and leasing office and other space for State agencies. The Board makes rules for administering the State Public School Construction Program and approves sums to be paid to each of the counties and Baltimore city. Vast sums of money are controlled by the Board of Public Works.

The Board of Public Works must meet at least four times a year on the first Wednesdays of January, April, July and October, in Annapolis. It can meet more often if necessary. In practice, meetings are scheduled every three weeks. Meetings may be attended by the public.

There is an Emergency Appropriation Fund controlled by the Board. This is used to help agencies that have run over their budget, if the Board feels that the extra money is deserved.

Sometimes, to buy land or to construct buildings, it is necessary for Maryland to borrow millions of dollars. To raise money, the Board of Public Works is allowed to set the interest rate on State bonds and to sell State bonds. In this way, the State borrows money.

Real property, that is, land or buildings and personal property of the State may be sold by the Board of Public Works. The Board also

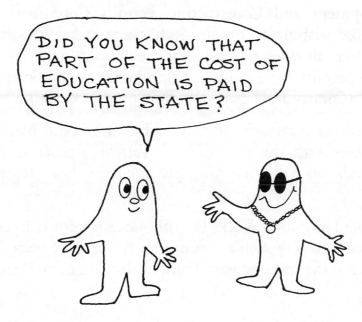

sets up many rules for the operation of State agencies. Also, the Board may approve or disapprove the creation of new jobs that are not on the budget.

Under the Board of Public Works are four offices:

Administration - office of the Secretary (of the Board of Public Works).

This office carries out the many administrative duties. For example, the preparation of agenda for the Board. (An agenda is a list of items to be discussed.)

There are many people and agencies that must be notified of Board actions. Careful records of meetings and actions must be kept. Grant programs must be administered. State agencies, news media and the public are given information.

Wetlands Administration is another office that carries out Board business. Anyone wishing to dredge or fill in wetlands must get a license from the Board of Public Works.

The Wetlands Administrator coordinates this program with other agencies, environmental groups and the public.

Development and Construction Permits Coordination works to advise those wishing to obtain State permits for construction. This office gathers all rules and laws and helps coordinate the granting or denial of permits for various developments in the State affected by State law. (County and city offices issue permits as well.)

Procurement Advisory Council advises the Board of Public Works on problems with the procurement (buying) process. The Council recommends ways to improve procurement law, regulations and process.

Our Board of Public Works is rather unusual, for Maryland is one of the few states having such a board. On it, the three State leaders work together. It is the most powerful arm of the Executive Department.

ALL SCHOOLS FUNDED BY THE STATE HAVE TO BE APPROVED BY PUBLIC WORKS.

NOW YOU TELL ME! MAYBE I CAN GET THEM TO DISAPPROVE FUNDING FOR MY SCHOOL .... RETROACTIVE!

CHAPTER 4

State Services Directed by the

Executive Branch of the State Government

Looking at the organizational chart of the Executive Branch of our State government we can see that there are many separate units to be supervised by the State leaders. These departments and commissions of Maryland usually have a central office which supervises the work of branch offices located in the counties and cities of the State.

In general, the State government provides us with the following services, under the supervision of the Executive Branch:

Leadership is provided by the State leaders, the Governor, the Lieutenant Governor, the Comptroller of the Treasury, the Attorney General, the Treasurer and the Secretary of State.

Money is provided for State services and government by collection of taxes and by borrowing and investment. This money is counted and records are kept on it. Plans for State spending are made each year, and the money required is paid out or disbursed.

Certain laws are published so that we may know the rules of the State. Laws to protect the consumer, the buyer or the customer are provided.

State employment is supervised with people being hired to do certain work for the State and being paid for work. Payments are made to retired workers.

There is a huge division for education. This helps educate Maryland citizens from pre-school days through university days. There are many special schools, too, in Maryland. Most of the colleges in Maryland receive State aid of some kind.

Health and mental hygiene is a concern of the State. Hospitals are provided for tubercular patients and to help people suffering from longlasting, "chronic" diseases. Maryland helps build hospitals and other centers affecting public health and contributes money to most of the hospitals in the State in some way. Maryland operates several mental hospitals and a psychiatric research center. Commissions are set up and asked to help the State program of public health in many ways; such as, by advising citizens on ways of keeping physically fit, or by working out ways of keeping our air and water clean.

Many programs of public welfare are provided by the State to help people who have no jobs, to train people to fill jobs, to help the handicapped find work, to help old people and to help groups of people who come into the State to harvest crops or to work at certain times of the year. (These last are called migrant workers.) Maryland's welfare programs are designed to help citizens of all races and religions to work well and to live happy, useful lives.

Maryland cares a great deal about young people who are in trouble and does its best to provide places for them to learn to become successful. This program of juvenile services includes projects such as training centers and camps for young people.

State prisons are now called correctional agencies. Today, the State does not just imprison people who have broken the law so that these people will not hurt others. Maryland also tries to train these people so that, when they are freed, they can earn a living and lead better, happier lives.

Through the Governor's Military Department, the Civil Defense Agency, and the Maryland State Police, the State government helps protect citizens from traffic hazards, storms, floods, fires and criminal acts.

The State Roads Commission and the Department of Motor Vehicles work to make our roads safer, to build new ones and to license and check motor vehicles. The Traffic Safety Division works with studies, research and training programs to make our highways safer.

Conservation of our natural resources in Maryland is the concern of several departments of our State government. People in these departments work to keep our beautiful Bay and our other waterways clean and to protect the fish, the game and the forests of our state. Our Parks system is a conservation-minded service of Maryland, as are the Maryland Geological Survey, the Bureau of Mines, the Department of Water Resources and the State Soil Conservation Committee.

Public improvements are made in Maryland by several groups, such as the Board of Architectural Review and the Art Commission that work under the Department of Public Improvements, the staff of the Superintendent of Public Buildings and Grounds, the Governor's Committee to Keep Maryland Beautiful and the Maryland Environmental Trust. These work to provide Maryland with well kept public buildings and grounds, to finance certain art projects and exhibits and to keep our natural beauty from being destroyed.

The State does a great deal of public planning. This includes planning for transit systems, zoning, regional planning for the future in terms of clean water and clean air, roads and other items. Also, plans must be made to keep up historical sites and, in some cases, to restore them.

Supervision of business is done by the State Banking Commission, Athletic Commission, Aviation Commission and many other commissions that check and regulate the various businesses in Maryland.

Labor and industrial relations groups in the State government check and administer the rules that govern the life of the Maryland worker. When he is hurt or old, there are State funds to help him.

Promotion of industry and agriculture is the concern of a very important section of Maryland's government. Offices of all kinds work to make land, water and workers fit together for profitable business in Maryland. These departments work, also, to let people all over the world know that Maryland has much to offer in plant sites, transportation, fine ports and desirable living for workers. Offices promote everything from apples, tobacco, poultry and seafood to tourism. These offices tell the world that Maryland is a fine convention site, a good place to spend a vacation and a good place to live.

Keeping our State records, our valuable historic buildings and sites safe, is the work of the Maryland State Library, the Hall of Records Commission, and the Maryland Historical Trust.

In the State government is the Maryland Veteran's Commission and the War Memorial Commission. These work for those who have served in our armed forces. These commissions also work to see that veterans are remembered in Maryland.

There are boards and commissions whose work it is to license and examine all sorts of occupations from lawyer to funeral director, from veterinarian to engineer, from psychologist to beauty operator. Almost every occupation demanding training and skill is licensed to make sure that the work is done by a well trained person.

EVEN TEACHERS?

YES, TYRONE. TEACHERS HAVE TO BE CERTIFIED BY THE STATE.

Interstate cooperation is the work of commissions and committees which study and act on an interstate, that is more than one state, basis. Their work ranges from decisions on nuclear energy sites to the use of the Potomac River Basin. These groups are in addition to the several bi-county agencies that work for more than one county to serve a certain area.

Miscellaneous commissions of all kinds bring State help to citizens. Whenever a need is felt, or a problem found, a commission is set up to study the item and work out a program to answer the need or to solve the problem.

To find out exactly what departments and commissions are at work, how to contact them and to find out what these do — consult the latest edition of the *Maryland Manual*, published every two years by the Maryland State Archives, P. O. Box 838, Annapolis, Maryland 21404.

The little kestrel or sparrow hawk

CHAPTER 5

The Legislative Branch

The General Assembly

A legislature is a group of people which has the authority to make laws for a political unit, such as a state or a nation. As does our United States government, Maryland also has a legislature made up of two "houses." We call our Maryland legislature the General Assembly. The "upper house" of the General Assembly is known as the Senate. The "lower house" is called the House of Delegates.

The presiding officer of the Senate (the person in charge of the meeting) is called the President of the Senate. The presiding officer of the House of Delegates is called the Speaker. Both houses elect their own officers, judge their own members and set rules for the conduct of their own business.

Our State is divided into twenty-four large political units. These are the twenty-three counties and Baltimore City.

Legislative districts differ from our twenty-four political units. A Constitutional amendment, ratified by the people on November 7, 1972, divided the State of Maryland into *47 legislative districts* for the election of the 188 members of the Senate and the House of Delegates. This *sets a limit* on the number of people elected to the General Assembly. If we had continued to elect legislators by population, as the number of people in the State grew, we would have so many legislators (senators and representatives) that it would be awkward to get so many people to agree. Also, there would be more people for us to pay, more office space and staff needed.

Each legislative district elects one senator and three delegates, for a total of 47 senators and 141 delegates.

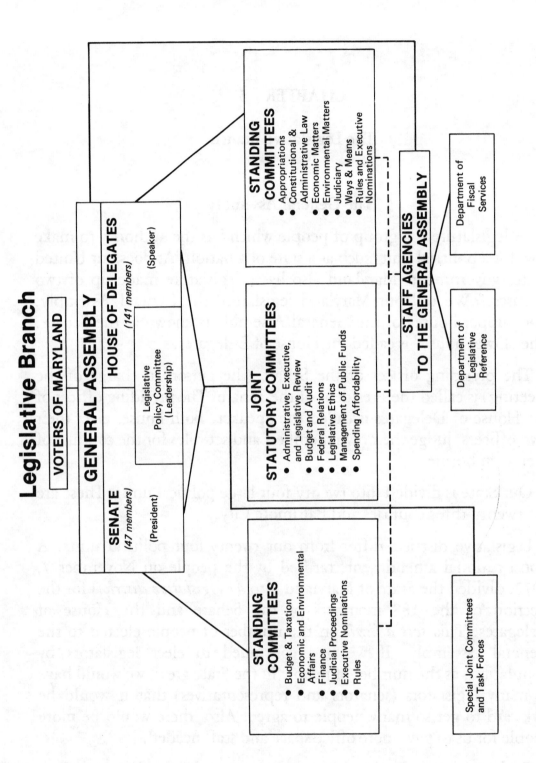

Legislative Branch

VOTERS OF MARYLAND

GENERAL ASSEMBLY

SENATE	HOUSE OF DELEGATES
(47 members)	*(141 members)*
(President)	*(Speaker)*

Legislative Policy Committee *(Leadership)*

STANDING COMMITTEES
- Budget & Taxation
- Economic and Environmental Affairs
- Finance
- Judicial Proceedings
- Executive Nominations
- Rules

JOINT STATUTORY COMMITTEES
- Administrative, Executive, and Legislative Review
- Budget and Audit
- Federal Relations
- Legislative Ethics
- Management of Public Funds
- Spending Affordability

STANDING COMMITTEES
- Appropriations
- Constitutional & Administrative Law
- Economic Matters
- Environmental Matters
- Judiciary
- Ways & Means
- Rules and Executive Nominations

Special Joint Committees and Task Forces

STAFF AGENCIES TO THE GENERAL ASSEMBLY

Department of Legislative Reference	Department of Fiscal Services

Material from the *Maryland Manual 1985-1986*, published by the State of Maryland, State Archives, Annapolis, MD.

118

Each district must consist of adjoining territory, be compact in form and of equal population. Each district may be divided into three delegate subdistricts or it can be one multi-member delegate subdistrict. There are other rules about legislative districts. The idea is to give equal parts of the population, equal representation in the General Assembly.

Maps of the legislative districts may be found in the *Maryland Manual* or obtained from your local election office.

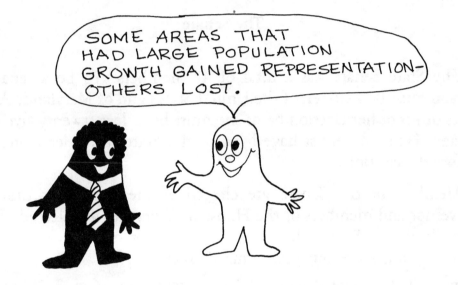

As directed by Article III, section 5, of the Constitution of Maryland, the Governor presented his Legislative Reapportionment Plan of 1982 to the General Assembly on January 13, 1982, and it become law February 26, 1982. This plan adjusted districts to reflect recent population counts. (Every ten years there is a national count, a census, taken. Example: 1980, 1990, 2000.)

To make the laws of Maryland, the General Assembly is required to hold sessions each year. These may not last longer than seventy days. The sessions begin on the third Wednesday of January, in Annapolis. The Governor may call the General Assembly into a special session at any time, but that special session may not last longer than thirty days.

The House of Delegates

The House of Delegates has a total of 141 members. Each delegate must be a citizen of Maryland and, of course, a citizen of the United States. He, or she, must be at least twenty-one years of age at the time of the election. The delegate must have lived in Maryland for at least one year before the election. Delegates serve four-year terms of office.

Members of the House of Delegates are elected at the same time the Governor is elected. There is no limit on the number of terms a delegate may serve.

The Senate

The State Senate has a total of 47 members. To be a senator a person must be a citizen of the United States and of Maryland. At the time of his or her election he or she must be at least twenty-five years of age. He or she must have lived in the State for at least one year before the election.

Members of the Senate are elected at the same that time the Governor and members of the House of Delegates are elected. There is no limit on the number of terms a senator may serve. Maryland State senators serve four-year terms of office.

Though by far the most members of the General Assembly are men, there are several women members in the House of Delegates and in the State Senate.

How Laws Are Written: How a Bill Becomes A Law

The way in which a bill (a proposed law) becomes a law can be quite a long procedure.

First, a bill is introduced by a member of one House of the General Assembly, which is the bill's "house of origin." (That is, either the Maryland House of Representatives or the Maryland Senate.) Bills may be introduced in either "house" of the General Assembly until the last thirty-five days of the session. Thereafter, they only may be introduced with the consent of two thirds of the membership.The members of that House read the bill. (The term "chamber" is also used to mean a "house" in the General Assembly.) The bill then goes to the proper committee to be studied and discussed.

THE LEGISLATIVE PROCESS:
HOW A BILL BECOMES A LAW

Upon request of a legislator, the Department of Legislative Reference drafts legislation in the form of a bill or a joint resolution. As a "prefiled bill," a bill or joint resolution may be introduced before the regular General Assembly session convenes in January. A bill is filed ("goes into the hopper") with the secretary of the Senate or the clerk of the House, is given a number, and is readied for its first reading on the floor.

First Reading: The reading clerk, when the session has convened, first reads the title of the bill. This is the first of three readings given the bill in the house where it is introduced. Then, the presiding officer assigns the bill to a standing committee. Bills may be introduced in either chamber until the last thirty-five days of the session. Thereafter, they only may be introduced with the consent of two-thirds of the membership.

Reference to Committee: The standing committees meet daily during the session to receive testimony and take action on bills assigned. Citizens are encouraged to present their views on proposed bills by mail or by personal appearance. The Department of Fiscal Services prepares a fiscal analysis for each bill and these fiscal notes are considered during the committee deliberations.

Second Reading and Floor Consideration: The bill is reported to the floor by the standing committee to which it was assigned. The report may be favorable, unfavorable, or without recommendation. If favorable, it may be with or without committee amendment. After consideration of committee amendments, the bill is then open to amendment from the floor. There, committee action may be reversed, although this happens infrequently.

Third Reading: The bill, with any adopted amendments, is then printed for third reading. No amendments may be presented on third reading. In the chamber of origin, a vote is taken to pass or reject the bill. To pass, the bill must receive a majority vote of the elected membership.

Second Chamber: The procedure followed is identical with that of the chamber in which the bill originated, except that amendments may be proposed during third reading as well as at second reading. If not amended in the second chamber, final passage may occur without reprinting.

Consideration of Bills Originating in one Chamber and Amended in the Second: If amended in the second chamber, the bill is returned to the chamber of origin for the sole purpose of permitting that house to accept the amendments. If the chamber of origin votes to concur with the amendments, the bill itself is voted on as amended and action is complete. The bill is reprinted, or enrolled, to include the added amendments before submitting it to the Governor.

If the chamber of origin votes to reject the amendments, the amending chamber may be asked to withdraw its amendments. If it refuses, either chamber may request that a conference committee be appointed to resolve the differences between the two chambers.

Conference Committee: Appointed by the Senate President and the House Speaker, a conference committee consists of three members of each house. The committee reports back to both chambers where its recommendations are adopted or rejected without amendment. If the report is adopted, the bill is voted upon for final passage in each house. If the report is rejected by either house, the bill fails.

Presentation of Bills to the Governor: All bills, except the budget bill and constitutional amendments, must be presented to the Governor within twenty days following adjournment of a session. The Governor may veto such bills within thirty days after presentation to him. If he does not veto a bill, it becomes law. The budget bill, however, becomes law upon its final passage and cannot be vetoed. Constitutional amendments become law only upon their ratification by the voters at the next general election.

Vetoed Bills: The power to override a veto rests with the General Assembly. If the Governor vetoes a bill during a regular session, the General Assembly immediately considers the Governor's veto message. If the Governor vetoes a bill presented after the session, the veto message must be considered immediately at the next regular or special session of the Legislature. The General Assembly may not override a veto during the first year of a new term. A three-fifths vote of the elected membership of both chambers is necessary to override a veto.

Material from the *Maryland Manual 1985-1986*, published by the State of Maryland, State Archives, Annapolis, MD.

THE PROGRESS OF A BILL

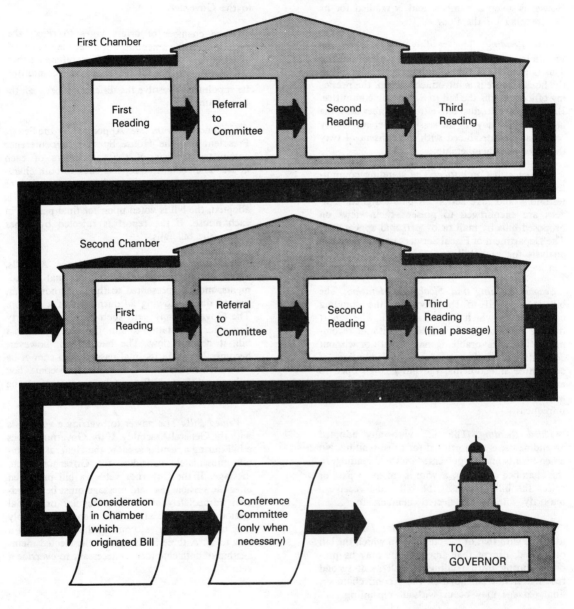

First Chamber

First Reading

Referral to Committee

Second Reading

Third Reading

Second Chamber

First Reading

Referral to Committee

Second Reading

Third Reading (final passage)

Consideration in Chamber which originated Bill

Conference Committee (only when necessary)

TO GOVERNOR

Material from the *Maryland Manual 1985-1986*, published by the State of Maryland, State Archives, Annapolis, MD.

SOURCES OF INFORMATION ON THE STATUS OF BILLS

Elected Officials. The most effective source of information on the status of a bill is often a constituent's State Senator or Delegate, who usually has information resources not available to the general public.

Department of Legislative Reference. The *Library* of the Department of Legislative Reference answers any request for information about the status of a bill.

Library (year-round)   841–3810
D.C. area: 858–3810

Information Desk, State House Ground Floor
841–3886
(during session only)   D.C. Area: 858–3886

The Department of Legislative Reference offers a subscription service known as the *Bin Service* to persons or organizations with a broad continuing need for bill information. Subscriptions are filed in Room G-17 of the Legislative Services Building (Phone: 841–3883; or from D.C. area: 858–3883).

Bin Service Subscription Rates:

Picked up in Annapolis —$20 for bills (first reader, third reader, enrolled); $5 for synopses, proceedings, hearing schedules.

Mailed Out —$500 for bills; $200 for synopses; $100 for proceedings; $50 for hearing schedules.

Newspapers. Newspapers often publish public hearing schedules of General Assembly committees and sometimes publish articles about bills introduced.

Bibliography: *Legislator's Handbook,* Department of Fiscal Services, Annapolis, 1982, 115 pp. *Student Legislative Handbook,* Cornelia Connelly, Maryland General Assembly, Annapolis, n.d., 31 pp. *Your Voice in Annapolis,* Maryland General Assembly, Annapolis, n.d., 16 pp. *Rules of the House of Delegates of Maryland,* Maryland General Assembly, 1982, 100 pp. *Rules of the Senate of Maryland,* Maryland General Assembly, 1983, 100 pp.

Material from the *Maryland Manual 1985-1986,* published by the State of Maryland, State Archives, Annapolis, MD.

During legislative sessions, much work is done by committees. Each House of the General Assembly has its own committees. Each of these committees considers bills which deal with a certain subject. Citizens are encouraged to present their views. The Department of Fiscal Services prepares a fiscal analysis of each bill.

If the committee members feel that a bill they are given needs changing, they amend it. The bill is then read again in the House of origin the second reading. There the members of that House vote for, or against, any amendments that may have been added in the committee. Another vote is then taken on whether or not to follow the recommendations of the committee on the bill. If the members of a committee do not want a bill to be voted on, they do not submit it to the House of origin. The bill "dies in committee." This action has the effect of rejection of the bill.

If submitted to the House of origin, and a majority of the members vote in favor of the bill, it goes back to the committee. Later, it is read a third time in the House of origin. If voted on favorably again, the bill goes to the other House where a similar procedure is followed. If a bill is approved by the second House, it then returns to the House of origin where any amendments added in the second House are voted on. If the Senate and House of Representatives disagree, a conference committee considers it. Made up of three members from each house, they may be able to work out a compromise version of the bill. If the amendments are agreed to by a majority of the members in the House of origin, the bill is submitted to the Governor for his approval. If the Governor signs the bill, it soon becomes a Maryland law.

The budget bill and Constitutional Amendments do not require the Governor's approval. It becomes law upon its final passage and cannot be vetoed. Constitutional Amendments become law upon their ratification by the voters at the next general election.

Vetoed Bills: The General Assembly has the power to set aside the governor's veto. A three-fifths vote of the elected membership of both chambers is needed to override a veto.

Checks and Balances

Our system of government in the United States and in the individual states is designed to give the power to pass laws to an entire Legislature and not just to one person or to one small group. A system of control to protect the people from one person or small group having too much control over the government is called a system of checks and balances. In Maryland, the system of checks and balances on the Legislative Branch includes:

Two houses in the General Assembly.   A three-time reading of each bill in both Houses.   The power of the legislature to confirm, or agree to, the Governor's appointments; that is, to his or her choice of persons for certain jobs in the State government.   The power of veto, or saying "no," given to the Governor. Also, the power of the legislature to override the Governor's veto and to pass the bill by a three-fifths vote in each house.   The power of review and referendum given to the public. (The right of the public to protest a certain law and ask that it be changed. The right to vote on Constitutional amendments.)   The power of the courts to test legislation.

Questions:

1. What is an election district?

2. Why is the State of Maryland divided into election districts?

3. Can election districts be changed? How?

4. Name Maryland's legislature. It is called the Maryland
   _____.

5. Name the two parts of Maryland's legislature.

6. In a primary election what are the political parties doing?

7. In a general election may a Republican vote for a Democrat or an independent candidate for office?

8. How often are elections held for Maryland State officials and legislators?

9. How often are elections held for national officers such as President of the United States? Is this at the same time as the Maryland State election of officers?

10. Does the Maryland General Assembly stay in session all year? How long is its session, usually?

11. Name three qualifications for persons who want to run for membership in the Maryland House of Delegates.

12. What is the practice of unit voting by electors at a national political convention?

13. Name four qualifications you need in order to vote in Maryland, please.

14. Name the three branches of our Maryland government, please.

15. What is the difference between the Maryland State Comptroller and the Maryland State Treasurer?

16. Give two examples of our system of ''checks and balances'' in Maryland's government.

17. How do the courts in Maryland test laws passed by the General Assembly and ratified by the people?

Legislative Agencies

Department of Legislative Reference

A part of the Legislative Branch of our Maryland government is the Department of Legislative Reference. This department gathers, sorts and indexes information on all questions of proposed legislation (law-making). In its offices are kept complete files on bills introduced in the General Assembly from 1918 to the present. Codes of Maryland laws are kept in a library. The laws and codes of laws from other states are also maintained in the library. Much other information gathering is done by this department for the use of any member of the General Assembly, the Governor or any State agency.

The Department operates through the Office of the Director and four divisions that provide: legislative services, statutory revision, research and information services, and computer and proofreading services.

The Legislative Division has trained staff members who assist the General Assembly in writing and reviewing nearly all bills and amendments introduced or considered by the General Assembly. Also, the Division staff helps many of the major working committees of the General Assembly, special joint committees, task forces and commissions. The Division staff also helps prepare informational materials and reports to be distributed to the General Assembly.

The Division of Statutory Revision is also known as the Code Revision Division. The Division's major work is the continuing preparation of a comprehensive revision and restatement of the statutory body of law of Maryland. This will be the first such complete revision since 1888. The object is to make the Code of Maryland easier to use and bring it up-to-date.

The Research Division has two functions. Research analysts provide scientific, economic, and policy analyses for committees, members and staff of the General Assembly. Legislative librarians provide reference and research services to the public.

The Research Division Library contains nearly 50,000 volumes of Maryland laws and related legislative and legal materials—laws and publications of other states, federal documents and general reference materials.

Bill status and other legislative information is provided by the Library. Through the Library, the Department serves as an official depository for the publications of Maryland State agencies and for all the local codes (compilations of laws) published by county and municipal governments. *Maryland Documents*, a list of State agency publications, is published monthly.

The Computer Division operates data processing equipment for the preparation of bills, the entry and maintenance of data into the bill status system, and the preparation of several Departmental publications. The Division provides certain proofreading services.

The Department of Fiscal Services was established in 1968 to succeed (take over the duties of) the Fiscal Research Bureau created in 1947. The present Department is the financial service arm of the

General Assembly. The Department operates under the policies and directives of the President of the Senate and the Speaker of the House of Delegates, the Legislative Policy Committee and the Joint Budget and Audit Committee.

It is, of course, most important that the General Assembly have current and complete information about the fiscal condition of Maryland and what implications new laws might have on the economic status of the State. So, the Department provides trained people to help the fiscal (financial) committees of the General Assembly and committees appointed by the legislature (General Assembly) to study taxation or other money matters.

The Department also studies and reviews all of the State's budgets while under development by the Executive branch and pending adoption by the Legislative branch.

The Department prepares reports on the fiscal impact of each session of the legislature and on many other money matters in the State: analysis of State debts, effectiveness of State agencies, and fiscal interrelationships. To inform the legislature and the executive branch data is collected and made available in the form of reports on a wide range of financial matters.

The Department provides support services to the General Assembly through printing, bill distribution, telecommunications and intern and page programs.

The Office of Legislative Auditor is responsible for conducting many audits (financial checks, investigation of accounting and data) of all departments, agencies and institutions of Maryland government. This Office audits offices of clerks of court and registers of wills. The General Assembly may be directed to make a management audit of a State agency or program and even private organizations receiving State funds. The Office also reviews the audit reports of all local governments and community colleges.

A modern state government is a huge and complex operation. Trained and experienced people are needed to help the legislators and the executives make decisions by keeping them well informed.

Finally, under the subject of legislative agencies we have three commissions.

Commission to Revise the Annotated Code of Maryland. The Governor appointed the Commission in 1970 to undertake the first reorganization and recodification of the *Annotated Code of Maryland* in almost 100 years. The Commission studies and revises the Public General Laws of Maryland to improve the organization, accessibility, utility and clarity of laws. Also, their work helps eliminate unconstitutional, obsolete and inconsistent or conflicting statutes.

The Commission submits proposals and recommendations to the General Assembly.

Staff services and support for the Commission are provided by the Division of Statutory Revision within the Department of Legislative Reference.

General Assembly Compensation Commission. The Commission was created by Constitutional Amendment, ratified November, 1970. It determines the compensation (payment) and allowances (such as staff, transportation, certain expenses) due members of the General Assembly. The legislature may reduce,but not increase, the amounts proposed by the Commission.

State Commission on Uniform State Laws. In 1896 the General Assembly established the "Commissioners for the Promotion of Uniformity of Legislation in the United States." In 1984, the Commissioners were renamed the State Commission on Uniform State Laws.

Every four years the Governor appoints three Commissioners who represent Maryland in the National Conference of Commissioners on Uniform State Laws. These people make recommendations to various state legislatures in an effort to make state laws more uniform. As noted earlier in this book, each state in the United States has its own laws.

CHAPTER 6

Our State Government: The Judicial Branch

As you can see by looking at the organizational chart for the Judicial Branch of Maryland's government, there are four levels of courts.

These are all higher courts than local courts concerned with matter of limited jurisdiction, such as most traffic violations and small fines for local ordinance violations, routine uncontested (not argued over) legal matters, wills and property matters.

When a case goes to trial then, it is first heard in one of Maryland's twelve District Courts.

The District Court has jurisdiction (power) in both criminal (including motor vehicle) and civil areas. It has little equity (justice between conflicting parties) jurisdiction. It has jurisdiction over juvenile cases only in Montgomery County.

The exclusive jurisdiction of the District Court generally includes all landlord/tenant cases; replevin (the process of recovering unlawfully detained personal property). Also, the District Court hears criminal cases if the possible penalty involved is less than three years in prison or not over a fine of $2,500, or both.

The District Court has concurrent (that means acting jointly, cooperatively, with equal authority) jurisdiction with the Circuit Courts (the next higher Maryland court) in civil cases over $2,500, but not over $10,000; and in misdemeanors and certain felonies. Are these legal terms hard to understand? Be sure to look up words that are not clear in the Glossary of Legal Terminology in the back of the book or in our word lists.

Since there are no juries provided in the District Court, a person entitled to, and who wants, a jury trial must go on to the Circuit Court.

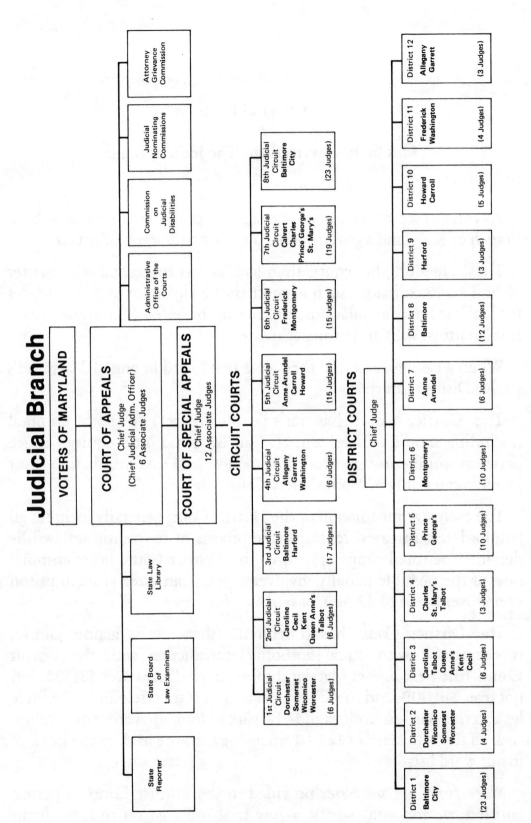

Judicial Branch

VOTERS OF MARYLAND

COURT OF APPEALS
Chief Judge
(Chief Judicial Adm. Officer)
6 Associate Judges

State Reporter

State Board of Law Examiners

State Law Library

Administrative Office of the Courts

Commission on Judicial Disabilities

Judicial Nominating Commissions

Attorney Grievance Commission

COURT OF SPECIAL APPEALS
Chief Judge
12 Associate Judges

CIRCUIT COURTS

| 1st Judicial Circuit
Dorchester
Somerset
Wicomico
Worcester
(6 Judges) | 2nd Judicial Circuit
Caroline
Cecil
Kent
Queen Anne's
Talbot
(6 Judges) | 3rd Judicial Circuit
Baltimore
Harford
(17 Judges) | 4th Judicial Circuit
Allegany
Garrett
Washington
(6 Judges) | 5th Judicial Circuit
Anne Arundel
Carroll
Howard
(15 Judges) | 6th Judicial Circuit
Frederick
Montgomery
(15 Judges) | 7th Judicial Circuit
Calvert
Charles
Prince George's
St. Mary's
(19 Judges) | 8th Judicial Circuit
Baltimore City
(23 Judges) |

DISTRICT COURTS

Chief Judge

| District 1
Baltimore City
(23 Judges) | District 2
Dorchester
Wicomico
Somerset
Worcester
(4 Judges) | District 3
Caroline
Talbot
Queen Anne's
Kent
Cecil
(6 Judges) | District 4
Charles
St. Mary's
Talbot
(3 Judges) | District 5
Prince George's
(10 Judges) | District 6
Montgomery
(10 Judges) | District 7
Anne Arundel
(6 Judges) | District 8
Baltimore
(12 Judges) | District 9
Harford
(3 Judges) | District 10
Howard
Carroll
(5 Judges) | District 11
Frederick
Washington
(4 Judges) | District 12
Allegany
Garrett
(3 Judges) |

Material from the *Maryland Manual 1985-1986*, published by the State of Maryland, State Archives, Annapolis, MD.

Judges of the District Courts are appointed by the Governor of Maryland with the advice and consent of the Maryland Senate. These judges serve ten-year terms or until they reach seventy years of age "whichever may first occur." (Constitution of Maryland, Article IV, Section 41D.) "If the ten year term of a judge shall expire before that judge shall have attained the age of seventy years, that judge shall be reappointed by the Governor, with the Senate's consent, for another ten year term or until he (or she) shall have attained the age of seventy years, whichever may first occur."

A Chief Judge of the Court of Appeals (the highest court in Maryland's government) names one judge of the District Court as Chief Judge of that Court.

If after the trial one of the parties involved in the case believes the decision of the District Court is unfair, that party can appeal to the next highest court, a circuit court.

Circuit Courts

Maryland is divided into eight Judicial Circuits:

> First—Counties of Worcester, Wicomico, Somerset and Dorchester.
>
> Second—Counties of Caroline, Talbot, Queen Anne's, Kent and Cecil.
>
> Third—Counties of Baltimore and Harford.
>
> Fourth—Counties of Allegany, Garrett and Washington.
>
> Fifth—Counties of Carroll, Howard and Anne Arundel.
>
> Sixth—Counties of Montgomery and Frederick.
>
> Seventh—Prince George's, Charles, Calvert and St. Mary's.
>
> Eighth—Baltimore City.

In most cases, one judge of the Circuit Court hears a case.

In each county and in Baltimore City, there is a Circuit Court. It is a trial court of general jurisdiction with broad powers. Generally, it handles the major civil cases and the more serious criminal matters.

Circuit Courts may decide appeals from the District Court and from certain administrative agencies.

Presently, there are 107 Circuit Court judges with at least one in each county. Unlike the other three levels of courts in Maryland, there is no chief judge for the Circuit Court. Instead, eight circuit administrative judges, appointed by the Chief Judge of Appeals, perform administrative duties in each of their respective circuits, with the aid of county administrative judges.

Each Circuit judge is first appointed to office by the Governor and then must stand for election. When elected, a judge serves a fifteen-year term of office.

If this Circuit Court decision is unacceptable to one of the parties — a petition may be sent to a higher Maryland Court, the Court of Special Appeals in Annapolis.

The Court of Special Appeals. The Court was created in 1966 to be Maryland's intermediate appellate court, to ease the caseload in the Court of Appeals (Maryland's highest State court).

The Court of Special Appeals sits in Annapolis and now consists of thirteen members.

Judges are elected from each of the six Appellate Judicial Circuits and from the State at large. Members are first appointed by the Governor and confirmed by the Senate of Maryland. After this, they run for election without formal opposition for a ten-year term of office.

The Court of Special Appeals generally has exclusive initial appellate jurisdiction over any reviewable decree, judgement, order or other actions of a Circuit Court. The Court of Special Appeals generally hears cases appealed from the Circuit Courts.

Judges sit in panels of three as a rule. The Court considers applications for permission to appeal in several matters—inmate grievances, denial of excessive bail—for example.

If one of the parties involved in a case heard before the Court of Special Appeals believes a correct and just decision has not been reached, that person may petition for a review of the case by Maryland's highest State court, the Court of Appeals.

If the Court of Appeals decides not to accept the case, not to review it, then the decision of the Court of Special Appeals stands.

The Court of Appeals of Maryland is the highest tribunal (court) in the State. It was created in 1776. Since 1851, the Court has sat (met) in Annapolis each September.

The Court has seven members. These judges are first appointed by the Governor and confirmed by the Maryland Senate. They next run for office on their records without opposition, for a ten-year term.

If the voters reject the keeping of a judge in office, or if the vote is tied, the office becomes vacant and must be filled by a new appointment.

The Chief Judge of the Court of Appeals is chosen by the Governor.

Due to laws effective January 1, 1975, the Court of Appeals hears cases almost exclusively on review. The Court may review a case decided by the Court of Special Appeals or may bring up for review cases filed in that court before they are decided there. The Court reviews, also, certain cases from the circuit court level.

Aside from reviewing cases — the Court of Appeals has other important work. The Court has the power to adopt rules for judges and courts in Maryland. It reviews recommendations from the State Board of Law Examiners and conducts disciplinary proceedings involving judges and lawyers. The Court admits lawyers to the practice of law in Maryland.

The Court of Appeals supervises the activities of the Attorney Grievance Commission which looks into matters involving possible misconduct of lawyers and investigation of requests for lawyers to again practice law in Maryland.

Clerks of the Courts

All of the Maryland courts we have just read about have clerks. This person maintains the docket (list of cases to be considered and the dates involved), receives briefs and transcripts of all cases filed with his or her particular court.

The clerk of the court maintains official custody of the decisions of the court, (takes them and files them) the Acts of the General Assembly, and all other records that must legally be filed with his or her court.

We have seen how Maryland courts work. There are other courts in Maryland —federal courts—not State courts.

For example, should the Maryland Court of Appeals decide to consider a case and then one of the parties is *still* not satisfied with the Court of Appeal's decision, a petition may be sent to a *federal court*, a U. S. District Court.

Federal Courts

As we discuss Maryland courts, we must also mention the fact that there are some federal judges and federal courts in Maryland, and concerned with state-level affairs.

U. S. District Court

The United States District Courts are trial courts with general federal jurisdiction. Each state has at least one district court.

If a person (or corporation, group, company) is not satisfied with the decisions of state courts and courts of appeal, that person may petition (ask) for a hearing of the matter by the United States District Court. Unless the matter is of federal concern (issue), or a constitutional issue—the U. S. District Court may not agree to hear the case, may not agree to review the decisions of the state courts.

U. S. District judges are appointed by the President of the United States with the advice and consent of the U. S. Senate.

If the person (or group, etc.) succeeds in getting the federal (U.S.) district court to review the case, yet does not like that decision—then the case may be appealed even higher to the U. S. Court of Appeals. The U. S. Courts of Appeal are empowered to review all decisions of the federal (U. S.) district courts.

The United States Courts of Appeals—are intermediate appellate courts created in 1891 to relieve overcrowding of the U. S. Supreme Court docket. The appeals courts are *empowered to review all decisions of federal district courts*, except in those few instances where direct review by the Supreme Court is mandated (required by U. S. law).

Appeals Court judges are appointed by the President of the United States with the advice and consent of the U. S. Senate.

The United States is divided into twelve judicial circuits (areas). Maryland is in the fourth judicial circuit, which also includes Virginia, West Virginia, North Carolina and South Carolina. Maryland's two members of the U. S. Court of Appeals maintain chambers (offices) in the U. S. Court House in Baltimore City.

Should the person (or company, etc.) appealing to the United States Court of Appeals still believe that a fair decision has not been made, there is one last chance for an appeal. That is by petitioning the United States Supreme Court to review the case.

The United States Supreme Court will consider, among its other duties, only cases of federal interest and those concerning possible conflict with the Constitution of the United States.

There are nine Justices of the United States Supreme Court. The President of the United States has the authority to select and appoint judges of the United States Supreme Court with the consent of the Senate. These judges are appointed for life or until the judge chooses to resign.

Qualifications for Judges

In Maryland, judges of all the Courts must be:

- citizens of Maryland
- qualified voters
- residents of Maryland for five years
- thirty years of age
- attorneys admitted to practice law in Maryland
- distinguished for integrity, wisdom and sound legal knowledge

Article IV of the Constitution of Maryland gives the details of the Maryland Judiciary Department, how judges are selected, paid, serve and retire.

Lawyers (Attorneys)

To become an attorney, a lawyer, one generally goes to college and earns a Bachelor of Arts or Bachelor of Science degree. Next, one applies for admission to a law school.

After graduation from law school (after three to four years of study) one takes an examination. Each state has its own bar examination plus a standard one called a "multi-state" examination.

Once past the examinations, one applies for "admission to the bar"—for permission to practice law in Maryland. To practice law in a state, one must be admitted to that state bar.

the dandelion

MARYLAND CONSERVATIONIST

Two historic kinds of transportation in Maryland, the train and the barge. View scenes like this at the B & O Railroad Museum in Baltimore City.

Photograph courtesy the Maryland Div. of Tourist Development.

SECTION III
COUNTY AND TOWN
Our Local Governments

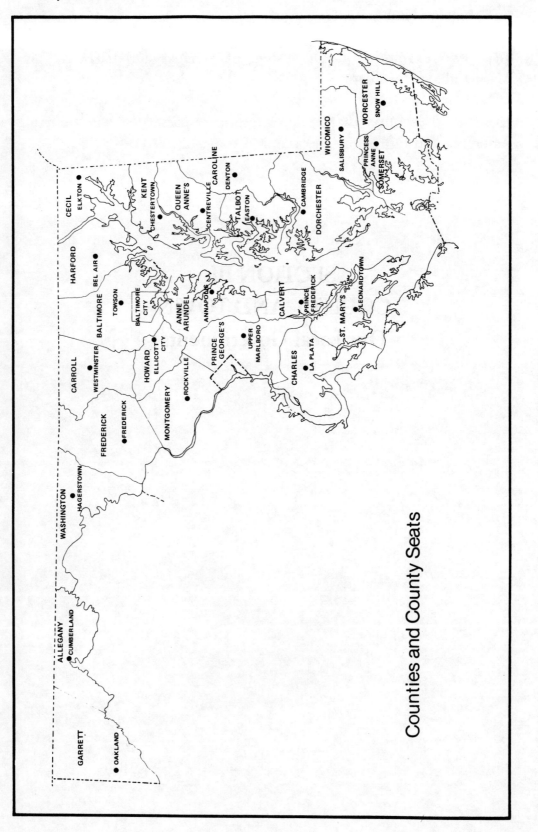

Counties and County Seats

Material from the *Maryland Manual 1985-1986*, published by the State of Maryland, State Archives, Annapolis, MD.

SECTION III   WORDS, WORDS, WORDS!!!

avocation, a hobby; something one does aside from one's work, often done for enjoyment. Example: gardening, photography.

board, a group of persons having managerial, supervisory or investigative powers.

commissioners, officials in charge of a government department; a **county commissioner** is an official who is a member of a **board of county commissioners.**

disburse, to pay out, to spend.

incorporated, united; formed into a legal corporation. Example: an incorporated town with its own government and services.

inherit, to receive from someone after that person's death; usually one inherits from a relative. One may also inherit something or some position if the former holder leaves or steps down.

municipal, relating to a town or city; an urban political unit.

optional, permitted a choice, not compulsory.

probate, to extablish that a will is genuine.

prosecutes, to seek to punish through an appeal to the courts.

rural, country area, farm area, not urban.

taxes, a charge, a fee, which must be paid by many citizens to pay for the governmental services they receive.

urban, pertaining to city or town areas, not rural.

vocation, the work in which a person is regularly employed. One's work or profession.

volunteers, people who work for a person or a cause due to interest or belief and who are not paid workers. Actions taken of one's free will.

zoning, to divide or plan (as in a city or county) areas into sections reserved for different purposes.

Washington Monument, Mount Vermon Place, Baltimore, Maryland. (This 1968 photograph courtesy J. H. Cromwell, C & P Telephone Company of Maryland.)

CHAPTER 1

Review of Maryland
County Governments

History. From the formation of the first colonial Maryland counties until 1798, the county court served as the administrative unit of county government. Then, the levy (tax mustering) court assumed (took over) its work. By 1827, *boards of county commissioners* began to replace the levy courts. These boards, quite alike, governed the counties until the mid-twentieth century (mid 1900's).

Today, twelve counties continue this form of government with a board of county commissioners serving executive and legislative functions. These counties are: Calvert, Caroline, Carroll, Cecil, Charles, Dorchester, Frederick, Garrett, Queen Anne's, St. Mary's, Somerset and Washington.

Since 1948, the citizens of several counties have used alternative modes of government. Eight counties adopted *charter governments:* Montgomery (1948), Baltimore (1956), Anne Arundel and Wicomico (1964), Howard (1968), Prince George's (1970), Harford (1972), and Talbot (1973). In these counties special departments, agencies and offices perform the work formerly done by the boards of county commissioners.

Three counties—Kent (1970), Allegany (1974), and Worcester (1976)—adopted optional powers of home rule, as provided for by Article XI-F of the Constitution of Maryland. These are called *Code Home Rule* county governments because details are given as to how these governments shall operate in Article 25B of the *Annotated Code of Maryland* (a compilation of Maryland laws).

Baltimore City became a government, separate from Baltimore County, with the ratification of the State Constitution of 1851.

While its original incorporation dates from 1796, the City operates today under its current charter of 1964. State provisions for Baltimore City government are given in Article XI of the Constitution of Maryland, and also in *the Annotated Code of Maryland.*

snipe

CHAPTER 2

Officers, Boards and Commissions Common to All Counties

All counties offer many services. Discussed below are some offices and services all Maryland county governments provide.

Boards of Education in about one-half of the Maryland counties are appointed by the Governor. The Board of Education members are elected by the voters in the other half. (Exact details are given in the *Annotated Code of Maryland*, Section 3-701, Title IV.)

These board members are in charge of the county school systems. They see that pre-school, elementary, middle school, high school and community college students are given the best teachers, buildings and supplies possible. Over half the money to educate people in the county comes from the county. The rest comes from the State and the federal government.

The State of Maryland is devoting a great deal of attention and money to kindergartens, county vocational centers and to special classes for handicapped children. Children are considered handicapped when they have a speech or hearing disorder, or are physically or mentally disabled. The help of the State is very welcome in these three kinds of schools because the schools are badly needed, and they are very expensive to build and to operate. Most counties also have teachers who visit students who are kept at home by a long illness.

Every county Board of Education must have a staff of people to administer the schools; to decide what to teach and how to teach it; to select books and materials with which to do teaching work; to hire, train and pay the people who staff the schools.

Boards of Social Services

These Boards of Social Services were formerly called the County Welfare Services. This county department helps people who cannot help themselves. Sometimes the person needing help is too sick to work, too old, or too young. Sometimes a person cannot seem to find work and must be supported by the people who do work and pay taxes.

County Health Boards

Members of the County Health Boards consist of members of the governing body of the county. There are many things to be done by the local health departments. You may remember getting polio shots and other inoculations from a County Health Service program. Clinics in the county are offices where people may go to get medical advice and treatment. A few counties operate hospitals and most contribute money to private hospitals that serve the county. Many of our Maryland counties have programs to help citizens suffering from mental illnesses.

Every county is working, too, to keep its air and waters clean. Men from the county department of health inspect wells, springs, and water supply systems to see if the water is safe to drink. Visiting nurses travel about the county helping those who are ill. Packing plants that put food into cans, or freeze it, for market are inspected by county health people. Other inspectors check bakeries and restaurants to be sure the food is cooked and served so that it is fresh and clean.

There are programs for elderly people in most Maryland counties. These help older citizens to get good housing, help them with their health problems and give them places where they can meet and work at crafts.

Community Action Committees

About half of our counties have special youth commissions which help young people head useful, happy lives.

All of our Maryland counties have programs to help low-income families. These are paid for, for the most part, by the Federal government. The programs help people learn to do work that will earn them a good living. It helps them find jobs; it helps them locate houses and apartments in which they can take pride. The members of these committees are appointed by the governing body of each county.

Departments of Public Safety

All of our counties have some sort of department of public safety. Baltimore City and many other cities and towns in Maryland have their own police departments.

In addition to the local police and the sheriff and his deputies, the Maryland State Police help protect the public in the counties. Their main job is patrolling and doing traffic safety work along State roads, but they also do other police work.

Both local and State law enforcement men and women do many things for us. They patrol our streets and highways to keep Maryland's millions of autos, trucks and busses moving safely. If a vehicle stops running or if there is an accident, the police are soon there to help.

In times of storm, flood, fire or when criminals threaten the public, the law enforcement men and women are there. It is work that needs people who are dependable and well trained—who have courage and good common sense.

Offices of Inspections and Permits

Most counties have offices that make inspections and give out permits.

A building inspector must be sure the land being dug away for foundations of buildings will not slide over the workers. While the building is going up, the inspector must be sure the builder has braced walls so they will not fall and hurt people near them. Then, too, when the building is finished, it must have been built in such a way that it is not likely to catch fire or to collapse. Inspectors check plans, electrical work and plumbing to make sure that all the work is done according to the county safety and health laws.

There are permits to be given to allow parades, carnivals, fireworks exhibitions, large gatherings; and to salesmen, called peddlers, who wish to travel about in the county with items to sell.

Somewhere in each county will be found an office in which one may apply for a license to build, to marry, to operate a business, or, to put on your dog!

Liquor Licensing Boards or Commissions

These departments carry out the laws of Maryland and of the county regarding the way in which liquors may be sold, by whom, to whom, where and when.

Fire Departments

Do you know that most of the firemen in our state are volunteers? They are not paid, but voluntarily dash off to the firehouse at all hours of the day and night to put out fires and save people. They spend many hours in training and practice.

In Baltimore City the firemen are all paid men because the city is so large and so much training and time is required of the firemen. Some of our larger towns and cities have paid firemen. In some counties there are both paid firemen and volunteer firemen. In some counties, there are mostly volunteer fire companies but some have a "skeleton crew" (a small group) of paid firemen.

Offices of Civil Defense

You might think that in times of peace the Office of Civil Defense would have nothing to do. This is not so. The people in this department are those who know where to put their hands on emergency equipment of all kinds. They can locate medical supplies and places where people can stay in emergencies. The Civil Defense people can get radios into action to keep in touch with places swept by fire, wind, water or riot, when telephone communication has been lost.

Most of us think of the office of Civil Defense as one which would direct us to an air raid shelter during an enemy air attack. However, the Office of Civil Defense is serving us now. For example, when a hurricane swept over Ocean City, Maryland, not long ago, it caused great damage. The Office of Civil Defense came in to help the homeless, to get food served and to treat people who were hurt in the storm.

The Civil Defense people are sometimes assisted by the Red Cross and other civil groups, and by State and federal organizations. About half of the cost of the county Civil Defense Office is paid by the federal government.

Departments of Public Works

This department provides county facilities. It also builds roads, new sewers, water supply facilities, airports and county bridges. It installs street lighting and traffic lights.

The department supervises what used to be called the county dump, but which is now known as a sanitary land fill. This chore may not sound very exciting, but it is very necessary. There are many kinds of cleaning-up jobs to be done in a modern county. Cars are abandoned by their owners and must be taken away, as well as old refrigerators and washing machines that are left about. The sides of the county roads must be trimmed and kept free of litter. The grounds of county properties must be mowed, planted and kept in good condition. Several counties collect trash for their residents. In some counties, leaves are collected in the fall in order to reduce air pollution from burning leaves. Streets must be cleared of snow in the winter.

The Department of Public Works provides for the upkeep of county roads, bridges and buildings. Several counties have built airports for citizens to use. Airports are often built with the financial assistance of a nearby city. The Baltimore-Washington International Airport was owned and operated by Baltimore City until July, 1968, when it was purchased by the State of Maryland.

Community Development

You probably know that in most counties there are programs to provide parks and recreation for the citizens. Often, this work is helped with money from the State and from a city government. Do you know that most counties also have a planning committee, or board that plans the future uses of land? To keep to this plan of orderly growth, the county commissioners, or councilmen, enforce zoning laws. Zoning means that certain kinds of work, housing and parks are kept in planned spaces. For example, it would not be practical to put a factory that sent out powerful-smelling fumes in the middle of a group of peaceful homes, would it? Planning and zoning help a county grow gracefully.

A new idea, and one that more and more counties are beginning to use, is that of "economic development." That is, many counties are setting up departments that will work to bring; a) more tourists into the county where they can enjoy themselves and spend money; b) more manufacturing and research plants into the county, so that county people can find good jobs near their homes.

Human Relations Committees

A large number of Maryland counties now have programs to work out good relations between groups of people in the county and to prevent injustices and disturbances.

Extension Services

In every county there are agents from the federal and State governments who can help both the farmer and the home owner to use their land well. Extension agents used to help the farmer most of the time. Now, they also help the city government with its planting of parks and parkways. They help the home owner with advice on grass and trees, on getting rid of insect pests and on what kinds of plants will be most successful in the area. That is, this job is becoming more and more "urban," or concerned with city and town problems.

Election Boards

Members of election boards are appointed by the Governor of Maryland to supervise the registration of voters and the elections held in the county. The county pays for this service.

Tax Offices

Services cost money, and to get money the county charges taxes. There are several kinds of county taxes:
 (a) Property taxes which bring in the largest part of the county income. (b) County individual income tax is collected by all twenty-three counties and Baltimore City. It is a part of the tax you pay to the State on your yearly state income tax report. (c) Businesses are taxed by the counties. (d) There are miscellaneous taxes, fees and charges which help the counties get money.

Judicial Services

The system of courts within the county is paid for by the county. In our section on the Judicial Branch of our Maryland government, we discussed these courts and what they do.

Local Officials

In each of Maryland's counties the following officers are elected, for a four-year term, by the voters in the county:

The Clerk of the Circuit Court keeps the records of the Circuit Court and records on land in the county. He or she issues licenses of various kinds.

The State's Attorney prosecutes cases in which the State of Maryland is interested.

The Sheriff often has the responsibility for general law enforcement in the county. Also, he sees that the county jail is properly run. He often serves the courts by delivering important official papers and orders.

The Register of Wills records wills, handles probate and probate fees and processes inheritance taxes. To probate a will is to declare it true and genuine.

Treasurers of the counties collect State and county taxes, disburse (send out) money and make financial reports. They also receive and disburse State and county funds for certain programs.

Public Defenders are appointed officials. These are attorneys who defend people accused of breaking the law and who have no money to pay for legal advice. This is a rather new office, but more and more counties have Public Defenders.

If they do not, a judge often appoints an attorney to help the defendant.

Hager House (1739 or 1740) home of the founder of Hagerstown, Maryland, Jonathan Hager. (This 1968 photograph courtesy J. H. Cromwell, C & P Telephone Company of Maryland.)

CHAPTER 3

How County Governments Operate

Government by County Commissioners

The governments of twelve of our counties are headed by Boards of County Commissioners. These people are elected by the voters for four-year terms.

The number of Commissioners for each county varies. (See the Constitution of 1867, Articles VII, XVII.) Individual county laws for those twelve counties are passed by the General Assembly. The State senators and delegates from each county usually have a great deal of influence over the passage of local laws for their county.

However, it is the county commissioners who levy, that is, charge, taxes on property in their respective counties. Also, the commissioners decide where new businesses and homes shall be placed on land in their county. This kind of planning is called "zoning." The commissioners must try to place buildings in which people work on easy-to-reach land, yet be sure that noise or smoke from these buildings will not annoy people living nearby. Plants where people work often need to be near roads, railroads, airports or waterways. The county commissioners must also plan for parks and play areas.

The county commissioners decide many things about the county roads. Old roads must be kept in good repair; new roads may need to be built; and, sometimes, roads must be made wider. The county commissioners check on the many county services which range from trash collection and sanitary landfills to the operation of the county police department and the running of the county jail! Look at the list of county services given in Chapter 1 of this Section.

Code Home Rule County Government

There is another type of government that can be adopted by counties in Maryland. In 1966, our State constitution was amended to allow a county to make its own laws through its Board of County Commissioners. This kind of county government would be known as "Code Home Rule." So far, it has been used by Kent, Allegany and Worcester counties, beginning in 1970, 1974 and 1976, respectively.

In counties with this type of government, if the commissioners passed a law which did not satisfy the people in the county, the people could petition for a referendum. To petition means to ask in writing with a certain number of voters' names signed to the request. The number needed is set by law. A referendum is an election held to decide whether or not to adopt a law. A referendum may also be held to decide other questions.

The General Assembly would still have power over many aspects of county government under the Code Home Rule plan, as it does over Charter Home Rule counties. The main advantage of adopting Code Home Rule government is that counties which would like their commissioners to make local laws do not need to write a charter. These charters are often very difficult to prepare. They are also very difficult to get voted into effect.

Charter County Governments

Anne Arundel, Baltimore, Howard, Harford, Montgomery, Prince George's, Talbot and Wicomico counties are the eight counties having a charter form of government.

Charter counties have a County Council which is made up of members elected by voters to serve four-year terms. The County Council in "charter counties" is the local legislature; that is, each County Council has the power to pass local laws for its county. This is important. In charter, or as it is sometimes called, "home rule," counties, the General Assembly of Maryland is limited as to the kinds of laws it may enact for one charter county. Of course, the General Assembly can still enact laws, known as general laws, that pertain (apply) to all counties.

The work of the highest local executive, the County Executive,

County Manager, or Administrative Director, although not completely identical (alike) in each case, is to supervise the departments of the county governments; to prepare a yearly budget; and to help choose people to head county departments. While both men and women are chosen for leading government positions in both local and state offices, most of the jobs are at present filled by men.

Agencies Operating in More Than One County

There are several groups that serve more than one county. Some are working to give counties orderly planning and zoning programs. Others work to prevent water and air pollution; still others are groups that serve more than one county to avoid duplication in library or animal rescue services.

Counties with the same problems often find it a good idea to join together to study the problem and, later, to take action to solve the problem.

These multi-county, or regional agencies cross county lines and sometimes state lines. The Maryland-National Capital Park and Planning Commission is an example of such a group. This commission helps with the planning and zoning programs and park programs in Montgomery and Prince George's counties. The Washington Suburban Sanitary Commission is another regional commission which is concerned with water supply and sewage treatment in Montgomery County, Prince George's County and part of Howard County. The Maryland Port Authority is a multi-county group which works for port development in the Baltimore area. Another group, called the Metropolitan Transit Authority, works on regional transit (transportation) problems in Prince George's and Montgomery counties. Other agencies deal with similar problems in the Baltimore area which includes Baltimore City, Baltimore County and Anne Arundel County.

The Maryland people serving on these regional, special governments, are usually appointed by the counties concerned or by the Governor.

President Ronald Reagan signing a bill into law.

Photograph by Pete Souza, courtesy The White House.

Chapter 4

The Government of Maryland's Towns and Cities

There are over 150 incorporated cities in Maryland. There are also many populated areas which are not incorporated. These unincorporated cities and towns include Dundalk, Silver Spring and Bethesda. Unincorporated places prefer to let the county governments provide the services they need. We can say then, that unincorporated towns and cities are governed by the county commissioners or the county council of the county in which it is located.

Because Baltimore City governs itself and is not located within any county, it will be discussed separately in this section.

Incorporated Towns and Cities

An incorporated town or city is known as a municipality. Municipal governments provide many local services such as police and fire protection, health and welfare services, public safety services and certain improvements for the town.

In Maryland, local government centers mainly around the county. Maryland grew up in this way from colonial times. Towns were scattered and populations were small. Later, as towns grew, sometimes services that the county government could not provide became necessary, such as paving of streets, street lighting or water supply. In these instances, to finance the building and upkeep of these things, a town might set up a municipal government. But town and city governments in Maryland, except for Baltimore City, are still controlled to a great extent by the county governments.

Each incorporated city or town has a mayor, or a president of the Town Commission, who serves as the highest officer for the municipality. An elected council, or commission, meets monthly. The dates of elections and the terms of office for these officials vary from town to town. However, the voluntary model for municipal government, which is contained in the Municipal Corporation Charter Act of 1955, provides that the mayor shall be elected in May of every second, odd-numbered year. So, there is some hope that one day municipal elections will be more uniform in date and in term of office!

The municipal council has the power to pass local ordinances, or rules, about the safety, health, welfare and improvement of the town. They also help regulate the police and fire departments and control the roads, parks, public buildings and other public works in the town.

Town and city services have to be paid for, and this means that the residents of the municipality must pay taxes to the municipal government. The state and county governments often help the municipal governments, however, with money for certain programs.

Questions:

1. There are three kinds of county governments in Maryland. Name and briefly explain each.

2. What kind of county government do you have in your county? (This question won't apply to those of you who live in Baltimore City.)

3. Is Baltimore City in a county?

4. What does ''administrative work'' mean in a school? In a county government?

5. Name as many county services as you can, please.

6. How is money raised to pay most county employees?

7. Some services are extended to the counties and cities by the State of Maryland and by the United States government. Are these called extension services? Name two, please.

8. Is the Code Home Rule type of county government rather like a like a county legislature? What about a Charter County government? Is it a legislature?

9. What is an incorporated town or city?

10. Who governs, and provides police and other services for, an unincorporated town or city or place?

11. How does Baltimore City get money to pay City workers?

12. Why is taxation a fair system for raising money for the many services we get in the United States, in Maryland, in our counties and our cities?

Annapolis Harbor.

THIS PLACE IS IN ANNAPOLIS. IT'S A NEAT PLACE TO VISIT.

St. Johns College.

SECTION IV
THE STORY OF THE CONSTITUTION OF MARYLAND

SECTION IV   WORDS, WORDS, WORDS!!!

abolition, to do away with some custom, practice, or law. To abolish it.

acting, serving temporarily for another.

adjournment, end of a meeting, a legislative session, or a class.

alimony, money paid to a marriage partner after a divorce to help that person live in their accustomed manner. Women receive alimony more often than men. Alimony today is being replaced in many cases by settlements, by one agreement.

allegiance, devotion or loyalty to a person, a group, a nation, or a cause; obligation of obedience and good faith owed by citizens to their governments.

archaic, ancient, very old, no longer in use; old fashioned.

barons, a member of the lowest grade of the British peerage; a title; a man of great power of some kind.

candidate, a person who has been selected as a candidate and is running for office.

census, a counting of the population of a place or a nation by its government. In the United States a census is taken every ten years.

colony, a body of people sent out by a country to settle another place. Example: Maryland was a British colony from 1634 to 1776.

committee, a group of people who are to consider and/or take action on some matter.

compensation, pay; repayment for some injury, loss or damage.

confederacy, a united group; allied. Example: the Confederate States of America, often called "the Confederacy."

consent, agreement.

conservative, tending to preserve laws and customs; slow to change; not radical.

constitutional convention , a group of persons selected to meet for the purpose of writing a new constitution.

declaration, a statement, a formal assertion.

delegates, persons elected or selected to represent others at some meeting.

democracy, a government by the people; rule of the majority; a belief in equality for all people.

deputy, someone authorized to act for another person.

dueling, a combat between two persons; one fought with weapons in the presence of witnesses.

emoluments, salary, wages, profit from one's employment or from an office held.

franchise, the right to vote; **enfranchised,** given the right to vote.

incumbent, one who is in office; one who holds an office at the time mentioned.

interim, a temporary thing, or action, or group.

ironic, relating to the humorous or sardonic use of words to express the opposite of what one really means; unexpected result.

merit system, hiring by means of tests offered to all applicants. The test must be passed to get the job.

monopoly, a commodity or service which is controlled by one person or group.

oath, a solemn appeal to some revered person or thing to bear witness to the truth of one's word or promise.

obsolete, out of date, no longer useful or appropriate.

parliament, an assembly of persons that makes up the supreme law-making (legislative) body of a country. A legislature.

poll tax, tax charged each person; each "poll," means, each head.

parole, a conditional release of a prisoner before his or her sentence is completed.

pension, sum paid regularly to a person after that person's retirement.

poll, (several meanings) to receive and record votes of; to receive (as votes) in an election; to question in a survey of opinions. Old meaning: one's head.

preamble, the first part of a formal document.

quorum, enough members of a board, committee, legislature or other group of people to legally vote on a proposal. The rules of the group set the number of members that make up a quorum.

radical, political tendency toward extreme change. The opposite of conservative.

repealed, removed; taken out of a constitution or a code of laws.

representative, one who acts for another or others; a delegate; **representative government** is one in which the people are represented by persons selected by vote to act for them.

republic, a government in which supreme power resides in a body of citizens entitled to vote and is exercised by elected officials and representatives responsible to the people.

revenue, income; money coming in. **Anticipated revenue,** is expected money, anticipated income.

suffrage, the right of voting; franchise; the exercise of the right to vote.

transition, a passing from one state, stage, place, office or subject, to another; change.

union, the formation of a single political unit from two or more independent units; for example---the United States of America is a union of states. **Unionists:** those favoring a union. Also: one side of the American Civil War, the United States side.

warrant, a guarantee, to attest, to secure, to sanction. Also, a legal document authorizing an officer to make an arrest, a seizure or a search.

CHAPTER 1

The Constitution of 1776

The story of the Constitution of Maryland is a dramatic one. Our Constitution is the very foundation of our State law. Oddly enough, many of us do not know much about it. Our present Constitution makes very interesting reading, with several surprises along the way. However, it makes one wonder how and why its many articles were written. What is the story of this important Maryland document?

The time was August of 1776. The colonies were in a state of rebellion. Maryland was without a constitution. The British government's Maryland Colonial Assembly had been ended in the period June 22, 1774 and July of 1775. This had been the government set in place over Maryland, a colony of Great Britain, by the British king. It was a peaceful takeover by a group of men who formed an interim government, called the Provincial Convention, which was established as a temporary measure to administer Maryland and fight the war against Britain. The revolutionary government consisted of representatives chosen and sent to Annapolis by men who governed the counties. Executive power to manage affairs for Maryland had been given to a Committee of Safety.

Then, on July 4, 1776, the Declaration of Independence was announced, officially breaking all ties between the British government and all thirteen colonies, now called the United States of America, including Maryland. Now, Maryland needed a state government—a permanent government. Maryland was no longer one of Britain's colonies.

So, on August 1, 1776, men in each county in Maryland chose men to represent them in a constitutional convention to write the first Maryland constitution. In so doing, they would be writing out a plan for the government of Maryland. These representatives, called delegates, were elected for a one-year term.

On August 14, 1776, just a few weeks after the announcement of the Declaration of Independence, the Maryland delegates met in Annapolis to tackle the problem of forming the new permanent government. (Actually, the Convention of 1776 was the government of Maryland and not in the modern sense a constitutional convention. A modern constitutional convention concentrates only on its work of writing a constitution.)

The governments of the newly formed states at this time would be very important because the new nation, the United States of America, was not yet very strong. With a strong central government lacking, state governments had a great deal of power and much responsibility. The delegates to the first Maryland Constitutional Convention had an imposing task before them.

SEE, THE PROBLEM WAS AMERICA WON THE WAR AND NOW SHE NEEDED A GOVERNMENT.

The men who met in Annapolis wanted to do several things. They wanted to discard many of the old methods of government that they felt had been unfair under the English government. However, they very much wanted to keep many laws and customs related to English Common Law which stressed men's individual rights and responsibilities. Then, to this they wanted to add something new, a representative form of government.

One of the first things the First Constitutional Convention did was to elect Matthew Tilghman as President. Then a committee was elected, by vote of the delegates, to prepare and submit to the Convention a State constitution including a declaration of rights. The men elected were: Matthew Tilghman, Charles Carroll of Annapolis, William Paca, Charles Carroll of Carrollton, George Plater, Samuel Chase and Robert Goldsborough. These men prepared the constitutional draft (proposed version), which they hoped would become the Constitution of Maryland and serve the people of the State well.

The first part of the Constitution of 1776 was the Preamble. It stated that, "We, the people of Maryland," intend to write a good constitution for the sure foundation of, and the security of, the State of Maryland.

Then, the writers of the Maryland Constitution prepared a Bill of Rights. This section has come down to us with almost no change. As you know, the first amendment to our United States Constitution is made up of a Bill of Rights. In comparison, our state and national bill of rights are quite similar. Both are based on laws of human rights which had slowly grown up in England over the years.

Today, we in the United States are so used to having these rights that it is hard for us to realize that in great areas of the world, these human rights are still not given to citizens. Nor were these rights always given here in Maryland; nor, before Maryland was settled, in England.

The fight for human rights for citizens in England covered several centuries and was hard won. In the year 1215, King John of England reluctantly granted certain rights to his barons, in a document called the "Magna Carta". Some rights were given to some people. Later, in

1689, the Parliament of England gained further rights which placed more power in the hands of the members of Parliament and made the King get the permission of Parliament before taking property or liberty from his subjects. Slowly, painfully, in England, the rights of the citizens were recognized.

In 1728, when Maryland was under English rule, in the Colonial Assembly of Maryland, the colonial Attorney General, Daniel Dulaney, and members of the Assembly declared that Maryland residents generally should have the same rights as free men living in England. Dulaney argued that both the Magna Carta and Maryland's original charter, dated 1632, gave the people of Maryland these freedoms and rights.

So, many years later, when the committee of Maryland men sat down in 1776 to write a Constitution for Maryland, they wanted first of all to write down the rights of the people of Maryland under the new government.

But what are these rights that the authors of our Maryland Constitution were so anxious to state plainly at the very beginning of the document? They are in simple words:

• The freedom to worship as one chooses. • The freedom of speech. • The freedom of the press. • The right to assemble peaceably. • The right to privacy of homes from search, from use by soldiers without permission, and the right to have property without its being unlawfully taken from individuals; also, the right not to be searched without a warrant and for a good reason. • The right to petition (ask) the government for fair treatment. • The right not to be tried unless accused of a crime by a Grand Jury. (A Grand Jury is a group of people chosen to decide whether or not the evidence against a person is enough to justify a trial.) • If accused of a crime, the right to have an attorney; the right to refuse to speak against oneself; and the right to trial by jury. (A jury is a group of people chosen to decide whether or not the person on trial is guilty.) If accused of a crime, the right to call and question witnesses. • Common law cases, those in which two parties disagree, also involve the right to trial by jury. • The right not to be charged unfair fines, or bail; nor must an individual be given cruel and unusual punishments.

With these rights, of course, come responsibilities. For example, when a citizen asks that the privacy of his home be respected, he must respect the privacy of other citizens. Or if a person wants the freedom to attend the church of his choice, he must respect the right of another person to attend whatever church that person wishes. It is an interesting thought that rights and responsibilities go together.

Next, the Maryland delegates on the committee wrote out a "Form of Government." This contained the following items:

•A governor was to be chosen each year by the General Assembly (not the voters). He was to serve no more than three terms consecutively; that is, one right after another. •The legislature of Maryland, called the Maryland General Assembly, was to consist of a House of Delegates and a Senate. •Four men from each county were

to be elected each year by the voters to go to the House of Delegates in Annapolis. Baltimore City and Annapolis each were to elect two delegates. Only male property owners could vote. Some black men could vote. •The Senate was to be made up of fifteen men, elected every five years. The senators were not elected directly by the voters, but were chosen by an electoral college. This was to be made up of two members from each county and one member each from Baltimore City and Annapolis. Only men were selected, no women! •The Sheriff, to be chosen for a three-year term, was the only locally elected officer. •The Governor's Council was to be quite a powerful group of men. It was to be made up of fifteen members, elected each year by the General Assembly. When the Governor appointed men to fill

State offices, except for the office of Sheriff, he was to get the approval of his Council on the choices. •Finally, to give equal voice to all sections of the State, regardless of population, there were to be two Treasurers and two Land Offices; one for the Eastern Shore and one for the Western Shore. Also, both of these sections would have separate terms of the Court of Appeals.

When the committee writing the first Maryland Constitution agreed upon a final version of their constitution, they had copies printed. These were sent throughout the counties in September so that the voters could look them over and tell the delegates what they thought of the proposed Constitution.

The Revolutionary War was being fought, and this delayed the final report to the Convention on the Maryland Constitution. By October, 1776, however, the Constitutional Convention was able to meet to discuss the proposed Constitution item by item.

It was not an easy task to decide just how the Constitution of Maryland should be worded. After all, fresh from English rule with its lack of representation, Marylanders wanted no such dictatorial government set up here. Then, too, there was always the chance that a person or a group of persons might gain power and force everyone else to obey them. The delegates working on the Constitution tried then to write into it many "checks and balances," so that the Governor's position would be a fairly weak one and so that the General Assembly would have the real power in Maryland. Then, as today, Maryland citizens wanted a way of peaceably changing either leaders or laws that did not satisfy the voters of the State. This is the ideal and beauty of our system of government. The words, "peaceful change," "law," and "justice," are the keystones of our freedoms.

There were long arguments and debates over what should be included. On September 17, 1776, the Convention ordered the revised, proposed document to be printed and distributed to the public. Many amendments had been added to the committee's version of the Maryland Constitution.

No mention was made in the Constitution of the possibility of a revising convention, but it could be amended. By November 3, 1776, the Declaration of Rights was agreed upon. On November 8, 1776, the Form of Government was also agreed to. The Convention then adopted the entire Constitution November 10, 1776.

Sandwiched in between the consideration of constitutional questions, the powers of government were used by the Maryland delegates in Annapolis, particularly with matters concerned with the public safety. A primary consideration, of course, was the conduct of the War of Independence (also called the American Revolution). Actually, the Convention of 1776 *was* the government of Maryland and not just a consitutional convention.

The Constitution of 1776 provided for its own amendment by a proposal passed by majority action of the General Assembly, with publication for three months before the next election of legislators and final confirmation by the following assembly. Should any amendment relate to the Eastern Shore, a vote by two-thirds of all the members of the assembly was required. No mention was made in the Constitution of the possibility of a revising convention.

THE FIRST CONSTITUTION WAS ADOPTED ON NOV. 10, 1776. IT INCLUDED NO POLL TAX AND POOR PEOPLE DID NOT HAVE TO PAY TAXES.

The finished document had some unusual features in its Declaration of Rights, though its list of rights was quite similar to that of Virginia, Pennsylvania and Delaware. Among items unique to Maryland was the one that allowed people to vote without paying a yearly fee known as a "poll tax." Another unusual item stated that paupers, people without money or goods, were not to be taxed.

Still other unusual items in our Maryland Declaration of Rights were the ones that forbade granting titles of nobility, stopped persons from holding more than one public office at a time, and outlawed monopolies. Ours was the first state constitution to order a rotation of office in the executive departments. Finally, our Declaration of Rights stated that the General Assembly must not declare any item in the Declaration no longer lawful. The writers of the Maryland Bill of Rights intended it to be a permanent list of human rights for the citizens of Maryland.

WHAT IS A POLL TAX?

IT'S A TAX YOU MUST PAY IN ORDER TO VOTE.

At first, the Constitution met the needs of the people of Maryland. There was not a great deal of industry as yet. Most of the population, in one way or another, lived off the land. So, for about three-quarters of a century, the Constitution of 1776 served the State with only a few changes. The most important changes made during those years were made in 1799, when election districts were set up for convenience in voting, and in 1805, when six judicial districts were created.

Government in those days was a fairly simple affair. However, it was not really a democratic government. Only an elite group made up of the wealthiest and most famous men governed. Nor could all free men vote! To vote, one not only had to be a *free* man over twenty-one years of age, but had to have at least fifty acres of land or property worth a certain amount. (This property qualification was later removed, by an act of the General Assembly introduced in 1801 and passed early in 1802.) Women could not vote at all.

The Amendment of 1837

Many citizens liked the aristocratic type of government and thought that it worked very well. Others wanted more voice in their government. They did not want the same group of powerful men holding the top government positions all of the time. Then, too, the different sections of Maryland were growing more and more apart.

Some were turning away from farming. Some social customs began to differ as more people came to Maryland from different European countries.

Finally, public opinion brought about the adoption of several important amendments to the Constitution. These were known as the Amendments of 1837. Under these amendments the Electoral College was done away with; and, for the first time, each county and Baltimore City had one State senator elected by the voters. These senators were now to serve a six-year term of office.

By the Amendments of 1837, the House of Delegates was changed. Now the counties with larger populations were given more delegates than the counties having less people. Other changes made by the Amendments were the abolition of the Governor's Council, the creation of the office of Secretary of State, and an increase in the Governor's power.

The State was divided into three gubernatorial districts. This was done to give the various sections of the State more equal power in the government. The Governor, under the Amendments of 1837, was to be elected from each of the three districts in turn. He was to serve a three-year term and was not to have the right to be re-elected.

The Amendments of 1837 reformed the government of Maryland into a more democratic system.

teal

Review Questions:

1. What were the men who wrote Maryland's first constitution doing? Choose one answer.

    a. They planned a government that would rule Maryland, protect property and make new laws as needed.

    b. They wanted to have a government exactly like the one in Great Britain.

    c. They hoped to set up a nobility of titled gentry to rule Maryland.

    d. They planned a true democracy in which every person living in Maryland could vote.

2. Look at the Maryland Constitution's Bill of Rights and compare it with the Bill of Rights in the Constitution of the United States. Discuss similarities and differences.

    You will find the Maryland Bill of Rights in the very first part of the Constitution of Maryland, Articles 1 through 46. You will notice some of these have been added or amended since 1776.

    The Bill of Rights of the Constitution of the United States is located in its first ten amendments (I through X).

3. Discuss how Maryland's first government as a state was not as democratic as it is today.

4. Why was the Electoral College changed to a vote by the people in 1837? Was it a more direct way of voters having a voice in the selection of people in Maryland government? Discuss this.

5. The Amendments of 1837: (Choose one correct answer.)

    a. Changed almost every part of the Maryland Constitution.

    b. Gave counties with larger populations more delegates than counties with less people.

    c. Made Maryland less democratic.

    d. Gave power to an Electoral College of men who were to choose Senators.

6. Look up the following words: (It might be a good idea to put each word and its definition on a separate card, or slip of paper, so you can build an alphabetical list of new words.)

    amendment, constitution, delegate, representative

7. Study your list of words for Section IV. Write sentences using at least ten of the words correctly.

CHAPTER 2

The Constitution of 1851

The Constitution of 1851 grew out of the growing struggle between the farmers, the manufacturers and the traders of Maryland. Population was shifting from the Eastern Shore and from the southern counties of Maryland, to those of the north and west. As it does to this day, representation in the General Assembly according to population caused anger in lightly peopled counties. At that time, it caused bitter resentment, too, because the southern counties wanted to keep slavery in force. If they did not have enough representatives in the General Assembly, the Assembly could vote to make slavery illegal. As the Civil War approached, Maryland was more and more divided over this question. In fact, the Eastern Shore of Maryland threatened to secede!

Only after long public debate about the need for a new basic law for Maryland and whether or not it was really legal (constitutionally), that the General Assembly finally voted to ask the voters if a constitutional convention should be called. The people voted "yes."

This debate and vote was in itself very important. It *established the right of the people of Maryland to call a constitutional convention*, to introduce new ideas into their government if they wished.

We must be careful, of course, in changing such a basic document, yet there should be a way that we can change the constitution. Changes should be openly discussed, well publicized and then voted on by the citizens. The people can then accept or reject constitutional changes.

Under the Constitution of 1851, many changes, some good, some bad, were made. First of all, the county court system was somewhat changed. Naturally, this upset the court system causing citizens to wonder, should they have to go to court for some reason, if justice would be properly administered.

Second, some reforms were made in the registration of voters to prevent fraud or cheating. For the first time, voters were asked to meet residence requirements. They had to have lived in the State and in their county for a certain length of time to be allowed to vote. To some, this idea seemed very unreasonable.

Third, the terms of state senators were reduced from six to four years, and not every senator had to stand for reelection at the same time.

Fourth, the office of Attorney General was abolished.

Fifth, by the terms of the Constitution of 1851, there was only one Treasurer, and a new office, the Comptroller of the Treasury, was created. He was to be elected by the voters and was to act as a control over the Treasury Department.

Sixth of the major changes made by the Constitution of 1851 was the increase of the Governor's term of office to a four-year term.

Important changes were also made in local governments. Baltimore City was separated from Baltimore County. Howard District, formerly a part of Anne Arundel County, now became Howard County.

Under the Constitution of 1851, there could be no amendments made except by constitutional convention. This made it an inflexible document.

When the Constitution of 1851 was completed, only fifty members of the Convention recommended it. It was, however, approved by the voters in June, 1851. The historian, Thomas J. Scharf, in his history of Maryland, stated that the voters actually did not know the provisions of the 1851 Constitution. They voted for it for the sake of change, simply because they were dissatisfied with the Constitution of 1776.

The Constitution of 1851 proved to be very unpopular. Because of its many faults, and because of the Civil War, it lasted only thirteen years.

Review Questions:

1. What very important idea (precedent) was established by the calling of the Constitutional Convention to write the Constitution of 1851?

2. What changes in Maryland's population caused some people to be dissatisfied with the Constitution of 1776?

3. How did population counts enter into question number 2?

4. Could the Maryland legislature (the General Assembly) vote to make slavery illegal in Maryland?

5. Name the six major changes made in the Constitution of Maryland by the writers of the Constitution of 1851.

deer in the hills . . .

Carroll County Farm Museum, Westminster, Maryland.
(Photograph courtesy J. H. Cromwell, C & P Telephone Company of Maryland.)

CHAPTER 3

The Constitution of 1864

In 1864, the people of Maryland voted to call another constitutional convention.

The Constitution of 1864, Maryland's third constitution, was written during the Civil War. As you know, this war was between the northern and southern states and was fought from 1861 to 1865. The Constitution of 1864 reflects the feeling of the Unionists, men who wanted the United States to remain one union of states. It shows their feelings of loyalty to the federal government and to the Constitution of the United States of America.

The Unionists had been successful in gaining votes. Maryland was a seriously divided state before and during the Civil War.

Names used by the two sides fighting the Civil War:

1. The Union	1. The Confederacy
2. The United States of America	2. The Confederate States of America (11 states seceded in 1860 and 1861)
3. The North	3. The South
4. "Yankees"	4. "Rebels"

The official choice of Maryland's government to be for the Union (the federal government, the national government of the United States) was interesting. True, many Marylanders sympathized with the South. Many southern Maryland people did not want to lose their workers who were not free. Still, the Union forces were on Maryland soil. Also, the United States government could not allow its capital city, Washington, D.C. to be encircled by rebel territory!

The Maryland Constitution of 1864 called for a strong oath (promise) of loyalty to the Union by every State official. Men who would not take this oath because they sympathized with the southern states could not hold office in Maryland. This oath and the way in which it was interpreted was the item that a few years later helped defeat the Constitution of 1864 and replace it with a new one. According to the *Baltimore Sun*, three-fourths of Maryland's voters were not allowed to vote, due to the strict and searching loyalty examinations!

185

Also written into the Constitution of 1864 was a provision making slavery illegal in Maryland. Why was this necessary? It was because the Emancipation Proclamation made by President Abraham Lincoln in November, 1863 which freed most of the slaves in the United States, applied only to those states in rebellion who were fighting the federal government, it did not apply to Maryland.

Though not a popular document, the Constitution of 1864 had some very good features. It gave the State the office of Lieutenant Governor and brought back the office of Attorney General, which had been abolished in 1851. An item of long-range importance, too, was the provision for a uniform State system of education in Maryland.

The Constitution of 1864 was adopted only with great difficulty. The voters turned it down in most counties but enough votes were gained from Union soldiers, taken in their camps outside the State, to adopt the Constitution.

The Constitution was written because of the need for reform in the social and political life of Maryland. Though so very unpopular with the people, it might have been successful if the State had not been in the middle of the bitter and tragic Civil War. Unfortunately, when the Constitution of 1864 was replaced by the Constitution of 1867, many of its good features were lost, along with its unpopular ones.

Questions:

1. Discuss the turmoil in Maryland in the 1860's.

2. Name some of the things that divided Maryland citizens during the civil war.

3. Discuss the fact that the Confederacy of Southern States decided to leave the union of American States, called the United States of America. How does this show the value of letting the majority rule? Is Bierut another example?

quail

*Old Senate Chamber, Maryland
State House.*

CHAPTER 4

The Constitution of 1867

The Constitution of 1867 is the one under which Maryland operates today, though much amended. It was written by the Democratic-Conservative Party which had regained control of the State after the Civil War. It was a conservative Constitution, careful not to break sharply with the past and stepping cautiously toward the future.

It began with a call for a constitutional convention in April, 1867. This was approved by a 10,000-vote majority, out of a total of 60,000 votes cast. Only Calvert, Carroll and Frederick Counties did not favor a constitutional convention. When the Constitution of 1867 had been written and was presented to the voters for approval (ratification), all the counties and Baltimore City voted for it by good-sized majorities.

Several changes were made by the 1867 document. The hated loyalty oath was replaced by a milder one. The new oath required only that candidates for public office swear to support the Constitution of the United States and the Constitution of Maryland.

Because so many people disliked the man who was the Lieutenant Governor at the time, that office was abolished. Minor changes were also made in the judiciary branch of the government.

The writers of the Constitution of 1867 reached back to the Constitution of 1776 for their Declaration of Rights. During the Civil War many rights had been denied many Maryland citizens. Writers of the Constitution of 1867 wanted to state the rights of Maryland citizens very plainly. In this section are forty-five articles, most of which are exactly as written in 1776.

The Form of Government, in the Constitution of 1867, was a section of 17 articles. These articles dealt with:
 I. Franchise and Elections II. Executive Department III. Legislative Department IV. Judiciary Department V. Attorney General and State's Attorney VI. Treasury Department VII. Sundry Officers VIII. Education IX. Militia and Military Affairs X. (Now vacant, repealed by Chapter 99, Acts of 1956) XI. City of Baltimore XII. Public Works XIII. New Counties XIV. Amendments to the Constitution XV. Miscellaneous XVI. The Referendum XVII. Quadrennial Elections.

The final provision in the Constitution was the usual one for the ratification (approval by the voters) of the document.

Amendments to the Constitution of 1867

Unlike the Constitution of the United States, amendments to the Constitution of Maryland replace items, and are not added on to the Constitution at the end. We should be *very* grateful indeed that this is so, for our Maryland Constitution has been amended over one hundred times! If these amendments were each added to the end of the Constitution, one would have to check back and forth and study a very long time to puzzle out the current meaning of each item! The story of our Maryland Constitution is not over. It continues to change with the changing needs of the State.

Questions:

1. Why was the "oath of allegiance" in the Constitution of 1867 so unpopular?

2. Was the provision for a free public school system kept in the Constitution of 1867?

3. Are amendments to the Constitution of Maryland added on to the end of the Constitution?

4. Was the Constitution of 1867 a radical or conservative one?

CHAPTER 5

The Constitution Convention of 1967

In 1965, Governor J. Millard Tawes appointed a twenty-seven member Constitutional Convention Commission. This Commission was to study the 1867 Constitution and the needs of the State to find out if the Constitution needed changing or rewriting. They were to report prior to the 1967 session of the General Assembly if there was, or was not, a need for a constitutional convention.

In September, 1965, the Commission reported to the Governor that, after carefully studying the Constituion of 1867 with all its amendments, and after considering the needs of modern Maryland, that a constituional convention should be called. The Commission felt that it would be better to write a new constitution than to try to revise and "patch up" the 1867 Constitution.

By May, 1967, the Commission had a copy of a basic, suggested constitution which they suggested be adopted by the Convention. Also submitted were comments on each part of the proposed constitution. This was to help guide delegates, elected from each county and from Baltimore City. These delegates were scheduled to gather in Annapolis on September 12, 1967, to write a new constitution for Maryland.

By January 10, 1968, the Fifth Constitutional Convention was over. The rewritten, final version of a new constitution was ready. It was printed. Copies were made available to the citizens of the state.

When the results of this referendum election came in, it was found that only Montgomery County and Prince George's County had voted for the proposed constitution. All of the other counties and Baltimore City voted against the document, and those votes were enough to defeat the proposed constitution. A book on the subject was written, the *Magnificent Failure: The Constitutional Convention of 1967-1968*, by John P. Wheeler, Jr., and Melissa Kinsey.1

1 *Magnificent Failure*, by John P. Wheeler, Jr., and Melissa Kinsey. NYC: National Municipal League, 1970.

THERE WAS ANOTHER CONSTITUTIONAL CONVENTION IN 1965 BUT THE PEOPLE VOTED AGAINST THE NEW CONSTITUTION.

BECAUSE IT HAD TOO MANY CHANGES TO THE GOVERNMENT AND PEOPLE ARE SLOW TO MAKE CHANGES.

CHAPTER 6

Changes Made to the Constitution of 1867
Since 1967

After all the shouting over the proposed Constitution of 1967, and its defeat by the voters, what happened? Something rather ironic.

In the years that followed, the much amended Constitution of 1867 was amended a great deal more! The work of the Constitutional Convention of 1967 had not all been in vain, for many of the items that the Constitution of 1967 had proposed were passed in the years that followed. Yes, at referendum elections the Constitution of Maryland was amended. In the years 1968 - 1984, the old document has been patched up, tucks have been taken in its fabric here and there. It has been remodeled like a beautiful old Victorian mansion. It keeps much of its special Maryland strength and charm, but has been modernized to better serve a modern state.

Let's take a look at the amendments voted into effect by the voters.

Referenda Questions: How Offered

The Constitution of Maryland provides in its Article XVII for elections every four years of state, county and city officials beginning with the year 1926. Examples: 1982, 1986, 1990, 1994.

National elections are held in between state elections every four years. Examples: 1984, 1988, 1992, 1996.

Questions can be offered to voters at any of these elections. Voters may vote "yes" and so ratify (agree to) a question, or vote "no" and reject the idea offered. In this way, amendments to the Constitution of Maryland are either ratified or rejected.

As we have seen, voters in Maryland decided against a revised constitution proposed on May 14, 1968.

Right away, the Maryland General Assembly set to work revising the Constitution of Maryland.

How Changes Are Made in the Constitution of Maryland

To change, add to, or subtract from, the Constitution of Maryland, the members of the General Assembly and the people of Maryland must abide by the provisions of Article XIV in the Constitution of Maryland.

This means that a member (or members) of the General Assembly must introduce "bills of amendment" to the General Assembly. If three-fifths of all the members elected to each of the two Houses agree by vote, the provisions of the bill are publicized extensively across the State before the next general election. If a majority of the voters vote for the bill then it is returned to the Governor and he or she proclaims the amendment adopted and it becomes a part of the Maryland Constitution.

This is a brief and incomplete description of how a constitutional change may be made. For more details, read Article XIV of the Constitution of Maryland, and also Article XVI, The Referendum, and Article XVIII, Provisions of Limited Duration.

Amendments Outlined

In the years following 1968, amendments changed the Constitution of Maryland by: modernizing its language, removing biased references to religion, sex and race, removing offices of some officials no longer needed. Briefly, the changes were designed to:

- Modernize the language of the document.
- Remove biased references to religion, race and sex.
- Set voter age at 18 (I,1).
  Voting rules (I,2).
- Clarify absentee voting procedures (I,1A).
- Governor's term of office is to begin in the January after his election (II,1).
- Create and define the office of Lieutenant Governor (II,1-6).
- Provide for filling offices in Executive Department when it is necessary to remove officers (II,6-7).

- Give the Governor 30 days to consider a bill (proposed law) (II,17).

- Provide a commission made up of legislators and the State Treasurer (II,21A).

- Authorize the State Treasurer to sell short term notes.

- Give more power to the Governor to make changes in the executive branch of the State government (II,24).

- Make legislative districts relate to populations in the districts (III,2-5).

- Allow General Assembly members to take office in January following their election (III,6).

- Set new qualifications for General Assembly members (III,9).

- Allow religious ministers to serve in the General Assembly (ratified November 7, 1978) (III,11).

- Set times to meet, pay and revise the length of sessions of the General Assembly (II,13-15).

- Give new ways to present and approve legislation amended (III,27-31).

- Clarify money and salary matters (III,34-35).

- Approve a state lottery (III,36).

- Repeal a dueling law (III,41).

- Amend sections of the Maryland Constitution referring to the "taking" of land for public purposes. (III,40D).

- See that the State of Maryland always has a balanced budget. Gives the General Assembly the right to cut judiciary budgets (III,52).

- To make many changes in the judiciary system. District Courts with appointed judges were added. Judges, except those of the Courts of Appeal, to be elected. Many rules passed to be certain judges are competent to serve. The new District Courts give Maryland a more uniform system of courts. Former "lower courts" such as Magistrate's Courts, People's Courts, Juvenile Courts and Justices of the Peace are deleted—their duties are taken over by the District Court (IV).

- Abolish several offices—County Surveyor, State Librarian and others (IV).
- Make several amendments relating to miscellaneous matters: local legislation; City of Baltimore affairs; clarifying Constitution amendment; and ways of removing elected officials accused of crimes (Articles XI, XIII, XIV, XV).

You can tell if, and when, a section has been amended by the footnotes in the Constitution of Maryland on sections that have been amended. For example, see Article I, Section 10. How many times has this section been amended? When?

Maryland State Comptroller Louis L. Goldstein (right) selling state bonds with the other members of the Board of Public Works, Governor Harry Hughes (center) and State Treasurer William S. James.

Students from Hurlock, Maryland, visit Senator Charles McC. Mathias, Jr., in his Capitol Hill office.

Photograph courtesy the U. S. Senate.

CHAPTER 7

Today's Constitution of Maryland

Would you rather tackle a cage full of tigers than study constitutions? That is an understandable first reaction. It's not that hard, however, when you see how plain is the general plan.

For example, our present Constitution of Maryland is set up this way. It is based on the original "form of government" written in 1776, with additions and changes. Look at the document as you read the following outline. See if you agree with what the outline says. (This is a very short overview. For details, see the exact wording of the Constitution.)

The first item in our Maryland Constitution is a STATEMENT of the Constitutional Convention which met, it states when and where they met and when the document they wrote was ratified (voted for by the people of Maryland).

Next comes the DECLARATION OF RIGHTS (Articles 1 through 46). This is a little confusing, since under the Declaration of Rights there are 46 "Articles," then, the Constitution starts off "Article I," and so on. So we specify "Bill" of Rights, Article 1 (or whatever one we're talking about, 1 through 46). If we say Article I (or any I through XVIII), using Roman numerals, we are referring to the main part, the body of the Constitution of Maryland. Still confusing? Here's a sort of Table of Contents:

STATEMENT

BILL OF RIGHTS, short Articles 1 through 46.

CONSTITUTION, Articles I through XVIII

To understand Roman Numerals, let us compare them with Arabic numbers like this:

ARABIC NUMBERS	ROMAN NUMBERS
1	I
2	II
3	III
4	IV
5	V
6	VI
7	VII
8	VIII
9	IX
10	X
11	XI
12	XII
13	XIII
14	XIV
15	XV
16	XVI
17	XVII
18	XVIII
19	XIX
20	XX
21	XXI
22	XXII
23	XXIII
24	XXIV
25	XXV
26	XXVI
27	XXVII
28	XXVIII

Next comes the CONSTITUTION, the "form of government." This is set up in Articles which have Sections.

These ARTICLES each have a subject:

Article I Elective Franchise

How elections are to be held, who may vote in elections, qualifications of candidates.

Article II Executive Department

Explains the powers of the Governor and his or her officers and staff. Tells how the Governor is to be elected and to serve (duties, conditions).

Article III Legislative Department

Explains the two branches of the Maryland General Assembly (the *Senate* and the *House of Delegates*). Tells how they are to be elected and to serve (duties and powers).

Explains how *laws* are to be made by the General Assembly.

Article IV Judiciary Department

This article is subdivided into Parts, and under the Parts, sections. It explains how Maryland courts are set up and how judges are selected, their powers, limits and how they are to serve.

Article V Attorney General and State's Attorneys

This article explains how these officers are to be elected (one Attorney General and State's Attorney in each county), their duties and powers.

Article VI Treasury Department

Explains that the Treasury Department shall consist of a Comptroller and Treasurer. Tells how the *Comptroller* of Maryland is to be elected and the *Treasurer* appointed. The Comptroller directs the fiscal (money) affairs of the State and the Treasurer receives and deposits the moneys of the State.

Article VII Sundry Officers

Explains how county commissioners are to be elected.

Senator Charles McC. Mathias, Jr.

204

U.S.F. Constellation, Inner Harbor.

Article VIII Education

Sets up a state-wide system of free public schools.

Article IX Militia and Military Affairs

Authority is given the General Assembly to call into service state military groups "as the exigency may require."

Article X

(Vacant)

Article XI City of Baltimore

This explains how the citizens of Baltimore shall elect their Mayor and members of the two branches of the Baltimore City Council. Authority given the Mayor and the City Council is described.

Explains how the city is operated and governed; how taxes raised for services by the Council and the Mayor.

Article XI-A Local Legislation

This article describes how petitions may be submitted by the voters; how city and county governments may be formed or changed and officers elected. Describes charter forms of county governments.

Article XI-B City of Baltimore — Land Development and Redevelopment

Powers are given the Mayor of Baltimore and the Baltimore City Council to acquire property and modify it to fit the needs of Baltimore City.

Article XI-C Off-Street Parking

This article empowers the City of Baltimore to acquire property, issue bonds to pay for the "development of the property into parking facilities."

Article XI-D Port Development

This article allows the Mayor and City Council of Baltimore to acquire and develop property on or near the Patapsco River to improve the Baltimore harbor or Port of Baltimore, with certain limits and conditions.

Article XI-E Municipal Corporations

Explains how municipal (city) governments may be set up or changed, and city taxes imposed.

Article XI-F Home Rule for Code Counties

Voters may choose a "code county" form of government. A code county is not a charter county. A code county may pass local laws and impose taxes — unless in conflict with the Constitution of Maryland or state law.

Article XI-G Residential Rehabilitation and Commercial Financing Loans

This article allows the Mayor and City Council of Baltimore to make, guarantee, and insure loans to persons or groups engaged in improving residential property in the City and for building or renovating buildings to be used for commercial purposes.

Article XI-H City of Baltimore Residential Financing Loans

This article empowers the Mayor and City Council of Baltimore to help by loans, loan guarantees or insurance of loans to those interested in building buildings for residential purposes.

Article XI-I City of Baltimore Industrial Financing Loans

Those who wish to build industrial facilities or buildings in Baltimore City may, under this article, obtain loans, get home loans insured or guaranteed by the Mayor and City Council of Baltimore.

Article XII Public Works

The Governor of Maryland, the Comptroller and Treasurer of Maryland are the Board of Public Works in the State.

They must meet regularly and supervise all Public Works, appoint Directors to guard the public interest.

Public Works are roadways; waterways; in some cases railways; bridges; certain buildings and other construction projects.

Article XII New Counties

The General Assembly may organize new counties, move county lines, change county seats, only with the consent of the majority of the voters living in the areas involved, and with certain minimum size and population limits.

Article XIV Amendments to the Constitution

Explains how the General Assembly may propose changes (amendments) in the Constitution of Maryland. (These amendments must be ratified by the voters in referendum elections before the changes may go into effect.)

Article XV Miscellaneous

This article is, as its title says, a group of miscellaneous items.

Section 1 has to do with persons holding various offices, and the records they must keep.

Section 2 explains that any elected official in Maryland who is convicted of a crime or who enters a plea of "no contest" to certain sorts of crime must be suspended. Reinstatement is provided for, should the conviction be overturned.

Section 3 says that no person advocating the overthrow of the government of the United States or of Maryland may hold office in Maryland.

Section 4 (vacant)

Section 5 allows the General Assembly to appoint persons to act for certain absent officials.

Section 6 (vacant)

Section 7 says that all general elections in the State shall be held "on the Tuesday next after the first Monday in the month of November, in the year they shall occur."

Article XVI The Referendum

This article explains the right of the people of Maryland to approve or reject by vote any Act of the General Assembly (excepting only emergency laws needed for public health and safety).

The ways these referendum elections are held, and when, are described in detail.

Further, the article explains how the people may petition the government of Maryland.

Article XVII Quadrennial Elections

This article provides for state and local elections every four years in November of every fourth year beginning with the year 1926. Examples: 1982, 1986, 1990, 1994, 1998.

(Note: National elections for the President and the United States Congress, are also every four years, but two years apart from the above-mentioned state elections. Examples: 1988, 1992, 1996, 2000.)

The article sets terms of office for state and other Maryland officials.

Article XVIII Provisions of Limited Duration

This article provides a place to insert items which are not permanent into the Constitution; items which, after a certain date, "drop out" of the Constitution. (An example might be when, after a certain date, some court or office will no longer exist.)

That is it. Yes, the articles to do with Baltimore City may, at first glance, seem a little difficult. Thinking about it, you can see the reasons for the articles — to provide incentives to people or organizations to build or rehabilitate places for Baltimore City citizens to live and work in. Simple? Right!

You can see that the Constitution of Maryland describes how State and local governments are set up, how officials are put into office, how taxes are imposed, how laws are made and generally "who does what."

Also, you can find many places in the Constitution of Maryland in which you can see provisions for the will of the people to be asked, their approval or rejection, by vote. Our Maryland government is based on the power of the people of Maryland.

The Constitution of the United States, in general, does the same thing as the Constitution of Maryland.

Powers not kept by the United States (federal) government are kept by state governments. Laws in the states vary widely. Each state legislature makes laws for that state. Also, some states (Maryland, for example) have laws that were originally based on the laws of England (Great Britain); while others have laws based originally on Spanish (example, California, Florida) or French (example, Louisiana) laws.

When we take the time out to think about history, constitutions, the lawmakers, the people who vote — it is quite interesting! And, very relevant to us.

You can see that constitutions and laws are ways we try to balance the powers that officials have; and how we try to let the citizens have power by their choosing officials, and by changing officials when the people wish to do so peaceably.

Constitution of Maryland

Annapolis, the United States Naval Academy. Midshipmen pass enroute to the weekly dress parade.

Bob Willis photo.

Courtesy Maryland Division of Tourism.

CONSTITUTION OF MARYLAND

ADOPTED BY THE CONVENTION

WHICH ASSEMBLED AT THE CITY OF ANNAPOLIS ON THE EIGHTH DAY OF MAY, EIGHTEEN HUNDRED AND SIXTY-SEVEN, AND ADJOURNED ON THE SEVENTEENTH DAY OF AUGUST, EIGHTEEN HUNDRED AND SIXTY-SEVEN, AND WAS RATIFIED BY THE PEOPLE ON THE EIGHTEENTH DAY OF SEPTEMBER, EIGHTEEN HUNDRED AND SIXTY-SEVEN, WITH AMENDMENTS TO AND INCLUDING NINETEEN HUNDRED AND EIGHTY-FOUR[1]

DECLARATION OF RIGHTS.

We, the People of the State of Maryland, grateful to Almighty God for our civil and religious liberty, and taking into our serious consideration the best means of establishing a good Constitution in this State for the sure foundation and more permanent security thereof, declare:

Article 1. That all Government of right originates from the People, is founded in compact only, and instituted solely for the good of the whole; and they have, at all times, the inalienable right to alter, reform or abolish their Form of Government in such manner as they may deem expedient.

Art. 2. The Constitution of the United States, and the Laws made, or which shall be made, in pursuance thereof, and all Treaties made, or which shall be made, under the authority of the United States, are, and shall be the Supreme Law of the State; and the Judges of this State, and all the People of this State, are, and shall be bound thereby; anything in the Constitution or Law of this State to the contrary notwithstanding.

Art. 3. The powers not delegated to the United States by the Constitution thereof, nor prohibited by it to the States, are reserved to the States respectively, or to the people thereof.

Art. 4. That the People of this State have the sole and exclusive right of regulating the internal government and police thereof, as a free, sovereign and independent State.

Art. 5. That the Inhabitants of Maryland are entitled to the Common Law of England, and the trial by Jury, according to the course of that Law, and to the benefit of such of the English statutes as existed on the Fourth day of July, seventeen hundred and seventy-six; and which, by experience, have been found applicable to their local and other circumstances, and have been introduced, used and practiced by the Courts of Law or Equity; and also of all Acts of Assembly in force on the first day of June, eighteen hundred and sixty-seven; except such as may have since expired, or may be inconsistent with the provisions of this Constitution; subject, nevertheless, to the revision of, and amendment or repeal by, the Legislature of this State. And the Inhabitants of Maryland are also entitled to all property derived to them from, or under the Charter granted by His Majesty Charles the First to Cæcilius Calvert, Baron of Baltimore.

Art. 6. That all persons invested with the Legislative or Executive powers of Government are the Trustees of the Public, and, as such, accountable for their conduct: Wherefore, whenever the ends of Government are perverted, and public liberty manifestly endangered, and all other means of redress are ineffectual, the People may, and of right ought, to reform the old, or establish a new Government; the doctrine of non-resistance against arbitrary power and oppression is absurd, slavish and destructive of the good and happiness of mankind.

Art. 7.[2] That the right of the People to participate in the Legislature is the best security of liberty and the foundation of all free Government; for this purpose, elections ought to be free and frequent; and every citizen having the qualifications prescribed by the Constitution, ought to have the right of suffrage.

Art. 8. That the Legislative, Executive and Judicial powers of Government ought to be forever separate and distinct from each other; and no person exercising the functions of one of said Departments shall assume or discharge the duties of any other.

Art. 9. That no power of suspending Laws or the execution of Laws, unless by, or derived from the Legislature, ought to be exercised, or allowed.

Art. 10. That freedom of speech and debate, or proceedings in the Legislature, ought not to be impeached in any Court of Judicature.

Art. 11. That Annapolis be the place of meeting of the Legislature; and the Legislature ought not to be convened, or held at any other place but from evident necessity.

Art. 12. That for redress of grievances, and for amending, strengthening and preserving the Laws, the Legislature ought to be frequently convened.

Art. 13. That every man hath a right to petition the Legislature for the redress of grievances in a peaceable and orderly manner.

Art. 14. That no aid, charge, tax, burthen or fees ought to be rated or levied, under any pretense, without the consent of the Legislature.

Art. 15.[3] That the levying of taxes by the poll is grievous and oppressive, and ought to be prohibited; that paupers ought not to be assessed for the support of the government; that the General Assembly shall, by uniform rules, provide for the separate assessment, classification and sub-classification of land, improvements on land and personal property, as it may deem proper; and all taxes thereafter provided to be levied by the State for the support of the general State Government, and by the Counties and by the City of Baltimore for their respective purposes, shall be uniform within each class or sub-class of land, improvements on land and personal property which the respective taxing powers may have directed to be subjected to the tax levy; yet fines, duties or taxes may properly and justly be imposed, or laid with a political view for the good government and benefit of the community.

Art. 16. That sanguinary Laws ought to be avoided as far as it is consistent with the safety of the State; and no Law to inflict cruel and unusual pains and penalties ought to be made in any case, or at any time, hereafter.

---

[1] Including amendments proposed by the General Assembly and adopted by the people through Nov. 6, 1984.

[2] Amended by Chapter 357, Acts of 1971, ratified Nov. 7, 1972.

[3] Amended by Chapter 390, Acts of 1914, ratified Nov. 2, 1915; Chapter 64, Acts of 1960, ratified Nov. 8, 1960.

NOTE: The following material (pp. 213-255) from the *Maryland Manual 1985-1986*, published by the State of Maryland, State Archives, Annapolis, MD.

Art. 17. That retrospective Laws, punishing acts committed before the existence of such Laws, and by them only declared criminal are oppressive, unjust and incompatible with liberty; wherefore, no *ex post facto* Law ought to be made; nor any retrospective oath or restriction be imposed, or required.

Art. 18. That no Law to attaint particular persons of treason or felony, ought to be made in any case, or at any time, hereafter.

Art. 19. That every man, for any injury done to him in his person or property, ought to have remedy by the course of the Law of the Land, and ought to have justice and right, freely without sale, fully without any denial, and speedily without delay, according to the Law of the Land.

Art. 20. That the trial of facts, where they arise, is one of the greatest securities of the lives, liberties and estate of the People.

Art. 21. That in all criminal prosecutions, every man hath a right to be informed of the accusation against him; to have a copy of the Indictment, or charge, in due time (if required) to prepare for his defence; to be allowed counsel; to be confronted with the witnesses against him; to have process for his witnesses; to examine the witnesses for and against him on oath; and to a speedy trial by an impartial jury, without whose unanimous consent he ought not to be found guilty.

Art. 22. That no man ought to be compelled to give evidence against himself in a criminal case.

Art. 23.[4] In the trial of all criminal cases, the Jury shall be the Judges of Law, as well as of fact, except that the Court may pass upon the sufficiency of the evidence to sustain a conviction.

The right of trial by Jury of all issues of fact in civil proceedings in the several Courts of Law in this State, where the amount in controversy exceeds the sum of five hundred dollars, shall be inviolably preserved.

Art. 24.[5] That no man ought to be taken or imprisoned or disseized of his freehold, liberties or privileges, or outlawed, or exiled, or, in any manner, destroyed, or deprived of his life, liberty or property, but by the judgment of his peers, or by the Law of the land.

Art. 25. That excessive bail ought not to be required, nor excessive fines imposed, nor cruel or unusual punishment inflicted, by the Courts of Law.

Art. 26. That all warrants, without oath or affirmation, to search suspected places, or to seize any person or property, are grievous and oppressive; and all general warrants to search suspected places, or to apprehend suspected persons, without naming or describing the place, or the person in special, are illegal, and ought not to be granted.

Art. 27. That no conviction shall work corruption of blood or forfeiture of estate.

Art. 28. That a well regulated Militia is the proper and natural defence of a free Government.

Art. 29. That Standing Armies are dangerous to liberty, and ought not to be raised, or kept up, without the consent of the Legislature.

Art. 30. That in all cases, and at all times, the military ought to be under strict subordination to, and control of, the civil power.

Art. 31. That no soldier shall, in time of peace, be quartered in any house, without the consent of the owner, nor in time of war, except in the manner prescribed by Law.

Art. 32. That no person except regular soldiers, marines, and mariners in the service of this State, or militia, when in actual service, ought, in any case, to be subject to, or punishable by Martial Law.

Art. 33. That the independency and uprightness of Judges are essential to the impartial administration of Justice, and a great security to the rights and liberties of the People: Wherefore, the Judges shall not be removed, except in the manner, and for the causes provided in this Constitution. No Judge shall hold any other office, civil, or military or political trust, or employment of any kind, whatsoever, under the Constitution or Laws of this State, or of the United States, or any of them; or receive fees, or perquisites of any kind, for the discharge of his official duties.

Art. 34.[6] That a long continuance in the Executive Departments of power or trust is dangerous to liberty; a rotation, therefore, in those departments is one of the best securities of permanent freedom.

Art. 35.[7] That no person shall hold, at the same time, more than one office of profit, created by the Constitution or Laws of this State; nor shall any person in public trust receive any present from any foreign Prince or State, or from the United States, or any of them, without the approbation of this State. The position of Notary Public shall not be considered an office of profit within the meaning of this Article.

Art. 36.[8] That as it is the duty of every man to worship God in such manner as he thinks most acceptable to Him, all persons are equally entitled to protection in their religious liberty; wherefore, no person ought by any law to be molested in his person or estate, on account of his religious persuasion, or profession, or for his religious practice, unless, under the color of religion, he shall disturb the good order, peace or safety of the State, or shall infringe the laws of morality, or injure others in their natural, civil or religious rights; nor ought any person to be compelled to frequent, or maintain, or contribute, unless on contract, to maintain, any place of worship, or any ministry; nor shall any person, otherwise competent, be deemed incompetent as a witness, or juror, on account of his religious belief; provided, he believes in the existence of God, and that under His dispensation such person will be held morally accountable for his acts, and be rewarded or punished therefor either in this world or in the world to come.

Nothing shall prohibit or require the making reference to belief in, reliance upon, or invoking the aid of God or a Supreme Being in any governmental or public document, proceeding, activity, ceremony, school, institution, or place.

Nothing in this article shall constitute an establishment of religion.

Art. 37. That no religious test ought ever to be required as a qualification for any office of profit or trust in this State, other than a declaration of belief in the existence of God; nor shall the Legislature prescribe any other oath of office than the oath prescribed by this Constitution.

Art. 38.[9] Vacant.

Art. 39. That the manner of administering an oath or affirmation to any person, ought to be such as those of the religious persuasion, profession, or denomination, of which he is a

---

[4] Amended by Chapter 407, Acts of 1949, ratified Nov. 7, 1950; Chapter 789, Acts of 1969, ratified Nov. 3, 1970. Transferred from Article XV, secs. 5 and 6, by Chapter 681, Acts of 1977, ratified Nov. 7, 1978.
[5] Amended by Chapter 681, Acts of 1977, ratified Nov. 7, 1978.

[6] Amended by Chapter 681, Acts of 1977, ratified Nov. 7, 1978.
[7] Amended by Chapter 129, Acts of 1964, ratified Nov. 8, 1964.
[8] Amended by Chapter 558, Acts of 1970, ratified Nov. 3, 1970.
[9] Amended by Chapter 623, Acts of 1947, ratified Nov. 2, 1948. Repealed by Chapter 681, Acts of 1977, ratified Nov. 7, 1978.

member, generally esteem the most effectual confirmation by the attestation of the Divine Being.

Art. 40. That the liberty of the press ought to be inviolably preserved; that every citizen of the State ought to be allowed to speak, write and publish his sentiments on all subjects, being responsible for the abuse of that privilege.

Art. 41. That monopolies are odious, contrary to the spirit of a free government and the principles of commerce, and ought not to be suffered.

Art. 42. That no title of nobility or hereditary honors ought to be granted in this State.

Art. 43.[10] That the Legislature ought to encourage the diffusion of knowlege and virtue, the extension of a judicious system of general education, the promotion of literature, the arts, sciences, agriculture, commerce and manufactures, and the general melioration of the condition of the People. The Legislature may provide that land actively devoted to farm or agricultural use shall be assessed on the basis of such use and shall not be assessed as if sub-divided.

Art. 44. That the provisions of the Constitution of the United States, and of this State, apply, as well in time of war, as in time of peace; and any departure therefrom, or violation thereof, under the plea of necessity, or any other plea, is subversive of good Government, and tends to anarchy and despotism.

Art. 45. This enumeration of Rights shall not be construed to impair or deny others retained by the People.

Art. 46.[11] Equality of rights under the law shall not be abridged or denied because of sex.

CONSTITUTION

ARTICLE I.

ELECTIVE FRANCHISE.

SECTION 1.[12] All elections shall be by ballot. Every citizen of the United States, of the age of 18 years or upwards, who is a resident of the State as of the time for the closing of registration next preceding the election, shall be entitled to vote in the ward or election district in which he resides at all elections to be held in this State. A person once entitled to vote in any election district, shall be entitled to vote there until he shall have acquired a residence in another election district or ward in this State.

SEC. 1A.[13] Vacant.

SEC. 2.[14] The General Assembly shall provide by law for a uniform registration of the names of all voters in this State, who possess the qualifications prescribed in this Article, which Registration shall be conclusive evidence to the Judges of Election of the right of every person, thus registered, to vote at any election thereafter held in this State; but no person shall vote, at

any election, Federal or State, hereafter to be held in this State, or at any municipal election in the City of Baltimore, unless his name appears in the list of registered voters; the names of all persons shall be added to the list of qualified voters by the officers of Registration, who have the qualifications prescribed in the first section of this Article, and who are not disqualified under the provisions of the second and third sections thereof.

SEC. 3.[15] The General Assembly of Maryland shall have power to provide by suitable enactment for voting by qualified voters of the State of Maryland who are absent at the time of any election in which they are entitled to vote and for voting by other qualified voters who are unable to vote personally and for the manner in which and the time and place at which such absent voters may vote, and for the canvass and return of their votes.

SEC. 4.[16] The General Assembly by law may regulate or prohibit the right to vote of a person convicted of infamous or other serious crime or under care or guardianship for mental disability.

SEC. 5.[17] It shall be the duty of the General Assembly to pass Laws to punish, with fine and imprisonment, any person, who shall remove into any election district, or precinct of any ward of the City of Baltimore, not for the purpose of acquiring a *bona fide* residence therein, but for the purpose of voting at an approaching election, or, who shall vote in any election district, or ward, in which he does not reside (except in the case provided for in this Article), or shall, at the same election, vote in more than one election district, or precinct, or shall vote, or offer to vote, in any name not his own, or in place of any other person of the same name, or shall vote in any county in which he does not reside.

SEC. 6.[18] If any person shall give, or offer to give, directly or indirectly, any bribe, present or reward, or any promise, or any security, for the payment or delivery of money, or any other thing, to induce any voter to refrain from casting his vote, or to prevent him in any way from voting, or to procure a vote for any candidate or person proposed, or voted for as the elector of President, and Vice President of the United States, or Representative in Congress or for any office of profit or trust, created by the Constitution or Laws of this State, or by the Ordinances, or Authority of the Mayor and City Council of Baltimore, the person giving, or offering to give and the person receiving the same, and any person who gives or causes to be given, an illegal vote, knowing it to be such, at any election to be hereafter held in this State, shall, on conviction in a Court of Law, in addition to the penalties now or hereafter to be imposed by law, be forever disqualified to hold any office of profit or trust, or to vote at any election thereafter. But the General Assembly may in its discretion remove the above penalty and all other penalties upon the vote seller so as to place the penalties for the purchase of votes on the vote buyer alone.

SEC. 7.[19] The General Assembly shall pass Laws necessary for the preservation of the purity of Elections.

---

[10] Amended by Chapter 65, Acts of 1960, ratified Nov. 8, 1960.

[11] Added by Chapter 366, Acts of 1972, ratified Nov. 7, 1972. Amended by Chapter 681, Acts of 1977, ratified Nov. 7, 1978.

[12] Amended by Chapter 99, Acts of 1956, ratified Nov. 6, 1956; Chapter 784, Acts of 1969, ratified Nov. 3, 1970; Chapter 681, Acts of 1977, ratified Nov. 7, 1978.

[13] Added by Chapter 20, Acts of 1918, ratified Nov. 5, 1918. Amended by Chapter 480, Acts of 1953, ratified Nov. 2, 1954; Chapter 100, Acts of 1956, ratified Nov. 6, 1956; Chapter 881, Acts of 1974, ratified Nov. 5, 1974. Renumbered as Art. I, sec. 3, by Chapter 681, Acts of 1977, ratified Nov. 7, 1978.

[14] Originally Article I, sec. 5, thus renumbered by Chapter 681, Acts of 1977, ratified Nov. 7, 1978. As sec. 5 it was amended by Chapter 99, Acts of 1956, ratified Nov. 6, 1956.

[15] Originally Article I, sec. 1A, thus renumbered by Chapter 681, Acts of 1977, ratified Nov. 7, 1978.

[16] Originally Article I, sec. 2, thus renumbered by Chapter 681, Acts of 1977, ratified Nov. 7, 1978. As sec. 2 it was amended by Chapter 368, Acts of 1972, ratified Nov. 7, 1972.

[17] Originally Article I, sec. 4, thus renumbered by Chapter 681, Acts of 1977, ratified Nov. 7, 1978.

[18] Originally Article I, sec. 3, thus renumbered by Chapter 681, Acts of 1977, ratified Nov. 7, 1978. As sec. 3 it was amended by Chapter 602, Acts of 1912, ratified Nov. 4, 1913.

[19] Transferred from Article III, sec. 42, by Chapter 681, Acts of 1977, ratified Nov. 7, 1978. Previous sec. 7 renumbered as Art. I, sec. 11, by same act and ratification.

SEC. 8.[20] The General Assembly, shall make provisions for all cases of contested elections of any of the officers, not herein provided for.

SEC. 9.[21] Every person elected, or appointed, to any office of profit or trust, under this Constitution, or under the Laws, made pursuant thereto, shall, before he enters upon the duties of such office, take and subscribe the following oath, or affirmation: I, _____, do swear, (or affirm, as the case may be), that I will support the Constitution of the United States; and that I will be faithful and bear true allegiance to the State of Maryland, and support the Constitution and Laws thereof; and that I will, to the best of my skill and judgment, diligently and faithfully, without partiality or prejudice, execute the office of_____ according to the Constitution and Laws of this State, (and, if a Governor, Senator, Member of the House of Delegates, or Judge,) that I will not directly or indirectly, receive the profits or any part of the profits of any other office during the term of my acting as_____ .

SEC. 10.[22] Any officer elected or appointed in pursuance of the provisions of this Constitution, may qualify, either according to the existing provisions of law, in relation to officers under the present Constitution, or before the Governor of the State, or before any Clerk of any Court of Record in any part of the State; but in case an officer shall qualify out of the County in which he resides, an official copy of his oath shall be filed and recorded in the Clerk's office of the Circuit Court of the County in which he may reside, or in the Clerk's office of the Superior Court of the City of Baltimore, if he shall reside therein. All words or phrases, used in creating public offices and positions under the Constitution and laws of this State, which denote the masculine gender shall be construed to include the feminine gender, unless the contrary intention is specifically expressed.

SEC. 11.[23] Every person, hereafter elected, or appointed, to office, in this State, who shall refuse, or neglect, to take the oath, or affirmation of office, provided for in the ninth section of this Article, shall be considered as having refused to accept the said office; and a new election, or appointment, shall be made, as in case of refusal to accept, or resignation of an office; and any person violating said oath, shall, on conviction thereof, in a Court of Law, in addition to the penalties now, or hereafter, to be imposed by Law, be thereafter incapable of holding any office of profit or trust in this State.

SEC. 12.[23a] Except as otherwise specifically provided herein, a person is ineligible to enter upon the duties of, or to continue to serve in, an elective office created by or pursuant to the provisions of this Constitution if the person was not a registered voter in this state on the date of the person's election or appointment to that term or if, at any time thereafter and prior to completion of the term, the person ceases to be a registered voter.

ARTICLE II.

EXECUTIVE DEPARTMENT.

SECTION 1.[24] The executive power of the State shall be vested

in a Governor, whose term of office shall commence on the third Wednesday of January next ensuing his election, and continue for four years, and until his successor shall have qualified; and a person who has served two consecutive popular elective terms of office as Governor shall be ineligible to succeed himself as Governor for the term immediately following the second of said two consecutive popular elective terms.

SEC. 1A.[25] There shall be a Lieutenant Governor, who shall have only the duties delegated to him by the Governor and shall have such compensation as the General Assembly shall provide by law, except that beginning in the year 1978 the salary of the Lieutenant Governor shall be as provided under Section 21A of this Article. No person who is ineligible under this Constitution to be elected Governor shall be eligible to hold the office of Lieutenant Governor.

SEC. 1B.[26] Each candidate who shall seek a nomination for Governor, under any method provided by law for such nomination, including primary elections, shall at the time of filing for said office designate a candidate for Lieutenant Governor, and the names of the said candidate for Governor and Lieutenant Governor shall be listed on the primary election ballot, or otherwise considered for nomination jointly with each other. No candidate for Governor may designate a candidate for Lieutenant Governor to contest for the said offices jointly with him without the consent of the said candidate for Lieutenant Governor, and no candidate for Lieutenant Governor may designate a candidate for Governor, to contest jointly for said offices with him without the consent of the said candidate for Governor, said consent to be in writing on a form provided for such purpose and filed at the time the said candidates shall file their certificates of candidacy, or other documents by which they seek nomination. In any election, including a primary election, candidates for Governor and Lieutenant Governor shall be listed jointly on the ballot, and a vote cast for the candidate for Governor shall also be cast for Lieutenant Governor jointly listed on the ballot with him, and the election of Governor, or the nomination of a candidate for Governor, also shall constitute the election for the same term, or the nomination, of the Lieutenant Governor who was listed on the ballot or was being considered jointly with him.

SEC. 2.[27] An election for Governor and Lieutenant Governor, under this Constitution, shall be held on the Tuesday next after the first Monday of November, in the year nineteen hundred and seventy-four, and on the same day and month in every fourth year thereafter, at the places of voting for Delegates to the General Assembly; and every person qualified to vote for Delegates, shall be qualified and entitled to vote for Governor and Lieutenant Governor; the election to be held in the same manner as the election of Delegates, and the returns thereof, under seal, to be addressed to the Speaker of the House of Delegates, and enclosed and transmitted to the Secretary of State, and delivered to said Speaker, at the commencement of the session of the General Assembly, next ensuing said election.

SEC. 3.[28] The Speaker of the House of Delegates shall then open the said Returns, in the presence of both Houses; and the persons having the highest number of votes for these offices, and being Constitutionally eligible, shall be the Governor and Lieutenant Governor, and shall qualify, in the manner herein prescribed, on the third Wednesday of January next ensuing his election, or as soon thereafter as may be practicable.

---

[20] Transferred from Article III, sec. 47, by Chapter 681, Acts of 1977, ratified Nov. 7, 1978.

[21] Originally Article I, sec. 6, renumbered by Chapter 681, Acts of 1977, ratified Nov. 7, 1978.

[22] Transferred from Article XV, sec. 10, by Chapter 681, Acts of 1977, ratified Nov. 7, 1978. As Art. XV, sec. 10, it was amended by Chapter 275, Acts of 1922, ratified Nov. 7, 1922.

[23] Originally Article I, sec. 7, thus renumbered and amended by Chapter 681, Acts of 1977, ratified Nov. 7, 1978.

[23a] Added by Chapter 788, Acts of 1984, ratified Nov. 6, 1984.

[24] Amended by Chapter 109, Acts of 1947, ratified Nov. 2, 1948; Chapter 161, Acts of 1964, ratified Nov. 3, 1964; Chapter 576, Acts of 1970, ratified Nov. 3, 1970.

[25] Amended by Chapter 532, Acts of 1970, ratified Nov. 3, 1970; Chapter 543, Acts of 1976, ratified Nov. 2, 1976.

[26] Added by Chapter 532, Acts of 1970, ratified Nov. 3, 1970.

[27] Amended by Chapter 99, Acts of 1956, ratified Nov. 6, 1956; Chapter 532, Acts of 1970, ratified Nov. 3, 1970.

[28] Amended by Chapter 161, Acts of 1964, ratified Nov. 3, 1964; Chapters 532 and 576, Acts of 1970, ratified Nov. 3, 1970.

SEC. 4.[29] If two or more sets of persons shall have the highest and an equal number of votes for Governor and Lieutenant Governor, one set of them shall be chosen Governor and Lieutenant Governor, by the Senate and House of Delegates; and all questions in relation to the eligibility of Governor and Lieutenant Governor, and to the Returns of said election, and to the number and legality of votes therein given, shall be determined by the House of Delegates; and if the person having the highest number of votes for Governor or for Lieutenant Governor or both of them, be ineligible, a person or persons shall be chosen by the Senate and House of Delegates in place of the ineligible person or persons. Every election of Governor or of Lieutenant Governor, or both, by the General Assembly shall be determined by a joint majority of the Senate and House of Delegates; and the vote shall be taken viva voce. But if two or more sets of persons shall have the highest and an equal number of votes, then, a second vote shall be taken, which shall be confined to the sets of persons having an equal number; and if the vote should again be equal, then the election of Governor and Lieutenant Governor shall be determined by lot between those sets, who shall have the highest and an equal number on the first vote.

SEC. 5.[30] A person to be eligible for the office of Governor or Lieutenant Governor must have attained the age of thirty years, and must have been a resident and registered voter of the State for five years next immediately preceding his election.

SEC. 6.[31] (a) If the Governor-elect is disqualified, resigns, or dies, the Lieutenant Governor-elect shall become Governor for the full term. If the Governor-elect fails to assume office for any other reason, the newly elected Lieutenant Governor shall become Lieutenant Governor and shall serve as acting Governor until the Governor-elect assumes office or until the office becomes vacant.

(b) The Lieutenant Governor shall serve as acting Governor when notified in writing by the Governor that the Governor will be temporarily unable to perform the duties of his office. The Lieutenant Governor also shall serve as acting Governor when the Governor is disabled but is unable to communicate to the Lieutenant Governor the fact of his inability to perform the duties of his office. In either event the Lieutenant Governor shall serve as acting Governor until notified in writing by the Governor that he is able to resume the duties of his office or until the office becomes vacant.

(c) The General Assembly, by the affirmative vote of three-fifths of all its members in joint session, may adopt a resolution declaring that the Governor or Lieutenant Governor is unable by reason of physical or mental disability to perform the duties of his office. When action is undertaken pursuant to this subsection of the Constitution, the officer who concludes that the other officer is unable, by reason of disability to perform the duties of his office shall have the power to call the General Assembly into Joint Session. The resolution, if adopted, shall be delivered to the Court of Appeals, which then shall have exclusive jurisdiction to determine whether that officer is unable by reason of the disability to perform the duties of his office. If the Court of Appeals determines that such officer is unable to discharge the duties of his office by reason of a permanent disability, the office shall be vacant. If the Court of Appeals determines that such officer is unable to discharge the duties of his office by reason of a temporary disability, it shall declare the office to be vacant during the time of the disability and the Court shall have continuing jurisdiction to determine when the disability has terminated. If the General Assembly and the Court of Appeals, acting in the same manner as described above, determine that the Governor-elect or Lieutenant Governor-elect is unable by reason of physical or mental disability to perform the duties of the office to which he has been elected, he shall be disqualified to assume office.

(d) When a vacancy occurs in the office of Governor, the Lieutenant Governor shall succeed to that office for the remainder of the term. When a vacancy occurs in the office of Lieutenant Governor, the Governor shall nominate a person who shall succeed to that office upon confirmation by the affirmative vote of a majority of all members of the General Assembly in joint session.

(e) If vacancies in the offices of Governor and Lieutenant Governor exist at the same time, the General Assembly shall convene forthwith, and the office of Governor shall be filled for the remainder of the term by the affirmative vote of a majority of all members of the General Assembly in joint session. The person so chosen as Governor by the General Assembly shall then nominate a person to succeed to the office of Lieutenant Governor, upon confirmation by the affirmative vote of a majority of all members of the General Assembly in the same joint session. The President of the Senate shall serve as acting Governor until the newly elected Governor has qualified. If a vacancy exists in the office of Lieutenant Governor, at a time when the Lieutenant Governor is authorized to serve as acting Governor, the President of the Senate shall serve as acting Governor. If there is a vacancy in the office of the President of the Senate at a time when he is authorized to serve as acting Governor, the Senate shall forthwith convene and fill the vacancy.

(f) When the Lieutenant Governor or a person elected by the General Assembly succeeds to the office of Governor, he shall have the title, powers, duties, and emoluments of that office; but when the Lieutenant Governor or the president of the Senate serves as acting Governor, he shall have only the powers and duties of that office. When the President of the Senate serves as acting Governor, he shall continue to be President of the Senate, but his duties as president shall be performed by such other person as the Senate shall select.

(g) The Court of Appeals shall have original and exclusive jurisdiction to adjudicate disputes or questions arising from the failure of the Governor-elect to take office, or the service of the Lieutenant Governor or President of the Senate as acting Governor, or the creation of a vacancy in the office of Governor or Lieutenant Governor by reason of disability, or the succession to the office of Governor or Lieutenant Governor, or the exercise of the powers and duties of a successor to the office of Governor.

SEC. 7.[32] The Legislature may provide by law, not inconsistent with Section 26 of Article III of this Constitution, for the impeachment of the Governor and Lieutenant Governor.

SEC. 7A.[33] Vacant.

SEC. 8. The Governor shall be the Commander-in-Chief of the land and naval forces of the State; and may call out the Militia to repel invasions, suppress insurrections, and enforce the execution of the Laws; but shall not take the command in person, without the consent of the Legislature.

SEC. 9. He shall take care that the Laws are faithfully executed.

SEC. 10. He shall nominate, and, by and with the advice and consent of the Senate, appoint all civil and military officers of the State, whose appointment, or election, is not otherwise herein provided for, unless a different mode of appointment be prescribed by the Law creating the office.

---

[29] Amended by Chapter 532, Acts of 1970, ratified Nov. 3, 1970.
[30] Amended by Chapter 532, Acts of 1970, ratified Nov. 3, 1970.
[31] Amended by Chapter 743, Acts of 1959, ratified Nov. 8, 1960; Chapter 532, Acts of 1970, ratified Nov. 3, 1970.

[32] Amended by Chapter 743, Acts of 1959, ratified Nov. 8, 1960; Chapter 532, Acts of 1970, ratified Nov. 3, 1970.
[33] Added by Chapter 532, Acts of 1970, ratified Nov. 3, 1970. Repealed by Chapter 681, Acts of 1977, ratified Nov. 7, 1978.

SEC. 11.[34] In case of any vacancy, during the recess of the Senate, in any office which the Governor has power to fill, he shall appoint some suitable person to said office, whose commission shall continue in force until the end of the next session of the Legislature, or until some other person is appointed to the same office, whichever shall first occur; and the nomination of the person thus appointed, during the recess, or, of some other person in his place, shall be made to the Senate on the first day of the next regular meeting of the Senate.

SEC. 12. No person, after being rejected by the Senate, shall be again nominated for the same office at the same session, unless at the request of the Senate; or, be appointed to the same office during the recess of the Legislature.

SEC. 13.[35] All civil officers nominated by the Governor and subject to confirmation by the Senate, shall be nominated to the Senate within forty days from the commencement of each regular session of the Legislature; and their term of office, except in cases otherwise provided for in this Constitution, shall commence on the first Monday of May next ensuing their appointment, and continue for two years, (unless removed from office), and until their successors, respectively, qualify according to Law.

SEC. 14. If a vacancy shall occur, during the session of the Senate, in any office which the Governor and the Senate have the power to fill, the Governor shall nominate to the Senate before its final adjournment, a proper person to fill said vacancy, unless such vacancy occurs within ten days before said final adjournment.

SEC. 15. The Governor may suspend or arrest any military officer of the State for disobedience of orders, or other military offense; and may remove him in pursuance of the sentence of a Court-Martial; and may remove for incompetency, or misconduct, all civil officers who received appointment from the Executive for a term of years.

SEC. 16. The Governor shall convene the Legislature, or the Senate alone, on extraordinary occasions; and whenever from the presence of an enemy, or from any other cause, the Seat of Government shall become an unsafe place for the meeting of the Legislature, he may direct their sessions to be held at some other convenient place.

SEC. 17.[36] To guard against hasty or partial legislation and encroachment of the Legislative Department upon the co-ordinate Executive and Judicial Departments, every Bill which shall have passed the House of Delegates and the Senate shall, before it becomes a law, be presented to the Governor of the State; if he approves he shall sign it, but if not he shall return it with his objections to the House in which it originated, which House shall enter the objections at large on its Journal and proceed to reconsider the Bill; if, after such reconsideration, three-fifths of the members elected to that House shall pass the Bill, it shall be sent with the objections to the other House, by which it shall likewise be reconsidered, and if it pass by three-fifths of the members elected to that House it shall become a law; but in all such cases the votes of both Houses shall be determined by yeas and nays, and the names of the persons voting for and against the Bill shall be entered on the Journal of each House respectively. If any Bill presented to the Governor while the General Assembly is in session shall not be returned by him with his objections within six days (Sundays excepted), the same shall be a law in like manner as if he signed it, unless the General

Assembly shall, by adjournment, prevent its return, in which case it shall not be a law.

Any Bill presented to the Governor within six days (Sundays excepted), prior to adjournment of any session of the General Assembly, or after such adjournment, shall become law without the Governor's signature unless it shall be vetoed by the Governor within 30 days after its presentment.

Any Bill so vetoed by the Governor shall be returned to the House in which it originated, immediately after said House shall have organized at the next regular or special session of the General Assembly. Said Bill may then be reconsidered according to the procedure specified hereinabove. Any Bill enacted over the veto of the Governor, or any Bill which shall become law as the result of the failure of the Governor to act within the time hereinabove specified, shall take effect 30 days after the Governor's veto is over-ridden, or on the date specified in the Bill, whichever is later, unless the Bill is an emergency measure, in which event it shall take effect when enacted. No such vetoed Bill shall be returned to the Legislature when a new General Assembly of Maryland has been elected and sworn since the passage of the vetoed Bill.

The Governor shall have power to disapprove of any item or items of any Bills making appropriations of money embracing distinct items, and the part or parts of the Bill approved shall be the law, and the item or items of appropriations disapproved shall be void unless repassed according to the rules or limitations prescribed for the passage of other Bills over the Executive veto.

SEC. 18. It shall be the duty of the Governor, semi-annually (and oftener, if he deem it expedient) to examine under oath the Treasurer and Comptroller of the State on all matters pertaining to their respective offices; and inspect and review their Bank and other Account Books.

SEC. 19. He shall, from time to time, inform the Legislature of the conditions of the State and recommend to their consideration such measures as he may judge necessary and expedient.

SEC. 20. He shall have power to grant reprieves and pardons, except in cases of impeachment, and in cases, in which he is prohibited by other Articles of this Constitution; and to remit fines and forfeitures for offences against the State; but shall not remit the principal or interest of any debt due the State, except in cases of fines and forfeitures; and before granting a *nolle prosequi*, or pardon, he shall give notice, in one or more newspapers, of the application made for it, and of the day on, or after which, his decision will be given; and in every case, in which he exercises this power, he shall report to either Branch of the Legislature, whenever required, the petitions, recommendations and reasons, which influenced his decision.

SEC. 21.[37] The Governor shall reside at the seat of government, and, from and after the fourth Wednesday in January 1967, shall receive for his services an annual salary of Twenty-five Thousand Dollars, except that beginning in the year 1978 the salary of the Governor shall be as provided in Section 21A of this Article.

SEC. 21A.[38] (a) The salaries of the Governor and Lieutenant Governor shall be as provided in this section.

(b) The Governor's Salary Commission is created. It consists of seven members: The State Treasurer; three appointed by the President of the Senate; and three appointed by the Speaker of the House of Delegates. Members of the General Assembly and officers and employees of the State or a political subdivision of the State are not eligible for appointment to the Commission. The members of the Commission shall elect a member to be chairman,

---

[34] Amended by Chapter 626, Acts of 1955, ratified Nov. 6, 1956.

[35] Amended by Chapter 99, Acts of 1956, ratified Nov. 6, 1956; Chapter 161, Acts of 1964, ratified Nov. 3, 1964; Chapter 576, Acts of 1970, ratified Nov. 3, 1970.

[36] Amended by Chapter 194, Acts of 1890, ratified Nov. 3, 1891; Chapter 714, Acts of 1949, ratified Nov. 7, 1950; Chapter 664, Acts of 1959, ratified Nov. 8, 1960; Chapter 883, Acts of 1974, ratified Nov. 5, 1974.

[37] Amended by Chapter 315, Acts of 1953, ratified Nov. 2, 1954; Chapter 641, Acts of 1965, ratified Nov. 8, 1966; Chapter 543, Acts of 1976, ratified Nov. 2, 1976.

[38] Added by Chapter 543, Acts of 1976, ratified Nov. 2, 1976.

and the concurrence of at least five members is required for any formal Commission action. The terms of members shall be for 4 years, except that the persons first appointed to the Commission shall serve from June 1, 1977 until May 31, 1980. The members of the Commission are eligible for reappointment. Members shall serve without compensation but shall be reimbursed for expenses incurred in carrying out responsibilities under this section.

(c) Within ten days after the commencement of the regular session of the General Assembly in 1978, and within ten days after the commencement of the regular session of the General Assembly each fourth year thereafter, the Commission shall make a written recommendation to the Governor, Lieutenant Governor, and other members of the General Assembly as to the salary of the Governor and Lieutenant Governor.

(d) The recommendation shall be introduced as a joint resolution in each house of the General Assembly not later than the fifteenth day of the session. The General Assembly may amend the joint resolution to decrease the recommended salaries, but may not amend the joint resolution to increase the recommended salaries. If the General Assembly fails to adopt a joint resolution in accordance with this section within 50 days after its introduction, the salaries recommended by the Commission shall apply. If the General Assembly amends the joint resolution in accordance with this section, the salaries specified in the joint resolution, as amended, shall apply. If the Commission recommends no salary change, a joint resolution shall not be introduced.

(e) The Commission may not recommend salaries lower than that received by the incumbent Governor at the time the recommendation is made; and the General Assembly may not amend the joint resolution to provide for salaries lower than that received by the incumbent Governor and Lieutenant Governor.

(f) A change in salary resulting from either Commission recommendation or amended joint resolution under this section shall take effect at the beginning of the next ensuing term of the Governor and Lieutenant Governor.

(g) Commission inaction or failure of the Commission to meet the requirements of this section with respect to proposing a change in salary for the Governor and Lieutenant Governor shall result in no change in salary.

SEC. 22.[39] A Secretary of State shall be appointed by the Governor, by and with the advice and consent of the Senate, who shall continue in office, unless sooner removed by the Governor, till the end of the official term of the Governor from whom he received his appointment, and receive such annual salary as the General Assembly may from time to time by law prescribe.

SEC. 23. The Secretary of State shall carefully keep and preserve a Record of all official acts and proceedings, which may at all times be inspected by a committee of either Branch of the Legislature; and he shall perform such other duties as may be prescribed by Law, or as may properly belong to his office, together with all clerical duty belonging to the Executive Department.

SEC. 24.[40] The Governor may make changes in the organization of the Executive Branch of the State Government, including the establishment or abolition of departments, offices, agencies, and instrumentalities, and the reallocation or reassignment of functions, powers, and duties among the departments, offices, agencies, and instrumentalities of the Executive Branch. Where these changes are inconsistent with existing law, or create new governmental programs they shall be set forth in executive orders in statutory form which shall be submitted to the General Assembly within the first ten days of a regular session. An

executive order that has been submitted shall become effective and have the force of law on the date designated in the Order unless specifically disapproved, within fifty days after submission, by a resolution of disapproval concurred in by a majority vote of all members of either House of the General Assembly. No executive order reorganizing the Executive Branch shall abolish any office established by this Constitution or shall change the powers and duties delegated to particular officers or departments by this Constitution.

ARTICLE III.

LEGISLATIVE DEPARTMENT.

SECTION 1. The Legislature shall consist of two distinct branches; a Senate, and a House of Delegates; and shall be styled the General Assembly of Maryland.

SEC. 2.[41] The membership of the Senate shall consist of forty-seven (47) Senators. The membership of the House of Delegates shall consist of one hundred forty-one (141) Delegates.

SEC. 3.[42] The State shall be divided by law into legislative districts for the election of members of the Senate and the House of Delegates. Each legislative district shall contain one (1) Senator and three (3) Delegates. Nothing herein shall prohibit the subdivision of any one or more of the legislative districts for the purpose of electing members of the House of Delegates into three (3) single-member delegate districts or one (1) single-member delegate district and one (1) multi-member delegate district.

SEC. 4.[43] Each legislative district shall consist of adjoining territory, be compact in form, and of substantially equal population. Due regard shall be given to natural boundaries and the boundaries of political subdivisions.

SEC. 5.[44] Following each decennial census of the United States and after public hearings, the Governor shall prepare a plan setting forth the boundaries of the legislative districts for electing of the members of the Senate and the House of Delegates.

The Governor shall present the plan to the President of the Senate and Speaker of the House of Delegates who shall introduce the Governor's plan as a joint resolution to the General Assembly, not later than the first day of its regular session in the second year following every census, and the Governor may call a special session for the presentation of his plan prior to the regular session. The plan shall conform to Sections 2, 3 and 4 of this Article. Following each decennial census the General Assembly may by joint resolution adopt a plan setting forth the boundaries of the legislative districts for the election of members of the Senate and the House of Delegates, which plan shall conform to Sections 2, 3 and 4 of this Article. If a plan has been adopted by the General Assembly by the 45th day after the opening of the regular session of the General Assembly in the second year following every census, the plan adopted by the General Assembly shall become law. If no plan has been adopted by the General Assembly for these purposes by the 45th day after the opening of

[39] Amended by Chapter 42, Acts of 1954, ratified Nov. 2, 1954.
[40] Added by Chapter 790, Acts of 1969, ratified Nov. 3, 1970.

[41] Amended by Chapter 469, Acts of 1900, ratified Nov. 5, 1901; Chapter 7, Acts of 1922, ratified Nov. 7, 1922; Chapter 99, Acts of 1956, ratified Nov. 6, 1956; Chapter 785, Acts of 1969, ratified Nov. 3, 1970; Chapter 363, Acts of 1972, ratified Nov. 7, 1972.
[42] Amended by Chapter 99, Acts of 1956, ratified Nov. 6, 1956; Chapter 785, Acts of 1969, ratified Nov. 3, 1970; Chapter 363, Acts of 1972, ratified Nov. 7, 1972.
[43] Amended by Chapter 432, Acts of 1900, ratified Nov. 5, 1901; Chapter 20, Acts of 1922, ratified Nov. 7, 1922; Chapter 99, Acts of 1956, ratified Nov. 6, 1956; Chapter 785, Acts of 1969, ratified Nov. 3, 1970; Chapter 363, Acts of 1972, ratified Nov. 7, 1972.
[44] Amended by Chapter 226, Acts of 1949, ratified Nov. 7, 1950; Chapter 99, Acts of 1956, ratified Nov. 6, 1956; Chapter 785, Acts of 1969, ratified Nov. 3, 1970; Chapter 363, Acts of 1972, ratified Nov. 7, 1972; Chapter 681, Acts of 1977, ratified Nov. 7, 1978.

the regular session of the General Assembly in the second year following every census, the Governor's plan presented to the General Assembly shall become law.

Upon petition of any registered voter, the Court of Appeals shall have original jurisdiction to review the legislative districting of the State and may grant appropriate relief, if it finds that the districting of the State is not consistent with requirements of either the Constitution of the United States of America, or the Constitution of Maryland. ·

SEC. 6.[45] A member of the General Assembly shall be elected by the registered voters of the legislative or delegate district from which he seeks election, to serve for a term of four years beginning on the second Wednesday of January following his election.

SEC. 7.[46] The election for Senators and Delegates shall take place on the Tuesday next, after the first Monday in the month of November, nineteen hundred and fifty-eight, and in every fourth year thereafter.

SEC. 8.[47] Vacant.

SEC. 9.[48] A person is eligible to serve as a Senator or Delegate, who on the date of his election, (1) is a citizen of the State of Maryland, (2) has resided therein for at least one year next preceding that date, and (3) if the district which he has been chosen to represent has been established for at least six months prior to the date of his election, has resided in that district for six months next preceding that date.

If the district which the person has been chosen to represent has been established less than six months prior to the date of his election, then, in addition to (1) and (2) above, he shall have resided in the district for as long as it has been established.

A person is eligible to serve as a Senator, if he has attained the age of twenty-five years, or as a Delegate, if he has attained the age of twenty-one years, on the date of his election.

SEC. 10. No member of Congress, or person holding any civil, or military office under the United States, shall be eligible as a Senator, or Delegate; and if any person shall after his election as Senator, or Delegate, be elected to Congress, or be appointed to any office, civil, or military, under the Government of the United States, his acceptance thereof, shall vacate his seat.

SEC. 11.[49] No person holding any civil office of profit, or trust, under this State shall be eligible as Senator or Delegate.

SEC. 12. No Collector, Receiver, or Holder of public money shall be eligible as Senator or Delegate, or to any office of profit, or trust, under this State, until he shall have accounted for, and paid into the Treasury all sums on the books thereof, charged to, and due by him.

SEC. 13.[50] (a) In case of death, disqualification, resignation, refusal to act, expulsion, or removal from the county or city for which he shall have been elected, of any person who shall have been chosen as a Delegate or Senator, or in case of a tie between two or more such qualified persons, the Governor shall appoint a

person to fill such vacancy from a person whose name shall be submitted to him in writing, within thirty days after the occurrence of the vacancy, by the Central Committee of the political party with which the Delegate or Senator, so vacating, had been affiliated in the County or District from which he or she was elected, provided that the appointee shall be of the same political party as the person whose office is to be filled; and it shall be the duty of the Governor to make said appointment within fifteen days after the submission thereof to him. If a name is not submitted by the Central Committee within thirty days after the occurrence of the vacancy, the Governor within another period of fifteen days shall appoint a person, who shall be of the same political party as the person whose office is to be filled, and who is otherwise properly qualified to hold the office of Delegate or Senator in the District or County. In the event there is no Central Committee in the County or District from which said vacancy is to be filled, the Governor shall within fifteen days after the occurrence of such vacancy appoint a person who is otherwise properly qualified to hold the office of Delegate or Senator in such District or County. In every case when any person is so appointed by the Governor, his appointment shall be deemed to be for the unexpired term of the person whose office has become vacant.

(b) In addition, and in submitting a name to the Governor to fill a vacancy in a legislative or delegate district, as the case may be, in any of the twenty-three counties of Maryland, the Central Committee or committees shall follow these provisions:

(1) If the vacancy occurs in a district having the same boundaries as a county, the Central Committee of the county shall submit the name of a resident of the district.

(2) If the vacancy occurs in a district which has boundaries comprising a portion of one county, the Central Committee of that county shall submit the name of a resident of the district.

(3) If the vacancy occurs in a district which has boundaries comprising a portion or all of two or more counties, the Central Committee of each county involved shall have one vote for submitting the name of a resident of the district; and if there is a tie vote between or among the Central Committees, the list of names there proposed shall be submitted to the Governor, and he shall make the appointment from the list.

SEC. 14.[51] The General Assembly shall meet on the second Wednesday of January, nineteen hundred and seventy-one, and on the same day in every year thereafter, and at no other time, unless convened by Proclamation of the Governor. A Proclamation convening the General Assembly in extraordinary session must be issued by the Governor if a majority of the members elected to the Senate and a majority of the members elected to the House of Delegates join in a petition to the Governor requesting that he convene the General Assembly in extraordinary session, and the Governor shall convene the General Assembly on the date specified in the petition. This section does not affect the Governor's power to convene the General Assembly in extraordinary session pursuant to Section 16 of Article II of this Constitution.

SEC. 15.[52] (1) The General Assembly may continue its session so long as in its judgment the public interest may require, for a period not longer than ninety days in each year. The ninety days shall be consecutive unless otherwise provided by law. The

[45] Amended by Chapter 99, Acts of 1956, ratified Nov. 6, 1956; Chapter 785, Acts of 1969, ratified Nov. 3, 1970; Chapter 681, Acts of 1977, ratified Nov. 7, 1978.
[46] Amended by Chapter 99, Acts of 1956, ratified Nov. 6, 1956.
[47] Repealed by Chapter 99, Acts of 1956, ratified Nov. 6, 1956.
[48] Amended by Chapter 880, Acts of 1974, ratified Nov. 5, 1974; Chapter 681, Acts of 1977, ratified Nov. 7, 1978.
[49] Thus amended by Chapter 681, Acts of 1977, ratified Nov. 7, 1978.
[50] Amended by Chapter 584, Acts of 1935, ratified Nov. 3, 1936; Chapter 162, Acts of 1966, ratified Nov. 8, 1966; Chapter 681, Acts of 1977, ratified Nov. 7, 1978.

[51] Amended by Chapter 497, Acts of 1947, ratified Nov. 2, 1948; Chapter 161, Acts of 1964, ratified Nov. 3, 1964; Chapter 576, Acts of 1970, ratified Nov. 3, 1970.
[52] Amended by Chapter 695, Acts of 1941, ratified Nov. 3, 1942; Chapter 497, Acts of 1947, ratified Nov. 2, 1948; Chapter 161, Acts of 1964, ratified Nov. 3, 1964; Chapter 576, Acts of 1970, ratified Nov. 3, 1970; Chapter 541, Acts of 1976, ratified Nov. 2, 1976; Chapter 681, Acts of 1977, ratified Nov. 7, 1978.

General Assembly may extend its session beyond ninety days, but not exceeding an additional thirty days, by resolution concurred in by a three-fifths vote of the membership in each House. When the General Assembly is convened by Proclamation of the Governor, the session shall not continue longer than thirty days, but no additional compensation other than mileage and other allowances provided by law shall be paid members of the General Assembly for special session.

(2) Any compensation and allowances paid to members of the General Assembly shall be as established by a commission known as the General Assembly Compensation Commission. The Commission shall consist of nine members, five of whom shall be appointed by the Governor, two of whom shall be appointed by the President of the Senate, and two of whom shall be appointed by the Speaker of the House of Delegates. Members of the General Assembly and officers and employees of the Government of the State of Maryland or of any county, city, or other governmental unit of the State shall not be eligible for appointment to the Commission. Members of the Commission shall be appointed for terms of four years commencing on June 1 of each gubernatorial election year. Members of the Commission are eligible for re-appointment. Any member of the Commission may be removed by the Governor prior to the expiration of his term for official misconduct, incompetence, or neglect of duty. The members shall serve without compensation but shall be reimbursed for expenses incurred in carrying out their responsibilities under this section. Decisions of the Commission must be concurred in by at least five members.

(3) Within 15 days after the beginning of the regular session of the General Assembly in 1974 and within 15 days after the beginning of the regular session in each fourth year thereafter, the Commission by formal resolution shall submit its determinations for compensation and allowances to the General Assembly. The General Assembly may reduce or reject, but shall not increase any item in the resolution. The resolution, with any reductions that shall have been concurred in by joint resolution of the General Assembly, shall take effect and have the force of law as of the beginning of the term of office of the next General Assembly. Rates of compensation and pensions shall be uniform for all members of the General Assembly, except that the officers of the Senate and the House of Delegates may receive higher compensation as determined by the General Assembly Compensation Commission. The provisions of the Compensation Commission resolution shall continue in force until superseded by any succeeding resolution.

(4) In no event shall the compensation and allowances be less than they were prior to the establishment of the Compensation Commission.

SEC. 16. No book, or other printed matter not appertaining to the business of the session, shall be purchased, or subscribed for, for the use of the members of the General Assembly, or be distributed among them, at the public expense.

SEC. 17. No Senator or Delegate, after qualifying as such, notwithstanding he may thereafter resign, shall during the whole period of time, for which he was elected, be eligible to any office, which shall have been created, or the salary, or profits of which shall have been increased, during such term.

SEC. 18. No Senator or Delegate shall be liable in any civil action, or criminal prosecution, whatever, for words spoken in debate.

SEC. 19.[53] Each House shall be judge of the qualifications and elections of its members, as prescribed by the Constitution and Laws of the State, and shall appoint its own officers, determine the rules of its own proceedings, punish a member for disorderly or disrespectful behaviour and with the consent of two-thirds of

its whole number of members elected, expel a member; but no member shall be expelled a second time for the same offence.

SEC. 20. A majority of the whole number of members elected to each House shall constitute a quorum for the transaction of business; but a smaller number may adjourn from day to day, and compel the attendance of absent members, in such manner, and under such penalties, as each House may prescribe.

SEC. 21. The doors of each House, and of the Committee of the Whole, shall be open, except when the business is such as ought to be kept secret.

SEC. 22. Each House shall keep a Journal of its proceedings, and cause the same to be published. The yeas and nays of members on any question, shall at the call of any five of them in the House of Delegates, or one in the Senate, be entered on the Journal.

SEC. 23. Each House may punish by imprisonment, during the session of the General Assembly, any person, not a member, for disrespectful, or disorderly behavior in its presence, or for obstructing any of its proceedings, or any of its officers in the execution of their duties; provided, such imprisonment shall not, at any one time, exceed ten days.

SEC. 24. The House of Delegates may inquire, on the oath of witnesses, into all complaints, grievances and offences, as the grand inquest of the State, and may commit any person, for any crime, to the public jail, there to remain, until discharged by due course of Law. They may examine and pass all accounts of the State, relating either to the collection or expenditure of the revenue, and appoint auditors to state and adjust the same. They may call for all public, or official papers and records, and send for persons, whom they may judge necessary in the course of their inquiries, concerning affairs relating to the public interest, and may direct all office bonds which shall be made payable to the State, to be sued for any breach thereof; and with a view to the more certain prevention, or correction of the abuses in the expenditures of the money of the State, the General Assembly shall create, at every session thereof, a Joint Standing Committee of the Senate and House of Delegates, who shall have power to send for persons, and examine them on oath, and call for Public, or Official Papers and Records, and whose duty it shall be to examine and report upon all contracts made for printing stationery, and purchases for the Public offices, and the Library, and all expenditures therein, and upon all matters of alleged abuse in expenditures, to which their attention may be called by Resolution of either House of the General Assembly.

SEC. 25. Neither House shall, without the consent of the other, adjourn for more than three days, at any one time, nor adjourn to any other place, than that in which the House shall be sitting, without the concurrent vote of two-thirds of the members present.

SEC. 26. The House of Delegates shall have the sole power of impeachment in all cases; but a majority of all the members elected must concur in the impeachment. All impeachments shall be tried by the Senate, and when sitting for that purpose, the Senators shall be on oath, or affirmation, to do justice according to the law and evidence; but no person shall be convicted without the concurrence of two-thirds of all the Senators elected.

SEC. 27.[54] Any bill may originate in either House of the General Assembly and be altered, amended or rejected by the other. No bill shall originate in either House during the last thirty-five calendar days of a regular session, unless two-thirds of the members elected thereto shall so determine by yeas and nays,

---

[53] Amended by Chapter 681, Acts of 1977, ratified Nov. 7, 1978.

[54] Amended by Chapter 497, Acts of 1912, ratified Nov. 4, 1913; Chapter 616, Acts of 1955, ratified Nov. 6, 1956; Chapter 161, Acts of 1964, ratified Nov. 3, 1964; Chapter 576, Acts of 1970, ratified Nov. 3, 1970; Chapter 369, Acts of 1972, ratified Nov. 7, 1972.

and in addition the two Houses by joint and similar rule may further regulate the right to introduce bills during this period; nor shall any bill become a law until it be read on three different days of the session in each House, unless two-thirds of the members elected to the House where such bill is pending shall so determine by yeas and nays, and no bill shall be read a third time until it shall have been actually engrossed or printed for a third reading.

Each House may adopt by rule a "consent calendar" procedure permitting bills to be read and voted upon as a single group on both second and third readings, provided that the members of each House be afforded reasonable notice of the bills to be placed upon each "consent calendar." Upon the objection of any member, any bill in question shall be removed from the "consent calendar."

SEC. 28.[55] No bill, nor single group of bills placed on the "consent calendar," shall become a Law unless it be passed in each House by a majority of the whole number of members elected, and on its final passage, the yeas and nays be recorded, and on final passage of the bills placed on the "consent calendar" the yeas and nays on the entire group of bills be recorded. A resolution requiring the action of both Houses shall be passed in the same manner.

SEC. 29. The style of all Laws of this State shall be, "Be it enacted by the General Assembly of Maryland:" and all Laws shall be passed by original bill; and every Law enacted by the General Assembly shall embrace but one subject, and that shall be described in its title; and no Law, nor section of Law, shall be revived, or amended by reference to its title, or section only; nor shall any Law be construed by reason of its title, to grant powers, or confer rights which are not expressly contained in the body of the Act; and it shall be the duty of the General Assembly, in amending any article, or section of the Code of Laws of this State, to enact the same, as the said article, or section would read when amended. And whenever the General Assembly shall enact any Public General Law, not amendatory of any section, or article in the said Code, it shall be the duty of the General Assembly to enact the same, in articles and sections, in the same manner, as the Code is arranged, and to provide for the publication of all additions and alterations, which may be made to the said Code.

SEC. 30.[56] Every bill, when passed by the General Assembly, and sealed with the Great Seal, shall be presented by the presiding officer of the House in which it originated to the Governor for his approval. All bills passed during a regular or special session shall be presented to the Governor for his approval no later than 20 days after adjournment. Within 30 days after presentment, if the Governor approves the bill, he shall sign the same in the presence of the presiding officers and Chief Clerks of the Senate and House of Delegates. Every Law shall be recorded in the office of the Court of Appeals, and in due time, be printed, published and certified under the Great Seal, to the several Courts, in the same manner as has been heretofore usual in this State.

SEC. 31.[57] A Law passed by the General Assembly shall take effect the first day of June next after the session at which it may be passed, unless it be otherwise expressly declared therein or provided for in this Constitution.

SEC. 32. No money shall be drawn from the Treasury of the State, by any order or resolution, nor except in accordance with an appropriation by Law; and every such Law shall distinctly specify the sum appropriated, and the object, to which it shall be applied; provided, that nothing herein contained, shall prevent the General Assembly from placing a contingent fund at the disposal of the Executive, who shall report to the General Assembly, at each Session, the amount expended, and the purposes to which it was applied. An accurate statement of the

receipts and expenditures of the public money, shall be attached to, and published with the Laws, after each regular Session of the General Assembly.

SEC. 33. The General Assembly shall not pass local, or special Laws, in any of the following enumerated cases, viz.: For extending the time for the collection of taxes; granting divorces; changing the name of any person; providing for the sale of real estate, belonging to minors, or other persons laboring under legal disabilities, by executors, administrators, guardians or trustees; giving effect to informal, or invalid deeds or wills; refunding money paid into the State Treasury, or releasing persons from their debts, or obligations to the State, unless recommended by the Governor, or officers of the Treasury Department. And the General Assembly shall pass no special Law, for any case, for which provision has been made, by an existing General Law. The General Assembly, at its first Session after the adoption of this Constitution, shall pass General Laws, providing for the cases enumerated in this section, which are not already adequately provided for, and for all other cases, where a General Law can be made applicable.

SEC. 34.[58] No debt shall be hereafter contracted by the General Assembly unless such debt shall be authorized by a law providing for the collection of an annual tax or taxes sufficient to pay the interest on such debt as it falls due, and also to discharge the principal thereof within fifteen years from the time of contracting the same; and the taxes laid for this purpose shall not be repealed or applied to any other object until the said debt and interest thereon shall be fully discharged. The annual tax or taxes required to be collected shall not be collected in the event that sufficient funds to pay the principal and interest on the debt are appropriated for this purpose in the annual State budget. The credit of the State shall not in any manner be given, or loaned to, or in aid of any individual association or corporation; nor shall the General Assembly have the power to involve the State in the construction of works of internal improvement which shall involve the faith or credit of the State, except in aid of the construction of works of internal improvement in the counties of St. Mary's, Charles and Calvert, which have had no direct advantage from such works as have been heretofore aided by the State; and provided that such aid, advances or appropriations shall not exceed in the aggregate the sum of five hundred thousand dollars. And they shall not use or appropriate the proceeds of the internal improvement companies, or of the State tax, now levied, or which may hereafter be levied, to pay off the public debt or to any other purpose until the interest and debt are fully paid or the sinking fund shall be equal to the amount of the outstanding debt; but the General Assembly may authorize the Board of Public Works to direct the State Treasurer to borrow in the name of the State, in anticipation of the collection of taxes or other revenues, including proceeds from the sale of bonds, such sum or sums as may be necessary to meet temporary deficiencies in the treasury, to preserve the best interest of the State in the conduct of the various State institutions, departments, bureaus, and agencies during each fiscal year. Subject to the approval of the Board of Public Works and as provided by law, the State Treasurer is authorized to make and sell short-term notes—in the name of the State, in anticipation of the collection of taxes or other revenues, including proceeds from the sale of bonds to meet temporary deficiencies in the Treasury, but such notes must only be made to provide for appropriations already made by the General Assembly. Any revenues anticipated for the purpose of short-term notes, made and sold under the authority of this section, must be so certain as to be readily estimable as to the time of receipt of the revenues and as to the amount of the revenues. The General Assembly may contract debts to any amount that may be necessary for the defense of the State, and provided

---

[55] Amended by Chapter 369, Acts of 1972, ratified Nov. 7, 1972.
[56] Amended by Chapter 883, Acts of 1974, ratified Nov. 5, 1974.
[57] Amended by Chapter 883, Acts of 1974, ratified Nov. 5, 1974.

[58] Amended by Chapter 327, Acts of 1924, ratified Nov. 4, 1924; Chapter 234, Acts of 1959, ratified Nov. 8, 1960; Chapter 372, Acts of 1972, ratified Nov. 7, 1972; Chapter 551, Acts of 1976, ratified Nov. 2, 1976; Chapter 600, Acts of 1982, ratified Nov. 2, 1982.

further that nothing in this section shall be construed to prohibit the raising of funds for the purpose of aiding or compensating in such manner or way as the General Assembly of the State shall deem proper, those citizens of the State who have served, with honor, their Country and State in time of War; provided, however, that such action of the General Assembly shall be effective only when submitted to and approved by a vote of the people of the State at the General Election next following the enactment of such legislation.

SEC. 35.[59] Extra compensation may not be granted or allowed by the General Assembly to any public Officer, Agent, Servant or Contractor, after the service has been rendered, or the contract entered into; nor may the salary or compensation of any public officer be increased or diminished during his term of office except those whose full term of office is fixed by law in excess of 4 years. However, after January 1, 1956, for services rendered after that date, the salary or compensation of any appointed public officer of the Mayor and City Council of Baltimore may be increased or diminished at any time during his term of office; except that as to officers in the Classified City Service, when the salary of any appointed public officer of the Mayor and City Council of Baltimore however, increased or decreased, it may not again be increased or decreased, as the case may be, during the term of such public officer.

SEC. 35A.[60] Nothing in this Constitution shall exempt the salary or compensation of any judge or other public officer from the imposition by the General Assembly of a non-discriminatory tax upon income.

SEC. 36.[61] No Lottery grant shall ever hereafter be authorized by the General Assembly, unless it is a lottery to be operated by and for the benefit of the State.

SEC. 37.[62] Vacant.

SEC. 38.[63] No person shall be imprisoned for debt, but a valid decree of a court of competent jurisdiction or agreement approved by decree of said court for the support of a spouse or dependent children, or for the support of an illegitimate child or children, or for alimony (either common law or as defined by statute), shall not constitute a debt within the meaning of this section.

SEC. 39.[64] The books, papers and accounts of all banks shall be open to inspection under such regulations as may be prescribed by law.

SEC. 40. The General Assembly shall enact no Law authorizing private property to be taken for public use without just compensation, as agreed upon between the parties, or awarded by a jury, being first paid or tendered to the party entitled to such compensation.

SEC. 40A.[65] The General Assembly shall enact no law authorizing private property to be taken for public use without just

compensation, to be agreed upon between the parties, or awarded by a jury, being first paid or tendered to the party entitled to such compensation, but where such property is situated in Baltimore City and is desired by this State or by the Mayor and City Council of Baltimore, the General Assembly may provide that such property may be taken immediately upon payment therefor to the owner or owners thereof by the State or by the Mayor and City Council of Baltimore, or into court, such amount as the State or the Mayor and City Council of Baltimore, as the case may be, shall estimate to be the fair value of said property, provided such legislation also requires the payment of any further sum that may subsequently be added by a jury; and further provided that the authority and procedure for the immediate taking of property as it applies to the Mayor and City Council of Baltimore on June 1, 1961, shall remain in force and effect to and including June 1, 1963, and where such property is situated in Baltimore County and is desired by Baltimore County, Maryland, the County Council of Baltimore County, Maryland, may provide for the appointment of an appraiser or appraisers by a Court of Record to value such property and that upon payment of the amount of such evaluation, to the party entitled to compensation, or into Court, and securing the payment of any further sum that may be awarded by a jury, such property may be taken; and where such property is situated in Montgomery County and in the judgment of and upon a finding by the County Council of said County that there is immediate need therefor for right of way for County roads or streets, the County Council may provide that such property may be taken immediately upon payment therefor to the owner or owners thereof, or into court, such amount as a licensed real estate broker appointed by the County Council shall estimate to be the fair market value of such property, provided that the Council shall secure the payment of any further sum that may subsequently be awarded by a jury. In the various municipal corporations within Cecil County, where in the judgment of and upon a finding by the governing body of said municipal corporation that there is immediate need therefor for right of way for municipal roads, streets and extension of municipal water and sewage facilities, the governing body may provide that such property may be taken immediately upon payment therefor to the owner or owners thereof, or into court, such amount as a licensed real estate broker appointed by the particular governing body shall estimate to be a fair market value of such property, provided that the municipal corporation shall secure the payment of any further sum that subsequently may be awarded by a jury. This section 40A shall not apply in Montgomery County or any of the various municipal corporations within Cecil County, if the property actually to be taken includes a building or buildings.

SEC. 40B.[66] The General Assembly shall enact no law authorizing private property to be taken for public use without just compensation, to be agreed upon between the parties or awarded by a jury, being first paid or tendered to the party entitled to such compensation, except that where such property in the judgment of the State Roads Commission is needed by the State for highway purposes, the General Assembly may provide that such property may be taken immediately upon payment therefor to the owner or owners thereof by said State Roads Commission, or into Court, such amount as said State Roads Commission shall estimate to be of the fair value of said property, provided such legislation also requires the payment of any further sum that may subsequently be awarded by a jury.

SEC. 40C.[67] The General Assembly shall enact no law authorizing private property to be taken for public use without just compensation, to be agreed upon between the parties or awarded by a jury, being first paid or tendered to the party entitled to such compensation, except that where such property, located in Prince George's County in this State, is in the judgment of the Washington Suburban Sanitary Commission needed for water supply, sewerage and drainage systems to be extended or

---

[59] Amended by Chapter 416, Acts of 1957, ratified Nov. 4, 1958; Chapter 547, Acts of 1976, ratified Nov. 2, 1976; Chapter 976, Acts of 1978, ratified Nov. 7, 1978.

[60] Added by Chapter 771, Acts of 1939, ratified Nov. 5, 1940.

[61] Amended by Chapter 364, Acts of 1972, ratified Nov. 7, 1972.

[62] Repealed by Chapter 681, Acts of 1977, ratified Nov. 7, 1978.

[63] Amended by Chapter 14, Acts of 1950, ratified Nov. 7, 1950; Chapter 121, Acts of 1962, ratified Nov. 6, 1962; Chapter 321, Acts of 1982, ratified Nov. 2, 1982.

[64] Amended by Chapter 151, Acts of Sp. Sess. of 1936, ratified Nov. 3, 1936.

[65] Amended by Chapter 402, Acts of 1912, ratified Nov. 4, 1913; Chapters 224 and 604, Acts of 1959, ratified Nov. 8, 1960; Chapter 329, Acts of 1961, ratified Nov. 6, 1962; Chapter 100, Acts of 1962, ratified Nov. 6, 1962; Chapter 304, Acts of 1966, ratified Nov. 8, 1966.

[66] Added by Chapter 607, Acts of 1941, ratified Nov. 3, 1942.

[67] Added by Chapter 781, Acts of 1965, ratified Nov. 8, 1966.

constructed by the said Commission, the General Assembly may provide that such property, except any building or buildings may be taken immediately upon payment therefor by the condemning authority to the owner or owners thereof or into the Court to the use of the person or persons entitled thereto, such amount as the condemning authority shall estimate to be the fair value of said property, provided such legislation requires that the condemning authority's estimate be not less than the appraised value of the property being taken as evaluated by at least one qualified appraiser, whose qualifications have been accepted by a Court of Record of this State, and also requires the payment of any further sum that may subsequently be awarded by a jury, and provided such legislation limits the condemning authority's utilization of the acquisition procedures specified in this section to occasions where it has acquired or is acquiring by purchase or other procedures one-half or more of the several takings of land or interests in land necessary for any given water supply, sewerage or drainage extension or construction project.

SEC. 40D.[68] Vacant.

SEC. 41.[69] Vacant.

SEC. 42.[70] Vacant.

SEC. 43. The property of the wife shall be protected from the debts of her husband.

SEC. 44.[71] Laws shall be passed by the General Assembly, to protect from execution a reasonable amount of the property of the debtor.

SEC. 45.[72] The General Assembly shall provide a simple and uniform system of charges in the offices of Clerks of Courts and Registers of Wills, in the Counties of this State and the City of Baltimore, and for the collection thereof; provided, the amount of compensation to any of the said officers in the various Counties and in the City of Baltimore shall be such as may be prescribed by law.

SEC. 46. The General Assembly shall have power to receive from the United States, any grant, or donation of land, money, or securities for any purpose designated by the United States, and shall administer, or distribute the same according to the conditions of the said grant.

SEC. 47.[73] Vacant.

SEC. 48.[74] Corporations may be formed under general laws, but shall not be created by Special Act, except for municipal purposes and except in cases where no general laws exist, providing for the creation of corporations of the same general character, as the corporation proposed to be created; and any act of incorporation passed in violation of this section shall be void. All charters granted, or adopted in pursuance of this section, and all charters heretofore granted and created, subject to repeal or modification, may be altered, from time to time, or be repealed; Provided, nothing herein contained shall be construed to extend to Banks, or the incorporation thereof. The General Assembly shall not alter or amend the charter, of any corporation existing at the time of the adoption of this Article, or pass any other general or special law for the benefit of such corporation, except upon the condition that such corporation shall surrender all claim to exemption from taxation or from the repeal or modification of its charter, and that

such corporation shall thereafter hold its charter subject to the provisions of this Constitution; and any corporation chartered by this State which shall accept, use, enjoy, or in any wise avail itself of any rights, privileges, or advantages that may hereafter be granted or conferred by any general or special Act, shall be conclusively presumed to have thereby surrendered any exemption from taxation to which it may be entitled under its charter, and shall be thereafter subject to taxation as if no such exemption has been granted by its charter.

SEC. 49. The General Assembly shall have power to regulate by Law, not inconsistent with this Constitution, all matters which relate to the Judges of election, time, place and manner of holding elections in this State, and of making returns thereof.

SEC. 50. It shall be the duty of the General Assembly, at its first session, held after the adoption of this Constitution, to provide by Law for the punishment, by fine, or imprisonment in the Penitentiary, or both, in the discretion of the Court, of any person, who shall bribe, or attempt to bribe, any Executive, or Judicial officer of the State of Maryland, or any member, or officer, of the General Assembly of the State of Maryland, or of any Municipal corporation in the State of Maryland, or any Executive officer of such corporation, in order to influence him in the performance of any of his official duties; and, also, to provide by Law for the punishment, by fine, or imprisonment in the Penitentiary, or both, in the discretion of the Court, of any of said officers, or members, who shall demand, or receive any bribe, fee, reward, or testimonial, for the performance of his official duties, or for neglecting, or failing to perform the same; and, also, to provide by Law for compelling any person, so bribing, or attempting to bribe, or so demanding, or receiving a bribe, fee, reward, or testimonial, to testify against any person, or persons, who may have committed any of said offenses; provided, that any person, so compelled to testify, shall be exempted from trial and punishment for the offense, of which he may have been guilty; and any person, convicted of such offence, shall, as part of the punishment thereof, be forever disfranchised and disqualified from holding any office of trust, or profit, in this State.

SEC. 51.[75] The personal property of residents of this State, shall be subject to taxation in the County or City where the resident *bona fide* resides for the greater part of the year for which the tax may or shall be levied, and not elsewhere, except goods and chattels permanently located, which shall be taxed in the City or County where they are so located, but the General Assembly may by law provide for the taxation of mortgages upon property in this State and the debts secured thereby, in the County or City where such property is situated.

SEC. 52.[76] (1) The General Assembly shall not appropriate any money out of the Treasury except in accordance with the provisions of this section.

(2) Every appropriation bill shall be either a Budget Bill, or a Supplementary Appropriation Bill, as hereinafter provided.

(3)[77] On the third Wednesday in January in each year, (except in the case of a newly elected Governor, and then not later than ten days after the convening of the General Assembly), unless such time shall be extended by the General Assembly, the Governor shall submit to the General Assembly a Budget for the next ensuing fiscal year. Each Budget shall contain a complete plan of proposed expenditures and estimated revenues for said fiscal year and shall show the estimated surplus or deficit of revenues at the end of the preceding fiscal year. Accompanying each Budget shall be a statement showing: (a) the revenues and expenditures for the preceding fiscal year; (b) the current assets,

---

[68] Repealed by Chapter 683, Acts of 1977, ratified Nov. 7, 1978.
[69] Repealed by Chapter 681, Acts of 1977, ratified Nov. 7, 1978.
[70] Transferred to Article I, sec. 7, by Chapter 681, Acts of 1977, ratified Nov. 7, 1978.
[71] Amended by Chapter 549, Acts of 1976, ratified Nov. 2, 1976.
[72] Amended by Chapter 509, Acts of 1941, ratified Nov. 3, 1942.
[73] Transferred to Article I, sec. 8, by Chapter 681, Acts of 1977, ratified Nov. 7, 1978.
[74] Amended by Chapter 195, Acts of 1890, ratified Nov. 3, 1891.

[75] Amended by Chapter 426, Acts of 1890, ratified Nov. 3, 1891.
[76] Amended by Chapter 159, Acts of 1916, ratified Nov. 7, 1916; Chapter 497, Acts of 1947, ratified Nov. 2, 1948.
[77] Amended by Chapter 725, Acts of 1955, ratified Nov. 6, 1956; Chapter 161, Acts of 1964, ratified Nov. 3, 1964.

liabilities, reserves and surplus or deficit of the State; (c) the debts and funds of the State; (d) an estimate of the State's financial condition as of the beginning and end of the preceding fiscal year; (e) any explanation the Governor may desire to make as to the important features of the Budget and any suggestions as to methods for reduction or increase of the State's revenue.

(4)[78] Each Budget shall embrace an estimate of all appropriations in such form and detail as the Governor shall determine or as may be prescribed by law, as follows: (a) for the General Assembly as certified to the Governor in the manner hereinafter provided; (b) for the Executive Department; (c) for the Judiciary Department, as provided by law, certified by the Comptroller; (d) to pay and discharge the principal and interest of the debt of the State in conformity with Section 34 of Article 3 of the Constitution, and all laws enacted in pursuance thereof; (e) for the salaries payable by the State and under the Constitution and laws of the State; (f) for the establishment and maintenance throughout the State of a thorough and efficient system of public schools in conformity with Article 8 of the Constitution and with the laws of the State; (g) for such other purposes as are set forth in the Constitution or laws of the State.

(5)[79] The Governor shall deliver to the presiding officer of each House the Budget and a bill for all the proposed appropriations of the Budget classified and in such form and detail as he shall determine or as may be prescribed by law; and the presiding officer of each House shall promptly cause said bill to be introduced therein, and such bill shall be known as the "Budget Bill." The Governor may, with the consent of the General Assembly, before final action thereon by the General Assembly, amend or supplement said Budget to correct an oversight, provide funds contingent on passage of pending legislation or, in case of an emergency, by delivering such an amendment or supplement to the presiding officers of both Houses; and such amendment or supplement shall thereby become a part of said Budget Bill as an addition to the items of said bill or as a modification of or a substitute for any item of said bill such amendment or supplement may affect.

(5a)[80] The Budget and the Budget Bill as submitted by the Governor to the General Assembly shall have a figure for the total of all proposed appropriations and a figure for the total of all estimated revenues available to pay the appropriations, and the figure for total proposed appropriations shall not exceed the figure for total estimated revenues. Neither the Governor in submitting an amendment or supplement to the Budget Bill nor the General Assembly in amending the Budget Bill shall thereby cause the figure for total proposed appropriations to exceed the figure for total estimated revenues, including any revisions, and in the Budget Bill as enacted the figure for total estimated revenues always shall be equal to or exceed the figure for total appropriations.

(6)[81] The General Assembly shall not amend the Budget Bill so as to affect either the obligations of the State under Section 34 of Article 3 of the Constitution, or the provisions made by the laws of the State for the establishment and maintenance of a system of public schools or the payment of any salaries required to be paid by the State of Maryland by the Constitution thereof; and the General Assembly may amend the bill by increasing or diminishing the items therein relating to the General Assembly, and by increasing or diminishing the items therein relating to the judiciary, but except as hereinbefore specified, may not alter the said bill except to strike out or reduce items therein, provided, however, that the salary or compensation of any public officer shall not be decreased during his term of office; and such bill,

when and as passed by both Houses, shall be a law immediately without further action by the Governor.

(7) The Governor and such representatives of the executive departments, boards, officers and commissions of the State expending or applying for State's moneys, as have been designated by the Governor for this purpose, shall have the right, and when requested by either House of the General Assembly, it shall be their duty to appear and be heard with respect to any Budget Bill during the consideration thereof, and to answer inquiries relative thereto.

(8)[82] Supplementary Appropriation Bill. Either House may consider other appropriations but both Houses shall not finally act upon such appropriations until after the Budget Bill has been finally acted upon by both Houses, and no such other appropriation shall be valid except in accordance with the provisions following: (a) Every such appropriation shall be embodied in a separate bill limited to some single work, object or purpose therein stated and called herein a Supplementary Appropriation Bill; (b) Each Supplementary Appropriation Bill shall provide the revenue necessary to pay the appropriation thereby made by a tax, direct or indirect, to be levied and collected as shall be directed in said bill; (c) No Supplementary Appropriation Bill shall become a law unless it be passed in each House by a vote of a majority of the whole number of the members elected, and the yeas and nays recorded on its final passage; (d) Each Supplementary Appropriation Bill shall be presented to the Governor of the State as provided in Section 17 of Article 2 of the Constitution and thereafter all the provisions of said section shall apply.

(9) Nothing in this section shall be construed as preventing the General Assembly from passing at any time, in accordance with the provisions of Section 28 of Article 3 of the Constitution and subject to the Governor's power of approval as provided in Section 17 of Article 2 of the Constitution, an appropriation bill to provide for the payment of any obligation of the State within the protection of Section 10 of Article 1 of the Constitution of the United States.

(10)[83] If the Budget Bill shall not have been finally acted upon by the Legislature seven days before the expiration of the regular session, the Governor shall issue a proclamation extending the session for some further period as may, in his judgment, be necessary for the passage of such bill; but no other matter than such bill shall be considered during such extended session except a provision for the cost thereof.

(11)[84] The Governor for the purpose of making up his Budget shall have the power, and it shall be his duty, to require from the proper State officials, including herein all executive departments, all executive and administrative offices, bureaus, boards, commissions and agencies, expending or supervising the expenditure of, and all institutions applying for State moneys and appropriations, such itemized estimates and other information, in such form and at such times as he shall direct, except that an estimate for a program required to be funded by a law which will be in effect during the fiscal year covered by the Budget and which was enacted before July 1 of the fiscal year prior thereto shall provide a level of funding not less than that prescribed in the law. The estimates for the Legislative Department, certified by the presiding officer of each House, of the Judiciary, as provided by law, certified by the Comptroller, and for the public schools, as provided by law, shall be transmitted to the Governor, in such form and at such times as he shall direct, and shall be included in the Budget without revision.

(12)[85] The Governor may provide for public hearings on all estimates and may require the attendance at such hearings of

---

[78] Amended by Chapter 20, Acts of 1952, ratified Nov. 4, 1952.
[79] Amended by Chapter 20, Acts of 1952, ratified Nov. 4, 1952.
[80] Added by Chapter 745, Acts of 1973, ratified Nov. 5, 1974.
[81] Amended by Chapter 373, Acts of 1972, ratified Nov. 7, 1972.

[82] Amended by Chapter 416, Acts of 1966, ratified Nov. 8, 1966.
[83] Amended by Chapter 576, Acts of 1970, ratified Nov. 3, 1970.
[84] Amended by Chapter 971, Acts of 1978, ratified Nov. 7, 1978.
[85] Amended by Chapter 971, Acts of 1978, ratified Nov. 7, 1978.

representatives of all agencies, and for all institutions applying for State moneys. After such public hearings he may, in his discretion, revise all estimates except those for the legislative and judiciary departments, and for the public schools, as provided by law, and except that he may not reduce an estimate for a program below a level of funding prescribed by a law which will be in effect during the fiscal year covered by the Budget, and which was enacted before July 1 of the fiscal year prior thereto.

(13) The General Assembly may, from time to time, enact such laws not inconsistent with this section, as may be necessary and proper to carry out its provisions.

(14) In the event of any inconsistency between any of the provisions of this Section and any of the other provisions of the Constitution, the provisions of this Section shall prevail. But nothing herein shall in any manner affect the provisions of Section 34 of Article 3 of the Constitution or of any laws heretofore or hereafter passed in pursuance thereof, or be construed as preventing the Governor from calling extraordinary sessions of the General Assembly, as provided by Section 16 of Article 2, or as preventing the General Assembly at such extraordinary sessions from considering any emergency appropriation or appropriations.

(15) If any item of any appropriation bill passed under the provisions of this Section shall be held invalid upon any ground, such invalidity shall not affect the legality of the bill or of any other item of such bill or bills.

SEC. 53.[86] Vacant.

SEC. 54.[87] No County of this State shall contract any debt, or obligation, in the construction of any Railroad, Canal, or other Work of Internal Improvement, nor give, or loan its credit to, or in aid of any association, or corporation, unless authorized by an Act of the General Assembly.

SEC. 55. The General Assembly shall pass no Law suspending the privilege of the Writ of *Habeas Corpus.*

SEC. 56. The General Assembly shall have power to pass all such Laws as may be necessary and proper for carrying into execution the powers vested, by this Constitution, in any Department, or office of the Government, and the duties imposed upon them thereby.

SEC. 57. The Legal Rate of Interest shall be Six per cent per annum, unless otherwise provided by the General Assembly.

SEC. 58.[88] The Legislature shall provide by Law for State and municipal taxation upon the revenues accruing from business done in the State by all foreign corporations.

SEC. 59.[89] The Legislature shall pass no law creating the office of "State Pension Commissioner", or establishing any general pension system within this State.

SEC. 60.[90] The General Assembly of Maryland shall have the power to provide by suitable general enactment (a) for the suspension of sentence by the Court in criminal cases; (b) for any form of the indeterminate sentence in criminal cases, and (c) for the release upon parole in whatever manner the General Assembly may prescribe, of convicts imprisoned under sentence for crimes.

SEC. 61.[91] (a) The General Assembly may authorize and

---

[86] Repealed by Chapter 681, Acts of 1977, ratified Nov. 7, 1978.
[87] Amended by Chapter 71, Acts of 1960, ratified Nov. 8, 1960.
[88] Amended by Chapter 99, Acts of 1956, ratified Nov. 6, 1956.
[89] Amended by Chapter 681, Acts of 1977, ratified Nov. 7, 1978.
[90] Added by Chapter 453, Acts of 1914, ratified Nov. 2, 1915.
[91] Added by Chapter 444, Acts of 1959, ratified Nov. 8, 1960.

empower any county or any municipal corporation, by public local law:

(1) To carry out urban renewal projects which shall be limited to slum clearance in slum or blighted areas and redevelopment or the rehabilitation of slum or blighted areas, and to include the acquisition, within the boundary lines of such county or municipal corporation, of land and property of every kind and any right, interest, franchise, easement or privilege therein, by purchase, lease, gift, condemnation or any other legal means. The term "slum area" shall mean any area where dwellings predominate which, by reason of depreciation, overcrowding, faulty arrangement or design, lack of ventilation, light or sanitary facilities, or any combination of these factors, are detrimental to the public safety, health or morals. The term "blighted area" shall mean an area in which a majority of buildings have declined in productivity by reason of obsolescence, depreciation or other causes to an extent they no longer justify fundamental repairs and adequate maintenance.

(2) To sell, lease, convey, transfer or otherwise dispose of any of said land or property, regardless of whether or not it has been developed, redeveloped, altered or improved and irrespective of the manner or means in or by which it may have been acquired, to any private, public or quasi public corporation, partnership, association, person or other legal entity.

No land or property taken by any county or any municipal corporation for any of the aforementioned purposes or in connection with the exercise of any of the powers which may be granted to such county or municipal corporation pursuant to this section by exercising the power of eminent domain shall be taken without just compensation, as agreed upon between the parties, or awarded by a jury, being first paid or tendered to the party entitled to such compensation.

All land or property needed, or taken by the exercise of the power of eminent domain, by any county or any municipal corporation for any of the aforementioned purposes or in connection with the exercise of any of the powers which may be granted pursuant to this Section is hereby declared to be needed or taken for public uses and purposes. Any or all of the activities authorized pursuant to this section shall constitute governmental functions undertaken for public uses and purposes and the power of taxation may be exercised, public funds expended and public credit extended in furtherance thereof.

(b) The General Assembly may grant to any county or any municipal corporation, by public local law, any and all additional power and authority necessary or proper to carry into full force and effect any and all of the specific powers authorized by this section and to fully accomplish any and all of the purposes and objects contemplated by the provisions of this section, provided such additional power or authority is not inconsistent with the terms and provisions of this section or with any other provision or provisions of the Constitution of Maryland.

(c) The General Assembly of Maryland, by public local law, may establish or authorize the establishment of a public body or agency to undertake in a county or municipal corporation (other than Baltimore City) the activities authorized by this section, and may provide that any or all of the powers, except the power of taxation, herein authorized to be granted to such county or municipal corporation shall be vested in such public body or agency or in any existing public body or agency.

(d) The General Assembly may place such other and further restrictions or limitations on the exercise of any of the powers provided for in this section, as it may deem proper and expedient.

(e) The provisions of this section are independent of, and shall in no way affect, the powers granted under Article XIB of the Constitution of Maryland, title "City of Baltimore—Land Development and Redevelopment." Also, the power provided in this section for the General Assembly to enact public local laws authorizing any municipal corporation or any county to carry out urban renewal projects prevails over the restrictions contained in Article XI-A "Local Legislation" and in Article XI-E "Municipal Corporations" of this Constitution.

ARTICLE IV.

JUDICIARY DEPARTMENT.

Part I—General Provisions.

SECTION 1.[92] The Judicial power of this State is vested in a Court of Appeals, such intermediate courts of appeal as the General Assembly may create by law, Circuit Courts, Orphans' Courts, and a District Court. These Courts shall be Courts of Record, and each shall have a seal to be used in the authentication of all process issuing from it.

SEC. 1A.[93] The several Courts existing in this State at the time of the adoption of this Constitution shall, until superseded under its provisions, continue with like powers and jurisdiction, and in the exercise thereof, both at Law and in Equity, in all respects, as if this Constitution had not been adopted; and when said Courts shall be so superseded, all causes, then depending in said Courts shall pass into the jurisdiction of the several Courts, by which they may, respectively, be superseded.

SEC. 2.[94] The Judges of all of the said Courts shall be citizens of the State of Maryland, and qualified voters under this Constitution, and shall have resided therein not less than five years, and not less than six months next preceding their election, or appointment, as the case may be, in the city, county, district, judicial circuit, intermediate appellate judicial circuit or appellate judicial circuit for which they may be, respectively, elected, or appointed. They shall be not less than thirty years of age at the time of their election, or appointment, and shall be selected from those who have been admitted to practice Law in this State, and who are most distinguished for integrity, wisdom and sound legal knowledge.

SEC. 3.[95] Except for Judges of the District Court, the Judges of the several Courts other than the Court of Appeals or any intermediate courts of appeal shall, subject to the provisions of Section 5 of this Article of the Constitution, be elected in Baltimore City and in each county, by the qualified voters of the city and of each county, respectively, all of the said Judges to be elected at the general election to be held on the Tuesday after the first Monday in November, as now provided for in the Constitution. Each of the said Judges shall hold his office for the term of fifteen years from the time of his election, and until his successor is elected and qualified, or until he shall have attained the age of seventy years, whichever may first happen, and be re-eligible thereto until he shall have attained the age of seventy years, and not after. In case of the inability of any of said Judges to discharge his duties with efficiency, by reason of continued sickness, or of physical or mental infirmity, it shall be in the power of the General Assembly, two-thirds of the members of each House concurring, with the approval of the Governor to retire said Judge from office.

SEC. 3A.[96] (a) Any former judge, except a former judge of the Orphans' Court, may be assigned by the Chief Judge of the Court of Appeals, upon approval of a majority of the court, to sit temporarily in any court of this State, except an Orphans' Court, as provided by law.

(b) The provisions of this section apply, notwithstanding provisions appearing elsewhere in this Article pertaining to retirement of judges upon attaining age 70.

SEC. 4. Any Judge shall be removed from office by the Governor, on conviction in a Court of Law, of incompetency, of wilful neglect of duty, misbehavior in office, or any other crime, or on impeachment, according to this Constitution, or the Laws of the State; or on the address of the General Assembly, two-thirds of each House concurring in such address, and the accused having been notified of the charges against him, and having had opportunity of making his defence.

SEC. 4A.[97] There is created a Commission on Judicial Disabilities composed of seven persons appointed by the Governor of Maryland. The members of the Commission shall be citizens and residents of this State. Four members of the Commission shall be appointed from among the judges of the appellate courts, the Circuit Courts, and the District Court; two members shall be appointed from among those persons who are admitted to practice of law in the State, who have been so engaged for at least fifteen years, and who are not judges of any court; and one member shall represent the public, who shall not be a judge, active or retired, and who is not admitted to the practice of law in this State. The term of office of each member shall be for four years commencing on January 1 following the expiration of his predecessor's term. Whenever any member of the Commission appointed from among judges in the State ceases to be a judge, when any member appointed from among those admitted to practice law becomes a judge, when any member representing the public becomes a judge or is admitted to the practice of law in this State, or when any member ceases to be a resident of the State, in such case the membership of this member shall forthwith terminate. Any vacancies on the Commission shall be filled for the unexpired term by the Governor in the same manner as for making of appointments to the Commission and subject to the same qualifications which were applicable to the person causing the vacancy. No member of the Commission shall receive any compensation for his services as such but shall be allowed any expenses necessarily incurred in the performance of his duties as such member.

SEC. 4B.[98] (a) The Commission on Judicial Disabilities has the power to investigate complaints against any judge of the Court of Appeals, any intermediate courts of appeal, the Circuit Courts, the District Court of Maryland, or the Orphans' Court; and to conduct hearings concerning such complaints, administer oaths and affirmations, issue process to compel the attendance of witnesses and the production of evidence, and require persons to testify and produce evidence by granting them immunity from prosecution or from penalty or forfeiture. The Commission has the power to issue a reprimand and the power to recommend to the Court of Appeals the removal, censure or other appropriate disciplining of a judge or, in an appropriate case, retirement. All proceedings, testimony, and evidence before the Commission shall be confidential and privileged, except as provided by rule of the Court of Appeals; the record and any proceeding filed with

---

[92] Amended by Chapter 10, Acts of 1966, ratified Nov. 8, 1966; Chapter 789, Acts of 1969, ratified Nov. 3, 1970; Chapter 681, Acts of 1977, ratified Nov. 7, 1978; Chapter 523, Acts of 1980, ratified Nov. 4, 1980.

[93] Transferred from Article XV, sec. 2, and amended by Chapter 681, Acts of 1977, ratified Nov. 7, 1978.

[94] Amended by Chapter 10, Acts of 1966, ratified Nov. 8, 1966; Chapter 789, Acts of 1969, ratified Nov. 3, 1970; Chapter 542, Acts of 1976, ratified Nov. 2, 1976.

[95] Amended by Chapter 479, Acts of 1931, ratified Nov. 8, 1932; Chapter 607, Acts of 1953, ratified Nov. 2, 1954; Chapter 10, Acts of 1966, ratified Nov. 8, 1966; Chapter 542, Acts of 1976, ratified Nov. 2, 1976; Chapter 681, Acts of 1977, ratified Nov. 7, 1978.

[96] Added by Chapter 546, Acts of 1976, ratified Nov. 2, 1976.

[97] Amended by Chapter 773, Acts of 1965, ratified Nov. 8, 1966; Chapter 789, Acts of 1969, ratified Nov. 3, 1970; Chapter 681, Acts of 1977, ratified Nov. 7, 1978; Chapter 523, Acts of 1980, ratified Nov. 4, 1980.

[98] Amended by Chapter 773, Acts of 1965, ratified Nov. 8, 1966; Chapter 789, Acts of 1969, ratified Nov. 3, 1970; Chapter 886, Acts of 1974, ratified Nov. 5, 1974; Chapter 523, Acts of 1980, ratified Nov. 4, 1980.

the Court of Appeals shall lose its confidential character, except as ordered by the Court of Appeals. No judge shall participate as a member of the Commission in any proceedings involving his own conduct, and the Governor shall appoint another judge as a substitute member of the Commission for those proceedings. The Court of Appeals shall prescribe by rule the means to implement and enforce the powers of the Commission and the practice and procedure before the Commission.

(b) Upon any recommendation of the Commission, the Court of Appeals, after a hearing and upon a finding of misconduct while in office, or of persistent failure to perform the duties of his office, or of conduct prejudicial to the proper administration of justice, may remove the judge from office or may censure or otherwise discipline him, or the Court of Appeals, after hearing and upon a finding of disability which is or is likely to become permanent and which seriously interferes with the performance of his duties, may retire the judge from office. A judge removed under this section, and his surviving spouse, shall have the rights and privileges accruing from his judicial service only to the extent prescribed by the order of removal. A judge retired under this section shall have the rights and privileges prescribed by law for other retired judges. No judge of the Court of Appeals shall sit in judgment in any hearing involving his own conduct.

(c) This section is alternative to, and cumulative with, the methods of retirement and removal provided in Sections 3 and 4 of this Article, and in Section 26 of Article III of this Constitution.

SEC. 5.[99] Upon every occurrence or recurrence of a vacancy through death, resignation, removal, disqualification by reason of age or otherwise, or expiration of the term of fifteen years of any judge of a circuit court, or creation of the office of any such judge, or in any other way, the Governor shall appoint a person duly qualified to fill said office, who shall hold the same until the election and qualification of his successor. His successor shall be elected at the first biennial general election for Representatives in Congress after the expiration of the term of fifteen years (if the vacancy occurred in that way) or the first such general election after one year after the occurrence of the vacancy in any other way than through expiration of such term. Except in case of reappointment of a judge upon expiration of his term of fifteen years, no person shall be appointed who will become disqualified by reason of age and thereby unable to continue to hold office until the prescribed time when his successor would have been elected.

SEC. 5A.[100] (a) A vacancy in the office of a judge of an appellate court, whether occasioned by the death, resignation, removal, retirement, disqualification by reason of age, or rejection by the voters of an incumbent, the creation of the office of a judge, or otherwise, shall be filled as provided in this section.

(b) Upon the occurrence of a vacancy the Governor shall appoint, by and with the advice and consent of the Senate, a person duly qualified to fill said office who shall hold the same until the election for continuance in office as provided in subsections (c) and (d).

(c) The continuance in office of a judge of the Court of Appeals is subject to approval or rejection by the registered voters of the appellate judicial circuit from which he was appointed at the next general election following the expiration of one year from the date of the occurrence of the vacancy which he was appointed to fill, and at the general election next occurring every ten years thereafter.

(d) The continuance in office of a judge of the Court of Special Appeals is subject to approval or rejection by the registered voters of the geographical area prescribed by law at the next general election following the expiration of one year from the date of the occurrence of the vacancy which he was appointed to fill, and at the general election next occurring every ten years thereafter.

(e) The approval or rejection by the registered voters of a judge as provided for in subsections (c) and (d) shall be a vote for the judge's retention in office for a term of ten years or his removal. The judge's name shall be on the appropriate ballot, without opposition, and the voters shall vote yes or no for his retention in office. If the voters reject the retention in office of a judge, or if the vote is tied, the office becomes vacant ten days after certification of the election returns.

(f) An appellate court judge shall retire when he attains his seventieth birthday.

(g) A member of the General Assembly who is otherwise qualified for appointment to judicial office is not disqualified by reason of his membership in a General Assembly which proposed or enacted any constitutional amendment or statute affecting the method of selection. Continuance in office, or retirement or removal of a judge, the creation or abolition of a court, an increase or decrease in the number of judges of any court, or an increase or decrease in the salary, pension or other allowances of any judge.

SEC. 6.[101] All Judges shall, by virtue of their offices, be Conservators of the Peace throughout the State; and no fees, or perquisites, commission, or reward of any kind shall be allowed to any Judge in this State, besides his annual salary, for the discharge of any Judicial duty.

SEC. 7. No Judge shall sit in any case wherein he may be interested, or where either of the parties may be connected with him, by affinity or consanguinity, within such degrees as now are, or may hereafter be prescribed by Law, or where he shall have been of counsel in the case.

SEC. 8.[102] (a) The parties to any cause may submit the same to the Court for determination without the aid of a jury.

(b) In all cases of presentments or indictments for offenses that are punishable by death, on suggestion in writing under oath of either of the parties to the proceedings that the party cannot have a fair and impartial trial in the court in which the proceedings may be pending, the court shall order and direct the record of proceedings in the presentment or indictment to be transmitted to some other court having jurisdiction in such case for trial.

(c) In all other cases of presentment or indictment, and in all suits or actions at law or issues from the Orphans' Court pending in any of the courts of law in this State which have jurisdiction over the cause or case, in addition to the suggestion in writing of either of the parties to the cause or case that the party cannot have a fair and impartial trial in the court in which the cause or case may be pending, it shall be necessary for the party making the suggestion to make it satisfactorily appear to the court that the suggestion is true, or that there is reasonable ground for the same; and thereupon the court shall order and direct the record of the proceedings in the cause or case to be transmitted to some other court, having jurisdiction in the cause or case, for trial. The right of removal also shall exist on suggestion in a cause or case in which all the judges of the court may be disqualified under the provisions of this Constitution to sit. The court to which the record of proceedings in such suit or action, issue, presentment or indictment is transmitted, shall hear and determine that cause or

[99] Amended by Chapter 417, Acts of 1880, ratified Nov. 8, 1881; Chapter 772, Acts of 1943, ratified Nov. 7, 1944; Chapter 703, Acts of 1945, ratified Nov. 5, 1946; Chapter 551, Acts of 1975, ratified Nov. 2, 1976; Chapter 523, Acts of 1980, ratified Nov. 4, 1980.
[100] Added by Chapter 551, Acts of 1975, ratified Nov. 2, 1976.

[101] Amended by Chapter 681, Acts of 1977, ratified Nov. 7, 1978.
[102] Amended by Chapter 364, Acts of 1874, ratified Nov. 2, 1875, and by Chapter 524, Acts of 1980, ratified Nov. 4, 1980.

case in the same manner as if it had been originally instituted in that court. The General Assembly shall modify the existing law as may be necessary to regulate and give force to this provision.

SEC. 9.[103] The Judge, or Judges of any Court, may appoint such officers for their respective Courts as may be found necessary. The General Assembly may provide, by Law, for compensation for all such officers; and the said Judge or Judges shall, from time to time, investigate the expenses, costs and charges of their respective courts, with a view to a change or reduction thereof, and report the result of such investigation to the General Assembly for its action.

SEC. 10. The Clerks of the several Courts, created, or continued by this Constitution, shall have charge and custody of the records and other papers, shall perform all the duties, and be allowed the fees, which appertain to their several offices, as the same now are, or may hereafter be regulated by Law. And the office and business of said Clerks, in all their departments, shall be subject to the visitorial power of the Judges of their respective Courts, who shall exercise the same, from time to time, so as to insure the faithful performance of the duties of said officers; and it shall be the duty of the Judges of said Courts respectively, to make, from time to time, such rules and regulations as may be necessary and proper for the government of said Clerks, and for the performance of the duties of their offices, which shall have the force of Law until repealed or modified by the General Assembly.

SEC. 11.[104] The election for Judges, hereinbefore provided, and all elections for Clerks, Registers of Wills, and other officers, provided in this Constitution, except State's Attorneys, shall be certified, and the returns made, by the Clerks of the Circuit Courts of the Counties, and the Clerk of the Superior Court of Baltimore City, respectively, to the Governor, who shall issue commissions to the different persons for the offices to which they shall have been, respectively, elected; and in all such elections for offices other than judges of an appellate court, the person having the greatest number of votes, shall be declared to be elected.

SEC. 12.[105] In case of any contested election for Judges, Clerks of the Courts of Law, and Registers of Wills, the Governor shall send the returns to the House of Delegates, which shall judge of the election and qualification of the candidates at such election; and if the judgment shall be against the one who has been returned elected, or the one who has been commissioned by the Governor, the House of Delegates shall order a new election within thirty days.

SEC. 13. All Public Commissions and Grants shall run thus: "The State of Maryland, etc.," and shall be signed by the Governor, with the Seal of the State annexed; all writs and process shall run in the same style, and be tested, sealed and signed, as heretofore, or as may hereafter be, provided by Law; and all indictments shall conclude, "against the peace, government and dignity of the State."

SEC. 13A.[106] Vacant.

Part II—Courts of Appeal.

SEC. 14.[107] The Court of Appeals shall be composed of seven judges, one from the First Appellate Judicial Circuit consisting of Cecil, Kent, Queen Anne's, Caroline, Talbot, Dorchester, Wicomico, Worcester and Somerset counties; one from the Second

Appellate Judicial Circuit consisting of Baltimore and Harford counties; one from the Third Appellate Judicial Circuit, consisting of Allegany, Frederick, Garrett, Montgomery and Washington counties; one from the Fourth Appellate Judicial Circuit, consisting of Prince George's, Calvert, Charles and St. Mary's counties; one from the Fifth Appellate Judicial Circuit, consisting of Anne Arundel, Carroll and Howard counties; and two from the Sixth Appellate Judicial Circuit, consisting of Baltimore City. The Judges of the Court of Appeals shall be residents of their respective Appellate Judicial Circuits. The term of each Judge of the Court of Appeals shall begin on the date of his qualification. One of the Judges of the Court of Appeals shall be designated by the Governor as the Chief Judge. The jurisdiction of the Court of Appeals shall be co-extensive with the limits of the State and such as now is or may hereafter be prescribed by law. It shall hold its sessions in the City of Annapolis at such time or times as it shall from time to time by rule prescribe. Its session or sessions shall continue not less than ten months in each year, if the business before it shall so require, and it shall be competent for the judges temporarily to transfer their sittings elsewhere upon sufficient cause. The salary of each Judge of the Court of Appeals shall be that now or hereafter prescribed by the General Assembly and shall not be diminished during his continuance in office. Five of the judges shall constitute a quorum, and five judges shall sit in each case unless the Court shall direct that an additional judge or judges sit for any case. The concurrence of a majority of those sitting shall be sufficient for the decision of any cause, and an equal division of those sitting in a case has the effect of affirming the decision appealed from if there is no application for reargument as hereinafter provided. In any case where there is an equal division or a three to two division of the Court a reargument before the full Court of seven judges shall be granted to the losing party upon application as a matter of right.

SEC. 14A.[108] The General Assembly may by law create such intermediate courts of appeal as may be necessary. The General Assembly may prescribe the intermediate appellate jurisdiction of these courts of appeal, and all other powers necessary for the operation of such courts.

SEC. 14B.[109] No member of the General Assembly at which the addition of Section 14A was proposed, if otherwise qualified, shall be ineligible for appointment or election as a judge of any intermediate court of appeal, established by law by the General Assembly pursuant to said Section 14A, by reason of his membership in such General Assembly.

SEC. 15.[110] Any Judge of the Court of Appeals or of an intermediate court of appeal who heard the cause below either as a trial Judge or as a Judge of any intermediate court of appeal as the case may be, shall not participate in the decision. In every case an opinion, in writing, shall be filed within three months after the argument or submission of the cause; and the judgment of the Court of Appeals shall be final and conclusive.

SEC. 16.[111] Provision shall be made by Law for publishing Reports of all causes, argued and determined in the Court of Appeals and in the intermediate courts of appeal, which the Judges thereof, respectively, shall designate as proper for publication.

SEC. 17.[112] There shall be a Clerk of the Court of Appeals, who shall be appointed by and shall hold his office at the pleasure of said Court of Appeals.

---

[103] Amended by Chapter 523, Acts of 1980, ratified Nov. 4, 1980.
[104] Amended by Chapter 551, Acts of 1975, ratified Nov. 2, 1976.
[105] Amended by Chapter 681, Acts of 1977, ratified Nov. 7, 1978.
[106] Added by Chapter 796, Acts of 1943, ratified Nov. 7, 1944. Repealed by Chapter 681, Acts of 1977, ratified Nov. 7, 1978.
[107] Amended by Chapter 772, Acts of 1943, ratified Nov. 7, 1944; Chapter 99, Acts of 1956, ratified Nov. 6, 1956; Chapter 11, Acts of 1960, ratified Nov. 8, 1960; Chapter 551, Acts of 1976, ratified Nov. 2, 1976; Chapter 681, Acts of 1977, ratified Nov. 7, 1978.

[108] Added by Chapter 10, Acts of 1966, ratified Nov. 8, 1966.
[109] Added by Chapter 10, Acts of 1966, ratified Nov. 8, 1966.
[110] Amended by Chapter 99, Acts of 1956, ratified Nov. 6, 1956; Chapter 10, Acts of 1966, ratified Nov. 8, 1966.
[111] Amended by Chapter 10, Acts of 1966, ratified Nov. 8, 1966.
[112] Amended by Chapter 40, Acts of 1939, ratified Nov. 5, 1940; Chapter 99, Acts of 1956, ratified Nov. 6, 1956.

SEC. 18.[113] (a) The Court of Appeals from time to time shall adopt rules and regulations concerning the practice and procedure in and the administration of the appellate courts and in the other courts of this State, which shall have the force of law until rescinded, changed or modified by the Court of Appeals or otherwise by law. The power of courts other than the Court of Appeals to make rules of practice and procedure, or administrative rules, shall be subject to the rules and regulations adopted by the Court of Appeals or otherwise by law.

(b)[114] The Chief Judge of the Court of Appeals shall be the administrative head of the judicial system of the State. He shall from time to time require, from each of the judges of the Circuit Courts, of the District Court and of any intermediate courts of appeal, reports as to the judicial work and business of each of the judges and their respective courts. He may, in case of a vacancy, or of the illness, disqualification or other absence of a judge or for the purpose of relieving an accumulation of business in any court assign any judge except a judge of the Orphans' Court to sit temporarily in any court except an Orphans' Court. Any judge assigned by the Chief Judge of the Court of Appeals pursuant to this section has all the power and authority pertaining to a judge of the court to which he is so assigned; and his power and authority shall continue with respect to all cases (including any motion, or other matters incidental thereto) which may come before him by virtue of such assignment until his action thereon shall be completed. In the absence of the Chief Judge of the Court of Appeals the provisions of this section shall be applicable to the senior judge present in the Court of Appeals. The powers of the Chief Judge set forth in this section shall be subject to any rule and regulation adopted by the Court of Appeals.

SEC. 18A.[115] Vacant.

Part IIA—Interim Provisions.

SEC. 18B.[116] (a) For the purpose of implementing the amendments to this article, dealing with the selection and tenure of appellate court judges, the following provisions shall govern.

(b) Each judge of an appellate court who is in office for an elected term on the effective date of these amendments, unless he dies, resigns, retires, or is otherwise lawfully removed, shall continue in office until the general election next after the end of his elected term, or until his seventieth birthday, whichever first occurs. His continuance in office is then subject to the provisions of section 5A (c) and (d) of this article, applicable to judges of that court, but in no event shall any judge continue in office after his seventieth birthday.

(c) Each judge of a court specified in subsection (b) who is in office on the effective date of these amendments, but who has not been elected to that office by the voters, shall, within fifteen days after the effective date of these amendments, be reappointed to that office. His continuance in office is then subject to the provisions of section 5A (c) and (d) of this article, applicable to judges of that court, but in no event shall any judge continue in office after his seventieth birthday.

Part III—Circuit Courts.

SEC. 19.[117] The State shall be divided into eight Judicial Circuits, in manner following, viz.: The Counties of Worcester, Wicomico, Somerset, and Dorchester, shall constitute the First Circuit; the Counties of Caroline, Talbot, Queen Anne's, Kent and Cecil, the Second; the Counties of Baltimore and Harford, the Third; the Counties of Allegany, Garrett, and Washington, the Fourth; the Counties of Carroll, Howard and Anne Arundel, the Fifth; the Counties of Montgomery and Frederick, the Sixth; the Counties of Prince George's, Charles, Calvert, and St. Mary's, the Seventh; and Baltimore City, the Eighth.

SEC. 20.[118] (a) There shall be a Circuit Court for each county and for Baltimore City. The Circuit Courts shall have and exercise, in the respective counties, and Baltimore City, all the power, authority and jurisdiction, original and appellate, which the Circuit Courts of the counties exercised on the effective date of these amendments, and the greater or lesser jurisdiction hereafter prescribed by law.

(b) The judges of the Circuit Courts for Montgomery and Harford counties shall each, alternately and in rotation and on schedules to be established by those judges, sit as an Orphans' Court for their County, and shall have and exercise all the power, authority and jurisdiction which the present Orphans' Courts now have and exercise, or which may hereafter be provided by law.

SEC. 21.[119] (a) Subject to the provisions of subsection (b) the General Assembly shall determine by law the number of judges of the circuit court in each county and circuit. These judges shall be selected in accordance with Sections 3 and 5 of this Article.

(b) There shall be at least four circuit court judges resident in each circuit, and at least one circuit court judge shall be resident in each county. There shall be at least two such judges resident in Anne Arundel County, at least three resident in Baltimore County, at least four resident in Prince George's County, and at least five resident in Montgomery County.

(c) The senior judge in length of service in each circuit shall be the chief judge of the circuit. The other judges shall be associate judges.

(d) Except as otherwise provided by law, one judge shall constitute a quorum for the transaction of any business.

(e) The terms of the circuit courts shall be determined by law.

(f) A person is not ineligible for appointment or election as a judge because he was a member of the General Assembly at a time when the number or salary of judges were increased or decreased.

SEC. 21A.[120] If the amendments to sections 3 and 21 of Article IV proposed by House Bill 972, Senate Bill 390 (1976) and the amendments to those sections proposed by House Bill 1048 (1976) are ratified by the voters at the election in Nov. 1976, the amendments to those sections proposed in House Bill 972, Senate Bill 390 (1976) shall take effect.

SEC. 22.[121] Where any Term is held, or trial conducted by less

---

[113] Amended by Chapter 772, Acts of 1943, ratified Nov. 7, 1944; Chapter 10, Acts of 1966, ratified Nov. 8, 1966; Chapter 789, Acts of 1969, ratified Nov. 3, 1970; Chapter 681, Acts of 1977, ratified Nov. 7, 1978; Chapter 523, Acts of 1980, ratified Nov. 4, 1980.

[114] Amended by Chapter 681, Acts of 1977, ratified Nov. 7, 1978; Chapter 523, Acts of 1980, ratified Nov. 4, 1980.

[115] Renumbered as sec. 18 by Chapter 681, Acts of 1977, ratified Nov. 7, 1978.

[116] Added by Chapter 551, Acts of 1975, ratified Nov. 2, 1976.

[117] Amended by Chapter 99, Acts of 1956, ratified Nov. 6, 1956.

[118] Amended by Chapter 744, Acts of 1963, ratified Nov. 3, 1964; Chapter 374, Acts of 1972, ratified Nov. 7, 1972; Chapter 681, Acts of 1977, ratified Nov. 7, 1978; Chapter 523, Acts of 1980, ratified Nov. 4, 1980.

[119] Amended by Chapter 515, Acts of 1912, ratified Nov. 4, 1913; Chapter 426, Acts of 1935, ratified Nov. 3, 1936; Chapter 494, Acts of 1937, ratified Nov. 8, 1938; Chapter 200, Acts of 1939, ratified Nov. 5, 1940; Chapter 494, Acts of 1941, ratified Nov. 3, 1942; Chapter 772, Acts of 1943, ratified Nov. 7, 1944; Chapter 607, Acts of 1953, ratified Nov. 2, 1954; Chapters 65 and 68, Acts of 1954, ratified Nov. 2, 1954; Chapters 642 and 761, Acts of 1959, ratified Nov. 8, 1960; Chapter 372, Acts of 1966, ratified Nov. 8, 1966; Chapter 542, Acts of 1976, ratified Nov. 2, 1976.

[120] Added by Chapter 542, Acts of 1976, ratified Nov. 2, 1976.

[121] Amended by Chapter 681, Acts of 1977, ratified Nov. 7, 1978.

than the whole number of said Circuit Judges, upon the decision or determination of any point, or question, by the Court, it shall be competent to the party, against whom the ruling or decision is made, upon motion, to have the point, or question reserved for the consideration of the three Judges of the Circuit, who shall constitute a court in *banc* for such purpose; and the motion for such reservation shall be entered of record, during the sitting, at which such decision may be made; and the several Circuit Courts shall regulate, by rules, the mode and manner of presenting such points, or questions to the court in *banc,* and the decision of the said Court in *banc* shall be the effective decision in the premises, and conclusive, as against the party, at whose motion said points, or questions were reserved; but such decision in *banc* shall not preclude the right of Appeal, or writ of error to the adverse party, in those cases, civil or criminal, in which appeal, or writ of error to the Court of Appeals may be allowed by Law. The right of having questions reserved shall not, however, apply to trials of Appeals from judgments of the District Court, nor to criminal cases below the grade of felony, except when the punishment is confinement in the Penitentiary; and this Section shall be subject to such provisions as may hereafter be made by Law.

SEC. 23.[122] The Judges of the respective Circuit Courts of this State shall render their decisions, in all cases argued before them, or submitted for their judgment, within two months after the same shall have been so argued or submitted.

SEC. 24.[123] The salary of each Chief Judge and of each Associate Judge of the Circuit Court shall not be diminished during his continuance in office.

SEC. 25.[124] There shall be a Clerk of the Circuit Court for each County and Baltimore City, who shall be elected by a plurality of the qualified voters of said County or City, and shall hold this office for four years from the time of his election, and until his successor is elected and qualified, and be re-eligible, subject to be removed for wilful neglect of duty or other misdemeanor in office, on conviction in a Court of Law. In case of a vacancy in the office of Clerk of a Circuit Court, the Judges of that Court may fill the vacancy until the general election for Delegates to the General Assembly, to be held next thereafter, when a successor shall be elected for the term of four years.

SEC. 26.[125] The Clerks shall appoint, subject to the confirmation of the Judges of their respective Courts, as many deputies under them, as the Judges shall deem necessary, to perform, together with themselves, the duties of the office, who shall be removable by the Judges for incompetency, or neglect of duty, and whose compensation shall be determined by law. In Washington County, all deputy clerks and other employees of the office of the clerk shall be appointed and be removable according to the merit system procedure established by law for these deputies and clerks. All deputy clerks and other employees of the office of the Clerk of the Criminal Court of Baltimore City, excepting the Clerks, shall be selected pursuant to and be removable according to a procedure established by law for these deputies and clerks.

Part IV—Courts of Baltimore City

SEC. 27.[126] Vacant.

SEC. 28.[127] Vacant.

SEC. 29.[128] Vacant.

SEC. 30.[129] Vacant.

SEC. 31.[130] Vacant.

SEC. 31A.[131] Vacant.

SEC. 32.[132] Vacant.

SEC. 33.[133] Vacant.

SEC. 34.[134] Vacant.

SEC. 35.[135] Vacant.

SEC. 36.[136] Vacant.

SEC. 37.[137] Vacant.

SEC. 38.[138] Vacant.

SEC. 39.[139] Vacant.

Part V—Orphans' Court.

SEC. 40.[140] The qualified voters of the City of Baltimore, and of the several Counties, except Montgomery County and Harford County, shall elect three Judges of the Orphans' Courts of City and Counties, respectively, who shall be citizens of the State and residents for the twelve months preceding, in the City or County for which they may be elected. They shall have all the powers now vested in the Orphans' Courts of the State, subject to such changes as the Legislature may prescribe. Each of the Judges shall be paid such compensation as may be regulated by Law, to be paid by the City or Counties, respectively. In case of a vacancy in the office of Judge of the Orphans' Court, the Governor shall appoint, subject to confirmation or rejection by the Senate, some suitable person to fill the vacancy for the residue of the term.

SEC. 41.[141] There shall be a Register of Wills in each county of the State, and the City of Baltimore, to be elected by the legal and qualified voters of said counties and city, respectively, who shall

---

[122] Amended by Chapter 523, Acts of 1980, ratified Nov. 4, 1980.
[123] Amended by Chapter 99, Acts of 1956, ratified Nov. 6, 1956.
[124] Amended by Chapter 99, Acts of 1956, ratified Nov. 6, 1956; Chapter 523, Acts of 1980, ratified Nov. 4, 1980.
[125] Amended by Chapter 376, Acts of 1972, ratified Nov. 7, 1972; Chapter 889, Acts of 1974, ratified Nov. 5, 1974; Chapter 523, Acts of 1980, ratified Nov. 4, 1980.
[126] Repealed by Chapter 523, Acts of 1980, ratified Nov. 4, 1980.
[127] Amended by Chapter 889, Acts of 1974, ratified Nov. 5, 1974. Repealed by Chapter 523, Acts of 1980, ratified Nov. 4, 1980.

[128] Amended by Chapter 889, Acts of 1974, ratified Nov. 5, 1974. Repealed by Chapter 523, Acts of 1980, ratified Nov. 4, 1980.
[129] Amended by Chapter 889, Acts of 1974, ratified Nov. 5, 1974. Repealed by Chapter 523, Acts of 1980, ratified Nov. 4, 1980.
[130] Amended by Chapter 889, Acts of 1974, ratified Nov. 5, 1974. Repealed by Chapter 523, Acts of 1980, ratified Nov. 4, 1980.
[131] Added by Chapter 116, Acts of 1924, ratified Nov. 2, 1926. Repealed by Chapter 617, Acts of 1968, ratified Nov. 5, 1968.
[132] Amended by Chapter 889, Acts of 1974, ratified Nov. 5, 1974. Repealed by Chapter 523, Acts of 1980, ratified Nov. 4, 1980.
[133] Amended by Chapter 889, Acts of 1974, ratified Nov. 5, 1974. Repealed by Chapter 523, Acts of 1980, ratified Nov. 4, 1980.
[134] Amended by Chapter 889, Acts of 1974, ratified Nov. 5, 1974. Repealed by Chapter 523, Acts of 1980, ratified Nov. 4, 1980.
[135] Amended by Chapter 889, Acts of 1974, ratified Nov. 5, 1974. Repealed by Chapter 523, Acts of 1980, ratified Nov. 4, 1980.
[136] Repealed by Chapter 681, Acts of 1977, ratified Nov. 7, 1978.
[137] Amended by Chapter 99, Acts of 1956, ratified Nov. 6, 1956; Chapter 889, Acts of 1974, ratified Nov. 5, 1974. Repealed by Chapter 523, Acts of 1980, ratified Nov. 4, 1980.
[138] Amended by Chapter 889, Acts of 1974, Nov. 5, 1974. Repealed by Chapter 523, Acts of 1980, ratified Nov. 4, 1980.
[139] Added by Chapter 313, Acts of 1892, ratified Nov. 7, 1893. Amended by Chapter 889, Acts of 1974, ratified Nov. 5, 1974. Repealed by Chapter 523, Acts of 1980, ratified Nov. 4, 1980.
[140] Amended by Chapters 99 and 124, Acts of 1956, ratified Nov. 6, 1956; Chapter 744, Acts of 1963, ratified Nov. 3, 1964; Chapter 374, Acts of 1972, ratified Nov. 7, 1972; Chapter 681, Acts of 1977, ratified Nov. 7, 1978.
[141] Amended by Chapter 99, Acts of 1956, ratified Nov. 6, 1956.

hold his office for four years from the time of his election and until his successor is elected and qualified; he shall be re-eligible, and subject at all times to removal for willful neglect of duty, or misdemeanor in office in the same manner that the Clerks of the Courts are removable. In the event of any vacancy in the office of the Register of Wills, said vacancy shall be filled by the Judges of the Orphans' Court, in which such vacancy occurs, until the next general election for Delegates to the General Assembly when a Register shall be elected to serve for four years thereafter.

Part VI—District Court.

SEC. 41A.[142] The District Court shall have the original jurisdiction prescribed by law. Jurisdiction of the District Court shall be uniform throughout the State; except that in Montgomery County and other counties and the City of Baltimore, the Court may have such jurisdiction over juvenile causes as is provided by law.

SEC. 41B.[143] The District Court shall consist of the number of judges prescribed by law. The State shall be divided by law into districts. Each district shall consist of one county or two or more entire and adjoining counties. The number of judges shall be allocated among the districts by law, and there shall be at least one District Court judge resident in each district. In any district containing more than one county, there shall be at least one District Court judge resident in each county in the district. Functional divisions of the District Court may be established in any district.

SEC. 41C.[144] Each District Court judge shall devote full time to his judicial duties, shall have the qualifications prescribed by Section 2 of this Article, and shall be a resident of the district in which he holds office. The number of judges for any district may be increased or decreased by the General Assembly from time to time, subject to the requirements of Section 41B of this Article, and any vacancy so created shall be filled as provided in Section 41D of this Article.

SEC. 41D.[145] The Governor, by and with the advice and consent of the Senate, shall appoint each judge of the District Court whenever for any reason a vacancy shall exist in the office. All hearings, deliberations, and debate on the confirmation of appointees of the Governor shall be public, and no hearings, deliberations or debate thereon shall be conducted by the Senate or any committee or subcommittee thereof in secret or executive session. Confirmation by the Senate shall be made upon a majority vote of all members of the Senate. A judge appointed by the Governor may take office upon qualification and before confirmation by the Senate, but shall cease to hold office at the close of the regular annual session of the General Assembly next following his appointment or during which he shall have been appointed by the Governor, if the Senate shall not have confirmed his appointment before then. Each judge appointed by the Governor and confirmed by the Senate shall hold the office for a term of ten years or until he shall have attained the age of seventy years whichever may first occur. If the ten year term of a judge shall expire before that judge shall have attained the age of

seventy years, that judge shall be reappointed by the Governor, with the Senate's consent, for another ten year term or until he shall have attained the age of seventy years, whichever may first occur. To the extent inconsistent herewith, the provisions of Section 3 and 5 of this Article shall not apply to judges of the District Court.

SEC. 41E. The Chief Judge of the Court of Appeals shall designate one judge of the District Court as Chief Judge of that Court, to serve as Chief Judge at his pleasure. The Chief Judge of the District Court may assign administrative duties to other judges of the District Court and shall perform such other duties in the administration of the District Court as may be prescribed by rule or by law.

SEC. 41F. The Chief Judge of the District Court shall appoint, to serve at his pleasure, a Chief Clerk of that Court. He shall also appoint, to serve at his pleasure, and upon the recommendation of the administrative judge of the district, a chief administrative clerk for each district. The chief clerk shall perform such duties in the administration of the District Court as may be assigned him by the chief judge or as may be prescribed by rule or by law. Each chief administrative clerk shall perform such duties in the administration of the District Court as may be assigned him by the administrative judge of his district or as may be prescribed by rule of law. There shall be in each County a clerk of the District Court whose appointment, term, and compensation shall be prescribed by law. The Chief Judge of the District Court, upon recommendation of the respective administrative judges, shall appoint such deputy clerks, constables, and other officers of the District Court as may be necessary. It shall be the duty of the General Assembly to prescribe by law a fixed compensation for all such officers.

SEC. 41G. There shall be district court commissioners in the number and with the qualifications and compensation prescribed by law. Commissioners in a district shall be appointed by and serve at the pleasure of the Administrative Judge of the district, subject to the approval of the Chief Judge of the District Court. Commissioners may exercise power only with respect to warrants of arrest, or bail or collateral or other terms of pre-trial release pending hearing, or incarceration pending hearing, and then only as prescribed by law or by rule.

SEC. 41H. The salary of a judge of the District Court shall not be reduced during his continuance in office.

SEC. 41-I.[146] For the purpose of implementing the amendments to Articles IV, XV and XVII of this Constitution, establishing the District Court, the following provisions shall govern.

(a) The provisions of Section 41D of this Article shall govern initial vacancies in the office of judge of the District Court. Each full-time judge of the People's Court of Baltimore City, the Municipal Court of Baltimore City, and of the People's Courts of Anne Arundel, Montgomery, Prince George's, Wicomico Counties and Baltimore County who is in office on the effective date of these amendments shall continue in office as a judge of the District Court in his district and county of residence (or in Baltimore City) for the remainder of the term for which he was elected or appointed, and if his term expires prior to January 1, 1971, such judge shall be re-appointed by the Governor, if the Senate consents, in accordance with the provisions of Section 41D of this Article, subject to the Provisions of the Constitution respecting age, removal and retirement; provided that the term of any such judge of a People's Court who would be ineligible for appointment as a judge of the District Court under this Article shall expire on the effective date of these amendments. Thereafter, retention of any judge who is retained in office pursuant to the preceding provisions of this subsection shall be pursuant to Section 41D of this Article. No People's Court judge, judge of the

---

[142] Referring to the People's Courts, this section originally was added by Chapter 163, Acts of 1939, ratified Nov. 5, 1940, and amended by Chapter 575, Acts of 1959, ratified Nov. 8, 1960. It was repealed and a new section concerning the District Court was enacted by Chapter 789, Acts of 1969, ratified Nov. 3, 1970, and amended by Chapter 544, Acts of 1976, ratified Nov. 2, 1976.

[143] Added by Chapter 163, Acts of 1939, ratified Nov. 5, 1940. Repealed and a new section enacted by Chapter 789, Acts of 1969, ratified Nov. 3, 1970.

[144] Added by Chapter 373, Acts of 1959, ratified Nov. 8, 1960. Repealed and a new section enacted by Chapter 789, Acts of 1969, ratified Nov. 3, 1970.

[145] Sections 41D through 41I added by Chapter 789, Acts of 1969, ratified Nov. 3, 1970.

[146] Amended by Chapter 681, Acts of 1977, ratified Nov. 7, 1978.

Housing Court of Baltimore County, or Justice of the Peace shall be appointed or elected or exercise any power or jurisdiction.

(b) Each full-time clerk of a justice of the peace designated as trial magistrate of a People's Court, of the Municipal Court of Baltimore City, and the chief constable of the People's Court of Baltimore City who is in office on the day before the first Monday in July, 1970, shall become a deputy clerk of the District Court on the first Monday in July 1970. The taking effect of the aforegoing amendments shall not of itself affect the tenure, term, status, retirement, or compensation of any person then holding public office, position, or employment in this State, except as provided in the amendments.

(c) All statutory references to justices of the peace designated as trial magistrates, to People's Courts, to the Municipal Court of Baltimore City or to the Housing Court of Baltimore County, shall be deemed to refer to the District Court in the appropriate district, county or Baltimore City, to the extent not inconsistent with this Constitution.

(d) No member of the General Assembly at which these amendments were proposed, or at which the number of or salary of any such judges may have been increased or decreased by the General Assembly from time to time, if otherwise qualified, is ineligible for appointment or election as a judge of the District Court by reason of his membership in the General Assembly.

SEC. 42.[147] Vacant.

SEC. 43.[148] Vacant.

Part VII—Sheriffs.

SEC. 44.[149] There shall be elected in each county and in Baltimore City one person, resident in said county or City, above the age of twenty-five years and for at least five years preceding his election a citizen of the State, to the office of Sheriff. He shall hold office for four years, until his successor is duly elected and qualified, give such bond, exercise such powers and perform such duties as now are or may hereafter be fixed by law.

In case of vacancy by death, resignation, refusal to serve, or neglect to qualify or give bond, or by disqualification or removal from the County or City, the Governor shall appoint a person to be Sheriff for the remainder of the official term.

The Sheriff in each county and in Baltimore City shall receive such salary or compensation and such expenses necessary to the conduct of his office as may be fixed by law. All fees collected by the Sheriff shall be accounted for and paid to the Treasury of the several counties and of Baltimore City, respectively.

SEC. 45.[150] Notaries Public may be appointed for each county and the city of Baltimore, in the manner, for the purpose, and with the powers now fixed, or which may hereafter be prescribed by Law.

ARTICLE V.

ATTORNEY-GENERAL AND STATE'S ATTORNEYS.

Attorney-General.

SEC. 1.[151] There shall be an Attorney-General elected by the qualified voters of the State, on general ticket, on the Tuesday next after the first Monday in the month of November, nineteen hundred and fifty-eight, and on the same day, in every fourth year thereafter, who shall hold his office for four years from the time of his election and qualification, and until his successor is elected and qualified, and shall be re-eligible thereto, and shall be subject to removal for incompetency, willful neglect of duty or misdemeanor in office, on conviction in a Court of Law.

SEC. 2. All elections for Attorney-General shall be certified to, and returns made thereof by the Clerks of the Circuit Courts for the several counties, and the Clerk of the Superior Court of Baltimore City, to the Governor of the State, whose duty it shall be to decide on the election and qualification of the person returned; and in case of a tie between two or more persons, to designate which of said persons shall qualify as Attorney-General, and to administer the oath of office to the person elected.

SEC. 3.[152] (a) The Attorney General shall:

(1) Prosecute and defend on the part of the State all cases pending in the Appellate Courts of the State, in the Supreme Court of the United States or the inferior Federal Courts, by or against the State, or in which the State may be interested, except those criminal appeals otherwise prescribed by the General Assembly.

(2) Investigate, commence, and prosecute or defend any civil or criminal suit or action or category of such suits or actions in any of the Federal Courts or in any Court of this State, or before administrative agencies and quasi legislative bodies, on the part of the State or in which the State may be interested, which the General Assembly by law or joint resolution, or the Governor, shall have directed or shall direct to be investigated, commenced and prosecuted or defended.

(3) When required by the General Assembly by law or joint resolution, or by the Governor, aid any State's Attorney or other authorized prosecuting officer in investigating, commencing, and prosecuting any criminal suit or action or category of such suits or actions brought by the State in any Court of this State.

(4) Give his opinion in writing whenever required by the General Assembly or either branch thereof, the Governor, the Comptroller, the Treasurer or any State's Attorney on any legal matter or subject.

(b) The Attorney General shall have and perform any other duties and possess any other powers, and appoint the number of deputies or assistants, as the General Assembly from time to time may prescribe by law.

(c) The Attorney General shall receive for his services the annual salary as the General Assembly from time to time may prescribe by law, but he may not receive any fees, perquisites or rewards whatever, in addition to his salary, for the performance of any official duty.

(d) The Governor may not employ any additional counsel, in any case whatever, unless authorized by the General Assembly.

SEC. 4. No person shall be eligible to the office of Attorney-General, who is not a citizen of this State, and a qualified voter therein, and has not resided and practiced Law in this State for at least ten years.

SEC. 5.[153] In case of vacancy in the office of Attorney-General, occasioned by death, resignation, removal from the State, or from office, or other disqualification, the Governor shall appoint a person to fill the vacancy for the residue of the term.

---

[147] Repealed by Chapter 789, Acts of 1969, ratified Nov. 3, 1970.

[148] Repealed by Chapter 789, Acts of 1969, ratified Nov. 3, 1970.

[149] Amended by Chapter 845, Acts of 1914, ratified Nov. 3, 1914; Chapter 786, Acts of 1945, ratified Nov. 5, 1946; Chapter 55, Acts of 1953, ratified Nov. 2, 1954; Chapter 681, Acts of 1977, ratified Nov. 7, 1978.

[150] Amended by Chapter 681, Acts of 1977, ratified Nov. 7, 1978.

[151] Amended by Chapter 99, Acts of 1956, ratified Nov. 6, 1956.

[152] Amended by Chapter 663, Acts of 1912, ratified Nov. 4, 1913; Chapter 10, Acts of 1966, ratified Nov. 8, 1966; Chapter 545, Acts of 1976, ratified Nov. 2, 1976.

[153] Amended by Chapter 681, Acts of 1977, ratified Nov. 7, 1978.

SEC. 6.[154] It shall be the duty of the Clerk of the Court of Appeals and the Clerks of any intermediate Courts of Appeal, respectively, whenever a case shall be brought into said Courts, in which the State is a party or has interest, immediately to notify the Attorney-General thereof.

The State's Attorneys.

SEC. 7.[155] There shall be an Attorney for the State in each county and the City of Baltimore, to be styled "The State's Attorney", who shall be elected by the voters thereof, respectively, and shall hold his office for four years from the first Monday in January next ensuing his election, and until his successor shall be elected and qualified; and shall be re-eligible thereto, and be subject to removal therefrom, for incompetency, willful neglect of duty, or misdemeanor in office, on conviction in a Court of Law, or by a vote of two-thirds of the Senate, on the recommendation of the Attorney-General.

SEC. 8. All elections for the State's Attorney shall be certified to, and Returns made thereof, by the Clerks of the said Counties and City, to the Judges thereof, having criminal jurisdiction, respectively, whose duty it shall be to decide upon the elections and qualifications of the Persons returned; and, in case of a tie between two or more persons, to designate which of said persons shall qualify as State's Attorney, and to administer the oaths of office to the Person elected.

SEC. 9.[156] The State's Attorney shall perform such duties and receive such salary as shall be prescribed by the General Assembly. If any State's Attorney shall receive any other fee or reward than such as is or may be allowed by law, he shall, on conviction thereof, be removed from office; provided, that the State's Attorney for Baltimore City shall have the power to appoint a Deputy and such other assistants as the Supreme Bench of Baltimore City may authorize or approve and until otherwise provided by the General Assembly, the said State's Attorney, Deputy and Assistants shall receive the following annual salaries: State's Attorney, seven thousand five hundred dollars; Deputy State's Attorney, five thousand dollars; Assistant State's Attorneys, four thousand dollars each; said salaries, or such salaries as the General Assembly may subsequently provide and such expenses for conducting the office of the State's Attorney as the Supreme Bench of Baltimore City may authorize or approve shall be paid by the Mayor and City Council of Baltimore to the extent that the total of them exceeds the fees of his office, or as the General Assembly shall otherwise provide, and the Mayor and City Council of Baltimore shall not be liable for appearance fees to the State's Attorney.

SEC. 10. No person shall be eligible to the office of State's Attorney, who has not been admitted to practice Law in this State, and who has not resided, for at least two years, in the county, or city, in which he may be elected.

SEC. 11.[157] In case of a vacancy in the office of State's Attorney, or of his removal from the county or city in which he shall have been elected, or on his conviction as herein specified, the Judge or Judges resident in the county or, if there be no resident Judge, the Judge or Judges having jurisdiction in the Circuit Court of the county in which the vacancy occurs, or by

the Supreme Bench of Baltimore City for a vacancy occurring in Baltimore City, shall appoint a person to fill the vacancy for the residue of the term.

SEC. 12.[158] The State's Attorney in each County, and the City of Baltimore, shall have authority to collect, and give receipt, in the name of the State, for such sums of money as may be collected by him, and forthwith make return of and pay over the same to the proper accounting officer. And the State's Attorney of each county, and the City of Baltimore, before he shall enter on the discharge of his duties, and from time to time thereafter, shall give such corporate surety bond as may hereafter be prescribed by Act of the General Assembly.

ARTICLE VI.

TREASURY DEPARTMENT.

SECTION 1.[159] There shall be a Treasury Department, consisting of a Comptroller chosen by the qualified electors of the State, who shall receive such salary as may be fixed by law; and a Treasurer, to be appointed on joint ballot by the two Houses of the Legislature at each regular session in which begins the term of the Governor, who shall receive such salary as may be fixed by law. The terms of office of the Comptroller and Treasurer shall be for four years, and until their successors shall qualify; and neither of the officers shall be allowed, or receive any fees, commissions or perquisites of any kind in addition to his salary for the performance of any duty or services whatsoever. In case of a vacancy in the office of the Comptroller by death or otherwise, the Governor, by and with the advice and consent of the Senate, shall fill such vacancy by appointment, to continue until another election and until the qualification of the successor. In case of a vacancy in the office of the Treasurer by death or otherwise, the Deputy Treasurer shall act as Treasurer until the next regular or extraordinary session of the Legislature following the creation of the vacancy, whereupon the Legislature shall choose a successor to serve for the duration of the unexpired term of office. The Comptroller and the Treasurer shall keep their offices at the seat of government, and shall take such oaths and enter into such bonds for the faithful discharge of their duties as are now or may hereafter be prescribed by law.

SEC. 2.[160] The Comptroller shall have the general superintendence of the fiscal affairs of the State; he shall digest and prepare plans for the improvement and management of the revenue, and for the support of the public credit; prepare and report estimates of the revenue and expenditures of the State; superintend and enforce the prompt collection of all taxes and revenues; adjust and settle, on terms prescribed by law, with delinquent collectors and receivers of taxes and State revenue; preserve all public accounts; and decide on the forms of keeping and stating accounts. He, or such of his deputies as may be authorized to do so by the Legislature, shall grant, under regulations prescribed by Law, all warrants for money to be paid out of the Treasury, in pursuance of appropriations by law, and countersign all checks drawn by the Treasurer upon any bank or banks in which the moneys of the State, may, from time to time, be deposited. He shall prescribe the formalities of the transfer of stock, or other evidence of the State debt, and countersign the same, without which such evidence shall not be valid; he shall make to the General Assembly full reports of all his proceedings, and of the state of the Treasury Department within ten days after the commencement of each session; and perform such other duties as shall be prescribed by law.

---

[154] Amended by Chapter 10, Acts of 1966, ratified Nov. 8, 1966; Chapter 681, Acts of 1977, ratified Nov. 7, 1978.
[155] Amended by Chapter 99, Acts of 1956, ratified Nov. 6, 1956; Chapter 681, Acts of 1977, ratified Nov. 7, 1978.
[156] Amended by Chapter 185, Acts of 1900, ratified Nov. 5, 1901; Chapter 624, Acts of 1912, ratified Nov. 4, 1913; Chapter 177, Acts of 1924, ratified Nov. 4, 1924; Chapter 490, Acts of 1943, ratified Nov. 7, 1944; Chapter 545, Acts of 1976, ratified Nov. 2, 1976.
[157] Amended by Chapter 522, Acts of 1957, ratified Nov. 4, 1958; Chapter 14, Acts of 1959, ratified Nov. 8, 1960; Chapter 681, Acts of 1977, ratified Nov. 7, 1978.

[158] Amended by Chapter 529, Acts of 1945, ratified Nov. 5, 1946.
[159] Amended by Chapter 141, Acts of 1922, ratified Nov. 7, 1922; Chapter 428, Acts of 1966, ratified Nov. 8, 1966; Chapter 640, Acts of 1976, ratified Nov. 2, 1976; Chapter 681, Acts of 1977, ratified Nov. 7, 1978.
[160] Amended by Chapter 632, Acts of 1973, ratified Nov. 5, 1974.

SEC. 3.[161] The Treasurer shall receive the moneys of the State, and, until otherwise prescribed by law, deposit them, as soon as received, to the credit of the State, in such bank or banks as he may, from time to time, with the approval of the Governor, select (the said bank or banks giving security, satisfactory to the Governor, for the safekeeping and forthcoming, when required of said deposits), and he or such of his deputies as may be authorized to do so by the Legislature shall disburse the same for the purposes of the State according to law, upon warrants drawn by the Comptroller, or his duly authorized deputy, and on checks countersigned by the Comptroller, or his duly authorized deputy. The Legislature may prescribe, by law, for the Treasurer to disburse the moneys of the State, by a system other than by the use of checks. The Treasurer or such of his deputies as may be authorized to do so by the Legislature shall take receipts for all moneys paid from the Treasury Department; and receipt for moneys received by him shall be endorsed upon warrants signed, by the Comptroller, or such deputy as may be authorized to do so by law, without which warrants, so signed, no acknowledgment of money received into the Treasury shall be valid; and upon warrants issued by the Comptroller, or his duly authorized deputy, the Treasurer shall make arrangements for the payment of the interest of the public debt, and for the purchase thereof, on account of the sinking fund. Every bond, certificate, or other evidence of the debt of the State shall be signed by the Treasurer, Chief Deputy Treasurer, or a Deputy Treasurer, and countersigned by the Comptroller, Chief Deputy Comptroller, or a Deputy Comptroller; and no new certificate or other evidence intended to replace another shall be issued until the old one shall be delivered to the Treasurer, and authority executed in due form for the transfer of the same filed in his office, and the transfer accordingly made on the books thereof, and the certificate or other evidence cancelled; but the Legislature may make provisions for the loss of certificates, or other evidences of the debt; and may prescribe, by law, the manner in which the Treasurer shall receive and keep the moneys of the State.

SEC. 4. The Treasurer shall render his Accounts, quarterly, to the Comptroller; and shall publish, monthly, in such newspapers as the Governor may direct, an abstract thereof, showing the amount of cash on hand, and the place, or places of deposit thereof; and on the third day of each regular session of the Legislature, he shall submit to the Senate and House of Delegates fair and accurate copies of all Accounts by him, from time to time, rendered and settled with the Comptroller. He shall, at all times, submit to the Comptroller the inspection of the money in his hands, and perform all other duties that shall be prescribed by Law.

SEC. 5. The Comptroller shall qualify, and enter on the duties of his office, on the third Monday of January next succeeding the time of his election, or as soon thereafter as practicable. And the Treasurer shall qualify within one month after his appointment by the Legislature.

SEC. 6.[162] Whenever during the recess of the Legislature charges shall be preferred to the Governor against the Comptroller or Treasurer, for incompetency, malfeasance in office, willful neglect of duty, or misappropriation of the funds of the State, it shall be the duty of the Governor forthwith to notify the party so charged, and fix a day for a hearing of said charges; and if, in the case of the Comptroller, from the evidence taken, under oath, on said hearing before the Governor, the said allegations shall be sustained, it shall be the duty of the Governor to remove the Comptroller and appoint another in his place, who shall hold the office for the unexpired term of the Comptroller so removed. However, if, in the case of the Treasurer, from the evidence taken

under oath in the hearing before the Governor, the allegations are sustained, it is the duty of the Governor to remove the Treasurer, and the Deputy Treasurer shall act as Treasurer until the next regular or extraordinary session of the Legislature following the appointment, whereupon a successor shall be chosen by the Legislature who shall serve for the unexpired term of the Treasurer so removed.

ARTICLE VII.

SUNDRY OFFICERS.

SECTION 1.[163] County Commissioners shall be elected on general ticket of each county by the qualified voters of the several counties of the State; their number in each county, their compensation, and their powers and duties shall be such as now or may be hereafter prescribed by law; and they shall be elected at such times, in such numbers, and for such periods not exceeding four years, as may be prescribed by law.

SEC. 2.[164] Vacant.

SEC. 3.[165] Vacant.

SEC. 4.[166] Vacant.

SEC. 5.[167] Vacant.

SEC. 6.[168] Vacant.

ARTICLE VIII.

EDUCATION.

SECTION 1. The General Assembly, at its First Session after the adoption of this Constitution, shall by Law establish throughout the State a thorough and efficient System of Free Public Schools; and shall provide by taxation, or otherwise, for their maintenance.

SEC. 2. The System of Public Schools, as now constituted, shall remain in force until the end of the said First Session of the General Assembly, and shall then expire; except so far as adopted, or continued by the General Assembly.

SEC. 3. The School Fund of the State shall be kept inviolate, and appropriated only to the purposes of Education.

ARTICLE IX.

MILITIA AND MILITARY AFFAIRS.

SECTION 1. The General Assembly shall make, from time to time, such provisions for organizing, equipping and disciplining the Militia, as the exigency may require, and pass such Laws to promote Volunteer Militia organizations as may afford them effectual encouragement.

SEC. 2. There shall be an Adjutant-General, appointed by the Governor, by and with the advice and consent of the Senate. He shall hold his office until the appointment and qualification of his successor, or until removed in pursuance of the sentence of a Court Martial. He shall perform such duties, and receive such compensation, or emoluments, as are now, or may be prescribed

[163] Amended by Chapter 255, Acts of 1890, ratified Nov. 3, 1891; Chapter 99, Acts of 1956, ratified Nov. 6, 1956; Chapter 681, Acts of 1977, ratified Nov. 7, 1978.
[164] Amended by Chapter 99, Acts of 1956, ratified Nov. 6, 1956. Repealed by Chapter 681, Acts of 1977, ratified Nov. 7, 1978.
[165] Amended by Chapter 97, Acts of 1958, ratified Nov. 4, 1958. Repealed by Chapter 681, Acts of 1977, ratified Nov. 7, 1978.
[166] Amended by Chapter 489, Acts of 1966, ratified Nov. 8, 1966. Repealed by Chapter 681, Acts of 1977, ratified Nov. 7, 1978.
[167] Repealed by Chapter 681, Acts of 1977, ratified Nov. 7, 1978.
[168] Repealed by Chapter 99, Acts of 1956, ratified Nov. 6, 1956.

[161] Amended by Chapter 133, Acts of 1929, ratified Nov. 4, 1930; Chapter 56, Acts of 1950, ratified Nov. 7, 1950; Chapter 7, Acts of 1965, ratified Nov. 8, 1966; Chapter 632, Acts of 1973, ratified Nov. 5, 1974.
[162] Amended by Chapter 640, Acts of 1975, ratified Nov. 2, 1976.

by Law. He shall discharge the duties of his office at the seat of Government, unless absent, under orders, on duty; and no other officer of the General Staff of the Militia shall receive salary or pay, except when on service, and mustered in with troops.

SEC. 3.[169] Vacant.

ARTICLE X.[170]

Vacant.

ARTICLE XI.[171]

CITY OF BALTIMORE.

SECTION 1. The Inhabitants of the City of Baltimore, qualified by Law to vote in said city for members of the House of Delegates, shall on the Tuesday after the first Monday of November, eighteen hundred and eighty-nine, and on the same day and month in every second year thereafter, elect a person to be Mayor of the City of Baltimore, who shall have such qualifications, receive such compensation, discharge such duties, and have such powers as are now, or may hereafter be prescribed by Law; and the term of whose office shall commence on the third Wednesday in the November of the year of his election, and shall continue for two years, and until his successor shall have qualified.

SEC. 2. The City Council of Baltimore shall consist of two branches, one of which shall be called the First Branch, and the other the Second Branch, and each shall consist of such number of members, having such qualification, receiving such compensation, performing such duties, possessing such powers, holding such terms of office, and elected in such manner, as are now, or may hereafter be prescribed by Law.

SEC. 3. An election for members of the First Branch of the City Council of Baltimore shall be held in the City of Baltimore on the Tuesday after the first Monday of November, eighteen hundred and eighty-nine, and on the same day in every year thereafter; and for members of the Second Branch on the Tuesday after the first Monday of November, eighteen hundred and eighty-nine, and on the same day in every second year thereafter; and the qualification for electors of the members of the City Council shall be the same as those prescribed for the electors of Mayor.

SEC. 4 The regular sessions of the City Council of Baltimore (which shall be annual), shall commence on the third Monday of January of each year, and shall not continue more than ninety days, exclusive of Sundays; but the Mayor may convene the City Council in extra session whenever, and as often as it may appear to him that the public good may require, but no called or extra session shall last longer than twenty days, exclusive of Sundays.

SEC. 5. No person elected and qualified as Mayor, or as a member of the City Council, shall during the term for which he was elected, hold any other office of profit or trust, created, or to be created, by the Mayor and City Council of Baltimore, or by any Law relating to the Corporation of Baltimore, or hold any employment, or position, the compensation of which shall be paid, directly or indirectly, out of the City Treasury; nor shall any such person be interested, directly or indirectly, in any contract, to which the City is a party; nor shall it be lawful for any person, holding any office, under the City, to be interested, while holding such office, in any contract, to which the City is a party.

SEC. 6. The Mayor shall, on conviction in a Court of Law, of wilful neglect of duty, or misbehavior in office, be removed from

office by the Governor of the State, and a successor shall thereafter be elected, as in a case of vacancy.

SEC. 7.[172] From and after the adoption of this Constitution, no debt except as hereinafter provided in this section, shall be created by the Mayor and City Council of Baltimore; nor shall the credit of the Mayor and City Council of Baltimore be given, or loaned to, or in aid of any individual, association, or corporation; nor shall the Mayor and City Council of Baltimore have the power to involve the City of Baltimore in the construction of works of internal improvement, nor in granting any aid thereto, which shall involve the faith and credit of the city, nor make any appropriation therefor, unless the debt or credit is authorized by an ordinance of the Mayor and City Council of Baltimore, submitted to the legal voters of the City of Baltimore, at such time and place as may be fixed by the ordinance, and approved by a majority of the votes cast at that time and place. An ordinance for the authorization of debt or credit as aforesaid may not be submitted to the legal voters of Baltimore City unless the proposed creation of debt or extension of credit is either (1) presented to and approved by a majority of the members of the General Assembly representing Baltimore City no later than the 30th day of the regular session of the General Assembly immediately preceding its submission to the voters, or (2) authorized by an Act of the General Assembly. The ordinance shall provide for the discharge of any such debt or credit within the period of 40 years from the time of contracting the same. The Mayor and City Council may, temporarily, borrow any amount of money to meet any deficiency in the City Treasury, and may borrow any amount at any time to provide for any emergency arising from the necessity of maintaining the police, or preserving the health, safety and sanitary condition of the City, and may make due and proper arrangements and agreements for the renewal and extension, in whole or in part, of any and all debts and obligations created according to law before the adoption of this Constitution.

The General Assembly may, from time to time, fix a limit upon the aggregate amount of bonds and other evidences of indebtedness of the City outstanding at any one time to the same extent as it fixes such a limit upon the indebtedness of the chartered counties.

SEC. 8. All Laws and Ordinances, now in force, applicable to the City of Baltimore, not inconsistent with this Article, shall be, and they are hereby continued until changed in due course of Law.

SEC. 9. The General Assembly may make such changes in this Article, except in Section seventh thereof, as it may deem best; and this Article shall not be so construed, or taken as to make the political corporation of Baltimore independent of, or free from the control, which the General Assembly of Maryland has over all such Corporations in this State.

ARTICLE XI-A.[173]

LOCAL LEGISLATION.

SECTION 1.[174] On demand of the Mayor of Baltimore and City Council of the City of Baltimore, or on petition bearing the signatures of not less than 20% of the registered voters of said City or any County (Provided, however, that in any case 10,000 signatures shall be sufficient to complete a petition), the Board of Election Supervisors of said City or County shall provide at the next general or congressional election, occurring after such demand or the filing of such petition, for the election of a charter board of eleven registered voters of said City or five registered voters in any such Counties. Nominations for members for said

---

[169] Repealed by Chapter 99, Acts of 1956, ratified Nov. 6, 1956.
[170] Repealed by Chapter 99, Acts of 1956, ratified Nov. 6, 1956.
[171] Amended by Chapter 397, Acts of 1888. See Section 9, Article XI, and the Charter of Baltimore City (1964 Edition), for changes in this Article made under the authority of Article 11A of the Constitution.

[172] Amended by Chapter 456, Acts of 1933, ratified Nov. 6, 1934; Chapter 739, Acts of 1982, ratified Nov. 2, 1982.
[173] Added by Chapter 416, Acts of 1914, ratified Nov. 2, 1915.
[174] Amended by Chapter 192, Acts of 1963, ratified Nov. 3, 1964.

charter board may be made not less than forty days prior to said election by the Mayor of Baltimore and City Council of the City of Baltimore or the County Commissioners of such County, or not less than twenty days prior to said election by petition bearing the signatures written in their own handwriting (and not by their mark) of not less than 5% of the registered voters of the said City of Baltimore or said County; provided, that in any case two thousand signatures of registered voters shall be sufficient to complete any such nominating petition, and if not more than eleven registered voters of the City of Baltimore or not more than five registered voters in any such County are so nominated their names shall not be printed on the ballot, but said eleven registered voters in the City of Baltimore or five in such County shall constitute said charter board from and after the date of said election. At said election the ballot shall contain the names of said nominees in alphabetical order without any indication of the source of their nomination, and shall also be so arranged as to permit the voter to vote for or against the creation of said charter board, but the vote cast against said creation shall not be held to bar the voter from expressing his choice among the nominees for said board, and if the majority of the votes cast for and against the creation of said charter board shall be against said creation the election of the members of said charter board shall be void; but if such majority shall be in favor of the creation of said charter board, then and in that event the eleven nominees of the City of Baltimore or five nominees in the County receiving the largest number of votes shall constitute the charter board, and said charter board, or a majority thereof, shall prepare within twelve months from the date of said election a charter or form of government for said city or such county and present the same to the Mayor of Baltimore or President of the Board of County Commissioners of such county, who shall publish the same in at least two newspapers of general circulation published in the City of Baltimore or County within thirty days after it shall be reported to him. Such charter shall be submitted to the voters of said City or County at the next general or Congressional election after the report of said charter to said Mayor of Baltimore or President of the Board of County Commissioners; and if a majority of the votes cast for and against the adoption of said charter shall be in favor of such adoption, the said charter from and after the thirtieth day from the date of such election shall become the law of said City or County, subject only to the Constitution and Public General Laws of this State, and any public local laws inconsistent with the provisions of said charter and any former charter of the City of Baltimore or County shall be thereby repealed.

SEC. 1A.[175] The procedure provided in this section for adoption of a charter may be used in any county in lieu of the procedures provided in Section 1 of this Article, and a charter adopted pursuant to this section has the effect of a charter adopted in accordance with the provisions of Section 1. The board of county commissioners of any county at any time may appoint a charter board. Said charter board shall be registered voters and shall consist of an uneven number of members, not fewer than five or more than nine. The board of county commissioners shall appoint a charter board within thirty days after receiving a petition signed by five percent of the registered voters of the county or by ten thousand voters of the county, whichever is the lesser number. If additional charter board members are nominated by petitions signed by three percent of the registered voters of the county or by two thousand registered voters, whichever is the lesser number, delivered to the board of county commissioners within sixty days after the charter board is appointed, the board of county commissioners shall call a special election not less than thirty or more than ninety days after receiving petitions, unless a regular election falls within the designated period. The appointees of the board of county commissioners and those nominated by petitions shall be placed on the ballot in alphabetical order without party designation. The voters may cast votes for, and elect a number of nominees equal to the number of charter board

members originally selected by the board of county commissioners, and those so elected are the charter board. The charter board, within twelve months from the date of its appointment, or if there was an election for some of its members, within twelve months from the date of the election, shall present a proposed charter for the county to the board of county commissioners, which shall publish it at least twice in one or more newspapers of general circulation in the county within thirty days after it is presented. The charter shall be submitted to the voters of the county at a special or regular election held not earlier than thirty days or later than ninety days after publication of the charter. If a majority of the votes cast for and against the adoption of the charter are in favor of its adoption, the charter shall become effective as the charter of the county on the thirtieth day after the election or such later date as shall be specified in the charter.

SEC. 2.[176] The General Assembly shall by public general law provide a grant of express powers for such County or Counties as may thereafter form a charter under the provisions of this Article. Such express powers granted to the Counties and the powers heretofore granted to the City of Baltimore, as set forth in Article 4, Section 6, Public Local Laws of Maryland, shall not be enlarged or extended by any charter formed under the provisions of this Article, but such powers may be extended, modified, amended or repealed by the General Assembly.

SEC. 3.[177] Every charter so formed shall provide for an elective legislative body in which shall be vested the lawmaking power of said City or County. Such legislative body in the City of Baltimore shall be known as the City Council of the City of Baltimore, and in any county shall be known as the County Council of the County. The chief executive officer, if any such charter shall provide for the election of such executive officer, or the presiding officer of said legislative body, if such charter shall not provide for the election of a chief executive officer, shall be known in the City of Baltimore as Mayor of Baltimore, and in any County as the President or Chairman of the County Council of the County, and all references in the Constitution and laws of this State to the Mayor of Baltimore and City Council of the City of Baltimore or to the County Commissioners of the Counties, shall be construed to refer to the Mayor of Baltimore and City Council of the City of Baltimore and to the President or Chairman and County Council herein provided for whenever such construction would be reasonable. From and after the adoption of a charter by the City of Baltimore, or any County of this State, as hereinbefore provided, the Mayor of Baltimore and City Council of the City of Baltimore or the County Council of said County, subject to the Constitution and Public General Laws of this State, shall have full power to enact local laws of said City or County including the power to repeal or amend local laws of said City or County enacted by the General Assembly, upon all matters covered by the express powers granted as above provided; provided that nothing herein contained shall be construed to authorize or empower the County Council of any County in this State to enact laws or regulations for any incorporated town, village, or municipality in said County, on any matter covered by the powers granted to said town, village, or municipality by the Act incorporating it, or any subsequent Act or Acts amendatory thereto. Provided, however, that the charters for the various Counties shall specify the number of days, not to exceed forty-five, which may but need not be consecutive, that the County Council of the Counties may sit in each year for the purpose of enacting legislation for such Counties, and all legislation shall be enacted at the times so designated for that purpose in the charter, and the title or a summary of all laws and ordinances proposed shall be published once a week for two successive weeks prior to enactment followed by publication once after enactment in at least one newspaper of general circulation in the county, so that the taxpayers and citizens may have notice thereof. The validity

[175] Added by Chapter 786, Acts of 1969, ratified Nov. 3, 1970.

[176] Amended by Chapter 681, Acts of 1977, ratified Nov. 7, 1978.
[177] Amended by Chapter 557, Acts of 1955, ratified Nov. 6, 1956; Chapter 371, Acts of 1972, ratified Nov. 7, 1972.

of emergency legislation shall not be affected if enacted prior to the completion of advertising thereof. These provisions concerning publication shall not apply to Baltimore City. All such local laws enacted by the Mayor of Baltimore and City Council of the City of Baltimore or the Council of the Counties as hereinbefore provided, shall be subject to the same rules of interpretation as those now applicable to the Public Local Laws of this State, except that in case of any conflict between said local law and any Public General Law now or hereafter enacted the Public General Law shall control.

SEC. 3A.[178] (a) The charter for the government of Anne Arundel, Baltimore, Montgomery, Prince George's and Howard counties under the provisions of this Article, either as adopted, or by amendment, may provide for the election of members of the county council by the voters of councilmanic districts therein established, or by the voters of the entire county, or by a combination of these methods of election.

(b) No amendment to the Montgomery County Charter authorized hereunder may affect the terms, powers, and duties of members of the Montgomery County Council in office or elected at the time of adoption of the Charter Amendment.

(c) Any proposed amendment to the Montgomery County Charter providing for the election of members of the county council by voters of councilmanic districts and approved by the voters prior to the 1984 General Election shall be null and void.

SEC. 4. From and after the adoption of a charter under the provisions of this Article by the City of Baltimore or any County of this State, no public local law shall be enacted by the General Assembly for said City or County on any subject covered by the express powers granted as above provided. Any law so drawn as to apply to two or more of the geographical sub-divisions of this State shall not be deemed a Local Law, within the meaning of this Act. The term "geographical sub-division" herein used shall be taken to mean the City of Baltimore or any of the Counties of this State.

SEC. 5.[179] Amendments to any charter adopted by the City of Baltimore or by any County of this State under the provisions of this Article may be proposed by a resolution of the Mayor of Baltimore and the City Council of the City of Baltimore, or the Council of the County, or by a petition signed by not less than 20% of the registered voters of the City or County, provided, however, that in any case 10,000 signatures shall be sufficient to complete a petition. A petition shall be filed with the Mayor of Baltimore or the President of the County Council. An amendment so proposed shall be submitted to the voters of the City or County at the next general or congressional election occurring after the passage of the resolution or the filing of the petition. If at the election the majority of the votes cast for and against the amendment shall be in favor thereof, the amendment shall be adopted and become a part of the charter of the City or County from and after the thirtieth day after said election. The amendments shall be published by the Mayor of Baltimore or President of the County Council once a week for five successive weeks prior to the election in at least one newspaper published in said City or County.

SEC. 6. The power heretofore conferred upon the General Assembly to prescribe the number, compensation, powers and duties of the County Commissioners in each county, and the power to make changes in Sections 1 to 6 inclusive, Article XI of this Constitution, when expressly granted as hereinbefore provided, are hereby transferred to the voters of each County and the voters of City of Baltimore, respectively, provided that said

powers so transferred shall be exercised only by the adoption or amendment of a charter as hereinbefore provided; and provided further that this Article shall not be construed to authorize the exercise of any powers in excess of those conferred by the Legislature upon said Counties or City as this Article sets forth.

SEC. 7.[180] The word "Petition" as used in this Article, means one or more sheets written or printed, or partly written and partly printed. There shall be attached to each paper of signatures filed with a petition an affidavit of the person procuring those signatures that the signatures were affixed in his presence and that, based upon the person's best knowledge and belief, every signature on the paper is genuine and bona fide and that the signers are registered voters at the address set opposite or below their names. The General Assembly shall prescribe by law the form of the petition, the manner for verifying its authenticity, and other administrative procedures which facilitate the petition process and which are not in conflict with this Article. The false signing of any name, or the signing of any fictitious name to said petition shall be forgery, and the making of any false affidavit in connection with said petition shall be perjury.

ARTICLE XI-B.[181]

CITY OF BALTIMORE—LAND DEVELOPMENT AND REDEVELOPMENT.

SECTION 1.[182] The General Assembly of Maryland, by public local law, may authorize and empower the Mayor and City Council of Baltimore:

(a) To acquire, within the boundary lines of Baltimore City, land and property of every kind, and any right, interest, franchise, easement or privilege therein, by purchase, lease, gift, condemnation or any other legal means, for development or redevelopment, including, but not limited to, the comprehensive renovation or rehabilitation thereof; and

(b) To sell, lease, convey, transfer or otherwise dispose of any of said land or property, regardless of whether or not it has been developed, redeveloped, altered or improved and irrespective of the manner or means in or by which it may have been acquired, to any private, public or quasi public corporation, partnership, association, person or other legal entity.

No land or property taken by the Mayor and City Council of Baltimore for any of the aforementioned purposes or in connection with the exercise of any of the powers which may be granted to the Mayor and City Council of Baltimore pursuant to this Article by exercising the power of eminent domain, shall be taken without just compensation, as agreed upon between the parties, or awarded by a jury, being first paid or tendered to the party entitled to such compensation.

All land or property needed, or taken by the exercise of the power of eminent domain, by the Mayor and City Council of Baltimore for any of the aforementioned purposes or in connection with the exercise of any of the powers which may be granted to the Mayor and City Council of Baltimore pursuant to this Article is hereby declared to be needed or taken for a public use.

SEC. 2.[183] The General Assembly of Maryland may grant to the Mayor and City Council of Baltimore any and all additional power and authority necessary or proper to carry into full force and effect any and all of the specific powers which the General Assembly is authorized to grant to the Mayor and City Council of Baltimore pursuant to this Article and to fully accomplish any and all of the purposes and objects contemplated by the

[178] Amended by Chapter 358, Acts of 1971, ratified Nov. 7, 1972; Chapter 785, Acts of 1975, ratified Nov. 2, 1976; Chapter 682, Acts of 1977, ratified Nov. 7, 1978; Chapter 136, Acts of 1980, ratified Nov. 4, 1980; Chapter 729, Acts of 1982, ratified Nov. 2, 1982.
[179] Amended by Chapter 681, Acts of 1977, ratified Nov. 7, 1978.
[180] Amended by Chapter 849, Acts of 1982, ratified Nov. 2, 1982.
[181] Added by Chapter 649, Acts of 1943, ratified Nov. 7, 1944.
[182] Amended by Chapter 659, Acts of 1945, ratified Nov. 5, 1946; Chapter 162, Acts of 1947, ratified Nov. 2, 1948.
[183] Amended by Chapter 162, Acts of 1947, ratified Nov. 2, 1948.

provisions of this Article, provided such additional power or authority is not inconsistent with the terms and provisions of this Article or with any other provision or provisions of the Constitution of Maryland. The General Assembly may place such other and further restrictions or limitations on the exercise of any of the powers which it may grant to the Mayor and City Council of Baltimore under the provisions of this Article as it may deem proper and expedient.

SEC. 3.[184] Vacant.

ARTICLE XI-C.[185]

OFF-STREET PARKING.

SECTION 1. The General Assembly of Maryland, by public local law, may authorize the Mayor and City Council of Baltimore:

(a) Within the City of Baltimore to acquire land and property of every kind, and any right, interest, franchise, easement or privilege therein, by purchase, lease, gift, condemnation or any other legal means, for storing, parking and servicing self-propelled vehicles, provided, that no petroleum products shall be sold or offered for sale at any entrance to or exit from, any land so acquired or at any entrance to, or exit from, any structure erected thereon, when any entrance to, or exit from, any such land or structure faces on a street or highway which is more than 25 feet wide from curb to curb; and

(b) To sell, lease, convey, transfer or otherwise dispose of any of said land or property, regardless of whether or not it has been developed, redeveloped, altered, or improved and irrespective of the manner or means in or by which it may have been acquired, to any private, public or quasi public corporation, partnership, association, person or other legal entity.

No land or property taken by the Mayor and City Council of Baltimore for any of the aforementioned purposes or in connection with the exercise of any of the powers which may be granted to the Mayor and City Council of Baltimore pursuant to this Article by exercising the power of eminent domain, shall be taken without just compensation, as agreed upon between the parties, or awarded by a jury, being first paid or tendered to the party entitled to such compensation.

All land or property needed, or taken by the exercise of the power of eminent domain, by the Mayor and City Council of Baltimore for any of the aforementioned purposes or in connection with the exercise of any of the powers which may be granted to the Mayor and City Council of Baltimore pursuant to this Article is hereby declared to be needed or taken for a public use.

SEC. 2. The General Assembly of Maryland may grant to the Mayor and City Council of Baltimore any and all additional power and authority necessary or proper to carry into full force and effect any and all of the specific powers which the General Assembly is authorized to grant to the Mayor and City Council of Baltimore pursuant to this Article and to fully accomplish any and all of the purposes and objects contemplated by the provisions of this Article, provided such additional power or authority is not inconsistent with the terms and provisions of this Article or with any other provision or provisions of the Constitution of Maryland. The General Assembly may place such other and further restrictions or limitations on the exercise of any of the powers which it may grant to the Mayor and City Council of Baltimore under the provisions of this Article as it may deem proper and expedient.

SEC. 3.[186] In addition to the powers granted and exercised under Sections 1 and 2, the Mayor and City Council of Baltimore

may, by ordinance, borrow money to finance the establishment, construction, erection, alteration, expansion, enlarging, improving, equipping, repairing, maintaining, operating, controlling, and regulating of off-street parking facilities owned or to be owned by the Mayor and City Council of Baltimore, and evidence such borrowing by the issuance of revenue bonds, notes or other obligations to be secured by a pledge of the revenues derived from such facilities, and may further pledge revenues collected from parking taxes, parking fees or charges, parking fines or any other revenue derived from the parking of motor vehicles in the City of Baltimore to or for the payment of such revenue bonds, notes or other obligations; and for such purposes the Commissioners of Finance are empowered to maintain a fund consisting of the revenue pledged herein. The bonds, notes or other obligations issued hereunder and the pledge of revenues, taxes, fees, charges or fines provided for herein shall not constitute a general obligation of nor a pledge of the faith and credit or taxing power of the Mayor and City Council of Baltimore and shall not constitute a debt of the Mayor and City Council of Baltimore within the meaning of Section 7 of Article XI of the Constitution of Maryland. The ordinance may prescribe the form and terms of the bonds, notes or other obligations, the time and manner of public or private sale thereof, and the method and terms of payment therefor, and may authorize the Commissioners of Finance by resolution to determine any matters hereinabove recited and to do any and all things necessary or appropriate in connection with the issuance and sale thereof.

ARTICLE XI-D.[187]

PORT DEVELOPMENT.

SECTION 1.[188] The General Assembly of Maryland, by public local law, may authorize the Mayor and City Council of Baltimore:

(a) To acquire land and property of every kind, and any right, interest, franchise, easement or privilege therein, in adjoining or in the vicinity of the Patapsco River or its tributaries, by purchase, lease, gift, condemnation or any other legal means, for or in connection with extending, developing or improving the harbor or port of Baltimore and its facilities and the highways and approaches thereto; and providing, further, that the Mayor and City Council of Baltimore shall not acquire any such land or property, or any such right, interest, franchise, easement or privilege therein, for any of said purposes, in any of the counties of this State without the prior consent and approval by resolution duly passed after a public hearing, by the governing body of the county in which such land or property, or such right, interest, franchise, easement or privilege therein, is situate; and provided, further, that Anne Arundel County shall retain jurisdiction and power to tax any land so acquired by the Mayor and City Council of Baltimore under the provisions of this Act.

(b) To sell, lease, convey, transfer or otherwise dispose of any of said land or property, regardless of whether or not it is undeveloped or has been developed, redeveloped, altered, or improved and irrespective of the manner or means in or by which it may have been acquired, to any private, public or quasi public corporation, partnership, association, person or other legal entity.

No land or property taken by the Mayor and City Council of Baltimore for any of the aforementioned purposes or in connection with the exercise of any of the powers which may be granted to the Mayor and City Council of Baltimore pursuant to this Article by exercising the power of eminent domain, shall be taken without just compensation, as agreed upon between the parties, or awarded by a jury, being first paid or tendered to the party entitled to such compensation.

---

[184] Repealed by Chapter 681, Acts of 1977, ratified Nov. 7, 1978.
[185] Added by Chapter 505, Acts of 1947, ratified Nov. 2, 1948.
[186] Added by Chapter 552, Acts of 1976, ratified Nov. 2, 1976.

[187] Added by Chapter 199, Acts of 1951, ratified Nov. 4, 1952.
[188] Amended by Chapter 754, Acts of 1953, ratified Nov. 2, 1954; Chapter 681, Acts of 1977, ratified Nov. 7, 1978.

All land or property needed, or taken by the exercise of the power of eminent domain, by the Mayor and City Council of Baltimore for any of the aforementioned purposes or in connection with the exercise of any of the powers which may be granted to the Mayor and City Council of Baltimore pursuant to this Article is hereby declared to be needed or taken for a public use.

SEC. 2.[189] The General Assembly of Maryland may grant to the Mayor and City Council of Baltimore any and all additional power and authority necessary or proper to carry into full force and effect any and all of the specified powers which the General Assembly is authorized to grant to the Mayor and City Council of Baltimore pursuant to this Article and to fully accomplish any and all of the purposes and objects contemplated by the provisions of this Article, provided such additional power or authority is not inconsistent with the terms and provisions of this Article or with any other provision or provisions of the Constitution of Maryland. The General Assembly may place such other and further restrictions or limitations on the exercise of any of the powers which it may grant to the Mayor and City Council of Baltimore under the provisions of this Article as it may deem proper and expedient.

SEC. 3.[190] Provided, however, that no public local law enacted under the provisions and authority of this Article shall be enacted or construed to authorize the Mayor and City Council of Baltimore to exercise or apply any of the powers or authority in this Article enumerated within the territorial limits of Howard County.

ARTICLE XI-E.[191]

MUNICIPAL CORPORATIONS.

SECTION 1. Except as provided elsewhere in this Article, the General Assembly shall not pass any law relating to the incorporation, organization, government, or affairs of those municipal corporations which are not authorized by Article 11–A of the Constitution to have a charter form of government which will be special or local in its terms or in its effect, but the General Assembly shall act in relation to the incorporation, organization, government, or affairs of any such municipal corporation only by general laws which shall in their terms and in their effect apply alike to all municipal corporations in one or more of the classes provided for in Section 2 of this Article. It shall be the duty of the General Assembly to provide by law the method by which new municipal corporations shall be formed.

SEC. 2. The General Assembly, by law, shall classify all such municipal corporations by grouping them into not more than four classes based on populations as determined by the most recent census made under the authority of the United States or the State of Maryland. No more than one such grouping of municipal corporations into four (or fewer) classes shall be in effect at any time, and the enactment of any such grouping of municipal corporations into four (or fewer) classes shall repeal any such grouping of municipal corporations into four (or fewer) classes then in effect. Municipal corporations shall be classified only as provided in this section and not otherwise.

SEC. 3. Any such municipal corporation, now existing or hereafter created, shall have the power and authority, (a) to amend or repeal an existing charter or local laws relating to the incorporation, organization, government, or affairs of said municipal corporation heretofore enacted by the General Assembly of Maryland, and (b) to adopt a new charter, and to amend or repeal any charter adopted under the provisions of this Article.

SEC. 4. The adoption of a new charter, the amendment of any charter or local laws, or the repeal of any part of a charter or local

laws shall be proposed either by a resolution of the legislative body of any such municipal corporation or by a petition containing the signatures of at least five per cent of the registered voters of a municipal corporation and filed with the legislative body of said municipal corporation. The General Assembly shall amplify the provisions of this section by general law in any manner not inconsistent with this Article.

SEC. 5. Notwithstanding any other provision in this Article, the General Assembly may enact, amend, or repeal local laws placing a maximum limit on the rate at which property taxes may be imposed by any such municipal corporation and regulating the maximum amount of debt which may be incurred by any municipal corporation. However, no such local law shall become effective in regard to a municipal corporation until and unless it shall have been approved at a regular or special municipal election by a majority of the voters of that municipal corporation voting on the question. No such municipal corporation shall levy any type of tax, license fee, franchise tax or fee which was not in effect in such municipal corporation on January 1, 1954, unless it shall receive the express authorization of the General Assembly for such purpose, by a general law which in its terms and its effect applies alike to all municipal corporations in one or more of the classes provided for in Section 2 of this Article. All charter provisions enacted under the authority of Section 3 of this Article shall be subject to any local laws enacted by the General Assembly and approved by the municipal voters under the provisions of this section.

SEC. 6. All charter provisions, or amendments thereto, adopted under the provisions of this Article, shall be subject to all applicable laws enacted by the General Assembly; except that any local laws, or amendments thereto, relating to the incorporation, organization, government, or affairs of any municipal corporation and enacted before this Article becomes effective, shall be subject to any charter provisions, or amendments thereto, adopted under the provisions of this Article. Any local law, or amendments thereto, relating to the incorporation, organization, government, or affairs of any municipal corporation and in effect at the time this Article becomes effective, shall be subject to any applicable State law enacted after this Article becomes effective. All laws enacted by the General Assembly and in effect at the time this Article becomes effective, shall remain in effect until amended or repealed in accordance with the provisions of this Constitution. Nothing in this Article shall be construed to authorize any municipal corporation by any amendment or addition to its charter, to permit any act which is prohibited by the laws of this State concerning the observance of the Sabbath Day or the manufacture, licensing or sale of alcoholic beverages.

ARTICLE XI-F.[192]

HOME RULE FOR CODE COUNTIES.

SECTION 1. For the purposes of this Article, (1) "code county" means a county which is not a charter county under Article 11A of this Constitution and has adopted the optional powers of home rule provided under this Article; and (2) "public local law" means a law applicable to the incorporation, organization, or government of a code county and contained in the county's code of public local laws; but this latter term specifically does not include (i) the charters of municipal corporations under Article 11E of this Constitution, (ii) the laws or charters of counties under Article 11A of this Constitution, (iii) laws, whether or not Statewide in application, in the code of public general laws, (iv) laws which apply to more than one county, and (v) ordinances and resolutions of the county government enacted under public local laws.

SEC. 2. The governing body of any county, by a vote of at least two-thirds of the members elected thereto, may propose by resolution that the county become a code county and be governed

---

[189] Amended by Chapter 754, Acts of 1953, ratified Nov. 2, 1954.
[190] Added by Chapter 754, Acts of 1953, ratified Nov. 2, 1954.
[191] Added by Chapter 53, Acts of 1954, ratified Nov. 2, 1954.

[192] Added by Chapter 493, Acts of 1965, ratified Nov. 8, 1966.

by the provisions of this Article. Upon the adoption of such a resolution, it shall be certified to the Board of Supervisors of Elections in the county, which Board (pursuant to the election laws of the State) shall submit to the voters of the county at the next ensuing general election the question whether the resolution shall be approved or rejected. If in the referendum a majority of those persons voting on this question vote for the resolution, the resolution is approved, and the county shall become a code county under the provisions of this Article, on the thirtieth day after the election. If in the referendum a majority of those persons voting on this question vote against the resolution, the resolution is rejected, and of no further effect.

Provided that if at the next ensuing general election there shall be submitted to the voters of the county a proposed charter under Article 11A of this Constitution, the proposed charter only shall be submitted to the voters at that next ensuing general election. If the proposed charter is adopted by the voters, this particular resolution to become a code county shall not be submitted to the voters and shall have no further effect. If the proposed charter is rejected by the voters, the code question under this Article shall be submitted to the voters at the general election two years later, and no charter question under Article 11A shall be submitted to the voters at that general election.

SEC. 3. Except as otherwise provided in this Article, a code county may enact, amend, or repeal a public local law of that county, following the procedure in this Article.

SEC. 4. Except as otherwise provided in this Article, the General Assembly shall not enact, amend, or repeal a public local law which is special or local in its terms or effect within a code county. The General Assembly may enact, amend, or repeal public local laws applicable to code counties only by general enactments which in term and effect apply alike to all code counties in one or more of the classes provided for in Section 5 of this Article.

SEC. 5. The General Assembly, by law, shall classify all code counties by grouping them into not more than four classes based either upon population as determined in the most recent Federal or State census or upon such other criteria as determined by the General Assembly to be appropriate. Not more than one such grouping of code counties into four (or fewer) classes may be in effect at any one time, and the enactment of any grouping of code counties into four (or fewer) classes repeals any other such grouping then in effect. Code counties may be classified only as provided in this section.

SEC. 6. A code county may enact, amend, or repeal a public local law of that county by a resolution of the board of county commissioners. The General Assembly may amplify the provisions of this section by general law in any manner not inconsistent with this Article.

SEC. 7. Any action of a code county in the enactment, amendment, or repeal of a public local law is subject to a referendum of the voters in the county, as in this section provided. The enactment, amendment, or repeal shall be effective unless a petition of the registered voters of the county requires that it be submitted to a referendum of the voters in the county. The General Assembly shall amplify the provisions of this section by general law in any manner not inconsistent with this Article, except that in any event the number of signatures required on such a petition shall not be fewer than five percentum (5%) of the voters in a county registered for county and State elections.

SEC. 8. Notwithstanding any other provisions of this Article, the General Assembly has exclusive power to enact, amend, or repeal any local law for a code county which (1) authorizes or places a maximum limit upon the rate of property taxes which may be imposed by the code county; or (2) authorizes or regulates the maximum amount of indebtedness which may be incurred by the code county. Public local laws enacted by the General

Assembly under this section prevail over any public local laws enacted by the code county under other sections in this Article.

SEC. 9. A code county shall not levy any type of tax, license fee, franchise tax, or fee which was not in effect or authorized in the code county at the time it came under the provisions of this Article, until an express authorization of the General Assembly has been enacted for this purpose by a general law which in its terms and effect applies alike to all code counties in one or more of the classes provided for in Section 5 of this Article.

SEC. 10. All laws enacted by the General Assembly and in effect when this Article was added to the Constitution shall remain in effect until amended or repealed under this Constitution. Every public local law enacted, amended, or repealed by a county under the provisions of this Article prevails over the previous public local law, except to the extent it is subject to an applicable law enacted by the General Assembly.

ARTICLE XI-G.[193]

CITY OF BALTIMORE—REHABILITATION AND IMPROVEMENT LOANS.

1.[194] The General Assembly of Maryland, by public local law, may authorize the Mayor and City Council of Baltimore:

(a) To make or contract to make financial loans to any person or other legal entity to be used for redevelopment or improvement of buildings or structures located within the boundaries of Baltimore City, which buildings or structures are to be used or occupied for residential purposes.

(b) To guarantee or insure financial loans made by third parties to any person or other legal entity to be used for or in connection with the rehabilitation, renovation or improvement of buildings or structures located within the boundaries of Baltimore City, which buildings or structures are to be used or occupied for residential purposes.

(c) To make or contract to make financial loans to any person or other legal entity to be used for or in connection with the purchase or acquisition of leasehold or fee simple interests in buildings or structures, and for construction, reconstruction, erection, development, rehabilitation, renovation, redevelopment or improvement of buildings or structures, located within the boundaries of Baltimore City, which buildings or structures are to be used or occupied for commercial purposes.

(d) To guarantee or insure financial loans made by third parties to any person or other legal entity to be used for or in connection with the purchase or acquistion of leasehold or fee simple interests in buildings or structures, and for construction, reconstruction, erection, development, rehabilitation, renovation, redevelopment or improvement of buildings or structures, located within the boundaries of Baltimore City, which buildings or structures are to be used or occupied for commercial purposes.

(e) Any and all financial loans made by the Mayor and City Council of Baltimore; any and all guarantees or insurance commitments made by the Mayor and City Council of Baltimore in connection with any of said loans; and any and all money used or expended by the Mayor and City Council of Baltimore in connection with said loans, guarantees, or insurance commitments, pursuant to the power and authority hereinabove vested in the municipality, and any and all acts performed by the Mayor and City Council of Baltimore in connection with any powers which may be granted to the Mayor and City Council of Baltimore pursuant to this Article, are all hereby declared to be needed, contracted for, expended or exercised for a public use.

[193] Added by Chapter 375, Acts of 1972, ratified Nov. 7, 1972.
[194] Amended by Chapter 133, Acts of 1974, ratified Nov. 5, 1974; Chapter 610, Acts of 1980, ratified Nov. 4, 1980.

(f) In the event of any conflict between the provisions of this Article and those of Article XI, Section 7, of the Constitution of Maryland, or any other provisions of said Constitution, then the provisions of this Article shall control.

2. The General Assembly of Maryland may grant to the Mayor and City Council of Baltimore any and all additional power and authority necessary or proper to carry into full force and effect any and all of the specific powers which the General Assembly is authorized to grant to the Mayor and City Council of Baltimore pursuant to this Article, and to fully accomplish any and all of the purposes and objects contemplated by the provisions of this Article, provided such additional power or authority is not inconsistent with the terms and provisions of this Article or with any other provision or provisions of the Constitution of Maryland, except as provided in this Article. The General Assembly may place such other and further restrictions or limitations on the exercise of any of the powers which it may grant to the Mayor and City Council of Baltimore under the provisions of this Article as it may deem proper and expedient.

ARTICLE XI-H.[195]

CITY OF BALTIMORE—RESIDENTIAL FINANCING LOANS.

1. The General Assembly of Maryland, by public local law, may authorize the Mayor and City Council of Baltimore:

(a) To make or contract to make financial loans to any person or other legal entity to be used for or in connection with the purchase, acquisition, construction, erection or development of buildings or structures, including any land necessary therefor, within the boundaries of Baltimore City, which buildings or structures are to be used or occupied for residential purposes.

(b) To guarantee or insure financial loans made by third parties to any person or other legal entity which are to be used for or in connection with the purchase, acquisition, construction, erection or development of buildings or structures, including any land necessary therefor, within the boundaries of Baltimore City, which buildings or structures are to be used or occupied for residential purposes.

(c) Any and all financial loans made by the Mayor and City Council of Baltimore; any and all guarantees or insurance commitments made by the Mayor and City Council of Baltimore in connection with any of the loans; and any and all money used or expended by the Mayor and City Council of Baltimore in connection with the loans, guarantees, or insurance commitments, pursuant to the power and authority hereinabove vested in the municipality, and any and all acts performed by the Mayor and City Council of Baltimore in connection with any powers which may be granted to the Mayor and City Council of Baltimore pursuant to this Article, are all declared to be needed, contracted for, expended or exercised for a public use.

(d) In the event of any conflict between the provisions of this Article and those of Article XI, Section 7, of the Constitution of Maryland, or any other provisions of the Constitution, then the provisions of this Article shall control.

2. The General Assembly of Maryland may grant to the Mayor and City Council of Baltimore any and all additional power and authority necessary or proper to carry into full force and effect any and all of the specific powers which the General Assembly of Maryland is authorized to grant to the Mayor and City Council of Baltimore pursuant to this Article, and to fully accomplish any and all of the purposes and objects contemplated by the provisions of this Article, provided such additional power or authority is not inconsistent with the terms and provisions of this Article or with any other provision or provisions of the Constitution of Maryland, except as provided in this Article. The General

Assembly may place such other and further restrictions or limitations on the exercise of any of the powers which it may grant to the Mayor and City Council of Baltimore under the provisions of this Article as it may deem proper and expedient.

ARTICLE XI-I.[196]

CITY OF BALTIMORE—INDUSTRIAL FINANCING LOANS.

1. The General Assembly of Maryland, by Public Local Law, may authorize the Mayor and City Council of Baltimore:

(a) To make or contract to make financial loans to any person or other legal entity to be used for or in connection with the purchase, acquisition, construction, reconstruction, erection, development, redevelopment, rehabilitation, renovation, modernization or improvement of buildings or structures, including any land necessary therefor, within the boundaries of Baltimore City, which buildings or structures are to be used or occupied for industrial purposes.

(b) To guarantee or insure financial loans made by third parties to any person or other legal entity which are to be used for or in connection with the purchase, acquisition, construction, reconstruction, erection, development, redevelopment, rehabilitation, renovation, modernization, or improvement of buildings or structures, including any land necessary therefor, within the boundaries of Baltimore City, which buildings or structures are to be used or occupied for industrial purposes.

(c) Any and all financial loans made by the Mayor and City Council of Baltimore; any and all guarantees or insurance commitments made by the Mayor and City Council of Baltimore in connection with any of the loans; and any and all money used or expended by the Mayor and City Council of Baltimore in connection with the loans, guarantees, or insurance commitments, pursuant to the power and authority hereinabove vested in the municipality, and any and all acts performed by the Mayor and City Council of Baltimore in connection with any powers which may be granted to the Mayor and City Council of Baltimore pursuant to this Article, are all declared to be needed, contracted for, expended or exercised for a public use.

(d) In the event of any conflict between the provisions of this Article and those of Article XI, Section 7, of the Constitution of Maryland, or any other provisions of the Constitution, then the provisions of this Article shall control.

2. The General Assembly of Maryland may grant to the Mayor and City Council of Baltimore any and all additional power and authority necessary or proper to carry into full force and effect any and all of the specific powers which the General Assembly of Maryland is authorized to grant to the Mayor and City Council of Baltimore pursuant to this Article, and to fully accomplish any and all of the purposes and objects contemplated by the provisions of this Article, provided such additional power or authority is not inconsistent with the terms and provisions of this Article or with any other provision or provisions of the Constitution of Maryland, except as provided in this Article. The General Assembly may place such other and further restrictions or limitations on the exercise of any of the powers which it may grant to the Mayor and City Council of Baltimore under the provisions of this Article as it may deem proper and expedient.

ARTICLE XII.

PUBLIC WORKS.

SECTION 1. The Governor, the Comptroller of the Treasury and the Treasurer, shall constitute the Board of Public Works in this State. They shall keep a journal of their proceedings, and shall hold regular sessions in the City of Annapolis, on the first

---

[195] Added by Chapter 888, Acts of 1974, ratified Nov. 5, 1974.

[196] Added by Chapter 553, Acts of 1976, ratified Nov. 2, 1976.

Wednesday in January, April, July and October, in each year, and oftener, if necessary; at which sessions they shall hear and determine such matters as affect the Public Works of the State, and as the General Assembly may confer upon them the power to decide.

SEC. 2.[197] They shall exercise a diligent and faithful supervision of all Public Works in which the State may be interested as Stockholder or Creditor, and shall appoint the Directors in every Railroad and Canal Company, in which the State has the legal power to appoint Directors, which said Directors shall represent the State in all meetings of the Stockholders of the respective Companies for which they are appointed or elected. They shall require the Directors of all said Public Works to guard the public interest, and prevent the establishment of tolls which shall discriminate against the interest of the citizens or products of this State, and from time to time, and as often as there shall be any change in the rates of toll on any of the said Works, to furnish the said Board of Public Works a schedule of such modified rates of toll, and so adjust them as to promote the agricultural interests of the State; they shall report to the General Assembly at each regular session, and recommend such legislation as they may deem necessary and requisite to promote or protect the interests of the State in the said Public Works; they shall perform such other duties as may be hereafter prescribed by Law, and a majority of them shall be competent to act. The Governor, Comptroller and Treasurer shall receive no additional salary for services rendered by them as members of the Board of Public Works.

SEC. 3.[198] The Board of Public Works is hereby authorized, subject to such regulations and conditions as the General Assembly may from time to time prescribe, to sell the State's interest in all works of Internal Improvement, whether as a stockholder or a creditor, and also the State's interest in any banking corporation, receiving in payment the bonds and registered debt now owing by the State, equal in amount to the price obtained for the State's said interest.

ARTICLE XIII.

NEW COUNTIES.

SECTION 1.[199] The General Assembly may provide, by Law, for organizing new Counties, locating and removing county seats, and changing county lines; but no new county shall be organized without the consent of the majority of the legal voters residing within the limits proposed to be formed into said new county; and whenever a new county shall be proposed to be formed out of portions of two or more counties, the consent of a majority of the legal voters of such part of each of said counties, respectively, shall be required; nor shall the lines of any county nor of Baltimore City be changed without the consent of a majority of the legal voters residing within the district, which under said proposed change, would form a part of a county or of Baltimore City different from that to which it belonged prior to said change; and no new county shall contain less than four hundred square miles, nor less than ten thousand inhabitants; nor shall any change be made in the limits of any county, whereby the population of said county would be reduced to less than ten thousand inhabitants, or its territory reduced to less than four hundred square miles. No county lines heretofore validly established shall be changed except in accordance with this section.

SEC. 2.[200] The General Assembly shall pass all such Laws as

may be necessary more fully to carry into effect the provisions of this Article.

ARTICLE XIV.

AMENDMENTS TO THE CONSTITUTION.

SEC. 1.[201] The General Assembly may propose amendments to this Constitution; provided that each amendment shall be embraced in a separate bill, embodying the Article or Section, as the same will stand when amended and passed by three-fifths of all the members elected to each of the two Houses, by yeas and nays, to be entered on the Journals with the proposed amendment. The requirement in this section that an amendment proposed by the General Assembly shall be embraced in a separate bill shall not be construed or applied to prevent the General Assembly from (1) proposing in one bill a series of amendments to the Constitution of Maryland for the general purpose of removing or correcting constitutional provisions which are obsolete, inaccurate, invalid, unconstitutional, or duplicative; or (2) embodying in a single Constitutional amendment one or more Articles of the Constitution so long as that Constitutional amendment embraces only a single subject. The bill or bills proposing amendment or amendments shall be publicized, either by publishing, by order of the Governor, in at least two newspapers, in each County, where so many may be published, and where not more than one may be published, then in that newspaper, and in three newspapers published in the City of Baltimore, once a week for four weeks, or as otherwise ordered by the Governor in a manner provided by law, immediately preceding the next ensuing general election, at which the proposed amendment or amendments shall be submitted, in a form to be prescribed by the General Assembly, to the qualified voters of the State for adoption or rejection. The votes cast for and against said proposed amendment or amendments, severally, shall be returned to the Governor, in the manner prescribed in other cases, and if it shall appear to the Governor that a majority of the votes cast at said election on said amendment or amendments, severally, were cast in favor thereof, the Governor shall, by his proclamation, declare the said amendment or amendments having received said majority of votes, to have been adopted by the people of Maryland as part of the Constitution thereof, and thenceforth said amendment or amendments shall be part of the said Constitution. If the General Assembly determines that a proposed Constitutional amendment affects only one county or the City of Baltimore, the proposed amendment shall be part of the Constitution if it receives a majority of the votes cast in the State and in the affected county or City of Baltimore, as the case may be. When two or more amendments shall be submitted to the voters of this State at the same election, they shall be so submitted as that each amendment shall be voted on separately.

SEC. 1A.[202] A proposed Constitutional amendment which, by provisions that are of limited duration, provides for a period of transition, or a unique schedule under which the terms of the amendment are to become effective, shall set forth those provisions in the amendment as a section or sections of a separate article, to be known as "provisions of limited duration", and state the date upon which or the circumstances under which those provisions shall expire. If the Constitutional amendment is adopted, those provisions of limited duration shall have the same force and effect as any other part of the Constitution, except that they shall remain a part of the Constitution only so long as their terms require. Each new section of the article known as "provisions of limited duration" shall refer to the title and section

[197] Amended by Chapter 99, Acts of 1956, ratified Nov. 6, 1956.

[198] Amended by Chapter 362, Acts of 1890, ratified Nov. 3, 1891.

[199] Amended by Chapter 618, Acts of 1947, ratified Nov. 2, 1948; Chapter 550, Acts of 1976, ratified Nov. 2, 1976; Chapter 681, Acts of 1977, ratified Nov. 7, 1978.

[200] Originally Article XIII, sec. 6, this section was renumbered with

the repeal of sections 2 through 5 by Chapter 681, Acts of 1977, ratified Nov. 7, 1978.

[201] Amended by Chapter 476, Acts of 1943, ratified Nov. 7, 1944; Chapter 367, Acts of 1972, ratified Nov. 7, 1972; Chapter 679, Acts of 1977, and Chapter 975, Acts of 1978, ratified Nov. 7, 1978.

[202] Added by Chapter 680, Acts of 1977, ratified Nov. 7, 1978.

of the other article of the Constitution of which it, temporarily, is a part.

SEC. 2.[203] It shall be the duty of the General Assembly to provide by Law for taking, at the general election to be held in the year nineteen hundred and seventy, and every twenty years thereafter, the sense of the People in regard to calling a Convention for altering this Constitution; and if a majority of voters at such election or elections shall vote for a Convention, the General Assembly, at its next session, shall provide by Law for the assembling of such convention, and for the election of Delegates thereto. Each County, and Legislative District of the City of Baltimore, shall have in such Convention a number of Delegates equal to its representation in both Houses at the time at which the Convention is called. But any Constitution, or change, or amendment of the existing Constitution, which may be adopted by such Convention, shall be submitted to the voters of this State, and shall have no effect unless the same shall have been adopted by a majority of the voters voting thereon.

ARTICLE XV.

MISCELLANEOUS.

SECTION 1.[204] Every person holding any office created by, or existing under the Constitution, or Laws of the State, or holding any appointment under any Court of this State, whose pay, or compensation is derived from fees, or moneys coming into his hands for the discharge of his official duties, or, in any way, growing out of, or connected with his office, shall keep a book in which shall be entered every sum, or sums of money, received by him, or on his account, as a payment or compensation for his performance of official duties, a copy of which entries in said book, verified by the oath of the officer, by whom it is directed to be kept, shall be returned yearly to the Comptroller of the State for his inspection, and that of the General Assembly of the State, to which the Comptroller shall, at each regular session thereof, make a report showing what officers have complied with this Section; and each of the said officers, when the amount received by him for the year shall exceed the sum which he is by Law entitled to retain, as his salary or compensation for the discharge of his duties, and for the expenses of his office, shall yearly pay over to the Treasurer of the State the amount of such excess, subject to such disposition thereof as the General Assembly may direct; if any of such officers shall fail to comply with the requisitions of this section for the period of thirty days after the expiration of each and every year of his office, such officer shall be deemed to have vacated his office, and the Governor shall declare the same vacant, and the vacancy therein shall be filled as in the case of vacancy for any other cause, and such officer shall be subject to suit by the State for the amount that ought to be paid into the Treasury.

SEC. 2.[205] Any elected official of the State, or of a county or of a municipal corporation who during his term of office is convicted of or enters a plea of *nolo contendere* to any crime which is a felony, or which is a misdemeanor related to his public duties and responsibilities and involves moral turpitude for which the penalty may be incarceration in any penal institution, shall be suspended by operation of law without pay or benefits from the elective office. During and for the period of suspension of the elected official, the appropriate governing body and/or official authorized by law to fill any vacancy in the elective office shall appoint a person to temporarily fill the elective office, provided that if the elective office is one for which automatic succession is provided by law, then in such event the person entitled to succeed

to the office shall temporarily fill the elective office. If the conviction becomes final, after judicial review or otherwise, such elected official shall be removed from the elective office by operation of Law and the office shall be deemed vacant. If the conviction of the elected official is reversed or overturned, the elected official shall be reinstated by operation of Law to the elective office for the remainder, if any, of the elective term of office during which he was so suspended or removed, and all pay and benefits shall be restored.

SEC. 3.[206] No person who is a member of an organization that advocates the overthrow of the Government of the United States or of the State of Maryland through force or violence shall be eligible to hold any office, be it elective or appointive, or any other position of profit or trust in the Government of or in the administration of the business of this State or of any county, municipality or other political subdivision of this State.

SEC. 4.[207] Vacant.

SEC. 5.[208] Except as the Constitution provides otherwise for any office, the General Assembly may provide by law for a person to act in place of any elected or appointed officer of the State who is unavailable to perform the duties of his office because he has become unable or is or will be absent.

SEC. 6.[209] Vacant.

SEC. 7.[210] All general elections in this State shall be held on the Tuesday next after the first Monday in the month of Nov., in the year in which they shall occur.

SEC. 8.[211] Vacant.

SEC. 9.[212] Vacant.

SEC. 10. [213] Vacant.

SEC. 11. [214] Vacant.

ARTICLE XVI.[215]

THE REFERENDUM.

SECTION 1. (a) The people reserve to themselves power known as The Referendum, by petition to have submitted to the registered voters of the State, to approve or reject at the polls, any Act, or part of any Act of the General Assembly, if approved by the Governor, or, if passed by the General Assembly over the veto of the Governor;

(b) The provisions of this Article shall be self-executing; provided that additional legislation in furtherance thereof and not in conflict therewith may be enacted.

---

[203] Amended by Chapter 99, Acts of 1956, ratified Nov. 6, 1956.

[204] Amended by Chapter 99, Acts of 1956, ratified Nov. 6, 1956; Chapter 681, Acts of 1977, ratified Nov. 7, 1978.

[205] Originally Article XV, sec. 3, renumbered by Chapter 681, Acts of 1977, ratified Nov. 7, 1978. As sec. 3 it was amended by Chapter 879, Acts of 1974, ratified Nov. 5, 1974.

[206] Originally Article XV, sec. 11, renumbered by Chapter 681, Acts of 1977, ratified Nov. 7, 1978. As sec. 11 it was added by Chapter 721, Acts of 1947, ratified Nov. 2, 1948.

[207] Transferred to Article XVII, sec. 8, by Chapter 681, Acts of 1977, ratified Nov. 7, 1978.

[208] Added by Chapter 974, Acts of 1978, ratified Nov. 7, 1978. The previous sec. 5 was transferred to Article 23 of the Declaration of Rights by Chapter 681, Acts of 1977, ratified Nov. 7, 1978.

[209] Transferred to Article 23 of the Declaration of Rights by Chapter 681, Acts of 1977, ratified Nov. 7, 1978.

[210] Amended by Chapter 99, Acts of 1956, ratified Nov. 6, 1956.

[211] Repealed by Chapter 99, Acts of 1956, ratified Nov. 6, 1956.

[212] Transferred to Article XVII, sec. 4, by Chapter 681, Acts of 1977, ratified Nov. 7, 1978.

[213] Transferred to Article I, sec. 10, by Chapter 681, Acts of 1977, ratified Nov. 7, 1978.

[214] Transferred to Article XV, sec. 3, by Chapter 681, Acts of 1977, ratified Nov. 7, 1978.

[215] Added by Chapter 673, Acts of 1914, ratified Nov. 2, 1915.

SEC. 2.[216] No law enacted by the General Assembly shall take effect until the first day of June next after the session at which it may be passed, unless it contains a Section declaring such law an emergency law and necessary for the immediate preservation of the public health or safety and is passed upon a yea and nay vote supported by three-fifths of all the members elected to each of the two Houses of the General Assembly. The effective date of a law other than an emergency law may be extended as provided in Section 3 (b) hereof. If before said first day of June there shall have been filed with the Secretary of State a petition to refer to a vote of the people any law or part of a law capable of referendum, as in this Article provided, the same shall be referred by the Secretary of State to such vote, and shall not become a law or take effect until thirty days after its approval by a majority of the electors voting thereon at the next ensuing election held throughout the State for Members of the House of Representatives of the United States. An emergency law shall remain in force notwithstanding such petition, but shall stand repealed thirty days after having been rejected by a majority of the qualified electors voting thereon. No measure creating or abolishing any office, or changing the salary, term or duty of any officer, or granting any franchise or special privilege, or creating any vested right or interest, shall be enacted as an emergency law. No law making any appropriation for maintaining the State Government, or for maintaining or aiding any public institution, not exceeding the next previous appropriation for the same purpose, shall be subject to rejection or repeal under this Section. The increase in any such appropriation for maintaining or aiding any public institution shall only take effect as in the case of other laws, and such increase or any part thereof specified in the petition, may be referred to a vote of the people upon petition.

SEC. 3.[217] (a) The referendum petition against an Act or part of an Act passed by the General Assembly, shall be sufficient if signed by three percent of the qualified voters of the State of Maryland, calculated upon the whole number of votes cast for Governor at the last preceding Gubernatorial election, of whom not more than half are residents of Baltimore City, or of any one County. However, any Public Local Law for any one County or the City of Baltimore, shall be referred by the Secretary of State only to the people of the County or City of Baltimore, upon a referendum petition of ten percent of the qualified voters of the County or City of Baltimore, as the case may be, calculated upon the whole number of votes cast respectively for Governor at the last preceding Gubernatorial election.

(b) If more than one-third, but less than the full number of signatures required to complete any referendum petition against any law passed by the General Assembly, be filed with the Secretary of State before the first day of June, the time for the law to take effect and for filing the remainder of signatures to complete the petition shall be extended to the thirtieth day of the same month, with like effect.

If an Act is passed less than 45 days prior to June 1, it may not become effective sooner than 31 days after its passage. To bring this Act to referendum, the first one-third of the required number of signatures to a petition shall be submitted within 30 days after its passage. If the first one-third of the required number of signatures is submitted to the Secretary of State within 30 days after its passage, the time for the Act to take effect and for filing the remainder of the signatures to complete the petition shall be extended for an additional 30 days.

(c) In this Article, "pass" or "passed" means any final action upon any Act or part of an Act by both Houses of the General Assembly; and "enact" or "enacted" means approval of an Act or part of an Act by the Governor.

(d) Signatures on a petition for referendum on an Act or part of an Act may be signed at any time after the Act or part of an Act is passed.

SEC. 4.[218] A petition may consist of several papers, but each paper shall contain the full text, or an accurate summary approved by the Attorney General, of the Act or part of Act petitioned. There shall be attached to each paper of signatures filed with a petition an affidavit of the person procuring those signatures that the signatures were affixed in his presence and that, based upon the person's best knowledge and belief, every signature on the paper is genuine and bona fide and that the signers are registered voters at the address set opposite or below their names. The General Assembly shall prescribe by law the form of the petition, the manner for verifying its authenticity, and other administrative procedures which facilitate the petition process and which are not in conflict with this Article.

SEC. 5. (a) The General Assembly shall provide for furnishing the voters of the State the text of all measures to be voted upon by the people; provided, that until otherwise provided by law the same shall be published in the manner prescribed by Article XIV of the Constitution for the publication of proposed Constitutional Amendments.

(b) All laws referred under the provisions of this Article shall be submitted separately on the ballots to the voters of the people, but if containing more than two hundred words, the full text shall not be printed on the official ballots, but the Secretary of State shall prepare and submit a ballot title of each such measure in such form as to present the purpose of said measure concisely and intelligently. The ballot title may be distinct from the legislative title, but in any case the legislative title shall be sufficient. Upon each of the ballots, following the ballot title or text, as the case may be, of each such measure, there shall be printed the words "For the referred law" and "Against the referred law," as the case may be. The votes cast for and against any such referred law shall be returned to the Governor in the manner prescribed with respect to proposed amendments to the Constitution under Article XIV of this Constitution, and the Governor shall proclaim the result of the election, and, if it shall appear that the majority of the votes cast on any such measure were cast in favor thereof, the Governor shall by his proclamation declare the same having received a majority of the votes to have been adopted by the people of Maryland as a part of the laws of the State, to take effect thirty days after such election, and in like manner and with like effect the Governor shall proclaim the result of the local election as to any Public Local Law which shall have been submitted to the voters of any County or of the City of Baltimore.

SEC. 6.[219] No law, licensing, regulating, prohibiting, or submitting to local option, the manufacture or sale of malt or spirituous liquors, shall be referred or repealed under the provisions of this Article.

ARTICLE XVII.[220]

QUADRENNIAL ELECTIONS.

SEC. 1.[221] The purpose of this Article is to reduce the number of elections by providing that all State and county elections shall be held only in every fourth year, and at the time provided by law for holding congressional elections, and to bring the terms of appointive officers into harmony with the changes effected in the time of the beginning of the terms of elective officers. The administrative and judicial officers of the State shall construe the provisions of this Article so as to effectuate that purpose. For the

---

[216] Amended by Chapter 681, Acts of 1977, ratified Nov. 7, 1978.
[217] Amended by Chapter 548, Acts of 1976, ratified Nov. 2, 1976. Sec. 3(a) previously amended by Chapter 6, Acts of 1962, ratified Nov. 6, 1962.

[218] Amended by Chapter 548, Acts of 1976, ratified Nov. 2, 1976; Chapter 849, Acts of 1982, ratified Nov. 2, 1982.
[219] Amended by Chapter 681, Acts of 1977, ratified Nov. 7, 1978.
[220] Added by Chapter 227, Acts of 1922, ratified Nov. 7, 1922.
[221] Originally Article XVII, sec. 11, transferred and amended by Chapter 681, Acts of 1977, ratified Nov. 7, 1978.

purpose of this Article only the word "officers" shall be construed to include those holding positions and other places of employment in the State and county governments whose terms are fixed by law, but it shall not include any appointments made by the Board of Public Works, nor appointments by the Governor for terms of three years.

SEC. 2.[222] Vacant.

SEC. 3.[223] All State and county officers elected by qualified voters (except judges of the Circuit Courts, judges of the Supreme Bench of Baltimore City, judges of the Court of Appeals and judges of any intermediate courts of appeal) shall hold office for terms of four years, and until their successors shall qualify.

SEC. 4.[224] The term of office of all Judges and other officers, for whose election provision is made by this Constitution, shall, except in cases otherwise expressly provided herein, commence from the time of their Election. All such officers shall qualify as soon after their election as practicable, and shall enter upon the duties of their respective offices immediately upon their qualification.

SEC. 5.[225] All officers to be appointed by the Governor shall hold office for the terms fixed by law. All officers appointed by County Commissioners shall hold office for terms of four years, unless otherwise duly changed by law.

SEC. 6.[226] The terms of the members of the Board of Supervisors of Elections of Baltimore City and of the several counties shall commence on the first Monday of June next ensuing their appointment.

SEC. 7.[227] Sections 1, 2, 3, and 5 of this Article do not apply or refer to members of any elective local board of education.

SEC. 8.[228] If at any election directed by this Constitution, any two or more candidates shall have the highest and an equal number of votes, a new election shall be ordered by the Governor, except in cases specially provided for by this Constitution.

SEC. 9.[229] In the event of any inconsistency between the provisions of this Article and any of the other provisions of the Constitution, the provisions of this Article shall prevail, and all other provisions shall be repealed or abrogated to the extent of such inconsistency.

SEC. 10.[230] Vacant.

---

[222] Left vacant by Chapter 681, Acts of 1977, ratified Nov. 7, 1978.

[223] Originally Article XVII, sec. 1(a), transferred and amended by Chapter 681, Acts of 1977, ratified Nov. 7, 1978. As sec. 1(a) it was amended by Chapter 10, Acts of 1966, ratified Nov. 8, 1966; Chapter 370, Acts of 1972, ratified Nov. 7, 1972.

[224] Originally Article XV, sec. 9, transferred and amended by Chapter 681, Acts of 1977, ratified Nov. 7, 1978.

[225] Originally Article XVII, sec. 4, transferred by Chapter 681, Acts of 1977, ratified Nov. 7, 1978. As sec. 4 it was amended by Chapter 99, Acts of 1956, ratified Nov. 6, 1956.

[226] Originally Article XVII, sec. 8, transferred by Chapter 681, Acts of 1977, ratified Nov. 7, 1978.

[227] Originally Article XVII, sec. 1(b), transferred and amended by Chapter 681, Acts of 1977, ratified Nov. 7, 1978. As sec. 1(b) it was amended by Chapter 10, Acts of 1966, ratified Nov. 8, 1966; Chapter 370, Acts of 1972, ratified Nov. 7, 1972.

[228] Transferred from Article XV, sec. 4, by Chapter 681, Acts of 1977, ratified Nov. 7, 1978.

[229] Transferred from Article XVII, sec. 13, by Chapter 681, Acts of 1977, ratified Nov. 7, 1978.

[230] Repealed by Chapter 99, Acts of 1956, ratified Nov. 6, 1956.

SEC. 11.[231] Vacant.

SEC. 12.[232] Vacant.

SEC. 13.[233] Vacant.

ARTICLE XVIII.[234]

PROVISIONS OF LIMITED DURATION.

1. Any provision of limited duration adopted pursuant to Article XIV is set forth below. As each expires, it shall stand repealed, and no further action shall be required to remove it from the Constitution.

2.[235] (a) For the purpose of implementing the amendments, proposed by Chapter 523 of the Acts of 1980 (H.B. 1729) (OLR3623) or (S.B. 784) (OLR0746), concerning the creation of a consolidated Circuit Court of Baltimore City, this section temporarily is a part of Article IV - Judiciary Department, secs. 5, 25, and 26 of the Constitution. This section shall expire (in accordance with Article XIV, sec. 1A of the Constitution), when, under the provisions of subsection (b) of this section, all of the judges of the Supreme Bench of Baltimore City who are serving on December 31, 1982 have completed their then existing terms, or have otherwise vacated their offices without completing those terms.

(b) Each judge of the Supreme Bench of Baltimore City, who is in office on December 31, 1982, shall continue in office as a judge of the Circuit Court for Baltimore City, for the remainder of the term to which he was appointed or elected, subject to the provisions of Article IV, sections 3, 4, 4A, 4B, and 5 of the Constitution.

(c) Each clerk and each deputy clerk of a court of the Supreme Bench of Baltimore City who is in office on December 31, 1982 shall become a deputy clerk of the Circuit Court for Baltimore City with no diminution of salary and as such shall occupy a position in the personnel merit system for the office of the clerk of the Circuit Court for Baltimore City. These persons shall serve subject to the provisions of Article IV, section 26 of the Constitution. Each person who otherwise has been employed in the office of a clerk of a court of the Supreme Bench of Baltimore City in a position authorized prior to June 30, 1982, shall become an employee of the office of the clerk of the Circuit Court for Baltimore City and occupy a position in the personnel merit system for that office, with no diminution in salary, subject to the provisions of Article IV, section 26 of the Constitution.

(d) At the primary and general elections occurring in 1982 in Baltimore City, there shall be nominated and elected one clerk who shall be designated as clerk of the Circuit Court for Baltimore City as created under the amendments proposed in section 2 of said Chapter 523, Acts of 1980. A clerk of one of the courts of the Supreme Bench of Baltimore City is eligible to run in this election.

(e) The amendments to Article IV and this Article XVIII of the Constitution (proposed by the above referenced Chapter 523 of the Acts of 1980) if approved by the voters at the general election in Nov., 1980, shall take effect on January 1, 1983.

---

[231] Amended and transferred to Article XVII, sec. 1, by Chapter 681, Acts of 1977, ratified Nov. 7, 1978.

[232] Repealed by Chapter 99, Acts of 1956, ratified Nov. 6, 1956.

[233] Transferred to Article XVII, sec. 9, by Chapter 681, Acts of 1977, ratified Nov. 7, 1978.

[234] Added by Chapter 680, Acts of 1977, ratified Nov. 7, 1978.

[235] Added by Chapter 523, Acts of 1980, ratified Nov. 4, 1980.

CONSTITUTION INDEX

Where no section numbers are given, the references are to articles in the Declaration of Rights.

SECTION V
THE GOVERNMENT OF
THE UNITED STATES OF AMERICA

CHAPTER 1

THE BIRTH OF A NEW NATION

Columbus Landing in the New World.

Since time began, people have gone from place to place in search of better ways to live.

A daring explorer, Christopher Columbus, sailed westward from Spain in 1492 looking for a new route to India. Instead of finding India, he discovered islands near the continent of North America.

The westward route discovered by Columbus opened the way to America, a new world. In the centuries that followed, millions of immigrants made the journey to this land that promised them a new way of life.

In this chapter you will learn about the early history of our country.

DISCUSS:

Why do people go to different lands to live?

MEETING NEW WORDS:

assembly: A gathering of people for some purpose; meeting of lawmakers

celebrate: To recognize and honor, as a holiday

charters: Official papers from a nation, or a state or city, granting certain rights and privileges and, sometimes, providing for a plan of government

colony: Newly-settled community that belongs to an older nation; settlement in a new land

committee: Group selected to do a special job

communities: Places where people live together, such as colonies, settlements, cities or towns

continent: One of the great bodies of land in the world

created: Made something new

NOTE: The following material, courtesy the Government Printing office, Washington, D.C. 20402 From *Our Government*, Book 3, M-163, revised 1973, U.S. Dept. of Justice.

delegate: Person sent to speak or act for others, usually at meetings; to give another person the right to do this; to give authority

endowed: Enriched, as with a gift; furnished; God-given; born with

establish: Set up; start; found

existence: State of being; living

impressed: Had a strong effect on the mind and feelings

inalienable: That which cannot be taken away

independence: Freedom from control by others

liberty: Freedom

limited: Kept within bounds

objected: Protested; opposed; was against

Parliament: British lawmaking body

possessions: Land or other things that a nation or person owns and holds

privilege: Right; benefit; favor

qualities: Characteristics; traits

recognized: Took notice of; identified; accepted

repealed: Did away with (a law)

representatives: Persons chosen to act for a group or groups of persons; delegates

rights: Things to which one has a just claim; any benefits or privileges given to a person by law or tradition

self-government: Government in which the people take part; home rule

settlement: Village built by persons in a new country

treaty: Formal agreement between nations

violated: Broken (a law, rule, agreement, promise, etc.)

Fill in the blank in each of the following sentences with the correct word from the above list:

1. The Americas _____ Columbus Day in October each year.

2. The first permanent _____ in the United States was at St. Augustine, Florida.

3. The Virginia colony had an _____ to make some of its own laws.

4. The _____ and the King governed the colonies in America.

5. American colonists wanted their own _____ in Parliament.

6. When the colonists objected to new taxes, Parliament _____ the Stamp Act.

7. By 1775 many colonists wanted their _____ from Great Britain.

8. In 1783 Great Britain and the United States signed a peace _____.

Outline Map of North America.

AS YOU READ

1. **Find out why people came to the continent of North America.**

2. **Find out why the colonists wanted their independence from Great Britain.**

THE BIRTH OF A NEW NATION

The part of the continent of North America that became the United States was blessed with many gifts. It had vast fields of fertile soil and enough rain and sunshine to produce good crops. There were forests for wood. Wild animals and birds lived in the forests. Along the seacoasts there were natural harbors. There were many broad rivers which made boat travel easy. Streams rushing down hills and down mountainsides helped to make the work of man easier. In the earth there were valuable minerals for man to find and use.

Early Indian Village.

On this continent there were people who lived in tribes. Columbus called them Indians because he thought he had reached India. They were the first Americans. Among the important American Indian tribes were the Algonquins, the Iroquois, and the Sioux. Each tribe was ruled by a chief. Some of the Indians and their tribes were peaceful and some were warlike, the same as people and countries today.

Christopher Columbus

Christopher Columbus, born in Genoa, Italy, was a sailor who believed the earth was round and that, by sailing westward, he would find a shorter route to India, land of spices, and other lands in Asia. He wanted to make a voyage to the west and needed money for the trip. He asked the rulers of several countries for help and, finally, Queen Isabella of Spain gave him three ships, sailors, and money for his trip. On August 3,

1492, Columbus and his men set out from Palos, Spain, in the three small ships: the *Nina*, the *Pinta*, and the *Santa Maria*.

Ten weeks later Columbus sighted land. On October 12, 1492, they landed on a small island in the Bahamas, several hundred miles southeast of what is now Florida. Still looking for the mainland of Asia, they sailed along the coasts of Cuba and Haiti. Although Columbus made three other voyages, he never found a westward route to Asia. However, he did discover a new world, America.

Every year, in October, the first landing of Columbus in the New World is celebrated in the Americas.

How America Was Named

Amerigo Vespucci, an Italian, was one of many explorers who wrote about the discoveries in the New World. When a German map maker read what Vespucci had written about one of his own voyages, he was so impressed that he named the new land "America," in honor of Amerigo Vespucci.

A Period of Discovery and Settlement

A period of discovery followed the daring voyage of Columbus. Men from Spain, France, Portugal, Holland, and England traveled across the western sea, which we now call the Atlantic Ocean. Each of these explorers claimed land in the New World for his country.

Although many people came to the New World in search of adventure, others were looking for the opportunity to worship God as they pleased. Some came to America because they wanted the opportunity to earn a better living. Others had heard that there was plenty of land in the New World and that poor people could become landowners. There were also those who wanted a voice in their government and believed they would have that opportunity in the new land across the western sea.

About 750,000 people crossed the ocean to America between 1600 and 1770 to make a new and better life for themselves in the New World. A great many of these immigrants had money to pay the cost of beginning this new life. Others without money were able to come to America only by promising to work for a certain number of years for the person who paid for their travel. At the end of that time, however, they too would be able to obtain and work land of their own.

Willing hands and alert minds were needed in the New World. The newcomers were usually hard-working and daring people. Even those who had to work to pay for their travel were selected for their strength and skills. These were the qualities of the people who helped to build the United States of America.

Colonies in North America

Many colonies were started in North America, but some of them did not succeed. To Spain belongs the honor of settling the first permanent colony in what is now the United States. This was a colony founded at St. Augustine, Florida. Other early colonists came from England. They were the next group to come in large enough numbers to form settlements that lasted. The King of England gave charters granting large areas of land in the New World to English companies and Englishmen who wished to organize groups of settlers to live and work in America.

The first successful English settlement was founded at Jamestown, Virginia, in the year 1607. In 1620 the Pilgrims, who had left England because they wanted to worship God in their own way, settled the colony of Plymouth, in Massachusetts. Other settlements were made by the Holland-Dutch in New York, the Swedes in Delaware, and the French in Louisiana. Although Pennsylvania was settled by English people, many Germans also came to live in that settlement. All of these colonies later came under British rule.

For almost 70 years, both in Europe and in the American colonies, Great Britain and France fought a series of wars, broken by only short periods of peace. The last war between the French and the British colonists, which began in 1754 and ended in 1763, was called the French and Indian War. As a result of this war, France lost almost all of her possessions in the New World to Great Britain.

Colonists Earned a Living by Fishing.

261

The Settlement of Jamestown.

In 1776 there were 13 British colonies in this part of America. They were:

Connecticut
Delaware
Georgia
Maryland
Massachusetts

New Hamp-
shire
New Jersey
New York
North Carolina

Pennsylvania
Rhode Island
South Carolina
Virginia

These 13 colonies later became the first 13 states—the United States of America.

King George III and the Parliament in London governed the British colonies in America. However, the early charters granted by the King gave the settlers "the rights of Englishmen."

The colonists had hoped that the King and Parliament would allow them the privilege of self-government. They wanted to have assemblies to make their own laws for the protection of the lives, families, properties, and freedoms of the colonists.

The King let the colonists elect representatives to make some of the laws for their own communities. But, he also sent governors from Great Britain to most of the colonies to see that British laws were obeyed. The governors collected taxes for the King on goods that the colonists brought in from other countries. Even under these conditions the colonists had a great deal of freedom and were quite content in the beginning.

After the French and Indian War, Great Britain decided to keep soldiers in the colonies. King George believed that the colonists should help to pay the cost of supporting the army. Great Britain was hard-pressed for money. The cost of the wars with France had been very high. The Parliament, to get money, passed the Stamp Act forcing the colonists to buy tax stamps for business and legal papers, as well as newspapers.

The King thought that the colonists were using goods on which taxes had not been paid. He ordered his officers to search for such goods. He even decided to tell the colonists what goods they could make, and with whom they could trade. He wanted them to trade only with the mother country, Great Britain.

All of these things angered the colonists. They stated that they could not be searched unless the officer gave them a written statement telling why the search was being made. They said that they did not like to be taxed against their wishes.

It was not that the colonists were against all taxes, for they did pay taxes on goods from other countries. However, they had no representatives in Parliament and all Englishman believed that they could be taxed only by their own representatives. The colonists believed that it was especially unfair to force them to pay taxes when they had no such representation. They claimed that, by these taxes, their rights as Englishmen were not being respected.

King George and Parliament at first refused to change the tax laws. Nevertheless, many people in the colonies would not buy the tax stamps and some colonists took the stamps and burned them. Within a year, friends of the colonists in Parliament were able to get the Stamp Act repealed.

A tax was then placed on all paint, paper, glass, lead, and tea brought into the colonies. The colonists once again objected to the new taxes and refused to buy these goods from Great Britain. As a result of their refusal to buy British goods, the King and Parliament finally agreed to repeal all of the taxes except the one on tea. The King kept this tax because he felt that there must always be at least one tax in force to show that he could tax the colonists.

In 1773 the British East India Company shipped millions of pounds of tea to the colonies. The colonists would not permit the tea to be removed from the ships. Several ships returned to Great Britain. In Boston, Massachusetts, the colonists boarded the ships and threw the tea into the harbor. Parliament then passed acts which closed the port of Boston and limited the freedom of the colonists.

The Colonists Meet

The colonists decided to meet to discuss the troubles they were having with Great Britain. They elected representatives who met in Philadelphia in the autumn of 1774. It was the First Continental Congress. All of the colonies, except Georgia, sent representatives to the meeting. The Congress sent a petition to King George asking him to respect the rights of the colonists. The King and Parliament refused.

The Second Continental Congress, made up of delegates from all 13 colonies, first met in Philadelphia on May 10, 1775. This Congress elected George Washington as commander in chief of the Continental Army and the colonists went to war against the British.

Declaration of Independence

Even though the colonists were at war with Great Britain, many of them hoped to remain British subjects. They believed that King George would change his mind about the new laws when he saw how determined they were to oppose them. The King decided to be even more firm and, to make matters worse, he hired German soldiers to fight the colonists in America.

More and more of the colonists and their leaders spoke of complete separation from Great Britain. One of the strongest arguments for independence came from the pen of Thomas Paine. In his

Colonists Show Displeasure at Unjust Taxation.

The Boston Tea Party.

pamphlet, *Common Sense*, he said that Americans had a natural right to their own government and called upon the people to break away from the mother country.

During the Second Continental Congress, Richard Henry Lee of Virginia made this motion, "Resolved: That these United Colonies are, and of right ought to be, free and independent states."

This motion was discussed by the delegates and a committee was appointed to write a Declaration of Independence.

Thomas Jefferson, a leading member of the committee, did most of the writing. On July 4, 1776, the Declaration of Independence was accepted by the Second Continental Congress, although it was not signed by all delegates until almost a month later.

The Declaration of Independence set forth ideas that were new to most people. It declared that all men are created equal, and that they are endowed by their Creator with certain inalienable rights, among which are life, liberty, and the pursuit of happiness. The Declaration also stated that governments are established to protect the rights of the people and that laws should not be made unless

An Early Town Meeting.

Washington Leading His Army.

the people agree to them. It further stated that when a government makes laws without their agreement, the people have every right to establish a new government. The Declaration listed the rights of the colonists which the King and the Parliament had violated and declared that the colonies were then separating from Great Britain and were free from all British control.

When the Second Continental Congress asked a committee to draw up a statement of independence, it recognized the independence already in existence in the colonies. The Declaration of Independence announced to the world the separation and independence of the colonies from Great Britain. The 13 colonies became the first 13 states. The United States of America was born!

The Revolutionary War

King George was angered by the Declaration of Independence and decided that Great Britain would continue to fight to keep the colonies.

The King's soldiers had good clothes and food, and were well trained. The American army under Washington was untrained. The men were poorly clothed and they used old guns. They did not always have enough food. Some of the soldiers had borrowed money so that their families could live while they were away at war. Other men wanted to go home to raise food for their families. General Washington tried in every way to get food, clothes, guns, and ammunition for his soldiers, but he was not very successful.

In CONGRESS, July 4, 1776.

The unanimous Declaration of the thirteen united States of America.

Facsimile of the Declaration of Independence.

Meanwhile, the King had trouble at home after the decision was made to fight to hold the colonies. Great Britain found herself at war with both Spain and France. At this time France also decided to send help to the colonists.

The Revolutionary War, also called the War for Independence, was a long and hard war. Freedom-loving people from many countries came to help the colonists. Lafayette, Rochambeau, and the German-born De Kalb came from France; Pulaski and Kosciusko from Poland; and Von Steuben from Germany. These men helped George Washington train and lead the American soldiers. In 1781 Washington, with the help of Lafayette, surrounded the British at Yorktown, Virginia. The French Navy joined in the fight at Yorktown against the British warships. After several weeks of fighting, the British commander, Lord Cornwallis, surrendered. This ended the actual war, but it was not until two years later that a peace treaty was signed between Great Britain and the new United States. By this treaty, the British recognized the United States as an independent nation.

Independence Day

In our American history July 4, 1776, marks the birth of the United States of America. The Fourth of July, Independence Day, is a national holiday. All the people in the United States celebrate this day.

Revolutionary War Battle Scene.

267

CAN YOU DO THIS?

In the list below find the word or words that can take the place of the underlined words in the sentences:

established
privilege
repealed
endowed
objected to
independence

1. Parliament did away with some tax laws.
2. The colonists protested the Stamp Act.
3. The American colonists fought for their freedom.
4. Many colonies were set up in the New World.
5. The colonists wanted the right of self-government.
6. The Declaration of Independence said that people were born with certain rights.

In the left column are the names of persons you have met in the chapter. Match the name with the words in the right-hand column that tell who the person was:

1. Thomas Paine
2. Amerigo Vespucci
3. Christopher Columbus
4. King George
5. Lafayette
6. George Washington
7. Thomas Jefferson

led the Continental Army.
wrote the pamphlet, *Common Sense.*
was the French leader who aided George Washington.
wrote most of the Declaration of Independence.
wrote about his trips to the New World which was later named for him.
landed in America in 1492.
taxed the colonies.

From the following list select the correct word(s) to complete each sentence:

Parliament
Continental Congress
thirteen (13)
George Washington
Pilgrims
Fourth of July
Declaration of Independence

1. There were _____ British colonies in America in 1776.
2. The _____ settled in Massachusetts.
3. The lawmaking body in Great Britain is called the _____.
4. We celebrate our nation's birthday on the _____.
5. The Continental Congress elected _____ to lead the army against the British.
6. The written statement sent to the King stating the rights of colonists was called the _____ _____.
7. The representatives who met to protect the rights of the people were called the _____. _____.

Talk about:

1. Why was Columbus' discovery so important?
2. What is meant by the statement in the Declaration that "all men are created equal"?

268

CHAPTER 2

PLANNING A NEW GOVERNMENT FOR A NEW NATION

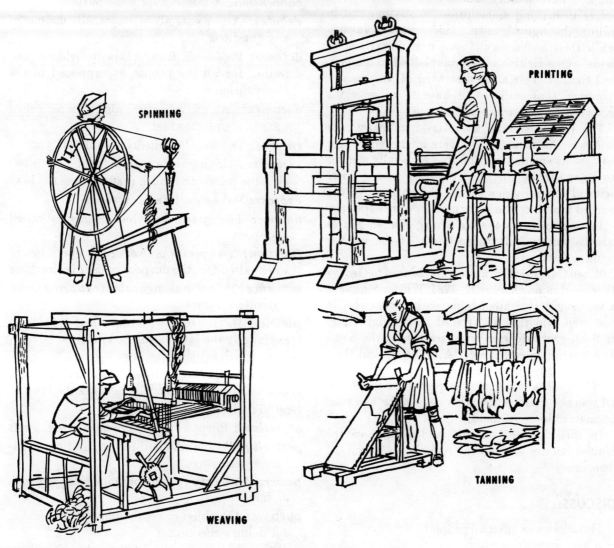

Some Colonial Industries.

Before the Revolutionary War, the British thought that the American colonies could not develop great statesmen who would be able to work with the statesmen of other governments. Great Britain forgot that struggles for freedom produce great leaders. Men such as Washington, Jefferson, and Franklin led the colonists in their struggle for independence, and they became great leaders and statesmen.

War affects all the people of a nation. The Revolutionary War increased the demand for guns, ammunition, clothing, food, and other supplies. There was an increase in iron, steel, and textile production. Spinning wheels hummed in newly-formed spinning clubs in towns and villages. Looms clattered, turning out more and more woolen, linen, and cotton cloth for uniforms and clothing. Great Britain had sold these goods to the colonies before the war. The young states were now gaining a new kind of independence by producing their own materials.

Throughout the war, patriotic women in the colonies were at work in many ways. They were active in making ammunition, in spying, and in aiding the fighting men. Some women farmed while their husbands and sons were on the battlefields. One British officer complained to his general that, if their army destroyed all the men in America, they still would have to conquer the women before the war would be won.

The people showed an interest in many new things at this time. They were interested in current events and politics, and they especially wanted to know about their local government. Their demand for daily news about the progress of the war led to an increase in the number of newspapers.

In these many ways the young United States was becoming fully independent of the mother country.

When General Cornwallis surrendered to George Washington on October 19, 1781, Washington sent a messenger to Philadelphia with the news. It has been said that he arrived at midnight, just as the night watchman was proclaiming the hour. The watchman called out, "All's well!" and then added, "Cornwallis is taken!"

"Cornwallis is taken" was very good news, but all was not well. Although a new nation had been born, troubles were ahead.

In this chapter you will read about how the United States became a republic, a form of democracy.

DISCUSS:

How does war affect all people?

MEETING NEW WORDS:

adopted: Accepted

affect: Act upon or influence; change in some way

appointed: Assigned, or named, to an office

approval: Acceptance; ratification

authority: Power or right to act or command

checks and balances: A system whereby each branch of government has some control over the other branches

coin: Make into money by stamping metal; metal money

commerce: Trade between persons or groups of persons, or states, or nations

convention: A meeting for some purpose

debates: Arguments about issues; discussions of any questions

defense: Protection from others; providing protection for all the people, as expressed in the Constitution

document: An official paper; also, a paper relied upon to prove some fact

enforce: To compel obedience (to a law)

executive: Having to do with enforcing the laws; also, the person or branch that enforces the laws

express: Make clear by acts or words

finance: The system by which money is raised and spent

function: To operate or work; the operation or work called for; the purpose or use of something

influence: Power to change; ability to bring about a result; pressure

judicial: Having to do with courts and judges and explaining the laws; also, the branch of government which explains the laws

legislative: Having to to with lawmaking; also, branch of government which makes the laws

levy: To place a tax on something

objectives: Purposes; results to be realized; goals

posterity: People who will live in the future; future generations

power: Authority to control; influence; strength or force

purpose: The object or result aimed at; the reason for doing something

ratified: Accepted and made official; approved

regulate: Make rules for something; govern according to rule

republic: A nation having a representative form of government

revolution: An overthrow of the government by the governed

supreme: Highest in rank; highest in authority and importance

trade: Buying and selling goods; commerce

tranquility: Condition of being calm, peaceful, or quiet

veto: Refuse to allow a bill to become a law by not signing it; refuse to approve; disapprove

wisdom: Knowledge and good judgment based on experience; being wise

Fill in the blank in each of the following sentences with the correct word from the above list:

1. Our Constitution was _____ by the states.

2. It was announced that the _____ of the meeting was to name a new leader.

3. The _____ branch of the government makes the laws.

4. Congress regulates _____ between the states and with foreign countries.

5. Men of great _____ wrote our Constitution.

6. In the United States only the government has authority to _____ money.

7. The President of our country has been given much _____ to act.

8. A committee was _____ to study the matter.

From the Portrait by Gilbert Stuart

George Washington.

AS YOU READ

1. **Find out why our country needed a plan of government.**

2. **Find out what checks and balances are in our Constitution.**

PLANNING A NEW GOVERNMENT FOR A NEW NATION

The Articles of Confederation

During the Revolutionary War, the members of the Second Continental Congress continued to hold meetings and to serve in the central government of the colonies. The Congress wanted to establish a simple framework of government for the colonies, which were soon to become states with the adoption of the Declaration of Independence. It appointed a committee in June 1776 to write a plan of confederation for the states. The committee called its plan "The Articles of Confederation." This plan was adopted by the Congress in 1777 and was sent to the states to be ratified by them. When the state of Maryland finally gave its approval in 1781, the Articles of Confederation went into effect.

The Articles of Confederation provided that the states were entering into a "firm league of friendship" and a "perpetual union for the common defense, the security of their liberties, and their mutual and general welfare." A Congress, made up of representatives from the 13 states, was to be the central government for the new United States under the Articles of Confederation.

This was the first step toward a republic.

What Freedom Brought

The new freedom of the states from Great Britain brought many changes and new responsibilities which had to be met by the Congress of the new Confederation.

No longer were there 13 colonies; there were 13 states.

No longer was there a single purpose—the fight for independence that united the states; new purposes were needed to keep them united.

No longer would the 13 colonies be protected by Great Britain; the states would have to protect themselves.

No longer would Great Britain control the trade of the colonies; the states would have to control their own trade.

No longer would money from Great Britain be used; the states would have to coin their own money.

The 13 struggling states, like young children without their mother, began to quarrel. Each state started to run its local government for its own good, rather than for the good of the whole nation.

The Articles of Confederation did not give enough power to the central government.

There was no executive officer to enforce the laws.

The Congress could levy taxes by asking the states for money, but it had no power to make the states pay the money.

The Congress could not control trade between the states.

The Congress had no good way to settle quarrels among the states.

A Critical Time in American History

Because of the weaknesses of the Articles of Confederation, the states began to drift apart and to distrust one another. As a result, some of the leading men of the states argued that there must be a stronger central government with enough authority to force the states to obey its laws. It was difficult to get started on such a plan of action. The Congress, the only central group representing the 13 states, finally suggested that the states arrange for a convention to change and strengthen the Articles of Confederation.

Alexander Hamilton.

The Constitutional Convention of 1787

The Constitutional Convention began its meetings in Independence Hall in Philadelphia on May 25, 1787. This was the same hall in which the Declaration of Independence had been signed almost 11 years earlier. The state governments had named more than 70 delegates to attend the convention, but only 55 actually attended. The convention soon decided that the Articles of Confederation could no longer serve as a framework for the government of the new United States, and that a new constitution would have to be written.

Great Men Lead the Convention

In 1787 the states sent some of their most able leaders to the Constitutional Convention in Philadelphia. These great men created one of the most famous and respected documents in the world, the Constitution of the United States. Among the great leaders were:

George Washington, who served as President of the convention through its long meetings. His wisdom and influence guided the delegates and held them together.

Benjamin Franklin, the elderly delegate from Pennsylvania, whose personality and good advice helped to keep the convention running smoothly.

James Madison, a Virginian who knew a great deal about governments and constitutional law. He is said to have written most of the Constitution with the able help of Gouverneur Morris, James Wilson, and Alexander Hamilton.

Alexander Hamilton, of New York, who was a student of finance and government. Although Hamilton opposed some of the ideas and provisions of the Constitution, he worked almost without sleep to have it adopted.

James Wilson, who was sent by Pennsylvania to the convention, was an authority in political and legal matters.

Gouverneur Morris, from Pennsylvania, who became responsible for the final wording of the Constitution because of his keen mind and ability to write.

These men and the other 49 delegates decided that everything which had been said and written at the convention should be kept secret until the Constitution was completed. Each delegate tried to represent the wishes of the people who had sent him to the convention and, at the same time, work for the good of all the people. All through the hot summer there were stormy debates, but these wise men learned to compromise. Each delegate, at times, gave up something he wanted in order to reach an agreement that would help the whole country.

The Objectives of the Constitution

The Preamble to the Constitution, in 52 words, stated the purposes and objectives of the new union of the states under the Constitution. The passing years have created many new needs which, in turn, have required changes to be made in the law. The writers of the Constitution provided a way in which these changes could be made. Such changes are called amendments. However, the purposes of our Constitution and the government it established have not changed.

Constitution of the United States of America

Preamble

We the People of the United States, in order to form a more perfect Union, establish justice, insure domestic tranquility, provide for the common defense, promote the general welfare, and secure the blessings of liberty to ourselves and our posterity, do ordain and establish this Constitution for the United States of America.

In these first words, the Preamble to the Constitution clearly states that the supreme power of government is in the hands of "We the People." Nearly every word in this opening paragraph of the Constitution expresses an important idea. It is well worth studying.

Some Old Ideas of Government Honored

In order to carry out the purposes and reach the objectives set forth in the Preamble, the delegates to the convention studied the plans of government used in England, in the former colonies, and in the states. The best ideas from each of these plans they wrote into the new Constitution.

New Ideas of Government Also Added

The delegates also found it necessary to write into the Constitution certain new ideas of government to assure that the aims and goals set forth in the Preamble would be reached.

The new Constitution provided for three branches of government:

The legislative branch, called Congress, which makes the laws,

The executive branch, headed by a President, which enforces the laws, and

The judicial branch, which is the system of courts and judges, that explains the laws.

The Constitution provided that the legislative branch would have two Houses, the House of Representatives and the Senate. Members of the House of Representatives were to be elected according to population. As a result, a state with more people would have more members in this House than would a state with fewer people, and it would, therefore, have greater power. In the Senate each state would have two Senators—each state would have equal power. Each House, however, would have equal rights in making the laws.

The new Congress would have authority to make laws governing all matters of national interest. It would have power to levy and collect taxes, regulate interstate and foreign commerce, spend money for common defense, and spend money for the general welfare. These were matters which would be of interest to all the states as a nation.

Each of the young 13 states would have to share much of its power with the new United States of America.

Checks and Balances in the Constitution

The delegates created a Constitution which was strong enough to bind the states together as a nation but which also left power in the hands of the people.

By dividing power among three branches of government,
  no one branch could control the government.

By having two Houses in Congress,
  no single group could make the laws.

By having the members of the House of Representatives elected according to the population of a state,
  the larger states would have more power in the House.

By having two Senators elected from each state,
  each state would have equal representation and power in the Senate.

By having a President with power to veto laws of Congress,
  unwise laws would be sent back to Congress to be studied again.

By creating the Supreme Court with final authority in law,
  the will of one high court would be final, rather than the clashing wills of the 13 states.

These are some of the checks and balances which were carefully written into the Constitution.

The Three Branches of the Federal Government.

LEGISLATIVE
THE CONGRESS

EXECUTIVE
THE PRESIDENT

JUDICIAL
THE SUPREME COURT

274

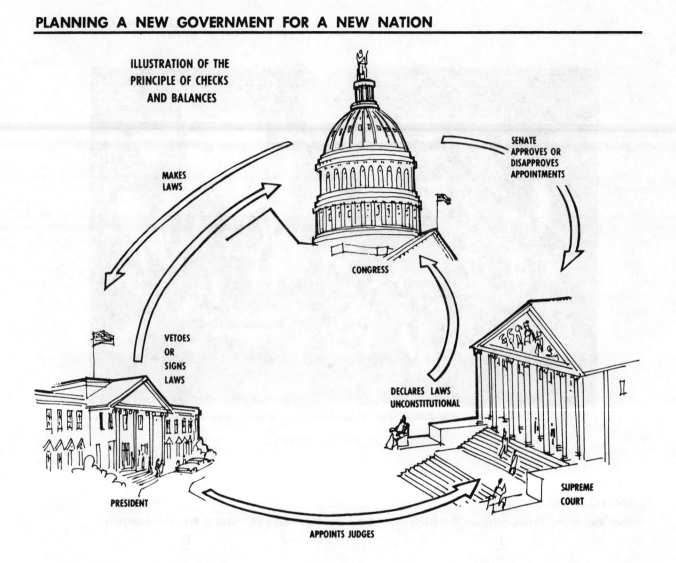

ILLUSTRATION OF THE
PRINCIPLE OF CHECKS
AND BALANCES

MAKES
LAWS

SENATE
APPROVES OR
DISAPPROVES
APPOINTMENTS

CONGRESS

VETOES
OR
SIGNS
LAWS

DECLARES LAWS
UNCONSTITUTIONAL

PRESIDENT

SUPREME
COURT

APPOINTS JUDGES

Signing and Ratifying the Constitution

Their work finally completed, on September 17, 1787, the delegates signed the Constitution. Of the 55 delegates attending the convention, only 39 actually signed the Constitution. It then had to be sent to the 13 states to be ratified by delegates selected by the people. Approval by nine states was necessary before it would become the law of the land.

Before the end of June 1788, nine states had ratified the Constitution. Some states felt that it was incomplete because it did not protect all the rights and freedoms of individuals. When these states were promised that the Constitution would be amended to protect these rights, they accepted the document. The two large states of Virginia and New York at first were undecided. By the end of July 1788, however, these states approved the Constitution. North Carolina ratified it in November 1789, and Rhode Island followed with its approval in the spring of 1790.

The United States of America began to function under the Constitution in 1789. It was the first country in the world which began life with a written Constitution assuring freedom to each of its citizens.

Signing of the Constitution.

CAN YOU DO THIS?
Select the word from column B which you can associate with the word from column A:

A	B
1. ratified	a. taxes
2. document	b. trade
3. judicial	c. approved
4. commerce	d. courts
5. checks	e. Constitution
6. levy	f. balances

Answer briefly:
1. What was the first step the colonists took toward a republic?
2. Why did the states begin to quarrel with each other?
3. What was the purpose of the Constitutional Convention?
4. Name three great leaders who attended the convention?
5. What are the three branches of our government?
6. What is the purpose of the checks and balances which are written into the Constitution?
7. What does the Constitution assure to each American citizen?

Talk about:
1. The purpose of the Preamble to the Constitution of the United States.
2. Why must people sometimes compromise with what they want?

CHAPTER 3

GIVING GOVERNMENT THE POWER TO WORK

The First Virginia Assembly.

The year was 1619. The place was Jamestown, Virginia, the first permanent English settlement in America. Twenty-two men, two elected by the people of each of Virginia's 11 boroughs, met in an assembly called the House of Burgesses. These delegates met to make laws for all the people of Virginia. Representative government had begun in America.

A year later a meeting much like the one at Jamestown was held aboard a little ship named the *Mayflower*, which brought the Pilgrims to America. The leaders of this little band of Pilgrims had asked all the men aboard the ship to help frame an agreement stating how the new colony at Plymouth would be governed. The agreement, called the Mayflower Compact, said that the men would make and obey "just and equal laws" for the good of their colony.

As shown here, self-government was part of the very beginning of English settlement in the New World.

In this chapter you will learn how our representative government received its power to delegate authority.

DISCUSS:

What is the meaning of representative government?

MEETING NEW WORDS:

ballot: A system of secret voting by the use of a printed form or a machine; the printed form itself

basically: Fundamentally; of first importance

277

The Mayflower Compact.

boroughs: Towns smaller than cities; also, divisions within larger cities

concerned: Interested in; related to; was about something

delegated authority: Power or right to act for another person or persons

efficiency: The way to get the best results with the least cost of time, money, and effort

indicated: Pointed out; showed

mayor: Chief executive of a city government

prohibited: Forbidden; not allowed

Fill in the blank in each of the following sentences with the correct word from the above list:

1. Some cities are divided into _____.
2. The people vote by _____ in most elections in the United States.
3. We should all be interested in _____ _____ in government.
4. The Senators _____ that they would vote for the law.
5. The chief of police acts under _____ _____ received from the mayor.
6. People _____ with good government vote for responsible representatives.

AS YOU READ

1. Look for the different ways of voting.
2. Look for some examples of delegated authority.

GIVING GOVERNMENT THE POWER TO WORK

As was the case with the Pilgrims, the laws in early America were made by all the men who were to obey the laws. As the number of people increased, it became impossible for all persons concerned with government to meet to make laws. Thus, when the colony in Virginia had grown to 11 boroughs, men had to be chosen by their neighbors to represent them in the House of Burgesses. Each man chosen was called a representative. When the population of the colony increased, each man in the House simply represented more colonists.

Choosing a representative is done by voting. When there are few voters, voting may be done by a show of hands. When the number of people voting is so large that all of them cannot meet in one room, written votes are usually cast at public places, called polls. The form on which the vote is recorded is called a ballot. Most voting in the United States is done by ballot. However, where the number of voters is very large, a voting machine may be used for recording votes.

Suppose that, in a recent election for Senator, people had a choice of voting for Tom Wells or Burt Hay. When the votes were counted, Wells had received 8,000 votes and Hay had received 10,000. This, of course, would indicate that the people had elected Burt Hay as Senator.

Until the next election for Senator, Mr. Hay's decisions as Senator will be the decisions of all the people he represents. When Mr. Hay's six-year term in the Senate is over, the people will probably re-elect him if they think he has done what they wanted done. If Mr. Hay has not carried out the wishes of the voters, they can, and probably will, elect a new Senator.

Final Authority

In a democracy, such as our republic, final authority in government rests with the people.

Because the people have the power to choose their representatives, they will always have the final power in governing themselves.

Delegated Authority

Often the word "authority" is used to mean power. Authority in government, under our democracy, means the power to act for the people. Such authority was given at Jamestown in 1619 when the voters gave their delegates power to act for them. This is called delegated authority.

A good example of delegated authority is that received by the mayor of a city. Among his duties is the protection of people and their property, and authority is given to him by the people to do whatever must be done to perform that duty. The mayor, in turn, delegates his authority to a chief of police who then has power

The Capitol of the United States represents Government of the people, by the people, and for the people.

to take action to assure that the police force does its work well and protects the people and their property. Should the police force not do its work properly, the mayor will call upon the police chief to explain why something was done, or was not done. Should the matter be serious enough, the mayor may even delegate his authority to a new chief of police. The mayor can delegate his authority, but not his responsibility. He will always be basically responsible for the efficiency of the police force in protecting the people and their property. If he has not properly used the authority delegated to him, the people will delegate their authority to a new mayor at the next election.

Authority delegated by the people can always be taken away by the people.

The men who drew up the Constitution of the United States did not have the power to tell the people to accept the Constitution. Therefore, it was presented to the people in each state so that they might vote for or against its approval. In turn, the people selected representatives to meet in state conventions for the purpose of deciding by vote whether or not the new plan of government should be accepted. The final power to accept the Constitution thus remained with the people of the United States.

Voting by Machine

Delegated Authority in Federal Government

The Federal government is another name for the government of the nation. The Federal government receives its basic power to govern from authority delegated to it in the Constitution and its amendments. When Congress, the President, or a Federal court takes action each must do so under and within the limits of delegated authority.

However, as stated earlier, authority delegated by the people can also be taken away by the people. The 18th Amendment to our Constitution prohibited the manufacture of, and trade in, intoxicating liquors and delegated authority to the Congress and the states to pass laws enforcing the amendment. This delegated authority was taken away from the Congress by the 21st Amendment, which repealed the 18th Amendment.

We have seen that the people of all the states, through the Federal Constitution, delegated to a Federal government the powers needed to govern the nation. Powers of government not delegated in this manner remained with the people of the several states.

The people of each state adopted a constitution which provides a general plan of government for the state. The constitution of each state declares

Voting by Paper Ballot

that the final authority in state government belongs to the people of that state. However, the state government, through the people, has only those powers not delegated to the Federal government.

Each state constitution makes provision for the same three branches of government as those of the Federal government. The people have delegated to an executive branch the authority to enforce the state laws. To a legislative branch has been delegated the authority to make state laws. To the state courts the people have delegated the authority to decide questions about the state law.

Just as the Federal Constitution provides a method by which it may be amended, each state constitution also indicates how it may be changed. For example, an important change in a state constitution took place in Nebraska. The constitution of this state had at one time divided the lawmaking branch into two legislative houses. Later, the people of Nebraska decided that one house would be better. They amended the state constitution to provide that the lawmaking branch should consist of only one legislative body. The constitution of every state can be amended to bring about changes in the state government in accordance with the wishes of the people.

Delegated Authority in Cities and Towns

The government of a state has the authority to govern its people, but only because they have delegated that power to it in a state constitution. The state government cannot govern the people properly unless a plan of government is provided for smaller communities within the state, such as cities and towns. The state government grants charters to the cities and towns for that purpose. In these charters the state government delegates to the communities a part of the authority to govern which it received from the people. Under such a charter, a community has the power to make local laws. Since the community's authority to make local laws is delegated by the state government, it cannot be greater than the authority of the state government. Consequently, the local laws passed by a community must agree with the constitution and laws of the state. Furthermore, since the state government received its power to govern from the people, it can be seen that the final authority in city and town governments also belongs to the people.

Government Power Is Delegated Authority

All government in the United States—Federal, state, and local—is government of the people, not one class or one group of people but *all* of the people; by the people, because the people elect the officers who carry on the work of the government; for the people, because the government is planned for the good of all the people.

CAN YOU DO THIS?

Select from the list below the word which best completes each sentence:

mayor	re-elect	provide
prohibit	delegated	basically

1. If a representative accomplishes what the people want done, they will probably ＿＿＿＿＿＿ him.
2. The Federal government may ＿＿＿＿＿＿＿ the levying of certain taxes by the states.
3. The mayor is ＿＿＿＿＿＿＿ responsible for good government in his city.
4. State constitutions also ＿＿＿＿＿＿＿ for a method of amendment.
5. Authority ＿＿＿＿＿＿＿ by the people may be taken away by the people.

Answer briefly:

1. What is a ballot?
2. What is meant by delegated authority?
3. What are the branches of state government?
4. Who has final authority in a state?
5. How does a state delegate authority to local communities?

Talk about:

1. Why do our citizens choose representatives?
2. What do we mean when we say that all government in the United States is government of, by, and for the people?

CHAPTER 4

CREATING THE NEW GOVERNMENT AND THE BILL OF RIGHTS

The Constitution grows in different ways. One way it grows is through decisions of the Federal courts. The decisions explain provisions that are not entirely clear and give to them their full meaning. They also apply provisions and principles of the Constitution to new situations.

The Constitution also grows by amendment. The first big growth took place with the addition of the first ten amendments. Each one of these amendments protects one or more of the rights of the people and they are, therefore, called the Bill of Rights. You will read about the Bill of Rights in this chapter.

DISCUSS:

How does the Constitution grow?

MEETING NEW WORDS:

accused: Charged a person with wrongdoing; also, the person so charged

administered: Directed the taking of (the oath of office); carried out

civil case: A law suit, not involving a crime, brought by or against a person, state, or nation (see criminal case) (explained in detail in chapter 13)

contained: Included; was a part of

crime: An act which is against the law; an unlawful act

criminal case: A law suit brought by the state or nation against a person accused of having committed a crime (see civil case) (explained in detail in chapter 13)

electors: Persons chosen by the voters for the purpose of electing the President and Vice President

excessive: Too large; beyond any degree or limit; extreme

guarantees: Promises; assurances given that something would be done

inauguration: Ceremony when President is sworn into office

included: Was among; formed a part of something

involves: Has to do with; concerns; includes

jury: A group of citizens who are chosen to listen to trials in a court and decide which side is right

legislature: Lawmaking body

quartering: Assignment of housing, as for soldiers

reserved: Saved, especially for a purpose

testify: Make a statement under oath in order to prove that something is true

trial: Hearing in a court of justice; judicial hearing

warrant: A legal document giving authority to do something

Fill in the blank in each of the following sentences with the correct word from the above list:

1. The colonists objected to the _____ _____ of soldiers in their homes.

2. All of the _____ cast their votes for George Washington.

3. An amendment to the Constitution prohibits _____ bail for accused persons.

4. The Constitution _____ freedom of speech.

5. A wife may not be forced to _____ against her husband.

6. In a criminal case the accused person has a right to a trial by _____ .

7. Thousands of people watched the _____ _____ of George Washington.

AS YOU READ

1. Make sure that you know the names of the two lawmaking bodies of the country.
2. Study how the Bill of Rights protects the people.

CREATING THE NEW GOVERNMENT AND THE BILL OF RIGHTS

After the Constitution had been accepted, its plan of government had to be put into effect. The first step in this direction was the election of a President and a new Congress. The Constitution stated how the members of the two Houses of Congress and a President should be chosen. It provided that the people of each state should elect persons to represent them in the House of Representatives, and that each state legislature should elect two Senators to the Senate. It also provided that the people should vote for electors, who would then vote for two persons—one to be President and one to be Vice President.

The First Election

The people of the states voted for the electors, who thereafter gathered and cast their votes for the President and the Vice President. George Washington received the vote of every elector. To date he has been the only President so honored. John Adams, having received the next highest number of votes, became Vice President.

George Washington Inaugurated April 30, 1789

George Washington had no desire to be President. After the war he wanted to live quietly at his home in Mount Vernon, Virginia. But his country wanted him to serve again—and needed him—so he accepted the responsibility of President of the new United States. On April 16, 1789, he left his home and went to New York City, at that time the capital of the nation. It was a long journey on horseback.

Washington's journey to New York must have made him happy—the towns through which he

Courtesy, The Mount Vernon Ladies Association

Mount Vernon.

284

PRESIDENT

SOLDIER

VIRGINIA PLANTER

Events in the Life of Washington.

passed gave great dinners in his honor; roads were lined with cheering crowds; children sang for him; guns in the villages were fired when he arrived, and again when he left.

He was met at the New Jersey coast by a large boat that had been sent from New York. It was hung with red and white bunting and was rowed by ship captains who were dressed in white. The guns of all the ships in the harbor sounded their welcome to the first President of the United States as the boat crossed the harbor to the city.

A new Congress had also been elected. It was to have met for the inauguration of the President on the 4th of March in 1789. Travel in those days was slow, however, and some of the members

of Congress were late in arriving in New York City. It was late in April before everything was ready for the inauguration.

The inauguration took place on the last day of April in Federal Hall. Robert Livingston, Chancellor of the state of New York, administered the oath of the office of President which the Constitution requires every President to take. George Washington, his hand on an open Bible, spoke the following words:

I do solemnly swear that I will faithfully execute the office of President of the United States, and will to the best of my ability, preserve, protect and defend the Constitution of the United States.

285

The Bible was raised and Washington kissed it as the seal of his pledge.

On April 30, 1789, the United States of America had its first President under the Constitution. The government provided for by the Constitution became a living government.

The President and the Congress Begin Their Work

The first work of the President and the new Congress was to organize the government which was so carefully planned by the writers of the Constitution.

Congress began its work by passing a law which provided for executive departments to assist and advise the President. To head these departments, the President appointed Alexander Hamilton as Secretary of the Treasury, Thomas Jefferson as Secretary of State, and Henry Knox as Secretary of War. The offices of Attorney General and Postmaster General were also created. To these positions the President appointed Edmund Randolph as Attorney General, and Samuel Osgood as Postmaster General. These men soon came to be known as the President's Cabinet, although there was no provision in the law for a Cabinet until over a hundred years had passed.

Congress also passed a law organizing the Federal courts. The President appointed the judges and, as required by the Constitution, the Senate approved the appointments.

Congress placed a tax on goods brought into the United States from other countries. This tax money helped to pay expenses of the new government.

The Congress Has a Problem

Some of the states had ratified the Constitution only when they were promised that a Bill of Rights would be added to it. State constitutions already contained such provisions, and many state leaders felt that the Federal Constitution should also guarantee in writing the rights and freedoms of the people.

When the new Congress met, some of its members thought that there should be no hurry to amend the Federal Constitution. However, James Madison, now elected to the House of Representatives, and other members of the Congress spoke

out in favor of adding the amendments immediately.

After much discussion, 12 amendments were approved by Congress and were sent to the states for acceptance. By 1791 ten of them were ratified and became law. These amendments were written into the Constitution as the Bill of Rights. The people were not only free, but they had a Constitution which included a Bill of Rights that guaranteed their freedom.

You will want to read every word of the first ten amendments to the Constitution. They are:

Amendment 1—Freedom of Religion, of Speech, and of the Press; Right to Assemble and Right of Petition

Guarantees freedom of religion, freedom of speech, and freedom of the press.

Guarantees the right to assemble peaceably, and the right to ask the government to change the laws.

Amendment 2—Right to Keep Arms

Gives the people the right to have weapons.

Amendment 3—Quartering of Soldiers

Provides that, in time of peace, no soldiers shall be placed in a private home without the approval of the owners.

Amendment 4—Warrants of Search and Seizure

Assures that there shall be no search or seizure of persons or things without the legal authority of a warrant, properly issued, setting forth the cause, and describing the person or place to be searched or the person(s) or thing(s) to be seized.

Amendment 5—Guarantees in Criminal Cases; Fair Price for Property

Guarantees that no person can be held to answer (brought to trial) for a serious crime without first having been accused by a Grand Jury, except persons actually in military service in time of war or public danger. (Members of the armed forces are tried by a military court without action by a Grand Jury.)

Facsimile of the Bill of Rights.

No person can be tried twice for the same crime.

No person in any criminal case shall have to testify against himself.

Life, liberty, or a person's property shall not be taken from him without a court trial.

Property will not be taken for public use without a fair price being paid for it.

Amendment 6—Rights of Accused Persons

Guarantees an accused person the right to a trial by jury.

Provides that a person accused of a crime must be told plainly the nature of the crime of which he is accused.

459-266 0 - 84 - 4 : QL 3

He has the right to have a lawyer to defend him.

An accused person has the right to hear and question those who say he has committed a crime.

All witnesses who testify against an accused person must do so in his presence.

He has the right to compel any person to appear in court as a witness to testify in his favor.

Amendment 7—Trial by Jury in Civil Cases

States that a trial by jury is guaranteed in any lawsuit which involves a claim of more than $20.

Amendment 8—Excessive Punishments

Prohibits excessive bail, excessive fines, and cruel and unusual punishments.

Amendment 9—Rights Reserved to the People

Declares that rights which the people may have had before the adoption of the Constitution are not taken away, nor do they have any lesser value, because they are not mentioned in the Constitution.

Amendment 10—Powers Reserved to the States

Declares that any powers not given to the Federal government, nor clearly taken away from the states, are reserved to the states, or to the people.

CAN YOU DO THIS?

Use each of the following phrases in a sentence of your own:

1. an accused person
2. a search warrant
3. administered the oath
4. witnesses for the accused
5. reserved to the states
6. contained in the Bill of Rights
7. a jury in civil cases

Answer these questions:

1. When was George Washington inaugurated?
2. How was Washington honored on his trip to New York City?
3. Who were the members of Washington's Cabinet?
4. What are the first ten amendments to the Constitution called?

After each of the statements below the boxes, write in the number of the amendment in which the statement can be found:

Amendment 1	Amendment 5	Amendment 6	Amendment 8
Freedom of Religion, of Speech, and of the Press	Criminal Cases	Rights of Accused Persons	Excessive Punishments

- A person cannot be forced to testify against himself. _____
- Citizens have the right to assemble peaceably. _____
- An accused person has the right to have a lawyer. _____
- An accused person cannot be required to post excessive bail. _____
- No person can be tried twice for certain crimes. _____
- The government cannot take property without paying a fair price for it. _____
- A person can go to the church of his own choosing. _____

Talk about:

Why is the Bill of Rights important to every American citizen?

CHAPTER 5

GROWTH OF THE CONSTITUTION

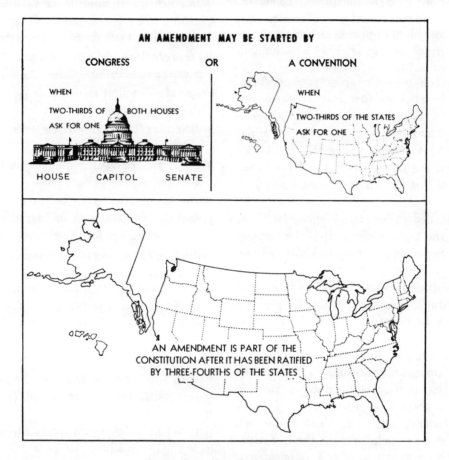

AN AMENDMENT MAY BE STARTED BY

CONGRESS OR A CONVENTION

WHEN TWO-THIRDS OF BOTH HOUSES ASK FOR ONE

HOUSE   CAPITOL   SENATE

WHEN TWO-THIRDS OF THE STATES ASK FOR ONE

AN AMENDMENT IS PART OF THE CONSTITUTION AFTER IT HAS BEEN RATIFIED BY THREE-FOURTHS OF THE STATES

Amending the Constitution.

An important question was raised at the Constitutional Convention: Should the Articles of Confederation be revised or should a new constitution be written? You know the answer to that question. A new constitution was written. To this day it continues to be the law upon which the framework of our government is based.

The Constitution was intended to be the fundamental law of the nation. It was planned to take care of the basic needs of the people for many years to come. Its writers recognized that, with the passing of time, changing conditions would require additional laws for the country. They, therefore, wrote the Constitution in a way which they believed would give Congress enough power to pass these laws without the need for a change in the Constitution. Nonetheless, they recognized that, as the nation grew, changes might also be needed in the fundamental law. To allow for this possibility, Article V was included in the Constitution. It describes the methods by which the Constitution may be amended.

Under the Articles of Confederation, amendments required approval by all of the states. A weakness of the Articles was that all of the states would never agree to needed changes. The writers of the Constitution made the amending process easier, and, at the same time, slow enough to allow for careful thought.

Amendments to the Constitution may be proposed by a two-thirds vote of both Houses of Congress, or by a national convention called by Congress at the request of two-thirds of the state legislatures. Amendments must be ratified by the legislatures of three-fourths of the states, or by special conventions in three-fourths of the states.

The Constitution was signed over 180 years ago. By 1791 the people had approved the original ten amendments. Since that time only 16 amendments have been added to the Constitution.

The Constitution gives Congress the general authority to make all laws that may be necessary for carrying out its legislative powers. This general authority makes the Constitution flexible. Laws passed by Congress under this authority have broadened the Constitution and have given it new meaning and growth by placing into effect its provisions.

However, no Federal or state law can last if it conflicts with the Constitution. It is the responsibility of the Supreme Court of the United States to determine whether a law conflicts or agrees with the Constitution. Court decisions interpreting the Constitution for this purpose have given added meaning to its provisions, and have also enabled it to grow without amendment.

Certain methods and practices have become a part of the American tradition. The methods by which political parties select persons to run for national offices are not set forth in the Constitution or a Federal law. Yet, these and other practices and customs help to make the Constitution's plan of government work and, in effect, are part of its unwritten growth.

The Constitution is the "supreme law of the land" and has survived because it is flexible and can, when necessary, be amended by the people to meet changing times.

You have read about the early growth of the Constitution, the Bill of Rights. This chapter tells how the Constitution continued to grow. It discusses Amendments 11 to 26 and explains why they were added.

DISCUSS:

Why has the Constitution of the United States survived?

MEETING NEW WORDS:

abolished: Did away with

confiscates: Takes by authority for public use

defines: Says clearly

due process of law: Regular legal steps assuring a fair hearing in accordance with the law

flexible: Not rigid; capable of taking care of new and different situations as they arise

interpretations: Explanations; the meanings given to something

original: The first in order or point of time; the first in existence

political reform: Improvement in the ideas and conditions of government

precedent: Something that may serve as a guide for later actions or decisions

previous: Earlier; gone before

principle: General rule or idea that can be used as a foundation for other rules or plans

reflecting: Showing; indicating

session: Meeting; period of meetings

social reform: Improvement in the ideas of health, living conditions, and welfare of the people

suffrage: The right to vote

Fill in the blank in each of the following sentences with the correct word from the above list:

1. When Washington refused to serve as President for a third term, he set a _____

2. That question was discussed at a _____ meeting.

3. When the government _____ private property, it must pay a fair price.

4. Since the _____ ten amendments were approved, only 16 more have been added to the Constitution.

5. The 14th Amendment _____ who is a citizen.

6. A _____ of Congress is held at least once a year.

7. The Constitution has strength and is also _____ in order to meet the changing needs of our nation.

AS YOU READ

1. Find out which amendments gave the right to vote to more people.
2. Look for the amendment that changed an amendment.

GROWTH OF THE CONSTITUTION

The Bill of Rights, which expresses the principle that the purpose of government is to protect the rights and liberties of the individual, has also grown since it was added to the Constitution in 1791. While the words of these first ten amendments remain unchanged, interpretations in court decisions have given them their fullest meanings to meet new conditions in the passing years.

Other amendments have been added to the Constitution as the need for them was expressed by the people. There are now 26 amendments to the Constitution, each reflecting a need of its time.

Amendments 11 to 26 are described below with an explanation of how they came into being.

Amendment 11—Power to Sue States (1795)

A state may not be sued in a Federal court by a citizen of another state or by a citizen of a foreign country. A person who has a claim against a state must bring his action in a court of that state.

> *The Supreme Court upheld the right of two citizens of South Carolina to sue Georgia in a Federal court for property confiscated by Georgia. The states believed that it was not proper for citizens of one state to sue another state in a Federal court. When this amendment was ratified, the Supreme Court's decision became ineffective.*

Amendment 12—Method of Electing President and Vice President (1804)

Electors must cast separate ballots for the President and the Vice President.

> *The Constitution provided for the election of the President and the Vice President by electors. Each elector voted for two persons on a single ballot. The person who received the most votes became President and the person who received the next high-*

> *est number of votes became Vice President. In the election of 1800, there was a tie between Thomas Jefferson and Aaron Burr. The members of the House of Representatives had to vote to decide between the two men. They finally chose Jefferson. This amendment made it impossible for such a situation to occur again.*

Amendment 13—Slavery Abolished (1865)

There shall be no slavery in the United States.

Amendment 14—Citizenship Defined (1868)

All persons born or naturalized in the United States are citizens of the United States. No state can limit the privileges of citizens or take away their life, liberty, or property rights without due process of law.

Amendment 15—Right to Vote (1870)

No citizen of the United States shall be denied the right to vote because of race, color, or previous condition of servitude.

> *Amendments 13, 14, and 15 deal with the status of slaves, and limit the power of the states. They are sometimes called the "National Supremacy Amendments" because they established the supremacy of the nation over the states in the matters described by the amendments. The Civil War, or the War Between the States, was fought to determine whether or not slavery would end and the states would remain united under the Constitution. In 1865, after 4 years of bitter struggle, the war ended and all slaves were freed. These three amendments grew out of this war. Congress was given the power to pass laws enforcing them.*

No amendments were added to the Constitution for more than 40 years. Then, in the space of 7 years, four amendments were ratified. These are sometimes called the "Progressive Amendments" because they reflect the spirit of political and social reform in the early 20th century.

Amendment 16—Tax on Incomes (1913)

Congress shall have the power to tax incomes without dividing such taxes among the states, and without regard to population.

POLITICAL WRITER

PRESIDENT

ARCHITECT

Jefferson as a Political Writer, as President, and as an Architect.

The Supreme Court had ruled that an income tax levied under a Federal law was a direct tax and must be divided among all of the states in accordance with their population. This decision made it impossible for the Federal government to tax people based upon their incomes in order to pay expenses of the government. The Supreme Court decision became ineffective when the 16th Amendment was ratified.

Amendment 17—Direct Election of Senators (1913)

Two Senators from each state shall be elected by the people of that state for a term of 6 years.

As first written, the Constitution provided that Senators were to be chosen by the state legislatures. This amendment made the Senators directly responsible to the voters.

Amendment 18—Prohibition (1919)

There shall be no manufacture, sale, or transportation of intoxicating liquors. Congress and the states shall have the power to pass laws enforcing this amendment.

There was a growing belief that the government should take a more active part in

helping the people to live better. The Federal government tried to do this by passing the 18th Amendment which regulated the use of intoxicating liquors.

Amendment 19—Suffrage for Women (1920)

The right of citizens to vote shall not be denied because of sex.

Efforts to give women the right to vote began in the early part of the 19th century. The great contributions made by women during World War I helped the passage of this amendment.

Amendment 20—Beginning of Presidential and Congressional Terms of Office (1933)

The President and the Vice President shall take office on January 20th and Congress shall begin its annual session on January 3rd, unless it provides for a different date.

For over a hundred years, the President and the Congress did not take office until long after the election. The Constitution provided that Congress should begin its yearly sessions in December. In the early days of the nation members who had been elected to a new Congress could not arrive in time for the opening session in December. As a result they did not take office until another session began a year later. In the meantime persons previously elected continued to make the laws. These lawmakers soon became known as "lame ducks" because they had lost the election.

This amendment abolished the "lame duck sessions" of Congress by changing the date on which the sessions of Congress should begin. It allowed the new Congress to begin at an earlier date to carry out the wishes of the people. The amendment also set January 20th, rather than March 4th, as the date for the inauguration of the President.

Amendment 21—Prohibition Ends (1933)

Amendment 18 is repealed. The carrying of intoxicating liquors into a state in violation of its laws continues to be prohibited.

Unlike other amendments, this one required ratification by state conventions, rather than by state legislatures. This requirement allowed each voter to express his own opinion on prohibition in the most direct manner.

Amendment 22—President Limited to Two Terms in Office (1951)

No person shall be elected to the office of President more than twice.

The Constitution did not limit the number of terms a President could serve. Washington set a two-term precedent. Franklin D. Roosevelt upset this precedent when he was elected in 1940 for a third term, and in 1944 for another term. This amendment established by law the two-term precedent.

Amendment 23—Voting Rights for Residents of the District of Columbia (1961)

Provides that the District shall appoint electors of the President and the Vice President.

Formerly, residents of the nation's capital could not vote in Presidential elections because the Constitution made no provision for electors in the District. These citizens wanted the same voting rights enjoyed by other citizens of the nation. They worked hard to have the Constitution amended and finally succeeded.

Amendment 24—Poll Tax Prohibited in Federal Elections (1964)

Provides that neither the United States nor any state can deny a citizen the right to vote in a primary or other election held for the purpose of choosing the President, the Vice President, or members of the Congress because he has not paid a poll tax or other tax.

Formerly, citizens living in a few states were not allowed to vote in such primaries or elections held within these states, unless they had first paid a sum of money called a poll tax. Now they are able to do so without paying the tax.

Amendment 25—Presidential Disability Defined (1967)

Provides that the Vice President shall become Acting President in the event of the President's illness or disability, and specifies how the President's disability shall be determined. Amendment also provides a method for filling the office of Vice President whenever there is a vacancy in that office.

The Constitution provides that the duties and powers of the President shall pass on to the Vice President in case of removal from office, or the death, resignation, or inability of the President to discharge the powers and duties of his office, but does not specify how that disability shall be determined. This amendment provides that the Vice President shall become Acting President under either one of two circumstances. It also provides that a new Vice President can be nominated by the President, and shall take office upon confirmation by a majority vote of both Houses of Congress. Formerly, if the Vice Presi-

dent died or succeeded to the Presidency, the office of Vice President remained vacant until the next Presidential election.

Amendment 26—Voting Rights Extended to 18-year-old Citizens (1971)

Provides that citizens cannot be denied the right to vote because of age if they are 18 years of age or older.

The qualifications for voting are not set by the Constitution but each state says which

of its citizens can vote. Most states had set the lowest age for voting at 21 years. This amendment lowered the age to 18 years for voting in all elections.

These amendments to the Constitution reflect the growth and changing conditions of our country. They also disclose the wisdom and skill of the writers of the Constitution who created a document with enough strength and flexibility to be able to serve the needs of a growing, democratic nation.

CAN YOU DO THIS?

Explain the meaning of each of the underlined words in the sentences below:

1. The most important principle of government is the protection of individual rights.
2. Interpretations in Supreme Court decisions have given new meanings to the Bill of Rights.
3. The Constitution gives the Federal government supremacy over the states in many matters.
4. The 20th Amendment abolished "lame duck sessions" of Congress.
5. The Constitution says that no man may be deprived of his liberty without due process of law.
6. The 23rd Amendment provides suffrage in Presidential elections for residents of Washington, D.C.

Complete the following sentences:

1. The _____ Amendment sets the date on which Congress shall begin its sessions.
2. The 21st Amendment ended _____
3. The 19th Amendment gave _____ to women.
4. The 17th Amendment provides for election of Senators by the _____
5. The 11th Amendment protects state governments from certain _____
6. The 26th Amendment gave voting rights to _____

Talk about:

1. What was the advantage of doing away with "lame duck congressmen"?
2. Why were the 16th, 17th, 18th, and 19th Amendments called the "Progressive Amendments"?

CHAPTER 6

VOTING—A RIGHT AND A DUTY

The truths set forth in the Declaration of Independence may be described as the foundation of the American way of life. To insure the rights of life, liberty, and the pursuit of happiness, the writers of the Constitution formed a democracy, a government deriving its "just powers from the consent of the governed."

The people of the United States are "the governed." They are governed by their own consent which they give when they vote. In a democracy the people first decide, and then make known by their votes, who will govern them and how they will be governed. You will read in this chapter about the political party system and the importance of voting.

DISCUSS:

How can the people in a democracy take part in government?

MEETING NEW WORDS:

acquainted: Informed about; have knowledge of

candidate: A person seeking office; a person who runs for office

consent: Approval; agreement

considered: Thought about; gave attention to; studied, or examined

deriving: Getting; receiving; obtaining

extension: Expansion; continuation; addition

frequently: Often; many times

insure: Make safe; guarantee; protect

majority: More than one-half

nominate: To name or choose a person to be considered for office

urge: Plead with; earnestly request

various: Different; several or many; a number of

Choose the correct meaning for each underlined word in the following sentences:

1. The writers of the Declaration of Independence wanted to <u>insure</u> certain rights of the people.

    guarantee   take away   prohibit

2. Our government is one <u>deriving</u> its power from the people.

    giving   deciding   getting

3. Citizens should be <u>acquainted</u> with the records of their political leaders.

    near by   have knowledge of   called by

4. We <u>frequently</u> meet our neighbors at political party meetings.

    often   never   once

5. Party members <u>nominate</u> candidates for President and Vice President at national conventions.

    name   defeat   crown

AS YOU READ

Find the answers to these questions:

1. How can a citizen learn more about a political party?

2. Why is the right to vote an important right?

295

VOTING—A RIGHT AND A DUTY

You have learned that the people of the United States have the final authority to govern. By voting, they delegate that authority to others who will then represent them in carrying on the work of the government.

Who Can Vote

After the Civil War the right to vote was given to former slaves. Under the 15th Amendment to the Constitution, no citizen can be refused the right to vote because of his race, color, or because he has been a slave. The 19th Amendment gave women the right to vote.

Not every citizen is eligible to vote, however, because each state can, and has, set up additional qualifications for voters. Common to all states are their laws requiring that a voter be a United States citizen, and a resident for a certain length of time in the place within the state wherein his vote will be cast. Under Federal law, a citizen cannot be denied the right to vote for President and Vice President because of failure to comply with that state's residence requirements for voting.

Each state sets a minimum age for voting, but the 26th Amendment provides that the minimum age cannot be set at an age over 18 years. Some state laws require that a citizen must be able to read and write before he can vote, but Federal law has suspended this requirement for voting in both Federal and state elections. That act allows a person to qualify for voting if he was educated in American-flag schools in which the predominant classroom language was other than English, or if he shows that he successfully completed the sixth primary grade in such a school.

You will always want to use your right to vote. You should find out what you must do to qualify under the law of the state in which you make your home. Most states also require a citizen to register before election day with election officials in the place where he lives. At that time, he must establish his qualifications to vote and have his name placed on a voting list. As soon as you become a citizen you should register to vote in the community where you make your home. Then, when election time comes, vote—and never fail to vote. It is your duty as a citizen to vote. In this way you use your authority to govern.

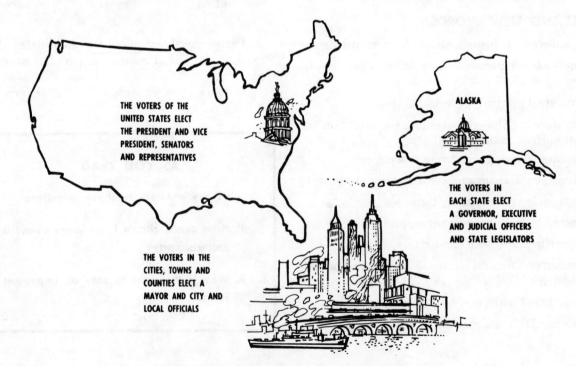

THE VOTERS OF THE UNITED STATES ELECT THE PRESIDENT AND VICE PRESIDENT, SENATORS AND REPRESENTATIVES

ALASKA

THE VOTERS IN EACH STATE ELECT A GOVERNOR, EXECUTIVE AND JUDICIAL OFFICERS AND STATE LEGISLATORS

THE VOTERS IN THE CITIES, TOWNS AND COUNTIES ELECT A MAYOR AND CITY AND LOCAL OFFICIALS

The Voters Elect Many Representatives.

How the Final Authority to Govern Is Used

By his vote a citizen influences the government in many ways. His vote helps to elect officers who make and enforce the laws of the nation, the state, and the city or town in which he lives.

As a qualified voter, you can vote for or against proposed amendments to the constitution of your state. Often you will be asked to vote on special issues concerning the spending of money for highways, schools, water sytems, or other public projects. State constitutions and city charters frequently declare that the right to borrow money above a certain amount must be decided by the voters. Sometimes a state legislature will be unwilling to take final action to pass an especially important law until the citizens first express their approval by voting for it.

When a citizen votes he indicates his own personal choice. However, the will of the majority of voters is expressed in the final results of most elections. A majority vote means more than one-half of the votes cast. Most elections and many public issues in the United States are decided by a majority vote.

In an election three or more candidates will often seek the same public office, and no one candidate may receive a majority of all votes cast. Sometimes, such an election will be decided by a plurality; that is, the winning candidate will be the one who receives the highest number of votes, even though he gets less than a majority. The difference between the number of votes cast for the winning candidate and the number given to the candidate receiving the next highest number of votes is called a plurality.

A citizen has a duty to vote, as well as a right to vote. He should give serious thought before making his choice of candidates. A good citizen votes in every election. Only in this way can we have a government by the people.

Forming Opinions

The decisions which a voter is required to make on important issues are a serious responsibility. Such decisions may affect our lives, liberty, and property. But, meeting the responsibility of

making decisions helps free people keep their freedoms. Every citizen has a duty to keep himself informed about candidates and issues. Before he forms opinions and makes decisions, he should read, listen, and think—then he can vote for what he believes is right.

Sharing Opinions

Although a citizen can and should vote as he wishes, he ought to be interested in what other people are thinking and saying. By obtaining the opinions of others concerning issues in government, the citizen can learn all sides of a question and this will help him make a good decision when he casts his vote. Citizens can learn about the opinions of others in many ways. Public issues and government matters can be discussed at home, in a person's neighborhood, and at work. Much can be learned about how others think by watching television, listening to the radio, and reading newspapers and other printed materials.

An intelligent voter reads more than one paper, magazine, or book, in order to get different opinions about candidates, party platforms, and issues.

A citizen of this country should want to know what other voters think about questions of the day, but the final decision as to how he will vote should be his own. However, his decision should be made only after he has heard all sides of the various questions.

The Political Party System

A citizen can also learn how others think by becoming acquainted with the political party system. A political party is a group of people who work together as an organization to get the kind of government action they believe in and want.

Political parties have helped to make our plan of government work. They are an extension of the democratic ideas first developed by the Constitution. Although the Constitution makes provisions for the election and appointment of persons to offices in government, it says nothing about how persons shall be nominated, or chosen to be considered, for these positions.   Nominees are usually chosen by political parties in accordance with methods and practices that have been developed over the years.   The methods by which candidates are nominated are just as much a part of our plan of government as if they had been written into the Constitution.   They are a part of the American tradition which has added to the growth of

the Constitution without its amendment.   Without them, provisions of the Constitution could not be put into effect.

Party Platform

Members and leaders of each party prepare a statement setting forth the aims and objectives of the party.   This statement is called the party

General Outline of the Organization of a Political Party.

298

A National Convention.

platform. The platform makes known the position of the party and its members on important public questions and affairs of government. It may call for more, fewer, or different taxes. It may recommend changes in the powers delegated by the people to their elected representatives.

Nomination of Candidates

Most men and women who seek election to public offices are nominated by a political party. Once they are nominated, they are called candidates for election.

Candidates of a political party may be nominated at a primary election. This is a special election at which the registered voters of each party are given an opportunity to choose candidates who will represent their party in a general election. In a primary election, citizens can vote only for the nominees of the party with which they are registered.

Candidates can also be nominated by a convention. Members of a political party select and send delegates to a meeting place. After considering the qualifications of possible candidates, the delegates choose those who will represent the party. The candidates for President and Vice President are nominated in this manner at a national convention.

A number of states allow a person to be nominated by petition. This is done by having qualified voters sign a petition requesting that a certain citizen's name be placed on the ballot. Men and women nominated in this way are called independent candidates.

The Voter and His Party

Each political party would like to have the voters elect its candidates to a majority of the public offices. Such a majority would give the party the power to carry out its aims and objectives as stated in the party platform.

Each political party tries to gain the support of as many voters as possible. One way used to gain public support is by holding meetings to which all voters are invited. Copies of the party platform are given to the voters at the meetings. Members and leaders of the party make speeches and urge the voters to elect its candidates. Booklets are also given out which show what the men in office have, or have not, done and what the candidates of the party promise to do if they are elected, or re-elected. A citizen may join any party and may attend its meetings and serve on committees. He can make speeches and give copies of the party platform to other voters. He can ask voters to support the candidates of his party.

CAN YOU DO THIS?

Explain the underlined part of each sentence:

1. What does consent of the governed mean?
2. What does support a candidate mean?
3. What does the extension of democratic ideas mean?
4. What does nominate a candidate mean?
5. What does sign a petition mean?

Answer the following questions:

1. Who is eligible to vote in the United States?
2. What are some of the issues that citizens are asked to vote on?
3. What is a majority vote?
4. What is meant by an independent candidate?
5. How can a citizen learn what other people think about candidates or issues?
6. What is meant by a party platform?

Talk about:

1. Why is voting a serious responsibility?
2. Why is it necessary to register?

Joining a political party is one of the most effective ways for a citizen to take part in government. However, it is not the only way. A citizen is not required to become a member of a political party. In fact, many wish to be, and they are, listed as independent voters. A voter is free to change to another party if he wishes to do so. He does this at registration time.

Election Day

After a candidate has been nominated to run for public office, he must be elected by the people. This is done at a general election. A general election is one in which only one candidate from among those nominated is chosen by the voters to fill the office for which they all ran.

In a general election a person may vote for the candidates of any party.

The Spirit of Democracy in the United States

The people of the United States decide public questions by votes—not by force. The voters may make a mistake and elect a person who does not perform his duty properly. They can correct this error in judgment by replacing him with another person at the next election for the office to which he was elected.

CHAPTER 7

ORGANIZATION OF THE CONGRESS

A long time ago a Greek slave, Aesop, became famous as a master storyteller. His stories, later called fables, always ended with a bit of wisdom.

One fable was about a family whose members had many quarrels. One day the father asked each of his ten sons to bring a stick to him. He tied the sticks in a bundle and asked each son, in turn, to break the bundle. None of the young men could break the bundle of sticks.

Next, the father untied the bundle and gave each son a stick to break. This, each son could do easily. He then told the sons that as long as they remain separated they can be easily defeated but, united, they would be a match for their enemies. "Union is strength!"

It is probable that the men who wrote the Constitution knew this fable of Aesop. Benjamin Franklin, one of these writers, is said to have remarked:

> *"We must indeed all hang together, or most assuredly we shall all hang separately."*

The men who drew up the Constitution firmly believed that one state alone, like one stick, could be easily destroyed. They knew that in a union of all the states there would be great strength. The Constitution was planned to guarantee such a union. As a result, the Federal government of our 50 states still operates within that framework.

This chapter outlines the organization of the legislative branch of our government, Congress.

DISCUSS:

What is the value of a union of small states?

MEETING NEW WORDS:

adjourn: End a meeting; continue until a later time

agriculture: Relating to farming and farmers

appropriation: Money set aside to pay for the cost of government and its related activities

defeated: Destroyed; beaten; disapproved

district: The part of a state which a Congressman (Representative) represents; geographical area set aside for a special purpose

preside: To be in charge of a meeting; conduct a meeting

similar: Alike in many, but not all, ways; basically or mostly the same

standing committee: A permanent committee

vested: Given to; placed with; conferred upon; belongs to

Fill in the blank in each of the following sentences with the correct word from the above list:

1. Senators and Representatives have _____ _____ responsibilities.

2. The _____ Committee studies problems about farming.

3. What time will the meeting _____?

4. The power to make laws is ＿＿＿＿＿＿
in Congress.

5. The Chairman asked for an additional
＿＿＿＿＿＿＿＿＿＿＿＿＿＿ to continue the
work of the committee.

6. The people of the 5th Congressional
＿＿＿＿＿＿＿＿＿＿＿ elected Mr. Randall.

7. The Chairman will ＿＿＿＿＿＿＿＿ at
the meeting.

8. The Foreign Relations Committee is a
＿＿＿＿＿＿＿＿＿＿＿＿＿＿ of the Senate.

AS YOU READ

1. Look for the differences between the Senate and the House of Representatives.

2. Find out what the Constitution says about the officers of the Senate and the House of Representatives.

ORGANIZATION OF THE CONGRESS

The first sentence of Article I of the Constitution says:

"All legislative powers herein granted shall be vested in a Congress of the United States, which shall consist of a Senate and House of Representatives."

By these words the first authority or power that "We the People" delegated in the Constitution, the legislative or lawmaking power, was given to Congress.

The Congress

A study of the two Houses of Congress will show that they are different and, at the same time, similar.

The Capitol Building.

Senate in Session

House in Session

Representation in the Senate

A Senator represents the people of the whole state.

There are 100 members in the Senate.

The people of the whole state elect two Senators.

Representation in the House of Representatives

A Representative acts for the people of the Congressional district of the state in which he is elected.

There are 435 members in the House of Representatives.

Representatives are elected according to the number of people residing in a state. However small the population may be, its people are guaranteed at least one Representative.

Qualifications of a Senator

A Senator must be at least 30 years of age.

He must have been a citizen of the United States for at least 9 years.

He must be a resident of the state from which he is elected.

Qualifications of a Representative

A Representative must be at least 25 years of age.

He must have been a citizen of the United States for at least 7 years.

He must be a resident of the state from which he is elected.

Term of Office of a Senator

Six years.

One-third of the Senators are elected every 2 years; in this way two-thirds of the Senators are always experienced legislators. They may be re-elected.

Term of Office of a Representative

Two years.

The term of office of all Representatives ends on the same day; if they wish to return to Congress, they must be re-elected.

Both Houses of Congress have equal authority in some matters. Each House has some power not given to the other. In Chapter 8 you will learn how their powers are similar and different.

When the Congress Meets

Since every 2 years one-third of the Senators and all of the Representatives are elected, the life of a Congress lasts for 2 years. The 20th Amendment provides that the Congress shall meet at noon on January 3rd of each year, unless by law it provides for a different day. This meeting of Congress is called a regular session, and it continues until the members of both Houses decide to adjourn. A special session is one called by the President to consider problems which are so important that they require immediate attention and cannot wait until the next regular session.

Senate and House Officers

The writers of the Constitution knew that the Senate and the House of Representatives would need officers to preside over their meetings and keep things running smoothly. They provided for certain officers and authorized each House of Congress to choose other needed officers.

Officers in the Senate

The Vice President of the United States is the President of the Senate and presides over its sessions.

The President of the Senate has no vote except in the case of a tie.

A President pro tempore presides if the Vice President is absent.

Additional officers are chosen by the Senators to perform other duties.

Officers in the House of Representatives

The Speaker of the House is chosen by its members and presides over its sessions.

By tradition the Speaker is a member of the political party to which most of the House members belong. As a result, he often has a great deal of influence in selecting members of important committees and in conducting the business of the House.

Additional officers are chosen by members of the House to perform other duties.

The members of each political party in each House of Congress select a "floor leader." He works to help pass laws which his party favors, and to defeat those laws which his party opposes. He is assisted by other Senators or Representatives who are members of his own party.

Senate and House Committees

A great deal of the work of both Houses of Congress is done by those legislators who are members of individual committees.

The Senate has 16 standing committees:

Aeronautical and Space Science
Agriculture and Forestry
Appropriations
Armed Services
Banking, Housing, and Urban Affairs
Commerce
District of Columbia
Finance
Foreign Relations
Government Operations
Interior and Insular Affairs
Judiciary
Labor and Public Welfare
Post Office and Civil Service
Public Works
Rules and Administration

The House of Representatives has 21 standing committees:

Agriculture
Appropriations
Armed Services
Banking and Currency
District of Columbia
Education and Labor
Foreign Affairs
Government Operations
House Administration
Interior and Insular Affairs

Internal Security
Interstate and Foreign Commerce
Judiciary
Merchant Marine and Fisheries
Post Office and Civil Service
Public Works
Rules
Science and Astronautics
Standards of Official Conduct
Veterans' Affairs
Ways and Means

From this study it can be seen that the Congress consists of a body of qualified Senators and Representatives, leaders who preside over the sessions of each legislative House, and committees of legislators whose main work is that of preparing bills for final action by the whole Congress.

CAN YOU DO THIS?

After each of the statements below the boxes, write in the House of Congress to which it relates:

The Senate	The House of Representatives

- Member must have lived in the United States for 9 years _____.
- Has at least one member from each state _____.
- Member must be 25 years of age _____.
- Members serve for 6 years _____.
- Term of all members ends on the same day _____.
- Each state elects two _____.
- One-third of members are elected every 2 years _____.
- Members serve for 2 years _____.
- Member must be 30 years of age _____.

Answer briefly:

1. When does a regular session of Congress meet?
2. What determines the total number of Representatives from each state?
3. Who presides over the Senate?
4. Who presides over the House of Representatives?
5. What work is done by the standing committees of Congress?

Talk about:

1. How does the organization of Congress carry out our principles of representative government?
2. Discuss the advantages of having all Representatives and only one-third of the Senators elected every 2 years.

The United States Capitol building in Washington, D.C.

CHAPTER 8

MAKING THE LAWS—THE LEGISLATIVE BRANCH

You will recall from Chapter 6 that the Federal Constitution was drawn up to provide only the broad outlines of the nation's government. No attempt was made to include in that document a complete and detailed description of the entire structure and operation of the government. Using foresight, the authors of the Constitution left many details of such matters to be developed over a period of time by the future government. They wisely reasoned that the persons elected to conduct the business of government would be in the best position to determine the exact machinery and procedures needed for this purpose.

The way in which Congress works and the legislative tools that it has created illustrate what has been said above. The Constitution provides for a Congress, consisting of the Senate and the House of Representatives, to make laws for the nation. It lists the qualifications of Senators and Representatives, states how they are to be elected, and grants them authority to pass laws concerning certain matters.

The Constitution, however, does not describe the exact process through which a bill must pass before it becomes a law. Nor does it mention the congressional committees which have become so important and necessary to the passage of legislation. The parts of the lawmaking procedure and the machinery which were not provided for by the fundamental law have been supplied by Congress because they are necessary to the performance of its authorized functions.

This chapter describes the matters listed in the Constitution concerning which the Congress may and may not pass laws. It also explains how Federal laws are passed by the Congress under a lawmaking system basically authorized by the Constitution and perfected throughout the years by the Congress itself.

DISCUSS:

How does your Congressman know the needs of the citizens he represents?

MEETING NEW WORDS:

assigned: Appointed; given for a purpose; allotted

confirm: Officially approve; ratify

convicts: Finds or proves guilty of a crime

general terms: Not detailed; broad provisions and meanings

impeachment: Accusation of serious misconduct by a government official in the performance of his public duties

implied: Not written or stated, but understood to exist or follow as a natural result of something already written or stated

introduce: Start; bring in

maintain: Keep up; support; pay the cost of

militia: Army of citizens trained for war or any other emergency; military force made up of citizens

participate: To take part in; have a share in

procedures: Ways of doing things; methods by which things are done

referred: Sent; turned over to

report: An account of something done, seen, heard, read, or considered; to furnish such an account

sources: Places from which anything comes; beginnings of; origins of

Pick out the word(s) below each sentence that gives the meaning of the underlined word(s). Explain the meaning of the sentence.

1. The Senator promised to introduce a bill for the benefit of the farmers.

    start   dissapprove   ratify

2. The Constitution did not provide the procedures for making laws.

    appropriations   methods   witnesses

3. Good citizens participate in their government by voting.

    play   manage   take part

4. The Constitution of the United States is written in general terms.

    not detailed   military terms   short loans

5. Congress will confirm the appointment of the ambassador.

    delay   approve   disagree with

AS YOU READ

1. Look for some things that Congress can and cannot do.
2. Study how a bill becomes a law.

MAKING THE LAWS—THE LEGISLATIVE BRANCH

Authority of the Congress to Legislate

The Constitution gives to the Congress certain specific powers and authorizes it to pass all laws which may be necessary to put these powers into use and make them effective in carrying on the business of the government for the people. By reason of these specific powers and this broad legislative authority, the Congress has other powers not specifically listed in the Constitution. Although not written into the Constitution, these other powers are implied because, without them, the Congress could not make full use of the specific powers.

Some powers delegated to the Congress by the Constitution may be grouped under various headings:

● *Money and Trade*

Under this heading Congress has the power to:

Provide for the coining of money and the regulation of its value

Borrow money

Levy and collect taxes

The broad authority to pass all laws necessary to make effective the specific powers to borrow money, and to levy and collect taxes, also gives Congress an implied power to organize a system of banks.

Regulate commerce among the states and with foreign countries

The writers of the Constitution probably realized that, with the natural growth of the nation, new kinds of commerce would appear and should be regulated by Congress. Consequently, this power is expressed in general terms. The meaning of commerce is neither explained nor limited. As a result, it has been possible to hold that the telephone, telegraph, radio, and television systems are engaged in commerce and that the Congress has the power to pass laws regulating their operation in the interest of all the people of the United States.

● *National Defense*

"We the People of the United States, in order to . . . provide for the common defense . . . do ordain and establish this Constitution for the United States of America."

To achieve this objective of the Preamble, certain specific and implied powers are delegated to the Congress. Under the heading of National Defense, Congress has the power to:

Provide for the common defense

Provide and maintain an Army, a Navy, and an Air Force

When the Constitution was written, the Founding Fathers could not have foreseen the possibility of an Air Force. However, the implied power of Congress to establish this branch of the armed forces under the broad national defense authority cannot be questioned.

Provide money for the armed forces, and regulate their size

Make rules governing the armed forces

Declare war

Aid in organizing and arming state militias (State National Guard units)

Call out the state militias in any national emergency

● *Other Authority*

Other specific and implied powers delegated to the Congress fall within no one group. Under the heading of Other Authority, Congress has the power to:

Establish requirements and procedures for the naturalization of aliens

Establish a system of post offices

Establish a system of weights and measures

Pass laws governing the place in which the seat of the United States government (District of Columbia) is located

● *The Similar Authority of Each House*

Most powers delegated by the Constitution are vested in both Houses equally. Both can introduce bills to use the delegated powers listed above, except those which relate to the raising of money. However, each House has the authority to consider and vote for or against bills which carry out such powers, including those which are concerned with the raising of money.

● *Different Authority of Each House*

Money bills cannot be introduced in the Senate. This very important power is given to the House of Representatives alone. Such bills must be proposed and passed first by the House of Representatives.

The Constitution also gives to each House additional powers not given to the other. The power of impeachment is given to the House of Representatives alone. Only the Senate, however, can try the official to determine whether he is guilty as accused. If the impeached official is found guilty by two-thirds of the Senate, he will be re-

moved from public office and, perhaps, brought to trial before a regular court in criminal proceedings.

The Senate alone has the power to confirm the President's selection of persons to serve as members of his Cabinet, or to fill other important positions in the government.

Another power not shared with the House of Representatives is the Senate's authority to ratify a treaty between the United States and a foreign nation. Unless a treaty is ratified, it does not become effective.

● *Authority Denied to Both Houses*

When the Constitution was written, the abuses which had caused the colonies to break away from Great Britain and declare their independence were fresh in the memories of its writers. They recalled all too clearly that the British King and Parliament had exercised lawmaking powers without the consent of the colonists. They were fearful that certain legislative powers given Congress might be used in a way that would be unfair and not in the best interests of the nation as a whole. To prevent this from happening, the Founding Fathers provided in the Constitution that Congress *shall not* have the power to:

Tax exports (goods shipped from one state to another or to a foreign country)

Pass trade laws favoring one state over another

Spend tax money unless a law has been passed authorizing it to be spent

The law must show how the money will be spent and, from time to time, Congress must issue a report telling how public money has been spent.

Pass a law to punish a person for an offense that was not a crime when it was committed

Pass a law to deprive a person in jail of the right to be taken before a judge for the purpose of determining whether there is sufficient basis under the law to keep him in jail

If the judge decides that there is no basis for holding the person in jail, he must be released.

Pass a law which convicts a person of an offense and sets forth his punishment

In effect, this provision guarantees the right of an accused person to have a hearing in court before a judge and, if he wishes it, a trial by jury.

How a Law Begins

A law begins as a proposal—a proposal to satisfy some public need or to solve a problem of the people through action by the lawmaking branch of the government. A proposal is called a bill when, in proper form, it is submitted by a legislator to Congress for consideration and action.

How a Bill Is Proposed

A bill can be submitted to the Congress only by a Senator or a Representative. However, a proposal of legislative action may come from any one of a number of different sources.

People or organizations may suggest to a Senator or Representative that there is need for a new law, or a Senator or Representative himself may decide that a new law is needed.

A standing committee of either House may prepare a bill to solve a problem relating to the work of that committee.

A special committee appointed to study a particular problem may suggest that a bill be passed.

The President may recommend legislation.

Committees Study All Bills

Before a Senator or Representative can vote intelligently for or against any bill, it is necessary that he understand its provisions, why the law is needed, and the effect that it will have upon the people it is expected to benefit. This requires a careful study of the bill

Thousands of bills are introduced in each House every year. Since it is not possible for every Senator and Representative to study all of these bills, much of the work is done by the standing committees and their subcommittees. Each House has its own committees.

Every bill introduced in Congress is assigned for study to a committee of the House in which it was introduced. The name of a committee describes the subject matter of the bills which are referred to it. For example, a bill introduced in the Senate and relating to labor matters would be assigned to the Labor and Public Welfare Committee of the Senate, as would a bill concerning social security.

Each standing committee has a chairman. More often than not, the committee chairman is a Senator or Representative who has served in Congress for many years. Usually he has had a great deal of experience with matters handled by the committee which he heads.

When the committee has finished its study of a bill, the bill is returned to the House from which it came, with a report of committee action. In this way, every member of each House has the benefit of the study made by its committees before he decides how to vote on a bill.

Examine the chart on the following page. It shows the steps that a bill must pass through from the time it is introduced until it is signed by the President and becomes a law.

Many bills never become laws. Some may be pigeon-holed and never acted upon by the committee. However, in the House of Representatives a majority of its members may sign a petition which will force the committee to return the bill to the whole House for debate and vote; in the Senate such a bill can be taken out of the committee when a majority of the Senators vote for such action. Other bills may be defeated by a final vote in either House of Congress. Still others may be defeated by a Presidential veto.

The President may veto a proposed law by refusing to sign it. When he vetoes a bill, the President returns it to the House which introduced it and tells why he opposes it. The bill can then be passed over the President's veto by a two-thirds vote of both Houses of Congress.

The President has 10 days in which to sign a bill. If he does not sign or veto it within that time, the bill becomes a law without his signature. If Congress adjourns within the 10 days allowed for the President to sign the bill, it does not become a law (unless he signs it within the 10 days). This is called a "pocket veto."

The people of the United States can participate in their government by recognizing the need for new laws and supporting Congress in its efforts to pass the necessary legislation.

HOW A BILL BECOMES A LAW

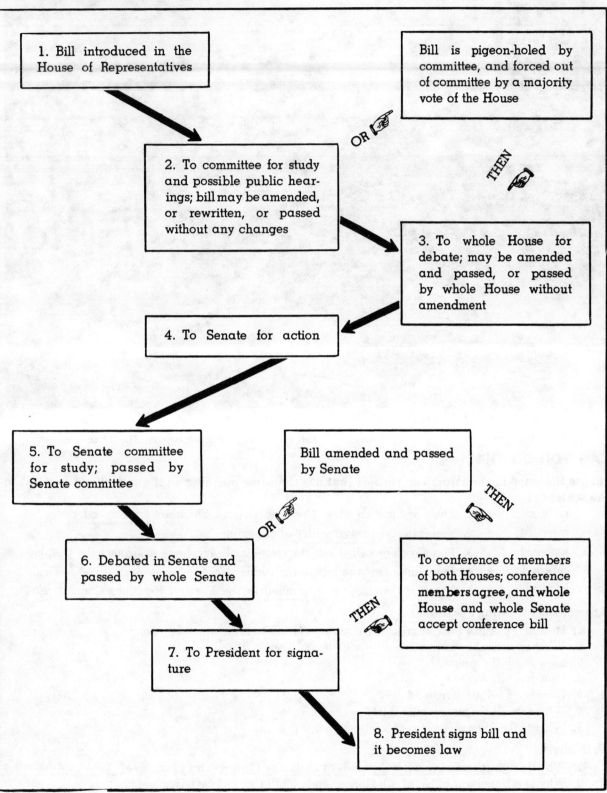

1. Bill introduced in the House of Representatives

Bill is pigeon-holed by committee, and forced out of committee by a majority vote of the House

2. To committee for study and possible public hearings; bill may be amended, or rewritten, or passed without any changes

OR ☞ THEN ☞

3. To whole House for debate; may be amended and passed, or passed by whole House without amendment

4. To Senate for action

5. To Senate committee for study; passed by Senate committee

Bill amended and passed by Senate

OR ☞ THEN ☞

6. Debated in Senate and passed by whole Senate

To conference of members of both Houses; conference members agree, and whole House and whole Senate accept conference bill

THEN ☞

7. To President for signature

8. President signs bill and it becomes law

President Ronald Reagan at his desk in the Oval Office, in the White House, Washington, D.C.   This Pete Souza photograph courtesy The White House.

CAN YOU DO THIS?

Choose the word in the column on the left that has the same meaning as the underlined word(s) in the sentence:

militia	1. The Constitution gives Congress powers which are <u>understood</u>.
convicted	2. The man was <u>proved guilty</u> of the crime.
assigned	3. The governor called out the state's <u>military force</u> to protect the people.
referred	4. The House <u>sent</u> the bill to the committee.
implied	5. The new Senator was <u>appointed</u> to the Foreign Relations Committee.

Answer the following questions:

1. How is it possible for Congress to pass laws relating to radio and television?
2. What is meant by "impeachment of a Federal officer"?
3. How is a bill proposed?
4. How is a bill vetoed?
5. How can a bill be defeated?
6. Where do all the money bills start?
7. What is the difference between a bill and a law?

Talk about:

1. Why does the Constitution list the kinds of authority Congress may not have?
2. Why is it important to have both Houses study a bill?

312

CHAPTER 9

THE PRESIDENT—THE EXECUTIVE BRANCH

Abraham Lincoln was one of the most beloved Presidents of the United States. He was President when the issues of slavery and secession were being decided. During this critical period, which saw the country involved in the Civil War, Lincoln led the fight to keep our nation together and to free the slaves.

Mr. Lincoln, our sixteenth President, was born in a tiny log cabin in Kentucky. His mother died when he was 9 years old. His stepmother encouraged "Abe," who was hungry for learning, to study and learn as much as he could. Although he attended school for a very short time, Lincoln educated himself by reading every book he could find or borrow.

Abraham Lincoln.

When he was a young man, Lincoln found a set of old law books in a barrel. His reading of these books led to the beginning of a law career. His law career led to politics, and politics led to the Presidency.

Abraham Lincoln was one of our greatest Presidents. Many of his words are written in the hearts of all Americans.

He made one of the nation's most famous speeches at the dedication of our national cemetery at the site of the battle of Gettysburg (Pennsylvania). Imagine that you are listening to this tall, thin man as he sadly begins:

"Fourscore and seven years ago our fathers brought forth on this continent a new nation, conceived in liberty, and dedicated to the proposition that all men are created equal...."

Look with him across the cold cemetery as he ends his speech with these stirring words:

".... that we here highly resolve that these dead shall not have died in vain, that this nation, under God, shall have a new birth of freedom, and that government
of the people,
by the people,
for the people,
shall not perish from the earth."

In this chapter you will read about the duties and powers of the President of the United States.

DISCUSS:

How can you help to educate yourself?

MEETING NEW WORDS:

agencies: Organized groups of officials or other persons selected to do some special job, or to administer a law or laws

campaign: Organized action to produce a certain result, such as winning an election; to take such action

313

The White House, Washington, D.C.

Photograph courtesy The White House.

crisis: A time when difficult decisions must be made; turning point

depression: A period of unemployment and widespread poverty

entitled: Given a claim or right to

injustice: Violation of a right; inequity; a wrong; unfairness

negotiate: Discuss and arrange terms; consult

nobility: People of high rank, title, or birth

pardons: Official orders forgiving a crime

popularity: Being liked by most people

prestige: Reputation, influence, or distinction based on what is known of one's abilities, achievements, opportunities, associations, etc.

reprieves: Temporary delays in carrying out punishment

secession: The right of a state to leave the Union

title: Name showing rank, position, or condition in life

Fill in each blank in the sentences below with the proper word from the list above:

1. The Secretary of State helps to _____ treaties with other countries.

2. During the Civil War _____ of the states was an issue.

3. In a time of national _____ the President is often given more power.

4. After a candidate has been nominated, he begins his _____ for office.

314

5. The office of the President carries with it much _____.

6. The President may grant _____ and pardons to persons convicted in Federal courts.

7. The lawyers knew that _____ might happen.

AS YOU READ

1. **Find out how a man becomes President.**
2. **Remember some of the duties and responsibilities of the President.**

THE PRESIDENT—THE EXECUTIVE BRANCH

In the 1600 block of Pennsylvania Avenue in Washington, the District of Columbia, there is only one house. It is the White House, the home of the President of the United States. In another country the home of the chief executive would be called a palace and the master of the house would have a title of nobility. Article I, Section 9, of the Constitution states that no person shall be granted a title of nobility by the United States. Therefore, it is "Mr. President," one of the citizens, who lives in the White House.

Article II of the Constitution gives the President the executive power to carry out the laws of the nation. It states that the President shall be a natural-born citizen, at least 35 years of age, and a resident of the United States for at least 14 years. The Constitution also provides for the payment of a salary to him, and describes his duties and powers. It further declares that the President shall be elected by electors chosen in a manner provided by the state legislatures and shall serve for a term of 4 years. Amendment 22 states that no President shall be elected more than twice.

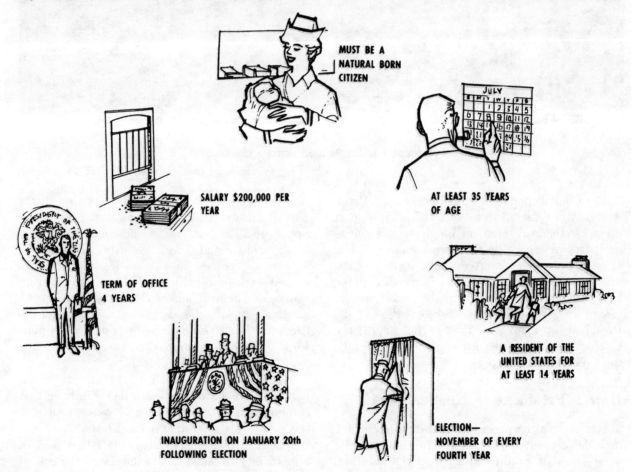

MUST BE A NATURAL BORN CITIZEN

AT LEAST 35 YEARS OF AGE

SALARY $200,000 PER YEAR

TERM OF OFFICE 4 YEARS

A RESIDENT OF THE UNITED STATES FOR AT LEAST 14 YEARS

INAUGURATION ON JANUARY 20th FOLLOWING ELECTION

ELECTION— NOVEMBER OF EVERY FOURTH YEAR

The President of the United States.

President Ronald Reagan visits a classroom.

Michael Evans photograph courtesy The White House.

The Constitution also describes how the President may be removed from office and provides that upon his removal, or upon his death, his duties shall be carried out by the Vice President. The Presidential Succession Act of 1947 provides that, in case of the death or removal from office of the President and Vice President, they shall be succeeded by (1) the Speaker of the House, (2) the President pro tempore of the Senate, and (3) the Cabinet members in the order, generally, in which their offices were created.

How a President Is Nominated

The nominating procedure is just as important in a democracy as the election procedure. The nomination of candidates answers the question, "Who will run for office?"

No single nominating procedure is used in the United States. Since 1840, however, the convention system has been used to nominate candidates for President and Vice President. During the summer of the year in which a President is to be elected, each political party holds a national convention. The members of the party in each state send delegates to the convention. They elect officers for the convention and agree on a party platform. The delegates are then ready to select the party's candidate for President.

There is first a roll call of the states. As the name of each state is called, a delegate from that state may offer the name of a person to represent the party as its candidate for President.

When the delegates of every state have had an opportunity to name their candidates, the roll of states is called again, and all of the delegates vote

316

to determine which one of the proposed candidates will receive the nomination. The candidate who receives a majority of the votes is nominated for the office of President.

The candidate for Vice President is chosen in the same way that the candidate for President is selected.

Candidates conduct their campaigns for the offices of President and Vice President until the election, which is held on the first Tuesday after the first Monday in November.

How a President Is Elected

The chief executive is chosen officially by the Presidential electors from all the states. Every state is entitled to have as many electors as it has Senators and Representatives in Congress. When the citizens of a state vote for President, they actually vote for a group of electors who have promised to choose as President a particular candidate. The voters have the opportunity to vote

for any one of the candidates because in every state there will be a group of electors for each candidate. The group of electors receiving the most votes becomes the electors for the state. After the citizens have voted, each group of electors chosen meets in its own state and votes for the President in accordance with the group's promise. By this indirect method, the voting citizens actually elect the President.

When Congress meets in January after the election, the members of the two Houses officially count the votes of the electors. The candidate who receives a majority of the total number of electoral votes is elected President. If no candidate receives a majority of the electoral votes, the House of Representatives chooses the President from among the three candidates who received the highest number of votes.

The Vice President is elected in the same way, and for the same 4-year term of office. Should no candidate for Vice President receive a majority of the electoral votes, the Senate chooses as Vice

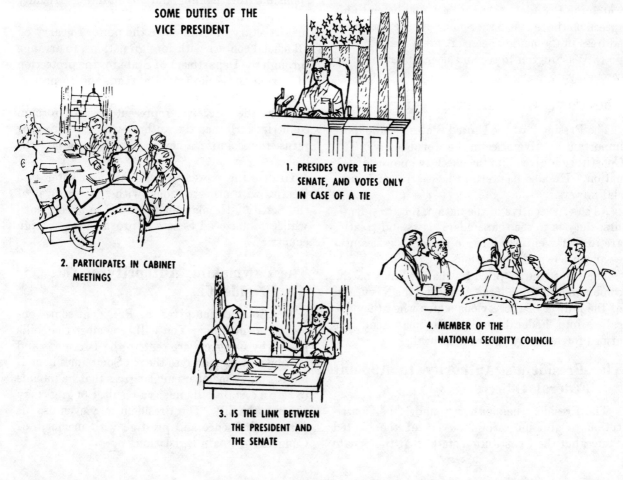

SOME DUTIES OF THE VICE PRESIDENT

1. PRESIDES OVER THE SENATE, AND VOTES ONLY IN CASE OF A TIE

2. PARTICIPATES IN CABINET MEETINGS

3. IS THE LINK BETWEEN THE PRESIDENT AND THE SENATE

4. MEMBER OF THE NATIONAL SECURITY COUNCIL

President one of the two candidates who received the highest number of votes.

Because the votes of the citizens actually elect the President, the people know who has been elected as soon as the votes for the electors have been counted. This is usually the day after the election.

The Presidential Inauguration

The day the President begins his term of office is known as Inauguration Day. On this day, the 20th of January following his election, the President takes the oath of office. It is administered to him by the Chief Justice of the United States.

The President repeats the oath which is required by the Constitution—the same oath taken by George Washington on April 30, 1789.

Following the oath, the new President makes a speech, called his inaugural address. In this speech he tells what he expects to do and what he would like to have done within the next four years. Many people hear this speech on the radio. Others watch the President take the oath and listen to his speech on the television. Some read the inaugural address in the newspapers. A great many people go to Washington to see and hear this impressive ceremony.

The Powers of the President

The President of the United States has the most important elective office in the world today. The Constitution gives him the executive power of the nation. He also has certain legislative and judicial powers.

As chief executive of the nation, the President's first duty is to see that Federal laws and treaties are properly enforced. In doing so, he issues necessary orders and instructions.

The Constitution provides that he shall be the commander in chief of the Army and the Navy, and of the militia of the various states when they are called into Federal service. He may send our armed forces to any part of the world.

The President's Authority to Appoint Federal Officers

The President has authority under the Constitution to appoint certain officers of the United States, but the Constitution states that the Senate must approve these appointments. Using this authority, the President appoints the heads of the 11 executive departments and some of their branches, members of independent executive agencies, and other Federal officials. There are many of these officers in the government. Before making appointments to Federal jobs in a particular state, the President often consults the Senators from that state, especially if they are of his political party. This is called "Senatorial Courtesy."

The President's Authority to Work with Foreign Countries

The President directs foreign relations through his power to nominate the Secretary of State, and the ambassadors, ministers, and consular officials who represent the United States abroad.

Government officers of foreign nations consider the President and his Secretary of State to be the representatives of the United States who are responsible for making and maintaining friendly relations with their countries. The President and his Secretary of State have the power to carry on all official contact with foreign nations, to arrange through the Department of State for the protection of our citizens who travel abroad, and to protect foreign persons traveling in the United States. The President receives representatives of foreign countries. He has the authority to recognize, or refuse to recognize, a new nation or a new government.

He has the power to negotiate and enter into treaties with other nations, with the approval of the Senate. He may make executive agreements, which do not need Senate approval, with foreign countries.

The Lawmaking Authority of the President

The Constitution gives the President some control in lawmaking. You will remember that bills passed by Congress are sent to the President and that he may sign or veto them. Sometimes he will tell his party members in Congress that he intends to veto a certain bill and, as a result, Congress may not pass the bill. The President may even use his personal influence and prestige with members of Congress to obtain legislation.

318

Courtesy, Cecil W. Stoughton

A President Addresses a Joint Session of the Congress.

Each year, as required by the Constitution, the President reports to the Congress on the state of the Union. In his State of the Union Message, he talks about the needs of the people, about our relations with other countries, and usually recommends legislation which he believes to be necessary for the nation. He may also send a special message to Congress for similar purposes. If necessary, he may call Congress into a special session, as provided by the Constitution, and recommend legislation to solve a particular problem. When Congress does not respond to his wishes, he may call upon the people directly for support. He does this through the press, radio, and television.

The Judicial Authority of the President

The President has the authority to select and appoint judges of the Supreme Court, and other Federal courts, provided the Senate approves his nominations.

Many of the 55 men who helped to frame the Constitution were very able lawyers. They had learned that sometimes even a judge may not be fair, or he may make an honest mistake. These wise leaders believed that injustice would not happen often, but they wanted someone to help the person wrongly convicted. Therefore, authority was given to the President to grant reprieves and pardons to persons convicted in Federal courts. He cannot, however, pardon lawbreakers who have been sentenced by a state court, nor can he pardon any government official for a Federal offense which resulted in his impeachment and conviction.

As you can see, the President has many powers. How he uses his powers determines whether he is a weak or strong leader. His personal popularity

319

with the people can help him win support for his programs. If he is serving during a time of national crisis, as in wartime or in a depression, he is usually given more power.

Although the President of the United States has great power because he is the executive authority of the nation, he remains "Mr. President," resident of the White House, whose work is to lead the nation and serve the will of the people.

CAN YOU DO THIS?

Explain the meaning of the underlined part of each of the following sentences:

1. The chief executive is chosen officially by Presidential electors.
2. The President reports on the state of the Union in his annual message to Congress.
3. The President of the United States has the most important elective office in the world today.
4. The Constitution says that no person shall be given a title of nobility.
5. The President's personal popularity with the people helps win support for his programs.
6. Even a judge may make an honest mistake.
7. Election day is the first Tuesday after the first Monday in November.

Answer "yes" or "no" to each of the following questions, and tell the reason(s) for your answer:

1. Is it the first duty of the President to make the laws of the nation?
2. Does the Vice President become President if the President dies?
3. Are the President and the Vice President elected by a direct vote of the people?
4. Is the President elected to serve for a certain number of years?
5. Can a naturalized citizen of the United States become President?
6. Does the President have authority to call special sessions of Congress?
7. Does "Senatorial Courtesy" mean the respect that the Senators pay to the President?

Talk about:

1. How are candidates for President nominated?
2. What is meant when it is said that a President may be a "strong" or "weak" leader?

CHAPTER 10

ADVISING THE PRESIDENT—THE CABINET

The newspapers are filled with examples of democracy in action. Read these familiar everyday headlines:

Senate Discusses New Treaty

NATO Chiefs Meet in Brussels

Government Hopes to Avoid Railroad Strike

New Interstate Highway Opened

Record Farm Production Last Year

New Income Tax Law Passed by House

If we read the stories under the headlines, we will notice that they concern problems relating to foreign affairs, national defense, labor unions, transportation, farm production, and income for the Federal government. We will also notice a common thread that runs through all the articles: The important role played by the President in helping to solve these problems. Actually, they are only a few of the many problems which are considered by our President, and this should make us realize how great his fund of knowledge must be if he is to handle them and all the other problems which he must help to solve. We should also realize the great amount of work which must be done to solve the problems described in the newspaper stories. No single individual, not even the President, could possibly know about and handle all of these matters without assistance. For this reason, the President has a Cabinet. Each member of the Cabinet is a skilled administrator and heads one

Washington and His Cabinet.

of the large executive departments. The members of the Cabinet are well informed concerning the matters handled by the departments they head, and they act as advisers to the President and assist him in solving problems relating to such matters.

This chapter tells about the work of the President's Cabinet.

DISCUSS:

Why is it important to get advice from others before making a decision?

MEETING NEW WORDS:

civil service: Having to do with working for the government of a nation or state

conservation: Preserving from harm or decay; protecting from loss or from being used up

counterfeit: Imitation; false; to make false money

duplication: The doing again of something that has already been done

estimates: Judgments or opinions about how much, how many, how good; evaluations

handicapped: Disabled; not able to do something because of a disadvantage or disability

initiate: Begin; set things going; introduce

national security: The safety of the nation

natural resources: Things that come from nature

patent: A government grant to a person stating that he is the only one allowed to make or sell a new invention for a certain number of years.

policy: Plan for present or future official action

prosecute: To take action to convict a person of a crime

research: Careful hunting for facts or truth

urban: Relating to cities and towns

vocational training: Education to prepare a person for some new job or kind of work

Fill in the blank in each of the following sentences with the correct word(s) listed in the other column:

1. The Secretary of State advises the President about foreign _____.

2. The Secretary of Defense is responsible for _____.

3. The Treasury Department has the duty to investigate and arrest persons who make or pass _____ money.

4. The Secretary of the Interior advises the President on matters regarding the _____ of our national resources.

5. As industry changes more _____ may be needed.

6. Most people who work for the government are _____ workers.

AS YOU READ

1. **Find out how the members of the President's Cabinet help him.**
2. **Learn about some of the duties of each department of the Federal government.**

ADVISING THE PRESIDENT—THE CABINET

The first Congress of the United States met in 1789. One of its first acts was to provide for a group of men to advise and assist President Washington. This group of advisers soon came to be known as the President's Cabinet. It consisted of a Secretary of State, a Secretary of the Treasury, and a Secretary of War, each of whom headed an executive department, and an Attorney General and a Postmaster General.

The President's Cabinet today has 11 members. The titles of these Cabinet members and the year in which their departments were officially created by Act of Congress are:

Secretary of State (1789)
Secretary of the Treasury (1789)
Secretary of Defense (First called Secretary of War (1789); Department of Defense (1949) includes former Departments of War (1789), Navy (1798), Air Force (1947))

322

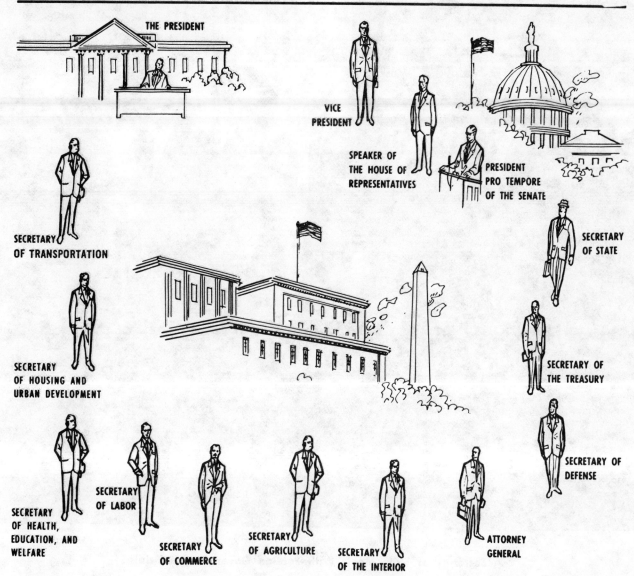

Succession to the Presidency.

Attorney General (The office of Attorney General (1789) heads the Department of Justice (1870))

Secretary of the Interior (1849)

Secretary of Agriculture (1862) (Commissioner of Agriculture renamed Secretary of Agriculture (1889))

Secretary of Commerce (1913) (First called Secretary of Commerce and Labor (1903)

Secretary of Labor (1913)

Secretary of Health, Education, and Welfare (1953)

Secretary of Housing and Urban Development (1965)

Secretary of Transportation (1966)

(*Note:* The office of Postmaster General (1789) headed the Post Office Department (1872). Department abolished by act of Congress and United States Postal Service established as an independent agency in 1971.)

Photo by Herbert J. Meyle

A Secretary of State Meets With Foreign Government Officials.

How Cabinet Members Are Chosen

Soon after he has been inaugurated, the President chooses his Cabinet. In appointing Cabinet members, the President is guided by a number of considerations. First, he chooses people who are experienced in the affairs of the departments which they are to head. Second, he selects men whose ideas of government are like his own, men who believe in the policies and program of his party. Third, he usually selects people from his own political party, although he is not required to do so. Finally, he tries to put together a Cabinet whose members come from different parts of the country. This is done in order to give all sections of the country representation in the executive branch of the Federal government. Appointments to the Cabinet, like appointments to all important Federal offices, must be approved by the Senate.

How the Cabinet Officer Does His Work

Cabinet members always keep in touch with the President. They do this by private conference, telephone, or messenger. The entire Cabinet meets with the President at his request, as often as necessary. In all of his contacts with the President, the Cabinet member suggests and advises. Guided by this advice, the President makes the final decision on all important matters of policy. He is basically responsible for the operation of the various executive departments of the government.

324

Each Cabinet member also administers the work of the executive department which he heads. He, too, has many assistants, some of whom are appointed by the President, and many others who are selected only after having passed a civil service examination to qualify for appointment. Some officers and employees work in branch offices of the executive departments which are located in many parts of the country.

Duties of the Cabinet

● *The Department of State*

The Secretary of State ranks as the executive officer next in importance to the President and the Vice President. The President relies on the Secretary and his department to initiate and develop the country's foreign policy and to recommend action to put it into effect. The Secretary and his assistants also represent the President in dealings with officials of countries all over the world.

The Department of State works in many ways to establish and maintain friendly and peaceful relations between the United States and foreign countries. The department acts, through United States representatives to the United Nations, with other countries to settle differences which might lead to war. It also assists the President in negotiating and carrying out treaties with foreign countries. Educational information activities abroad, and foreign student and teacher exchange programs, are also planned and supervised by this department to further the general objectives.

State Department representatives who are assigned abroad meet with citizens of foreign countries who wish to come to the United States, and issue permits (visas) allowing them to apply for admission to this country.

This department issues United States passports to citizens who desire to travel abroad for pleasure or business. It also helps our businessmen by reporting on trade conditions and acting in a general way as agent for United States business interests abroad.

● *The Department of the Treasury*

The Secretary of the Treasury is the President's adviser on the financial affairs of our country. He is in charge of collecting and managing the funds of the United States.

The Department of the Treasury handles more money than any other organization in the world. It is responsible for the coining and printing of the nation's money, bonds, and stamps; the borrowing of money as directed by Congress; and the payment of all debts of the nation. The collection of Federal taxes, including taxes on many kinds of goods brought into the country, is a further responsibility of the Treasury Department.

The Secret Service, under direction of the Secretary of the Treasury, is responsible for the guarding of the President and his family, as well as other high government officials. However, another very important duty of this agency is the investigation and arrest of persons who are believed to have made or passed counterfeit money.

Other units of the Treasury Department guard the seacoasts and the land borders of the United States to protect shipping and prevent the bringing of goods into the country without the payment of taxes; still other units administer laws relating to alcohol, tobacco, and firearms.

● *The Department of Defense*

The Secretary of Defense, as a member of the President's Cabinet, is adviser to the President on all military matters. He is responsible for our national defense and national security. He establishes general policies for, and supervises, all branches of the armed forces, as well as certain nonmilitary activities; prevents duplication and overlapping in the purchase of military supplies, and directs the preparation of the budget estimates for the armed forces.

The Department of Defense is subdivided into three military departments, the Department of the Army, the Department of the Navy, and the Department of the Air Force. Each of these departments is headed by a secretary who does not, however, have the rank of a Cabinet member. Each military department has many responsibilities relating to its branch of the armed forces and, as required by its own functions,

Recruits and trains officers and enlisted personnel, and makes provision for obtaining military equipment and weapons for their use,

325

Immigration and Naturalization
Service Port Receptionist and
Immigration Officer Greet an
Arriving Passenger.

Acquires and maintains forts, camps, naval bases and air bases, as appropriate to their particular operation,

Conducts research on new weapons, and

Participates in space programs which relate to military matters.

● *The Department of Justice*

The Attorney General advises the President in all legal matters pertaining to the Federal government.

The Department of Justice assists the President by providing the means to enforce Federal laws. The Attorney General is the chief legal officer of the nation and he, or his assistants, represent the United States in all proceedings before the Supreme Court. The President is assisted by this department in protecting rights guaranteed by the Constitution.

Under the supervision of the Department of Justice is the Federal Bureau of Investigation which conducts investigations to determine whether Federal laws have been violated. The department takes action to prosecute and convict persons who are accused of Federal violations. It maintains and supervises Federal institutions in which lawbreakers are imprisoned as punishment for their crimes.

Another important function of the Justice Department is the administration and enforcement of the immigration and naturalization laws.

United States Department of Justice
Building.

• *The Department of the Interior*

The Secretary of the Interior advises the President on matters relating to the development and conservation of our natural resources, and matters relating to island possessions of the United States.

The Department of the Interior administers and enforces the Federal laws relating to the public lands of the United States including, among others, our national parks and lands reserved for fish and wildlife conservation. It supervises the operation of power plants which provide electricity for large parts of the country; helps to develop operating procedures and safety programs for removal from the earth of its natural resources, such as coal, gas, oil, etc.

The Department of the Interior administers many Federal laws relating to the island possessions of the United States. It is responsible also for the welfare of American Indians living on reservations in the United States.

• *The Department of Agriculture*

The Secretary of Agriculture keeps the President advised concerning problems of the American farmer. One of the ways he carries on research, education, and conservation projects relating to agriculture is by working in close cooperation with state research stations.

The Department of Agriculture helps farmers learn the best ways to develop better crops and livestock by teaching them the science of soil care, and helping them to fight plant and animal diseases. It gives them information about the supply and prices of farm products and helps them obtain a fair price for their products. This department assists in financing the construction of rural electric systems, and provides a credit system for farmers.

• *The Department of Commerce*

The Secretary of Commerce advises the President concerning the nation's business affairs. He promotes and develops the foreign and domestic commerce of the United States.

The Department of Commerce collects information and publishes reports on goods produced, exported, imported, and stocked in the United States; establishes and maintains official standards of weights and measures; and issues patents and administers patent laws. This department also issues official weather reports and forecasts;

Assistance to Farmers.

studies the seacoasts and rivers and reports on tides and currents to safeguard shipping; studies transportation and travel, both in the United States and abroad; and takes the census of the nation every 10 years.

• *The Department of Labor*

The Secretary of Labor advises the President on the welfare of the wage earners in the United States. He tries to improve working conditions as directed by laws of Congress.

The Department of Labor administers and enforces the labor laws including those relating to the wages, hours of work, working conditions and welfare of young people who work and women who work. It helps to set up and enforce safety programs, and tries to prevent or settle strikes. It administers the programs of unemployment insurance and workmen's compensation. This department collects information and publishes reports about employment, wages, and the welfare of workers.

• *The Department of Health, Education, and Welfare*

The Secretary of Health, Education, and Welfare advises the President on matters regarding the general welfare of the people. He acts to improve the mental and physical health of the people through research and the efficient and proper use of new knowledge.

327

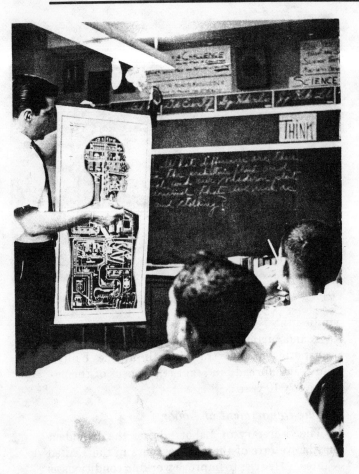

Improving Education.

The Department of Health, Education, and Welfare works through a Public Health Service to prevent and control disease, and through the Food and Drug Administration to assure the purity and quality of the foods, drugs, and cosmetics we use. The department provides vocational training for physically handicapped persons, including war-disabled civilians. It administers the various social security programs throughout the United States. The Department of Health, Education, and Welfare helps to improve education in our country.

• The Department of Housing and Urban Development

The Secretary of Housing and Urban Development advises the President with respect to Federal programs and activities relating to housing and urban development.

The Department of Housing and Urban Development is concerned with housing, urban development and urban transportation, including the encouragement of private homebuilding and mortgage lending, and the furnishing of information to aid state, county and other local governments in solving community and metropolitan development problems.

• The Department of Transportation

The Secretary of Transportation, the newest member of the President's Cabinet, is the President's principal adviser on all transportation matters.

The Department of Transportation conducts research in the field of transportation to find safer, faster, and cheaper ways of moving people and freight throughout the United States. In order to establish transportation policies which will serve the needs of the public, as well as of private industry, labor, and the national defense, the department seeks the cooperation of Federal, state, and local governments on transportation problems.

The work of the executive departments, under the administration of members of the President's Cabinet, affects every individual in this country. If a person is serving in the armed forces, his activities are regulated by the Department of Defense. If he is a farmer, he has direct contact with the Department of Agriculture. If he has an income, he may pay income taxes to the Internal Revenue Service of the Department of the Treasury. Should he be an alien, he will be in touch with the Immigration and Naturalization Service, of the Department of Justice, from the time of his application for admission to the United States until he is granted citizenship.

In addition to the 11 executive departments, there are many independent agencies in the Federal government, each one having certain duties and responsibilities, as indicated often by their names. They are, to name a few, the Atomic Energy Commission, Farm Credit Administration, Federal Communications Commission, Labor Relations Board, Small Business Administration, the Civil Service Commission and the United States Postal Service.

Good citizens will always use their right to vote and will elect a President who they believe will appoint the most capable men to Cabinet positions and to head the independent agencies.

CAN YOU DO THIS?

Select the word under each sentence which best completes the sentence:

1. The committee chairman will _____ a discussion of the bill.

   initiate   research   classify

2. The Department of Commerce issues _____ and administers laws relating to them.

   reports   visas   patents

3. Doctors depend upon _____ in order to win their fight against disease.

   lawyers   research   books

4. If you do that work, it will be a _____ of what was done earlier.

   duplication   service   policy

5. Budget _____ for the armed forces are prepared under the direction of the Secretary of Defense.

   estimates   programs   opinions

Answer the following questions:

1. The head of which department advises the President about legal matters?
2. In which department is the Weather Service?
3. How does the Department of Health, Education, and Welfare help the people?
4. Which department helps farmers develop better crops and livestock?
5. How many Cabinet members are there?
6. How are the Cabinet members chosen?
7. Which department coins money?
8. Which department works with the United Nations?
9. Which department maintains our national parks?

Talk about:

1. For what reasons was the President's Cabinet enlarged?
2. How does each Federal department affect the daily life of the people?

The Supreme Court Building, designed by Cass Gilbert, is our symbol of equal justice under the law. It was completed in 1935.

Courtesy U.S. House of Representatives

CHAPTER 11

INTERPRETING THE LAWS—THE JUDICIAL BRANCH

You must recall certain things if you are to understand one of the most important duties of the judicial branch of the government. The Federal Constitution gave specific powers to Congress and, in addition, gave it authority to pass all laws which might be necessary to use those powers. This last authority is so broad and general that it is possible for Congress to make a mistake and use that authority to pass a law which it has no power to pass. Furthermore, laws passed by Congress are not always clear and, in enforcing them, the executive branch of the government may give them meaning not intended by Congress. Such laws and their enforcement might take away rights or freedoms of the people.

The government created by the Constitution protects these rights and freedoms through a system of Federal courts. The Constitution provides that:

> *"The judicial power of the United States shall be vested in one Supreme Court, and in such inferior courts as the Congress may from time to time ordain and establish."*

The Supreme Court of the United States meets in the Supreme Court Building in Washington, D.C. It is a beautiful building of white marble. The figures over the entrance represent our national ideas of law and liberty. Above the main entrance appear the words, "Equal Justice Under Law."

The Supreme Court, made up of a Chief Justice and eight Associate Justices, is usually in

Judge Samuel Chase of Maryland, served on the Supreme Court for fifteen years. A colorful and controversial figure. He served his country in many capacities during the American Revolution and afterwards. George Washington nominated him to the Supreme Court January 26, 1796 and Chase served until his death in 1811.

Photograph courtesy Division of Tourist Development, Maryland Dept. of Economic and Community Development.

session from October to June. One of the most important duties of the justices is to decide whether laws passed by the Congress agree with the Constitution. The justices do this by interpreting and explaining the laws of Congress and the provisions of the Constitution. Should the Supreme Court decide that the Constitution does not give Congress the power to pass a certain law, the court declares that law to be unconstitutional. Such a law can no longer be enforced by the President and his executive officers.

John Marshall, a brilliant lawyer who also fought under Washington during the War for Independence, was Chief Justice of the Supreme Court when it was first decided in 1803 that the Supreme Court had the authority to declare that a law passed by Congress did not agree with the Constitution. Nonetheless, Chief Justice Marshall himself believed that the Founding Fathers intended the Federal government to be a strong government, and that it should have enough power to govern the nation for the benefit of the people. He interpreted the Constitution in a way that gave the government this needed strength without destroying the rights and freedoms of the people. It has been said that he gave life and power to the Constitution.

William Howard Taft, another great Chief Justice of the Supreme Court, said that the reason for the existence of the courts is to promote the happiness of all the people by the speedy and careful administration of justice. He believed that the courts were created to help individuals who seek justice.

As you study this chapter, you will learn how the judicial branch of our government serves the people and protects their freedom.

DISCUSS:

How do the Federal courts help to preserve freedom?

MEETING NEW WORDS:

appeal: To request a higher court to review a lower court's decision; also, the request itself

award: Money or some other thing of value given in payment of a claim decided in one's favor

customs: Taxes or money charged on something imported or brought into the country from another country; import taxes

diplomatic: Having to do with the official activities of government officials who work with representatives of other countries

dispute: Quarrel; argument; difference of opinion

jurisdiction: Authority of the government or an agency of the government to exercise control over people or property; authority of a court to hear and decide a criminal or civil case

resign: To give up a position or job

self-restraint: A restriction by a person of his own actions; self-control

Fill in the blank in each of the following sentences with the proper word from the list above:

1. Supreme Court has _____ in cases which involve the interpretation of the Constitution.

2. The members of the Health Committee asked the chairman to _____.

3. He has never lost his _____ even in a time of national crisis.

4. The court granted an _____ of $2,000 after he proved his claim against the government.

5. A _____ between two people about property rights may be taken to court in a civil case.

6. When a decision is made by the Supreme Court, no further _____ is possible.

7. Our _____ officials represent the United States in foreign countries.

AS YOU READ

1. **Find out how the Supreme Court and our system of courts help to preserve our freedom.**
2. **Find out how court decisions may be appealed.**

INTERPRETING THE LAWS—THE JUDICIAL BRANCH

The Supreme Court alone is named and created by Article III of the Constitution. However, the Constitution also gives Congress the authority to establish other courts, and to increase or decrease their number, as the need may arise. From time to time Congress has used that authority to create

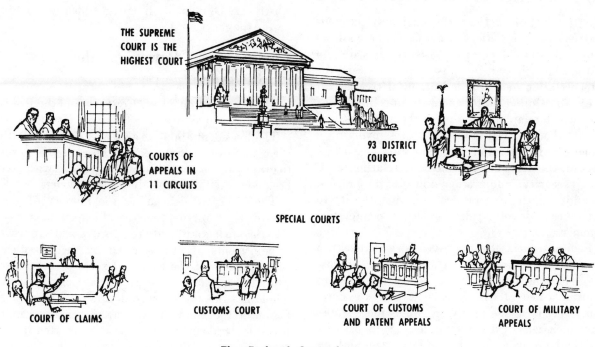

THE SUPREME COURT IS THE HIGHEST COURT

COURTS OF APPEALS IN 11 CIRCUITS

93 DISTRICT COURTS

SPECIAL COURTS

COURT OF CLAIMS

CUSTOMS COURT

COURT OF CUSTOMS AND PATENT APPEALS

COURT OF MILITARY APPEALS

The Federal Court System.

the lower Federal courts which exist today.

By creating the Supreme Court and authorizing the establishment of other Federal courts, the Constitution created the judicial power; that is, the power to hear and decide the two classes of cases—criminal and civil.

Certain things which a person may do will harm other persons. To protect all the people from the effect of these acts, the Congress passed laws making them crimes. The laws provide for the punishment of persons who commit these acts. If a person breaks one of these laws, the Federal government will prosecute him in court. This is called a criminal case. Persons convicted in a criminal case may be punished by imprisonment. You will remember that Amendment 6 of the Constitution guarantees a trial by jury to every person accused of a crime.

It is also possible for a person to take some action which affects the rights of another person. Such action, however, may not be a crime because no criminal law has been broken. In such a case one person can sue the other person in court. This is called a civil case. A person who is found to be wrong in a civil case is never punished by being sent to prison, as in a criminal case, but the court

may make him pay a certain sum of money to the other person. Such money payment is called damages.

The Judges of the Federal Courts

An independent judiciary, free from control by the King, was proposed in England during the 17th century. The authors of the Constitution adopted this idea when they included in the fundamental law provisions regulating the appointment of judges to the Supreme Court and the lower Federal courts.

The Founding Fathers provided that the President shall appoint all Federal judges, with the consent of the Senate, and that a Federal judge shall hold office during "good behavior." He can be removed from office only by Congress upon impeachment for, and conviction of, "high crimes and misdemeanors." Otherwise, every judge is appointed for life, or until he chooses to resign. The Constitution provides further that the salary of a Federal judge shall not be reduced while he is in office. The judges, therefore, are independent and cannot be influenced by other branches of the government, or by any person or group of persons.

The Authority of the Federal Courts

Article III of the Constitution gives to the Federal courts jurisdiction in a case because of its subject matter. Upon this basis, the jurisdiction of the courts may include cases which concern the interpretation of the Constitution, of treaties between the United States and foreign countries, of laws which relate to shipping on the high seas, and of all other Federal laws. All cases involving a violation of Federal criminal laws are heard in a Federal court. They include cases relating to internal security, immigration, and customs matters. In addition, the Federal courts have authority to handle cases involving laws relating to interstate commerce.

Federal courts also are given jurisdiction in a case because it involves certain parties. A case involving the United States as a party must be heard in a Federal court. Also heard in a Federal court may be a case involving two or more states, or two citizens of different states. Suits between a foreign government or one of its citizens and one of our states may be heard in a Federal court.

The Supreme Court

The Chief Justice and the eight Associate Justices of the Supreme Court sit as a group. When the court hears a case, it is decided by a majority vote of the justices.

The Supreme Court is primarily an appellate court; that is, a court which hears appeals from decisions made in cases which began in a lower court. The Constitution, however, provides that in all cases affecting foreign diplomatic officials, such as ambassadors and other public ministers and consuls, the Supreme Court shall have original jurisdiction. This means that such cases can be heard only in the Supreme Court. Because the authority in these cases comes from the Constitution, Congress cannot take it away from the court.

The Supreme Court has the power to declare that a law passed by Congress and approved by the President is unconstitutional. It also has the authority to decide whether a state constitution or a state law agrees or disagrees with the Federal Constitution. The decision of this, the highest Federal court, is final. With a final decision there can be no further appeals.

The Supreme Court has developed a tradition of self-restraint, and is generally very careful in declaring state or Federal actions unconstitutional.

It does not consider all new laws, but only those which may be involved in a case which is brought before the court for decision.

Checking the Power of the Supreme Court

The Constitution grants Congress and the President some control over the Supreme Court.

The President appoints all Federal judges, with the consent of the Senate. He also has the power to grant pardons and reprieves to persons who have been convicted of crimes in Federal courts.

The Congress determines the number of justices of the Supreme Court, and it fixes their pay. The Senate has authority to approve or disapprove appointments of men selected by the President to be justices of the court. Except as otherwise provided in the Constitution, the Congress as a whole has the authority to decide what cases will begin in the Supreme Court, rather than in a lower Federal court, and what cases started in the lower Federal courts may be appealed to the Supreme Court. However, the court is allowed to decide which of the appealed cases it will consider. If the Supreme Court refuses to hear a case appealed to it, the decision of the lower court thereby becomes final.

Other Federal Courts

Not long after the inauguration of George Washington as our first President, Congress used the authority given to it in the Constitution and passed the Judiciary Act of September 24, 1789. This act established a system of lower Federal courts, which consisted of 13 district courts and three circuit courts. As the country grew and the need for more courts arose, additional courts were created by Congress. Today each state has at least one district court, and the larger states have two or more such courts.

The United States courts of appeals were established in 1891 to relieve the Supreme Court of many of the cases which were being appealed to it from the district courts. At the present time, the country is divided into 11 judicial circuits, each having a circuit court of appeals. Each court of appeals has from three to 15 judges. One justice of the Supreme Court is also assigned as a circuit justice for each circuit.

The lowest Federal courts are the United States district courts. They have original jurisdiction in all cases that may be heard by the Federal courts, except those which come within the original jurisdiction of the Supreme Court, or the jurisdiction of special courts. District court cases are usually heard by a single judge and sometimes with a jury. Usually an appeal from the decision of a district court may be taken to a United States court of appeals for the judicial circuit within which the district court is located. In some cases, a further appeal may be taken to the Supreme Court.

Congress also recognized the need for special courts. It set up the United States Court of Claims in 1855, a kind of court called the Board of United States General Appraisers in 1890, and the United States Court of Customs and Patent Appeals in 1909. In 1926 the name of the Board of United States General Appraisers was changed to the United States Customs Court. The United States Court of Military Appeals was established in 1950.

During the early days of our country, a person who had a reasonable money claim against the government of the United States had to ask Congress to pay the claim. The United States Court of Claims was established to relieve Congress of the burden of deciding whether such a claim should be paid. This court consists of a Chief Judge and four Associate Judges who meet in Washington. The awards of this court cannot be paid until Congress appropriates the money to pay them.

The United States Customs Court hears and settles disputes that arise out of decisions by customs officers relating to customs matters. For example, decisions as to the rate of tax on, or the value for tax purposes of, the article imported may be reviewed by this court. Appeals from these decisions are heard by the United States Court of Customs and Patent Appeals, as are appeals from decisions relating to patent matters. An inventor, for example, who has been denied a patent by the Patent Office may bring his appeal in this court.

Members of the armed forces who are accused of misconduct may be tried by court-martial (a military court). Decisions in the more serious cases can be appealed to the United States Court of Military Appeals.

Final appeal of decisions in cases arising in the special courts may be taken to the Supreme Court, except decisions of the Court of Military Appeals. Decisions of this court are final.

The Federal Courts and the People

The chief purpose of the Federal courts, and all courts, is to help the people settle their disputes and differences fairly and peaceably. The courts provide justice for all. The people may not always like the laws, but it is their duty to obey them as they are explained by the courts. When the people do not like the laws, they can elect representatives who will change them. Any change in a law must be made in the manner provided for by our plan of government.

It is the duty of the courts to make sure that all laws agree with the Constitution of the United States.

The judicial branch is the balance wheel in our system of government. It helps to maintain the correct constitutional relationships between the executive and legislative branches of the Federal government, and also between the nation and the states.

CAN YOU DO THIS?

The following sentences are separated into two parts. Match the first part of each sentence in Column A with its other part in Column B:

Column A	Column B
1. Article III of the Constitution describes the	a. relating to shipping on the high seas.
2. Violations of Federal law	b. that a law passed by Congress is unconstitutional.
3. Federal courts have jurisdiction over cases	c. were originally handled by Congress.
4. Claims against the government of the United States	d. are handled by the Federal courts.
5. The Supreme Court can declare	e. is never sent to prison.
6. A person found wrong in a civil case	f. Federal courts and their authority.

Answer the following questions:

1. Which court is the only one named in the Constitution?
2. What is an appellate court?
3. Who hears cases in a United States district court?
4. Who has the power to establish lower Federal courts?
5. How many Federal judicial circuits are there in the United States?
6. What did John Marshall do to strengthen the Federal government?
7. How could the executive branch, in enforcing a law, give it a meaning not intended by Congress?
8. Why are the judges of Federal courts independent and free from influence by others?

Talk about:

1. What are the special courts and their duties?
2. Why is a system of courts necessary in a democracy?

SECTION VI

DOCUMENTS

The Declaration of Independence

In Congress, July 4, 1776

The Unanimous Declaration of the Thirteen United States of America

When in the course of human events, it becomes necessary for one people to dissolve the political bands which have connected them with another, and to assume among the powers of the earth, the separate and equal station to which the laws of Nature and of Nature's God entitle them, a decent respect to the opinions of mankind requires that they should declare the causes which impel them to the separation.

We hold these truths to be self-evident, that all men are created equal, that they are endowed by their Creator with certain unalienable rights, that among these are life, liberty and the pursuit of happiness. That to secure these rights, governments are instituted among men, deriving their just powers from the consent of the governed,—That whenever any form of government becomes destructive of these ends, it is the right of the people to alter or to abolish it, and to institute new government, laying its foundation on such principles and organizing its powers in such form, as to them shall seem most likely to effect their safety and happiness. Prudence, indeed, will dictate that governments long established should not be changed for light and transient causes; and accordingly all experience hath shown, that mankind are more disposed to suffer, while evils are sufferable, than to right themselves by abolishing the forms to which they are accustomed. But when a long train of abuses and usurpations, pursuing invariably the same object evinces a design to reduce them under absolute despotism, it is their right, it is their duty, to throw off such government, and to provide new guards for their future security.—Such has been the patient sufferance of these colonies; and such is now the necessity which constrains them to alter their former systems of government. The history of the present King of Great Britain is a history of repeated injuries and usurpations, all having in direct object the establishment of an absolute tyranny over these states. To prove this, let facts be submitted to a candid world.

He has refused his assent to laws, the most wholesome and necessary for the public good.

He has forbidden his governors to pass laws of immediate and pressing importance, unless suspended in their operation till his assent should be obtained; and when so suspended, he has utterly neglected to attend to them.

He has refused to pass other laws for the accommodation of large districts of people, unless those people would relinquish the right of representation in the legislature, a right inestimable to them and formidable to tyrants only.

He has called together legislative bodies at places unusual, uncomfortable, and distant from the depository of their public records, for the sole purpose of fatiguing them into compliance with his measures.

He has dissolved Representative Houses repeatedly, for opposing with manly firmness his invasion on the rights of the people.

He has refused for a long time, after such dissolutions, to cause others to be elected; whereby the legislative powers, incapable of annihilation, have returned to the people at large for their exercise; the state remaining in the meantime exposed to all the dangers of invasion from without, and convulsions within.

He has endeavoured to prevent the population of these states; for that purpose obstructing the laws for naturalization of foreigners; refusing to pass others to encourage their migrations hither, and raising the conditions of new appropriations of lands.

337

He has obstructed the administration of justice, by refusing his assent to laws for establishing judiciary powers.

He has made judges dependent on his will alone, for the tenure of their offices, and the amount and payment of their salaries.

He has erected a multitude of new offices, and sent hither swarms of officers to harass our people, and eat out their substance.

He has kept among us, in times of peace, standing armies without the consent of our legislatures.

He has affected to render the military independent of and superior to the civil power.

He has combined with others to subject us to a jurisdiction foreign to our constitution, and unacknowledged by our laws; giving his assent to their acts of pretended legislation:

For quartering large bodies of armed troops among us:

For protecting them, by a mock trial, from punishment for any murders which they should commit on the inhabitants of these states:

For cutting off our trade with all parts of the world:

For imposing taxes on us without our consent:

For depriving us in many cases, of the benefits of trial by jury:

For transporting us beyond seas to be tried for pretended offenses:

For abolishing the free system of English laws in a neighbouring province, establishing therein an arbitrary government, and enlarging its boundaries so as to render it at once an example and fit instrument for introducing the same absolute rule into these colonies:

For taking away our charters, abolishing our most valuable laws, and altering fundamentally the forms of our governments.

For suspending our own legislatures, and declaring themselves invested with power to legislate for us in all cases whatsoever.

He has abdicated government here, by declaring us out of his protection and waging war against us.

He has plundered our seas, ravaged our coasts, burnt our towns, and destroyed the lives of our people.

He is at this time transporting large armies of foreign mercenaries to complete the works of death, desolation and tyranny, already begun with circumstances of cruelty and perfidy scarcely paralleled in the most barbarous ages and totally unworthy the head of a civilized nation.

He has constrained our fellow citizens taken captive on the high seas to bear arms against their country, to become the executioners of their friends and brethren, or to fall themselves by their hands.

He has excited domestic insurrections amongst us, and has endeavoured to bring on the inhabitants of our frontiers, the merciless Indian savages, whose known rule of warfare is an undistinguished destruction of all ages, sexes, and conditions.

In every stage of these oppressions we have petitioned for redress in the most humble terms: Our repeated petitions have been answered only by repeated injury. A prince, whose character is thus marked by every act which may define a tyrant, is unfit to be the ruler of a free people.

Nor have we been wanting in attentions to our British brethren. We have warned them from time to time of attempts by their legislature to extend an unwarrantable jurisdiction over us. We have reminded them of the circumstances of our emigration and settlement here. We have appealed to their native justice and magnanimity, and we have conjured them by the ties of our common kindred to disavow these usurpations, which, would inevitably interrupt our connections and correspondence. They too have been deaf to the voice of justice and of consanguinity. We must, therefore, acquiesce in the necessary which denounces our separation, and hold them, as we hold the rest of mankind, enemies in war, in peace friends.

WE, THEREFORE, the Representatives of the United States of America, in General Congress, Assembled, appealing to the Supreme Judge of the world for the rectitude of our intentions, do, in the name, and by authority of the good people of these colonies, solemnly publish and declare, That these United Colonies are, and of right ought to be FREE AND INDEPENDENT STATES; that they are absolved from all allegiance to the British Crown, and that all political connection between them and the state of Great Britain, is and ought to be totally dissolved; and that as free and independent states, they have full power to levy war, conclude peace, contract alliances, establish commerce, and to do all other acts and things which independent states may of right do. And for the support of this Declaration, with a firm reliance on the protection of Divine Providence, we mutually pledge to each other our lives, our fortunes, and our sacred honor.

JOHN HANCOCK.

New Hampshire

JOSIAH BARTLETT   MATTHEW THORNTON
WM. WHIPPLE

Massachusetts Bay

SAML ADAMS   ROBT TREAT PAINE
JOHN ADAMS   ELBRIDGE GERRY

Rhode Island

STEP. HOPKINS   WILLIAM ELLERY

Connecticut

ROGER SHERMAN   WM. WILLIAMS
SAML HUNTINGTON   OLIVER WOLCOTT

New York

WM FLOYD   FRANS. LEWIS
PHIL. LIVINGSTON   LEWIS MORRIS

New Jersey

RICHD. STOCKTON   JOHN HART
JNO WITHERSPOON   ABRA CLARK
FRAS. HOPKINSON

Pennsylvania

ROBT MORRIS   JAS. SMITH
BENJAMIN RUSH   GEO. TAYLOR
BENJA. FRANKLIN   JAMES WILSON
JOHN MORTON   GEO. ROSS
GEO. CLYMER

Delaware

CAESAR RODNEY   THO M'KEAN
GEO READ

Maryland

SAMUEL CHASE   CHARLES CARROLL
WM. PACA   of Carrollton
THOS. STONE

Virginia

GEORGE WYTHE   THOS. NELSON Jr.
RICHARD HENRY LEE   FRANCIS LIGHTFOOT LEE
TH JEFFERSON   CARTER BRAXTON
BENJA. HARRISON

North Carolina

WM HOOPER   JOHN PENN
JOSEPH HEWES

South Carolina

EDWARD RUTLEDGE   THOS HEYWARD JUNR.
THOMAS LYNCH JUNR.   ARTHUR MIDDLETON

Georgia

BUTTON GWINNETT   GEO WALTON
LYMAN HALL

The Constitution of the United States of America

Preamble

WE THE PEOPLE of the United States, in order to form a more perfect Union, establish justice, insure domestic tranquillity, provide for the common defense, promote the general welfare, and secure the blessings of liberty to ourselves and our posterity, do ordain and establish this Constitution for the United States of America.

Article I

Section 1. All legislative powers herein granted shall be vested in a Congress of the United States, which shall consist of a Senate and House of Representatives.

Section 2. The House of Representatives shall be composed of members chosen every second year by the people of the several states, and the electors in each state shall have the qualifications requisite for electors of the most numerous branch of the state legislature.

No person shall be a Representative who shall not have attained to the age of twenty-five years, and been seven years a citizen of the United States, and who shall not, when elected, be an inhabitant of that state in which he shall be chosen.

Representatives and direct taxes shall be apportioned among the several states which may be included within this Union, according to their respective numbers, which shall be determined by adding to the whole number of free persons, including those bound to service for a term of years, and excluding Indians not taxed, three-fifths of all other persons. The actual enumeration shall be made within three years after the first meeting of the Congress of the United States, and within every subsequent term of ten years, in such manner as they shall by law direct. The number of Representatives shall not exceed one for every thirty thousand, but each state shall have at least one representative; and until such enumeration shall be made, the state of New Hampshire shall be entitled to choose three, Massachusetts eight, Rhode Island and Providence Plantations one, Connecticut five, New York six, New Jersey four, Pennsylvania eight, Delaware one, Maryland six, Virginia ten, North Carolina five, South Carolina five, and Georgia three.

When vacancies happen in the representation from any state, the executive authority thereof shall issue writs of election to fill such vacancies.

The House of Representatives shall choose their Speaker and other officers; and shall have the sole power of impeachment.

Section 3. The Senate of the United States shall be composed of two Senators from each state, chosen by the legislature thereof, for six years and each Senator shall have one vote.

Immediately after they shall be assembled in consequence of the first election, they shall be divided as equally as may be into three classes. The seats of the Senators of the first class shall be vacated at the expiration of the second year, of the second class at the expiration of the fourth year, and of the third class at the expiration of the sixth year, so that one-third may be chosen every second year; and if vacancies happen by resignation, or otherwise, during the recess of the legislature of any state, the executive thereof may make temporary appointments until the next meeting of the legislature, which shall then fill such vacancies.

No person shall be a Senator who shall not have attained to the age of thirty years, and been nine years a citizen of the United States, and who shall not, when elected, be an inhabitant of that state for which he shall be chosen.

The Vice President of the United States shall be President of the Senate, but shall have no vote, unless they be equally divided.

The Senate shall choose their other officers, and also a President pro tempore, in the absence of the

Vice President, or when he shall exercise the office of President of the United States.

The Senate shall have the sole power to try all impeachments. When sitting for that purpose, they shall be on oath or affirmation. When the President of the United States is tried, the Chief Justice shall preside: And no person shall be convicted without the concurrence of two-thirds of the members present.

Judgment in cases of impeachment shall not extend further than to removal from office, and disqualification to hold and enjoy any office of honor, trust or profit under the United States: but the party convicted shall nevertheless be liable and subject to indictment, trial, judgment and punishment, according to law.

Section 4. The times, places and manner of holding elections for Senators and Representatives, shall be prescribed in each state by the legislature thereof; but the Congress may at any time by law make or alter such regulations, except as to the places of choosing Senators.

The Congress shall assemble at least once in every year, and such meeting shall be on the first Monday in December, unless they shall by law appoint a different day.

Section 5. Each House shall be the judge of the elections, returns and qualifications of its own members, and a majority of each shall constitute a quorum to do business; but a smaller number may adjourn from day to day, and may be authorized to compel the attendance of absent members, in such manner, and under such penalties as each House may provide.

Each House may determine the rules of its proceedings, punish its members for disorderly behaviour, and, with the concurrence of two-thirds, expel a member.

Each House shall keep a journal of its proceedings, and from time to time publish the same, excepting such parts as may in their judgment require secrecy; and the yeas and nays of the members of either House on any question shall, at the desire of one-fifth of those present, be entered on the journal.

Neither House, during the session of Congress, shall, without the consent of the other, adjourn for more than three days, nor to any other place than that in which the two Houses shall be sitting.

Section 6. The Senators and Representatives shall receive a compensation for their services, to be ascertained by law, and paid out of the Treasury of the United States. They shall in all cases, except treason, felony and breach of the peace, be privileged from arrest during their attendance at the session of their respective Houses, and in going to and returning from the same; and for any speech or debate in either House, they shall not be questioned in any other place.

No Senator or Representative shall, during the time for which he was elected, be appointed to any civil office under the authority of the United States, which shall have been created, or the emoluments whereof shall have been increased during such time; and no person holding any office under the United States, shall be a member of either House during his continuance in office.

Section 7. All bills for raising revenue shall originate in the House of Representatives; but the Senate may propose or concur with amendments as on other bills.

Every bill which shall have passed the House of Representatives and the Senate, shall, before it becomes a law, be presented to the President of the United States; if he approves he shall sign it, but if not he shall return it, with his objections to that House in which it shall have originated, who shall enter the objections at large on their journal, and proceed to reconsider it. If after such reconsideration two thirds of that House shall agree to pass the bill, it shall be sent, together with the objections, to the other House, by which it shall likewise be reconsidered, and if approved by two thirds of that House, it shall become a law. But in all such cases the votes of both Houses shall be determined by yeas and nays, and the names of the persons voting for and against the bill shall be entered on the journal of each House respectively. If any bill shall not be returned by the President within ten days (Sundays excepted) after it shall have been presented to him, the same shall be a law, in like manner as if he had signed it, unless the Congress by their adjournment prevent its return, in which case it shall not be a law.

Every order, resolution, or vote to which the concurrence of the Senate and House of Representatives may be necessary (except on a question of adjournment) shall be presented to the President of the United States; and before the same shall take effect, shall be approved by him, or being disapproved by him, shall be repassed by two thirds of the Senate and House of Representatives, according to the rules and limitations prescribed in the case of a bill.

Section 8. The Congress shall have power to lay and collect taxes, duties, imposts and excises, to pay the debts and provide for the common defense and general welfare of the United States; but all duties, imposts and excises shall be uniform throughout the United States;

To borrow money on the credit of the United States;

To regulate commerce with foreign nations, and among the several States, and with the Indian tribes;

To establish a uniform rule of naturalization, and uniform laws on the subject of bankruptcies throughout the United States;

To coin money, regulate the value thereof, and of foreign coin, and fix the standard of weights and measures;

To provide for the punishment of counterfeiting the securities and current coin of the United States;

To establish post offices and post roads;

To promote the progress of science and useful arts, by securing for limited times to authors and inventors the exclusive right to their respective writings and discoveries;

To constitute tribunals inferior to the Supreme Court;

To define and punish piracies and felonies committed on the high seas, and offenses against the law of nations;

To declare war, grant letters of marque and reprisal, and make rules concerning captures on land and water;

To raise and support armies, but no appropriation of money to that use shall be for a longer term than two years;

To provide and maintain a Navy;

To make rules for the government and regulation of the land and naval forces;

To provide for calling forth the militia to execute the laws of the Union, suppress insurrections and repel invasions;

To provide for organizing, arming, and disciplining, the militia, and for governing such part of them as may be employed in the service of the United States, reserving to the states respectively, the appointment of the officers, and the authority of training the militia according to the discipline prescribed by Congress;

To exercise exclusive legislation in all cases whatsoever, over such District (not exceeding ten miles square) as may, by cession of particular states, and the acceptance of Congress, become the seat of the government of the United States, and to exercise like authority over all places purchased by the consent of the legislature of the state in which the same shall be, for the erection of forts, magazines, arsenals, dock-yards, and other needful buildings;—and

To make all laws which shall be necessary and proper for carrying into execution the foregoing powers, and all other powers vested by this Constitution in the government of the United States, or in any department or officer thereof.

Section 9. The migration or importation of such persons as any of the states now existing shall think proper to admit, shall not be prohibited by the Congress prior to the year one thousand eight hundred and eight, but a tax or duty may be imposed on such importation, not exceeding ten dollars for each person.

The privilege of the writ of habeas corpus shall not be suspended, unless when in cases of rebellion or invasion the public safety may require it.

No bill of attainder or ex post facto law shall be passed.

No capitation, or other direct, tax shall be laid, unless in proportion to the census or enumeration herein before directed to be taken.

No tax or duty shall be laid on articles exported from any state.

No preference shall be given by any regulation of commerce or revenue to the ports of one state over those of another: nor shall vessels bound to, or from, one state, be obliged to enter, clear, or pay duties in another.

No money shall be drawn from the Treasury, but in consequence of appropriations made by law; and a regular statement and account of the receipts and expenditures of all public money shall be published from time to time.

No title of nobility shall be granted by the United States: And no person holding any office of profit or trust under them, shall, without the consent of the Congress, accept of any present, emolument, office, or title, of any kind whatever, from any King, Prince, or foreign state.

Section 10. No state shall enter into any treaty, alliance, or confederation; grant letters of marque and reprisal; coin money; emit bills of credit; make any thing but gold and silver coin a tender in payment of debts; pass any bill of attainder, ex post facto law, or law impairing the obligation of contracts, or grant any title of nobility.

No state shall, without the consent of the Congress, lay any imposts or duties on imports or exports, except what may be absolutely necessary for executing its inspection laws; and the net produce of all duties and imposts, laid by any state on imports or exports, shall be for the use of the Treasury of the United States; and all such laws shall be subject to the revision and control of the Congress.

No state shall, without the consent of Congress, lay any duty of tonnage, keep troops, or ships of war in time of peace, enter into any agreement or compact with another state, or with a foreign power, or engage in war, unless actually invaded, or in such imminent danger as will not admit of delay.

Article II

Section 1. The executive power shall be vested in a President of the United States of America. He shall hold his office during the term of four years, and, together with the Vice President, chosen for the same term, be elected, as follows:

Each state, shall appoint, in such manner as the legislature thereof may direct, a number of electors, equal to the whole number of Senators and Representatives to which the state may be entitled in the Congress; but no Senator or Representative, or person holding an office of trust or profit under the United States, shall be appointed an elector.

The electors shall meet in their respective states, and vote by ballot for two persons, of whom one at least shall not be an inhabitant of the same state with themselves. And they shall make a list of all the persons voted for, and of the number of votes for each; which list they shall sign and certify, and transmit sealed to the seat of the government of the United States, directed to the President of the Senate. The President of the Senate

shall, in the presence of the Senate and House of Representatives, open all the certificates, and the votes shall then be counted. The person having the greatest number of votes shall be the President, if such number be a majority of the whole number of electors appointed; and if there be more than one who have such majority, and have an equal number of votes, then the House of Representatives shall immediately choose by ballot one of them for President; and if no person have a majority, then from the five highest on the list the said House shall in like manner choose the President. But in choosing the President, the votes shall be taken by states, the representation from each state having one vote; a quorum for this purpose shall consist of a member or members from two thirds of the states, and a majority of all the states shall be necessary to a choice.

In every case, after the choice of the President, the person having the greatest number of votes of the electors shall be the Vice President. But if there should remain two or more who have equal votes, the Senate shall choose from them by ballot the Vice President.

The Congress may determine the time of choosing the electors, and the day on which they shall give their votes; which day shall be the same throughout the United States.

No person except a natural born citizen, or a citizen of the United States, at the time of the adoption of this Constitution, shall be eligible to the office of President; neither shall any person be eligible to that office who shall not have attained to the age of thirty-five years, and been fourteen years a resident within the United States.

In case of the removal of the President from office, or of his death, resignation, or inability to discharge the powers and duties of the said office, the same shall devolve on the Vice President, and the Congress may by law provide for the case of removal, death, resignation, or inability, both of the President and Vice President, declaring what officer shall then act as President, and such officer shall act accordingly, until the disability be removed, or a President shall be elected.

The President shall, at stated times, receive for his services, a compensation, which shall neither be increased nor diminished during the period for which he shall have been elected, and he shall not receive within that period any other emolument from the United States, or any of them.

Before he enters on the execution of his office, he shall take the following oath or affirmation:—"I do solemnly swear (or affirm) that I will faithfully execute the office of President of the United States, and will to the best of my ability, preserve, protect and defend the Constitution of the United States."

Section 2. The President shall be commander in chief of the Army and Navy of the United States, and of the militia of the several States, when called into the actual service of the United States; he may require the opinion, in writing, of the principal officer in each of the executive departments, upon any subject relating to the duties of their respective offices, and he shall have power to grant reprieves and pardons for offenses against the United States, except in cases of impeachment.

He shall have power, by and with the advice and consent of the Senate, to make treaties, provided two thirds of the Senators present concur; and he shall nominate, and by and with the advice and consent of the Senate, shall appoint ambassadors, other public ministers and consuls, judges of the Supreme Court, and all other officers of the United States, whose appointments are not herein otherwise provided for, and which shall be established by law: but the Congress may by law vest the appointment of such inferior officers, as they think proper, in the President alone, in the courts of law, or in the heads of departments.

The President shall have power to fill up all vacancies that may happen during the recess of the Senate, by granting commissions which shall expire at the end of their next session.

Section 3. He shall from time to time give to the Congress information of the state of the Union, and recommend to their consideration such measures as he shall judge necessary and expedient; he may, on extraordinary occasions, convene both Houses, or either of them, and in case of disagreement between them, with respect to the time of adjournment, he may adjourn them to such time as he shall think proper; he shall receive ambassadors and other public ministers; he shall take care that the laws be faithfully executed, and shall commission all the officers of the United States.

Section 4. The President, Vice President and all civil officers of the United States, shall be re-moved from office on impeachment for, and conviction of, treason, bribery, or other high crimes and misdemeanors.

Article III

Section 1. The judicial power of the United States, shall be vested in one Supreme Court, and in such inferior courts as the Congress may from time to time ordain and establish. The judges, both of the supreme and inferior courts, shall hold their offices during good behaviour, and shall, at stated times, receive for their services, a compensation, which shall not be diminished during their continuance in office.

Section 2. The judicial power shall extend to all cases, in law and equity, arising under this Constitution, the laws of the United States, and treaties made, or which shall be made, under their authority;—to all cases affecting ambassadors, other public ministers and consuls;—to all cases of admiralty and maritime jurisdiction;—to controversies to which the United States shall be a party;—to controversies between two or more states;—between a state and citizens of another state;—between citizens of different states,—between citizens of the same state claiming lands under grants of different states, and between a state, or the citizens thereof, and foreign states, citizens or subjects.

In all cases affecting ambassadors, other public ministers and consuls, and those in which a state shall be a party, the Supreme Court shall have original jurisdiction. In all the other cases before mentioned, the Supreme Court shall have appellate jurisdiction, both as to law and fact, with such exceptions, and under such regulations as the Congress shall make.

The trial of all crimes, except in cases of impeachment, shall be by jury; and such trial shall be held in the state where the said crimes shall have been committed; but when not committed within any state, the trial shall be at such place or places as the Congress may by law have directed.

Section 3. Treason against the United States, shall consist only in levying war against them, or in adhering to their enemies, giving them aid and comfort. No person shall be convicted of treason unless on the testimony of two witnesses to the same overt act, or on confession in open court.

The Congress shall have power to declare the punishment of treason, but no attainder of treason shall work corruption of blood, or forfeiture except during the life of the person attained.

Article IV

Section 1. Full faith and credit shall be given in each state to the public acts, records, and judicial proceedings of every other state. And the Congress may by general laws prescribe the manner in which such acts, records and proceedings shall be proved, and the effect thereof.

Section 2. The citizens of each state shall be entitled to all privileges and immunities of citizens in the several states.

A person charged in any state with treason, felony, or other crime, who shall flee from justice, and be found in another state, shall on demand of the executive authority of the state from which he fled, be delivered up, to be removed to the state having jurisdiction of the crime.

No person held to service or labour in one state, under the laws thereof, escaping into another, shall, in consequence of any law or regulation therein, be discharged from such service or labour, but shall be delivered up on claim of the party to whom such service or labour may be due.

Section 3. New states may be admitted by the Congress into this Union; but no new state shall be formed or erected within the jurisdiction of any other state; nor any state be formed by the junction of two or more states, or parts of states, without the consent of the legislature of the states concerned as well as of the Congress.

The Congress shall have power to dispose of and make all needful rules and regulations respecting the territory or other property belonging to the United States; and nothing in this Constitution shall be so construed as to prejudice any claims of the United States, or of any particular state.

Section 4. The United States shall guarantee to every state in this Union a republican form of government, and shall protect each of them against invasion; and on application of the legislature, or of the executive (when the legislature cannot be convened) against domestic violence.

Article V

The Congress, whenever two thirds of both Houses shall deem it necessary, shall propose amendments to this Constitution, or on the application of the legislatures of two thirds of the several states, shall call a convention for proposing amendments, which, in either case, shall be valid to all intents and purposes, as part of this Constitution, when ratified by the legislatures of three fourths of the several States, or by conventions in three fourths thereof, as the one or the other mode of ratification may be proposed by the Congress; provided that no amendment which may be made prior to the year one thousand eight hundred and eight shall in any manner affect the first and fourth clauses in the Ninth Section of the First Article; and that no state, without its consent, shall be deprived of its equal suffrage in the Senate.

Article VI

All debts contracted and engagements entered into, before the adoption of this Constitution, shall be as valid against the United States under this Constitution, as under the Confederation.

This Constitution, and the laws of the United States which shall be made in pursuance thereof; and all treaties made, or which shall be made, under the authority of the United States, shall be the supreme law of the land; and the judges in every state shall be bound thereby, any thing in the Constitution or laws of any State to the contrary notwithstanding.

The Senators and Representatives before mentioned, and the members of the several state legislatures, and all executive and judicial officers, both of the United States and of the several states, shall be bound by oath or affirmation, to support this Constitution; but no religious test shall ever be required as a qualification to any office or public trust under the United States.

Article VII

The ratification of the conventions of nine states shall be sufficient for the establishment of this Constitution between the states so ratifying the same.

Done in convention by the unanimous consent of the states present the seventeenth day of September in the year of our Lord one thousand seven hundred and eighty seven and of the independence of the United States of America the twelfth. In witness whereof we have hereunto subscribed our names,

Go. WASHINGTON—*Presid't*,
and deputy from Virginia

Attest WILLIAM JACKSON *Secretary*

New Hampshire
JOHN LANGDON   NICHOLAS GILMAN

Massachusetts
NATHANIEL GORHAM   RUFUS KING

Connecticut
WM. SAML. JOHNSON   ROGER SHERMAN

New York
ALEXANDER HAMILTON

New Jersey
WIL: LIVINGSTON   WM. PATERSON
DAVID BREARLEY   JONA: DAYTON

Pennsylvania
B FRANKLIN   THOS. FITZSIMONS
THOMAS MIFFLIN   JARED INGERSOLL
ROBT MORRIS   JAMES WILSON
GEO. CLYMER   GOUV MORRIS

Delaware
GEO: READ   RICHARD BASSETT
GUNNING BEDFORD JUN   JACO: BROOM
JOHN DICKINSON

Maryland
JAMES MCHENRY   DANL CARROLL
DAN OF ST THOS.
  JENIFER

Virginia
JOHN BLAIR—   JAMES MADISON JR.

North Carolina
WM. BLOUNT   HU WILLIAMSON
RICHD. DOBBS SPAIGHT

South Carolina
J. RUTLEDGE   CHARLES PINCKNEY
CHARLES COTESWORTH   PIERCE BUTLER
  PINCKNEY

Georgia
WILLIAM FEW   ABR BALDWIN

Amendments

Article I

Congress shall make no law respecting an establishment of religion, or prohibiting the free exercise thereof; or abridging the freedom of speech, or of the press; or the right of the people peaceably to assemble, and to petition the government for a redress of grievances.

Article II

A well-regulated militia, being necessary to the security of a free state, the right of the people to keep and bear arms, shall not be infringed.

Article III

No soldier shall, in time of peace be quartered in any house, without the consent of the owner, nor in time of war, but in a manner to be prescribed by law.

Article IV

Tht right of the people to be secure in their persons, houses, papers, and effects, against unreasonable searches and seizures, shall not be violated, and no warrants shall issue, but upon probable cause, supported by oath or affirmation, and particularly describing the place to be searched, and the persons or things to be seized.

Article V

No person shall be held to answer for a capital, or otherwise infamous crime, unless on a presentment or indictment of a Grand Jury, except in cases arising in the land or naval forces, or in the militia, when in actual service in time of war or public danger; nor shall any person be subject for the same offense to be twice put in jeopardy of life or limb; nor shall be compelled in any criminal case to be a witness against himself, nor be deprived of life, liberty, or property, without due process of law; nor shall private property be taken for public use, without just compensation.

Article VI

In all criminal prosecutions, the accused shall enjoy the right to a speedy and public trial, by an impartial jury of the state and district wherein the crime shall have been committed, which district shall have been previously ascertained by law, and to be informed of the nature and cause of the accusation; to be confronted with the witnesses against him; to have compulsory process for obtaining witnesses in his favor, and to have the assistance of counsel for his defense.

Article VII

In suits at common law, where the value in controversy shall exceed twenty dollars, the right of trial by jury shall be preserved, and no fact tried by a jury, shall be otherwise reexamined in any court of the United States, than according to the rules of the common law.

Article VIII

Excessive bail shall not be required, nor excessive fines imposed, nor cruel and unusual punishments inflicted.

Article IX

The enumeration in the Constitution, of certain rights, shall not be construed to deny or disparage others retained by the people.

Article X

The powers not delegated to the United States by the Constitution, nor prohibited by it to the states, are reserved to the states respectively, or to the people.

Article XI

The judicial power of the United States shall not be construed to extend to any suit in law or equity, commenced or prosecuted against one of the United States by citizens of another state, or by citizens or subjects of any foreign state.

Article XII

The electors shall meet in their respective states, and vote by ballot for President and Vice President, one of whom, at least, shall not be an inhabitant of the same state with themselves; they shall name in their ballots the person voted for as President, and in distinct ballots the person voted for as Vice President, and they shall make distinct lists of all persons voted for as President, and of all persons voted for as Vice President, and of the number of votes for each, which lists they shall sign and certify, and transmit sealed to the seat of the government of the United States, directed to the President of the Senate;— The President of the Senate shall, in the presence of the Senate and House of Representatives, open all the certificates and the votes shall then be counted;—The person having the greatest number of votes for President, shall be the President, if such number be a majority of the whole number of electors appointed; and if no person have such majority, then from the persons having the highest numbers not exceeding three on the list of those voted for as President, the House of Representatives shall choose immediately, by ballot, the President. But in choosing the President, the votes shall be taken by states, the representation from each state having one vote; a quorum for this purpose shall consist of a member or members from two-thirds of the states, and a majority of all the states shall be necessary to a choice. And if the House of Representatives shall not choose a President whenever the right of choice shall devolve upon them, before the fourth day of March next following, then the Vice President shall act as President, as in the case of the death or other constitutional disability of the President.—The person having the greatest number of votes as Vice President, shall be the Vice President, if such number be a majority of the whole number of electors appointed, and if no person have a majority, then from the two highest numbers on the list, the Senate shall choose the Vice President; a quorum for the purpose shall consist of two-thirds of the whole number of Senators, and a majority of the whole number shall be necessary to a choice. But no person constitutionally ineligible to the office of President shall be eligible to that of Vice President of the United States.

Article XIII

Section 1. Neither slavery nor involuntary servitude, except as a punishment for crime whereof the party shall have been duly convicted, shall exist within the United States, or any place subject to their jurisdiction.

Section 2. Congress shall have power to enforce this article by appropriate legislation.

Article XIV

Section 1. All persons born or naturalized in the United States, and subject to the jurisdiction thereof, are citizens of the United States and of the state wherein they reside. No state shall make or enforce any law which shall abridge the privileges or immunities of citizens of the United States; nor shall any state deprive any person of life, liberty, or property, without due process of law; nor deny to any person within its jurisdiction the equal protection of the laws.

Section 2. Representatives shall be apportioned among the several states according to their respective numbers, counting the whole number of persons in each state, excluding Indians not taxed. But when the right to vote at any election for the choice of electors for President and Vice President of the United States, Representatives in Congress, the executive and judicial officers of a state, or the members of the legislature thereof, is denied to any of the male inhabitants of such state, being twenty-one years of age, and citizens of the United States, or in any way abridged, except for participation in rebellion, or other crime, the basis of representation therein shall be reduced in the proportion which the number of such male citizens shall bear to the whole number of male citizens twenty-one years of age in such state.

Section 3. No person shall be a Senator or Representative in Congress, or elector of President and Vice President, or hold any office, civil or military, under the United States, or under any state, who, having previously taken an oath, as a member of Congress, or as an officer of the United States, or as a member of any state legislature, or as an executive or judicial officer of any state, to support the Constitution of the United States, shall have engaged in insurrection or rebellion against the same, or given aid or comfort to the enemies thereof. But Congress may by a vote of two-thirds of each house, remove such disability.

Section 4. The validity of the public debt of the United States, authorized by law, including debts incurred for payment of pensions and bounties for services in suppressing insurrection or rebellion, shall not be questioned. But neither the United States nor any state shall assume or pay any debt or obligation incurred in aid of insurrection or rebellion against the United States, or any claim for the loss or emancipation of any slave; but all such debts, obligations and claims shall be held illegal and void.

Section 5. The Congress shall have power to enforce, by appropriate legislation, the provisions of this article.

Article XV

Section 1. The right of citizens of the United States to vote shall not be denied or abridged by the United States or by any state on account of race, color, or previous condition of servitude.

Section 2. The Congress shall have power to enforce this article by appropriate legislation.

Article XVI

The Congress shall have power to lay and collect taxes on incomes, from whatever source derived, without apportionment among the several states, and without regard to any census or enumeration.

Article XVII

Section 1. The Senate of the United States shall be composed of two Senators from each state, elected by the people thereof, for six years; and each Senator shall have one vote. The electors in each state shall have the qualifications requisite for electors of the most numerous branch of the state legislature.

Section 2. When vacancies happen in the representation of any state in the Senate, the executive authority of such state shall issue writs of election to fill such vacancies: *Provided*, That the legislature of any state may empower the executive thereof to make temporary appointments until the people fill the vacancies by election as the legislature may direct.

Section 3. This amendment shall not be so construed as to affect the election or term of any Senator chosen before it becomes valid as part of the Constitution.

Article XVIII

Section 1. After one year from the ratification of this article the manufacture, sale, or transportation of intoxicating liquors within, the importation thereof into, or the exportation thereof from the United States and all territory subject to the jurisdiction thereof for beverage purposes is hereby prohibited.

Section 2. The Congress and the several states shall have concurrent power to enforce this article by appropriate legislation.

Section 3. This article shall be inoperative unless it shall have been ratified as an amendment to the Constitution by the legislatures of the several states, as provided in the Constitution, within seven years from the date of the submission hereof to the states by the Congress.

Article XIX

Section 1. The right of citizens of the United States to vote shall not be denied or abridged by the United States or by any state on account of sex.

Section 2. Congress shall have power to enforce this article by appropriate legislation.

Article XX

Section 1. The terms of the President and Vice President shall end at noon on the 20th day of January, and the terms of Senators and Representatives at noon on the 3d day of January, of the years in which such terms would have ended if this article had not been ratified; and the terms of their successors shall then begin.

Section 2. The Congress shall assemble at least once in every year, and such meeting shall begin at noon on the 3d day of January, unless they shall by law appoint a different day.

Section 3. If, at the time fixed for the beginning of the term of the President, the President elect shall have died, the Vice President elect shall become President. If a President shall not have been chosen before the time fixed for the beginning of his term, or if the President elect shall have failed to qualify, then the Vice President elect shall act as President until a President shall have qualified; and the Congress may by law provide for the case wherein neither a President elect nor a Vice President elect shall have qualified, declaring who shall then act as President, or the manner in which one who is to act shall be selected, and such person shall act accordingly until a President or Vice President shall have qualified.

Section 4. The Congress may by law provide for the case of the death of any of the persons from whom the House of Representatives may choose a President whenever the right of choice shall have devolved upon them, and for the case of the death of any of the persons from whom the Senate may choose a Vice President whenever the right of choice shall have devolved upon them.

Section 5. Sections 1 and 2 shall take effect on the 15th day of October following the ratification of this article.

Section 6. This article shall be inoperative unless it shall have been ratified as an amendment to the Constitution by the legislatures of three-fourths of the several states within seven years from the date of its submission.

Article XXI

Section 1. The eighteenth article of amendment to the Constitution of the United States is hereby repealed.

Section 2. The transportation or importation into any state, territory, or possession of the United States for delivery or use therein of intoxicating liquors, in violation of the laws thereof, is hereby prohibited.

Section 3. This article shall be inoperative unless it shall have been ratified as an amendment to the Constitution by conventions in the several states, as provided in the Constitution, within seven years from the date of the submission hereof to the states by the Congress.

Article XXII

Section 1. No person shall be elected to the office of the President more than twice, and no person who has held the office of President, or acted as President, for more than two years of a term

to which some other person was elected President shall be elected to the office of the President more than once. But this Article shall not apply to any person holding the office of President when this Article was proposed by the Congress, and shall not prevent any person who may be holding the office of President, or acting as President, during the term within which this Article becomes operative from holding the office of President or acting as President during the remainder of such term.

Section 2. This Article shall be inoperative unless it shall have been ratified as an amendment to the Constitution by the legislatures of three-fourths of the several states within seven years from the date of its submission to the states by the Congress.

Article XXIII

Section 1. The District constituting the seat of government of the United States shall appoint in such manner as the Congress may direct:

A number of electors of President and Vice President equal to the whole number of Senators and Representatives in Congress to which the District would be entitled if it were a state, but in no event more than the least populous state; they shall be in addition to those appointed by the states, but they shall be considered, for the purposes of the election of President and Vice President, to be electors appointed by a state; and they shall meet in the District and perform such duties as provided by the twelfth article of amendment.

Section 2. The Congress shall have power to enforce this article by appropriate legislation.

Article XXIV

Section 1. The right of citizens of the United States to vote in any primary or other election for President or Vice President, for electors for President or Vice President, or for Senator or Representative in Congress, shall not be denied or abridged by the United States or any State by reason of failure to pay any poll tax or other tax.

Section 2. The Congress shall have power to enforce this article by appropriate legislation.

Article XXV

Section 1. In case of the removal of the President from office or of his death or resignation, the Vice President shall become President.

Section 2. Whenever there is a vacancy in the office of the Vice President, the President shall nominate a Vice President who shall take office upon confirmation by a majority vote of both Houses of Congress.

Section 3. Whenever the President transmits to the President pro tempore of the Senate and the Speaker of the House of Representatives his written declaration that he is unable to discharge the powers and duties of his office, and until he transmits to them a written declaration to the contrary, such powers and duties shall be discharged by the Vice President as Acting President.

Section 4. Whenever the Vice President and a majority of either the principal officers of the executive departments or of such other body as Congress may by law provide, transmit to the President pro tempore of the Senate and the Speaker of the House of Representatives their written declaration that the President is unable to discharge the powers and duties of his office, the Vice President shall immediately assume the powers and duties of the office as Acting President.

Thereafter, when the President transmits to the President pro tempore of the Senate and the Speaker of the House of Representatives his written declaration that no inability exists, he shall resume the powers and duties of his office unless the Vice President and a majority of either the principal officers of the executive department or of such other body as Congress may by law provide, transmit within four days to the President pro tempore of the Senate and the Speaker of the House of Representatives their written declaration that the President is unable to discharge the powers and duties of his office. Thereupon Congress shall decide the issue, assembling within forty-eight hours for that purpose if not in session. If the Congress, within twenty-one days after receipt of the latter written declaration, or, if Congress is not in session, within twenty-one days after Congress is required to assemble, determines by two-thirds vote of both Houses that the President is unable to discharge the powers and duties of his office, the Vice President shall continue to discharge the same as Acting President; otherwise, the President shall resume the powers and duties of his office.

Article XXVI

Section 1. The right of citizens of the United States, who are eighteen years of age or older, to vote shall not be denied or abridged by the United States or by any State on account of age.

Section 2. The Congress shall have power to enforce this article by appropriate legislation.

The Charter of Maryland was the 1632 agreement by which Maryland was granted to Cecil Calvert for purposes of English colonization and development as a British colony.

This copy courtesy the Maryland Hall of Records.

CHARTER OF MARYLAND

TRANSLATED FROM THE LATIN ORIGINAL

CHARLES, by the grace of God, of *England, Scotland, France, and Ireland,* KING, Defender of the Faith, &c. To ALL to whom these Presents shall come, GREETING.

II. WHEREAS, our well beloved and right trusty Subject CÆCILIUS CALVERT, Baron of BALTIMORE, in our Kingdom of *Ireland,* Son and Heir of GEORGE CALVERT, Knight, late Baron of BALTIMORE in our said Kingdom of *Ireland,* treading in the Steps of his Father, being animated with a laudable, and pious Zeal for extending the *Christian Religion,* and also the Territories of our Empire, hath humbly besought leave of US, that he may transport by his own Industry, and Expense, a numerous Colony of the *English* Nation, to a certain region, hereinafter described, in a Country hitherto uncultivated, in the parts of *America,* and partly occupied by Savages, having no Knowledge of the Divine Being, and that all that Region, with some certain Privileges, and Jurisdiction, appertaining unto the wholesome Government, and State of his Colony and Region aforesaid, may by our Royal Highness be given, granted, and confirmed unto him, and his heirs.

III. KNOW YE therefore, that WE, encouraging with our Royal Favour, the pious and noble Purpose of the aforesaid Baron of Baltimore, of our special Grace, certain Knowledge, and mere Motion, have GIVEN, GRANTED, and CONFIRMED, and by this our present CHAPTER, for US, our Heirs, and Successors, do GIVE, GRANT, AND CONFIRM, unto the aforesaid CÆCILIUS, now Baron of BALTIMORE, his Heirs, and Assigns, all that Part of the Peninsula, or *Chersonese,* lying in the Parts of *America,* between the Ocean on the East, and the Bay of *Chesapeake* on the West, divided from the Residue thereof by a Right Line drawn from the Promontory, or Head-Land, called *Watkin's Point,* situate upon the Bay aforesaid, near the River of *Wighco,* on the West, unto the Main Ocean on the East; and between that Boundary on the South, unto that Part of the Bay of *Delaware* on the North, which lieth under the Fortieth Degree of North Latitude from the æquinoctial, where *New-England* is terminated: And all the Tract of that Land within the Metes underwritten (*that is to say*) passing from the said Bay, called *Delaware Bay,* in a right line, by the degree aforesaid, unto the true Meridian of the first Fountain of the River of *Pattowmack,* thence verging toward the South, unto the further Bank of the said River, and following the same on the West and South, unto a certain place called *Cinquack,* situate near the Mouth of the said River, where it disembogues into the aforesaid Bay of *Chesapeake,* and thence by the shortest line unto the aforesaid Promontory or Place called *Watkin's Point;* so that the whole Tract of Land, divided by the Line aforesaid, between the Main Ocean, and *Watkin's Point,* unto the Promontory called *Cape-Charles,* and every the Appendages thereof, may entirely remain excepted for ever to US, our Heirs and Successors.

IV. ALSO WE do GRANT, and likewise CONFIRM unto the said Baron of BALTIMORE, his Heirs, and Assigns, all Islands and Islets within the Limits aforesaid, all and singular the Islands, and Islets, from the Eastern Shore of the aforesaid Region, toward the East, which have been, or shall be formed in the Sea, situate within Ten marine Leagues from the said Shore; with all and singular the Ports, Harbors, Bays, Rivers, and Straits belonging to the Region or Islands aforesaid, and all the Soil, Plains, Woods, Mountains, Marshes, Lakes, Rivers, Bays, and Straits, situate, or being within the Metes, Bounds, and Limits aforesaid, with the Fishings of every kind of Fish, as well of Whales, Sturgeons, and other royal Fish, as of other Fish, in the Sea, Bays, Straits, or Rivers, within the Premisses, and the Fish there taken: And moreover all Veins, Mines, and Quarries, as well opened as hidden, already found, or that shall be found within the Region,

Islands, or Limits aforesaid, of Gold, Silver, Gems, and precious Stones, and any other whatsoever, whether they be of Stones, or Metals, or of any other Thing, or Matter whatsoever: And furthermore the PATRONAGES, and ADVOWSONS of all churches which (with the increasing Worship and Religion of CHRIST) within the said Region, Islands, Islets, and Limits aforesaid, hereafter shall happen to be built, together with Licence and Faculty of erecting and founding Churches, Chapels, and Places of Worship, in convenient and suitable Places, within the Premisses, and of causing the same to be dedicated and consecrated according to the Ecclesiastical Laws of our Kingdom of *England,* with all, and singular such, and as ample Rights, Jurisdictions, Privileges, Prerogatives, Royalties, Liberties, Immunities, and royal Rights, and temporal Franchises whatsoever, as well by Sea as by Land, within the Region, Island, Islets, and Limits aforesaid, to be had, exercised, used, and enjoyed, as any Bishop of *Durham,* within the Bishoprick or County Palatine of *Durham,* in our Kingdom of *England,* ever heretofore hath had, held, used, or enjoyed, or of Right could, or ought to have, hold, use or enjoy.

V. AND WE do by these presents, for US, our Heirs and Successors, MAKE, CREATE and CONSTITUTE HIM, the now Baron of BALTIMORE, and his Heirs, the TRUE and ABSOLUTE LORDS and PROPRIETARIES of the Region aforesaid, and of all other the Premisses (except the before excepted) saving always the Faith and Allegiance and Sovereign Dominion due to US, our Heirs, and Successors; to HAVE, HOLD, POSSESS, and ENJOY the aforesaid Region, Islands, Islets, and other the Premisses, unto the aforesaid now Baron of BALTIMORE, and to his Heirs and Assigns, to the sole and proper Behoof and Use of him, the now Baron of BALTIMORE, his Heirs and Assigns, forever. To HOLD of US, our Heirs and Successors, Kings of *England,* as of our Castle of *Windsor,* in our County of *Berks,* in free and common SOCCAGE, by Fealty only for all Services, and not *in Capite,* nor by Knight's Service, YIELDING therefore unto US, our Heirs and Successors, TWO INDIAN ARROWS of those Parts, to be delivered at the said Castle of *Windsor,* every Year, on Tuesday in Easter-week: and also the fifth Part of all Gold and Silver Ore, which shall happen from Time to Time, to be found within the aforesaid Limits.

VI. Now, That the aforesaid Region, thus by us granted and described, may be eminently distinguished above all other Regions of that Territory, and decorated with more ample Titles, KNOW YE, that WE, of our more especial Grace, certain Knowledge, and mere Motion, have thought fit that the said Region and Islands be erected into a PROVINCE, as out of the Plenitude of our royal Power and Prerogative, WE do, for Us, our Heirs and Successors, ERECT and INCORPORATE the same into a PROVINCE, and nominate the same MARYLAND, by which name WE will that it shall from henceforth be called.

VII. AND forasmuch as WE have above made and ordained the aforesaid now Baron of BALTIMORE, the true LORD and PROPRIETARY of the whole PROVINCE aforesaid, KNOW YE therefore further, that WE, for Us, our Heirs and Successors do grant unto the said now Baron, (in whose Fidelity, Prudence, Justice, and provident Circumspection of Mind, WE repose the greatest Confidence) and to his Heirs, for the good and happy Government of the said PROVINCE, free, full, and absolute Power, by the Tenor of these Presents, to Ordain, Make, and Enact LAWS, of what kind soever, according to their sound Discretions, whether relating to the Public State of the said PROVINCE,

NOTE: The following material (pp. 352-355) from the *Maryland Manual 1985-1986,* published by the State of Maryland, State Archives, Annapolis, MD.

or the private Utility of Individuals, of and with the Advice, Assent, and Approbation of the Free-Men of the same PROVINCE, or of the great Part of them, or of their Delegates or Deputies, whom WE will shall be called together for the framing of LAWS, when, and as often as Need shall require, by the aforesaid now Baron of BALTIMORE, and his Heirs, and in the Form which shall seem best to him or them, and the same to publish under the Seal of the aforesaid now Baron of BALTIMORE, and his Heirs, and duly to execute the same upon all Persons, for the Time being, within the aforesaid PROVINCE, and the Limits thereof, or under his or their Government and Power, in Sailing toward MARYLAND, or thence Returning, Outwardbound, either to *England*, or elsewhere, whether to any other Part of Our, or of any foreign Dominions, wheresoever established, by the Imposition of Fines, Imprisonment, and other Punishment whatsoever; even if it be necessary, and the Quality of the Offence require it, by Privation of Member, or Life, by him the aforesaid now Baron of BALTIMORE, and his Heirs, or by his or their Deputy, Lieutenant, Judges, Justices, Magistrates, Officers, and Ministers, to be constituted and appointed according to the Tenor and true Intent of these Presents, and to constitute and ordain Judges, Justices, Magistrates and Officers, of what Kind, for what Cause, and with what Power soever, within that Land, and the Sea of those Parts, and in such Form as to the said now Baron of BALTIMORE, or his Heirs, shall seem most fitting: And also to Remit, Release, Pardon, and Abolish, all Crimes and Offences whatsoever against such Laws, whether before, or after Judgment passed; to do all and singular other Things belonging to the Completion of Justice, and to Courts, Prætorian Judicatories, and Tribunals, judicial Forms and Modes of Proceedings, although express Mention thereof in these Presents be not made; and, by Judges by them delegated, to award Process, hold Pleas, and determine in those Courts, Prætorian Judicatories, and Tribunals, in all Actions, Suits, Causes, and Matters whatsoever, as well Criminal as Personal, Real and Mixed, and Prætorian: Which said Laws, so to be published as above said, WE will, enjoin, charge, and command, to be the most absolute and firm in Law, and to be kept in those Parts by all the Subjects and Liege-Men of US, our Heirs and Successors, so far as they concern them, and to be inviolably observed under the Penalties therein expressed, or to be expressed. So NEVERTHELESS, that the Laws aforesaid be Consonant to Reason, and be not repugnant or contrary, but (so far as conveniently may be) agreeable to the Laws, Statutes, Customs and rights of this Our Kingdom of *England*.

VIII. AND FORASMUCH as, in the Government of so great a PROVINCE, sudden Accidents may frequently happen, to which it will be necessary to apply a Remedy, before the Freeholders of the said PROVINCE, their Delegates, or Deputies, can be called together for the framing of Laws; neither will it be fit that so great a number of People should immediately, on such emergent Occasion, be called together, WE THEREFORE, for the better Government of so great a PROVINCE, do Will and Ordain, and by these Presents, for US, our Heirs and Successors, do grant unto the said now Baron of BALTIMORE, and to his Heirs, that the aforesaid now Baron of BALTIMORE, and his Heirs, by themselves, or by their Magistrates and Officers, thereunto duly to be constituted as aforesaid, may, and can make and constitute fit and wholesom Ordinances from Time to Time, to be kept and observed within the PROVINCE aforesaid, as well for the Conservation of the Peace, as for the Better Government of the People inhabiting therein, and publickly to notify the same to all Persons whom the same in anywise do or may affect. Which Ordinances WE will to be inviolably observed within the said PROVINCE, under the Pains to be expressed in the same. So that the said Ordinances be Consonant to Reason, and be not repugnant nor contrary, but (so far as conveniently may be done) agreeable to the Laws, Statutes, or Rights of our Kingdom of *England:* and so that the same Ordinances do not, in any Sort, extend to oblige, bind, charge, or take away the Right or Interest of any Person or Persons, of, or in Member, Life, Freehold, Goods or Chattels.

IX. FURTHERMORE, that the New Colony may more happily increase by a Multitude of People resorting thither, and at the same Time may be more firmly secured from the Incursions of Savages, or of other Enemies, Pirates, and Ravagers: WE therefore, for US, our Heirs and Successors, do by these Presents give and grant Power, Licence and Liberty, to all the Liege-Men and Subjects, present and future, of US, our Heirs and Successors, except such to whom it shall be expressly forbidden, to transport themselves and their Families to the said PROVINCE with fitting Vessels, and suitable provisions, and therein to settle, dwell, and inhabit; and to build and fortify Castles, Forts, and other Places of Strength, at the Appointment of the aforesaid now Baron of BALTIMORE, and his Heirs, for the Public and their own Defense; the Statute of Fugitives, or any other whatsoever to the contrary of the Premisses in any wise notwithstanding.

X. WE will also, out of our more abundant Grace, for US, our Heirs and Successors, do firmly charge, constitute, ordain, and commend, that the said PROVINCE be of our Allegiance; and that all and singular the Subjects and Liege-men of US, our Heirs and Successors, transplanted, or hereafter to be transplanted into the PROVINCE aforesaid, and the children of them, and of others their Descendants, whether already born there, or hereafter to be born, be and shall be natives and Liege-Men of US, our Heirs and Successors, of our Kingdom of *England* and *Ireland;* and in all Things shall be held, treated, reputed, and esteemed as the faithful Liege-Men of US, and our Heirs and Successors, born within our Kingdom of *England;* also Lands, Tenements, Revenues, Services, and other Hereditaments whatsoever, within our Kingdom of *England*, and other our Dominions, to inherit, or otherwise purchase, receive, take, have, hold, buy, and possess, and the same to use and enjoy, and the same to give, sell, alien and bequeath; and likewise all Privileges, Franchises and Liberties of this our Kingdom of *England*, freely, quietly, and peaceably to have and possess, and the same may use and enjoy in the same Manner as our Liege-Men born, or to be born within our same Kingdom of *England*, without Impediment, Molestation, Vexation, Impeachment, or Grievance of US, or any of our Heirs or Successors; any Statute, Act, Ordinance, or Provisions to the contrary thereof, notwithstanding.

XI. FURTHERMORE, That our Subjects may be incited to undertake this Expedition with a ready and chearful Mind: KNOW YE, that WE, of our especial Grace, certain Knowledge, and mere Motion, do, by the Tenor of these Presents, give and grant, as well to the aforesaid Baron of BALTIMORE, and to his Heirs, as to all other Persons who shall from Time to Time repair to the said Province, either for the sake of Inhabiting, or of Trading with the Inhabitants of the Province aforesaid, full License to Ship and Lade in any the Ports of US, our Heirs and Successors, all and singular their Goods, as well moveable as immoveable, Wares and Merchandise, likewise Grain of what Sort soever, and other Things whatsoever necessary for Food and Clothing, by the Laws and Statutes of our Kingdoms and Dominions, not prohibited to be transported out of the said Kingdoms; and the same to transport, by themselves, or their Servants or Assigns, into the said PROVINCE, without the Impediment or Molestation of US, our Heirs or Successors, or of any officers of US, our Heirs or Successors, (SAVING unto Us, our Heirs and Successors, the Impositions, Subsidies, Customs, and other Dues payable for the same Goods and Merchandizes) any Statute, Act, Ordinance, or other Thing whatsoever to the contrary notwithstanding.

XII. BUT BECAUSE, that in so remote a Region, placed among so many barbarous Nations, the Incursions as well of the Barbarians themselves, as of other Enemies, Pirates and Ravagers, probably will be feared, THEREFORE WE have Given, and for US, our Heirs, and Successors, do Give by these Presents, as full and unrestrained Power, as any Captain-General of an Army ever hath had, unto the aforesaid now Baron of BALTIMORE, and to his Heirs and Assigns, by themselves or by their Captains, or other Officers, to summon to their Standards, or to array all Men, of whatsoever Condition, or wheresoever born, for the Time being, in the said Province of MARYLAND, to wage War, and to pursue, even beyond the Limits of their Province, the Enemies and Ravagers aforesaid, infesting those Parts by Land and by Sea, and (if GOD shall grant it) to vanquish and captivate them, and the Captives to put to Death, or, according to their Discretion, to save, and to do all other and singular the Things which appertain, or have been accustomed to appertain unto the Authority and Office of a Captain-General of an Army.

XIII. We also WILL, and by this our CHARTER, do Give unto the aforesaid now Baron of BALTIMORE, and to his Heirs, and Assigns, Power, Liberty and Authority, that, in Case of Rebellion, sudden Tumult, or Sedition, if any (which GOD forbid) should happen to arise, whether upon Land within the PROVINCE aforesaid, or upon the High Sea in making a Voyage to the said PROVINCE of MARYLAND, or in returning thence, they may, by themselves, or by their Captains, or other Officers, thereunto deputed under their Seals (to whom WE, for US, our Heirs and Successors, by these Presents, do Give and Grant the fullest Power and Authority) exercise Martial Law as freely, and in as ample Manner and Form, as any Captain-General of an Army, by virtue of his Office may, or hath accustomed to use the same, against the seditious Authors of Innovations in those Parts, withdrawing themselves from the Government of him or them, refusing to serve in War, flying over to the Enemy, exceeding their Leave of Absence, Deserters, or otherwise howsoever offending against the Rule, Law, or Discipline of War.

XIV. MOREOVER, lest in so remote and far distant a Region, every Access to Honours and Dignities may seem to be precluded, and utterly barred to, Men well born, who are preparing to engage in the present Expedition, and desirous of deserving well, both in Peace and War, of US, and our Kingdoms; for this Cause, WE, for US, our Heirs and Successors, do give free and plenary Power to the aforesaid now Baron of BALTIMORE, and to his Heirs and Assigns, to confer Favours, Rewards and Honours, upon such Subjects, inhabiting within the PROVINCE aforesaid, as shall be well deserving, and to adorn them with whatsoever Titles and Dignities they shall appoint; (so that they be not such as are now used in *England*) also to erect and incorporate Towns into BUROUGHS, and Buroughs into CITIES, with suitable Privileges and Immunities, according to the Merits of the Inhabitants, and Convenience of the places; and to do all and singular other Things in the Premises, which to him or them shall seem fitting and convenient; even although they shall be such as, in their own Nature, require a more special Commandment and Warrant than in these Presents may be expressed.

XV. WE WILL also, and by these Presents do, for US, our Heirs and Successors, give and grant Licence by this our CHARTER, unto the aforesaid now Baron of BALTIMORE, his Heirs and Assigns, and to all Persons whatsoever, who are, or shall be Residents and Inhabitants of the PROVINCE aforesaid, freely to import and unlade, by themselves, their Servants, Factors or Assigns, all Wares and Merchandizes whatsoever, which shall be collected out of the Fruits and Commodities of the said PROVINCE, whether the Product of the Land or the Sea, into any the Ports whatsoever of US, our Heirs and Successors, of *England* or *Ireland,* or otherwise to dispose of the same there; and, if Need be, within One Year, to be computed immediately from the Time of unlading thereof, to lade the same Merchandizes again, in the same, or other Ships, and to export the same to any other Countries they shall think proper, whether belonging to US, or any foreign Power which shall be in Amity with US, our Heirs or Successors: Provided always, that they be bound to pay for the same to US, our Heirs and Successors, such Customs and Impositions, Subsidies and Taxes, as our other Subjects of our Kingdom of *England,* for the Time being shall be bound to pay, beyond which WE WILL that the Inhabitants of the aforesaid PROVINCE of the said Land, called MARYLAND, shall not be burdened.

XVI. AND FURTHERMORE, of our more ample special Grace, and of our certain Knowledge, and mere Motion, WE do, for US,

our Heirs and Successors, grant unto the aforesaid now Baron of BALTIMORE, his Heirs and Assigns, full and absolute Power and Authority to make, erect, and constitute, within the PROVINCE of MARYLAND, and the islands and Islets aforesaid, such, and so many Sea-Ports, Harbours, Creeks, and other Places of Unlading and Discharge of Goods and Merchandizes out of Ships, Boats, and other Vessels, and of Lading in the same, and in so many, and such places, and with such Rights, Jurisdictions, Liberties, and Privileges, unto such Ports respecting, as to him or them shall seem most expedient: And, that all and every the Ships, Boats, and other Vessels whatsoever, coming to, or going from the PROVINCE aforesaid, for the Sake of Merchandizing, shall be laden and unladen at such Ports only as shall be so erected and constituted by the said now Baron of BALTIMORE, his Heirs and Assigns, any Usage, Custom, or any other Thing whatsoever to the contrary notwithstanding. SAVING always to US, our Heirs and Successors, and to all the Subjects of our Kingdoms of *England* and *Ireland,* of US, our Heirs and Successors, the Liberty of Fishing for Sea-Fish as well in the Sea, Bays, Straits and navigable Rivers, as in the Harbours, Bays, and Creeks of the PROVINCE aforesaid; and the Privilege of Salting and Drying Fish on the Shores of the same PROVINCE; and, for that Cause, to cut down and take Hedging-Wood and Twigs there growing, and to build Huts and Cabins, necessary in this Behalf, in the same Manner as heretofore they reasonably might, or have used to do. Which Liberties and Privileges, the said Subjects of US, our Heirs and Successors, shall enjoy, without notable Damage or Injury in any wise to be done to the aforesaid now Baron of BALTIMORE, his Heirs or Assigns, or to the Residents and Inhabitants of the same PROVINCE in the Ports, Creeks, and Shores aforesaid, and especially in the Woods and Trees there growing. And if any Person shall do damage or Injury of this kind, he shall incur the Peril and Pain of the heavy Displeasure of US, our Heirs and Successors, and of the due Chastisement of the Laws, besides making Satisfaction.

XVII. MOREOVER, WE will, appoint, and ordain, and by these Presents, for US, our Heirs and Successors, do grant unto the aforesaid now Baron of BALTIMORE, his Heirs and Assigns, that the same Baron of BALTIMORE, his Heirs and Assigns, from Time to Time, for ever, shall have, and enjoy the Taxes and Subsidies payable, or arising within the Ports, Harbours, and other Creeks and Places aforesaid, within the PROVINCE aforesaid, for Wares bought and sold, and Things there to be laden, and unladen, to be reasonably assessed by them, and the People there as aforesaid, on emergent Occasion; to Whom WE grant Power by these Presents, for US, our Heirs and Successors, to assess and impose the said taxes and Subsidies there, upon just Cause, and in due Proportion.

XVIII. AND FURTHERMORE, of our special Grace, and certain Knowledge, and mere Motion, WE have given, granted, and confirmed, and by these Presents, for US, our Heirs and Successors, do give, grant, and confirm, unto the aforesaid now Baron of BALTIMORE, his Heirs and Assigns, full and absolute Licence, Power, and Authority, that he, the aforesaid now Baron of BALTIMORE, his Heirs and Assigns, from Time to Time hereafter, for ever, may and can, at his or their Will and Pleasure, assign, alien, grant, demise, or enfeoff so many, such, and proportionate Parts and Parcels of the Premises, to any Person or Persons willing to purchase the same, as they shall think convenient, to have and to hold to the same Person or Persons willing to take or purchase to same, and his and their Heirs and Assigns, in Fee-Simple, or Fee-tail, or for Term of Life, Lives, or Years; to hold of the aforesaid now Baron of BALTIMORE, his Heirs and Assigns, by so many, such, and so great Services, Customs and Rents OF THIS KIND, as to the same now Baron of Baltimore, his Heirs and Assigns, shall seem fit and agreeable, and not immediately of US, our Heirs or Successors. And WE do give, and by these Presents, for US, our Heirs and Successors, do grant to the same Person and Persons, and to each and every of them, Licence, Authority and Power, that such Person and Persons, may take the premises, or any Parcel thereof, of the aforesaid now Baron of BALTIMORE, his Heirs and Assigns, and hold the same to them and their Assigns, or their Heirs, of the aforesaid Baron of BALTIMORE, his Heirs and Assigns, of what Estate of Inheritance soever, in Fee-simple or Fee-tail, or otherwise, as to them and the now Baron of BALTIMORE, his Heirs and Assigns, shall seem expedient; the Statute made in the Parliament of Lord EDWARD, son of King HENRY, late King of *England,* our Progenitor, commonly called the "STATUTE QUIA EMPTORES TERRARUM," heretofore published in our Kingdom of *England,* or any other Statute, Act, Ordinance, Usage, Law, or Custom, or any other Thing, Cause or Matter, to the contrary thereof, heretofore had, done, published, ordained or provided to the contrary thereof notwithstanding.

XIX. WE also, by these Presents, do give and grant Licence to the same Baron of BALTIMORE, and to his Heirs, to erect any Parcels of Land with the PROVINCE aforesaid, into Manors, and in every of those Manors, to have and to hold a Court-Baron, and all Things which to a Court-Baron do belong; and to have and to keep View of Frank-Pledge, for the Conservation of the Peace and Better Government of those Parts, by themselves and their Stewards, or by the Lords, for the Time being to be deputed of other of those Manors when they shall be constituted, and in the same to exercise all Things to the View of Frank-Pledge belonging.

XX. AND FURTHER WE will, and do, by these Presents, for US, our Heirs and Successors, covenant and grant to, and with the aforesaid now Baron of BALTIMORE, his Heirs and Assigns, that WE, our Heirs, and Successors, at no Time hereafter, will impose, or make or cause to be imposed, any Impositions, Customs, or other Taxations, Quotas or Contributions whatsoever, in or upon the Residents or Inhabitants of the PROVINCE aforesaid for their Goods, Lands, or Tenements within the same PROVINCE, or upon any tenements, lands, goods or chattels within the PROVINCE aforesaid, or in upon any Goods or Merchandizes within the PROVINCE aforesaid, or within the Ports or Harbours of the said PROVINCE, to be laden or unladen: And WE Will and do, for US, our Heirs and Successors, enjoin and command that this our Declaration shall, from Time to Time, be received and allowed in all our Courts and Prætorian Judicatories, and before all the Judges whatsoever of US, our Heirs and Successors, for a Sufficient and lawful Discharge, Payment, and Acquittance thereof, charging all and singular the Officers and Ministers of US, our Heirs and Successors, and enjoining them, under our heavy Displeasure, that they do not at any Time presume to attempt any Thing to the contrary of the Premisses, or that may in any wise contravene the same, but that they, at all Times, as is fitting, do aid and assist the aforesaid now Baron of BALTIMORE, and his Heirs, and the aforesaid Inhabitants and Merchants of the PROVINCE of MARYLAND aforesaid, and

their Servants and Ministers, Factors and Assigns, in the fullest Use and Enjoyment of this our CHARTER.

XXI. AND FURTHERMORE WE WILL, and by these Presents, for US, our Heirs and Successors, do grant unto the aforesaid now Baron of BALTIMORE, his Heirs and Assigns, and to the Freeholders and Inhabitants of the said PROVINCE, both present and to come, and to every one of them, that the said PROVINCE, and the Freeholders or Inhabitants of the said Colony or Country, shall not henceforth be held or reputed a member or Part of the Land of *Virginia,* or of any other Colony already transported, or hereafter to be transported, or be dependent on the same, or subordinate in any kind of Government, from which WE do separate both the said PROVINCE, and Inhabitants thereof, and by these presents do WILL to be distinct, and that they may be immediately subject to our Crown of England, and dependent on the same for ever.

XXII. AND if, peradventure, hereafter it may happen, that any Doubts or Questions should arise concerning the true Sense and Meaning of any Word, Clause, or Sentence, contained in this our present CHARTER, WE will, charge and command, THAT Interpretation to be applied, always, and in all Things, and in all our Courts and Judicatories whatsoever, to obtain which shall be judged to be the more beneficial, profitable, and favourable to the aforesaid now Baron of BALTIMORE, his Heirs and Assigns: PROVIDED always, that no Interpretation thereof be made, whereby GOD'S holy and true Christian Religion, or the Allegiance due to US, our Heirs and Successors, may in any wise suffer by Change, Prejudice, or Diminution; although express Mention be not made in these Presents of the true yearly Value or Certainty of the Premisses, or any Part thereof, or of other Gifts and Grants made by US, our Heirs and Predecessors, unto the said now Lord BALTIMORE, or any Statute, Act, Ordinance, Provision, Proclamation or Restraint, heretofore had, made, published, ordained or provided, or any other Thing, Cause, or Matter Whatsoever, to the contrary thereof in any wise notwithstanding.

XXIII. NOW WITNESS whereof WE have caused these our Letters to be made Patent. WITNESS OURSELF at *Westminister,* the Twentieth Day of *June,* in the Eighth Year of our Reign. (June 20, 1632).

Bibliographic Note: This translation of the Maryland Charter is taken from the Reverend Thomas Bacon, *The Laws of Maryland* (Annapolis, 1765). Bacon was unaware of the earliest printed translation of the Charter, which was published in London in 1635 as part of a promotional pamphlet entitled *A Relation of Maryland.* A facsimile edition of the 1635 Charter is available from the Maryland State Archives, P.O. Box 828, Annapolis, MD 21404.

SELECTED BIBLIOGRAPHY

Constitution of Maryland with Amendments to January 1, 1985, published by the Maryland Secretary of State, edited by the State Department of Legislative Reference, Maryland, 1985.

Contemporary Local Government in Maryland, by Jean E. Spencer, Bureau of Governmental Research, College of Business and Public Administration, University of Maryland, College Park, Md., 1965.

Counties of Maryland, by J. H. Cromwell, C & P Telephone Company of Maryland, Baltimore, MD., 1966.

Governor of Maryland, A Constitutional Study, by Charles James Rohr, Ph.D., Johns Hopkins Press, Baltimore, Md., 1932.

History of Maryland, Province and State, by Matthew Page Andrews, Tradition Press, Hatboro, Pa., 1965. (A facsimile copy of the 1929 edition.)

History of Maryland, Volumes I, II and III, by J. Thomas Scharf, Tradition Press, Hatboro, Pa., 1967. (A facsimile copy of the 1879 edition.)

Judicial Process in Maryland, by Elbert M. Byrd, Jr., Bureau of Governmental Research, College of Business and Public Administration, University of Maryland, College Park, Md., 1961.

The Legislative Process in Maryland: A Study of the General Assembly, second edition, by George A. Bell and Jean E. Spencer, Bureau of Governmental Research, University of Maryland, College Park, Md., 1963.

Magnificent Failure: The Constitutional Convention of 1967-1968, John P. Wheeler and Melissa Kinsey, State of Maryland, 1968.

Maryland Manual, 1985-1986, Gregory A. Stiverson, editor, Hall of Records Commission, Hall of Records, Annapolis, Md., 1985.

Maryland Personality Parade, Volume I, by Vera F. Rollo, Maryland Historical Press, Lanham, Md., 1967.

Maryland State Government, Volume I, 1960-1961, by J. H. Cromwell, C & P Telephone Company of Maryland, Baltimore, Md., 1961.

Maryland State Government, Volume II, 1961-1963, by J. H. Cromwell, C & P Telephone Company of Maryland, Baltimore, Md., 1963.

Registration and Election Laws of Maryland 1968, published by the Maryland Secretary of State, with instructions prepared by the Maryland Attorney General, printed by the Michie Company, Charlottesville, Va., 1968.

Resource Guide on the Maryland Constitutional Convention, Maryland State Department of Education, Baltimore, Md., 1967.

Senator Charles Mathias with students and faculty from a Maryland school on the steps of the United States Capitol.

GLOSSARY

NOTE: Due to space limitations, the definitions given here are narrow and include only the meaning of the words as they are used in the text of this book.

Abolish To do away with.

Adjourn To close a meeting or a court until another time or day.

Adopt To accept; to take and put into practice.

Amendment A change for the better by adding, omitting or changing.

Appeal To call for the rehearing of a court case.

Appellate court One which re-examines evidence.

Appoint To place in office.

Apportionment A just division; a division into shares.

Appropriation Money set aside for a specific use.

Aristocratic Having the thoughts and habits common to the ruling or privileged class.

Authority Legal or rightful power.

Bail The security given in order to obtain the release of a prisoner.

Ballots Votes or papers used in voting.

Bill (legislative) Proposed law submitted to a legislature for enactment.

Board A Council or authorized assembly.

Bond 1) A promise to pay money should a prisoner not return for trial; 2) a promise to pay back money plus interest in a certain time.

Bribe Something given a person in a position of trust in order to influence him.

Budget A statement or plan for income and expenses for a certain period of time.

Bureau A government office or department.

Candidate One being offered as suitable to fill a position or an office.

Chairman One who heads a committee; the presiding officer of a committee.

Charge (as with duty) A command to perform a duty; a task assigned.

Circuit A regular journey from place to place in pursuit of one's calling.

Civil Belonging to civic affairs, not military.

Collateral Something worth money which is given as security.

Commission A written warrant or authority giving certain powers and authorizing the performance of certain duties.

Committee A group of persons who are to take action on a certain matter.

Condemn (people) Sentence to punishment or execution; (property such as land or buildings) to pronounce to be taken for public use under the right of eminent domain.

Consecutive Following one another without a break.

Conservative Opposed to change, moderate.

Constitution Fundamental law of a nation or state or other groups, usually written.

Consumer One who uses goods.

Convict To find guilty; a description of a prisoner.

Convention A body of representatives meeting for a common purpose.

Coroner A public official whose duty it is to inquire into the cause of any death which appears to be due to unnatural causes.

Court The place where justice is administered.

Crime Act of lawbreaking. *Felony-*Serious crime such as murder, robbery or manslaughter. *Misdemeanor-*A crime thought to be less serious than a felony.

Delegate A member of the House of Delegates; one sent to represent others.

Disburse To pay out.

Documents Official or original papers.

Duel A combat, usually formal, between two persons with deadly weapons.

Electoral College A group of elected persons who have the power to select a higher official such as a President.

Elisor One who will act in place of the county sheriff or similar official if necessary.

Eminent domain Power of a government over property inside its borders, to take it for a necessary public use, reasonable payment being made.

Evidence Facts shown in order to prove the truth of a statement.

Executive Any person charged with administrative or executive work.

Ex officio Because of an office; by reason of one's office.

Extradition Surrender of a person by one state to another.

Federal Pertaining to the government of a union of states.

Fine Payment of money made as a punishment; to punish by making a person pay.

Fiscal Of public monies; of financial matters.

Franchise A positive right to do something.

Fund A store of money for a certain purpose.

General Assembly Legislature, as of Maryland.

General Election (General Election Day) The election held to elect national officers.

Gubernatorial Pertaining to the governor.

Habeas corpus Legal, written authorization, used to bring a person before a court or judge.

Hearing A listening to arguments; a trial.

House (as in legislatures) A body of persons forming an assembly.

Impeach To accuse a person of wrongdoing.

Incorporate To form or unite into a legal organization.

Investment Money put into business in order to earn a profit.

Judge One who decides by reason of knowledge and/or authority.

Jurisdiction Sphere, or area, of authority; the right to hear a case of law.

Jury A number of persons who must give a true answer, or verdict, on some matter submitted to them, after hearing arguments and being shown evidence.

Justice of the Peace A local magistrate.

Legislature Group in a state given power to make, repeal or change laws.

Libel To make a false report or statement to damage a person; to slander.

License Written permission to act or to carry on a business.

Lottery A scheme for giving prizes by choosing chances from all those sold. A gambling scheme in which chances are sold.

Magistrate A person with power; a public official who decides certain matters.

Majority The greater number.

Maryland Annotated Code Laws of Maryland gathered together in volumes.

Mayor Chief executive of a city; person holding the office of mayor.

Military Having to do with war, arms or soldiers; not civil.

Militia A body of citizens trained in military matters but called to service only in emergencies.

Minority The smaller number.

Monopoly Exclusive possession of anything; exclusive control of some service or thing.

Mortgage A promise to pay secured by property such as buildings or land.

Municipal Pertaining to a city or town government.

Non compos mentis Not of sound mind.

Notary or *notary public* A public officer who attests, or states, to signatures or papers as being authentic.

Oath A solemn promise or statement.

Ordinance A local law; a city law.

Penalty A loss due to breaking a law; a punishment.

Pending Not yet decided.

Petition A formal, written request to a government for action.

Poll A place where votes are cast or recorded.

Poll tax A "head tax"; a tax on every individual; sometimes must be paid in order to be allowed to vote.

Population The number of people in a place.

Primary election A preliminary election in which voters directly nominate (put forward) for office the candidates of their own political party.

Proclamation A public notice by an official of an order; a formal statement of facts.

Prohibit To forbid, to stop or to prevent.

Prosecute To bring before a court of law.

Quorum The number of persons in a group needed to do business legally.

Ratify To approve.

Recess To stop business for a short time; a short intermission.

Referendum A vote on a law or question by the voters. A way of finding out the will of the people.

Registration (of voters) A record or list of voters. To register to vote, one must meet certain requirements.

Representative A person who is selected to speak or act for others. A member of the U. S. House of Representatives.

Reprieve To delay a punishment.

Resident One who lives in a certain place or claims a certain place as his legal residence.

Resolution (of legislatures) A formal expression of opinion of an assembly, adopted by vote. Often used to honor deserving persons.

Revenue A source of income; the yearly money which comes into a treasury from taxes.

Rural Of the country, rustic, not urban.

Salary A certain amount of money regularly paid to someone for his work.

Secretary 1) One who attends to correspondence, records, etc. 2) An officer of a state who manages a particular department of the government.

Solicitor An attorney, a lawyer; a law officer of a city or department.

Subpoena A writ (written order) commanding a person to appear in court.

Tax Money charged people and businesses to pay for the operation and services of a government.

Tie (election) To have an equal score or equal number of votes; no one winner.

Transit Passage through or over; as, rapid transit from city to city.

Urban Belonging to a city or town, not rural.

Witness One who has personal knowledge of something; one who can be asked to give evidence; to see or experience something personally.

INDEX

President and Mrs. Ronald Reagan.

Michael Evans photo courtesy The White House.

As a father of three children, Mr. Goldstein is committed to quality education in Maryland.

U.S. Senator from Maryland Paul S. Sarbanes.

A view from the bell tower of St. Ignatius Church, Charles County, Maryland.

Photograph courtesy the Office of Tourist Development,
Maryland Dept. of Economic and Community Development.

DATE DUE			
DEC 2 3 1999			